Independent Journey

1817

HARPER & ROW, PUBLISHERS, New York
Cambridge, Hagerstown, Philadelphia, San Francisco,
London, Mexico City, São Paulo, Sydney

Independent Journey

THE LIFE OF

WILLIAM O. DOUGLAS

by James F. Simon

To David, Lauren, Sara and Marcia
and to
the memory of my father,
Richard U. Simon, Sr.

Excerpts from *Of Men and Mountains* by William O. Douglas, Copyright 1950 by William O. Douglas, Reprinted by permission of Harper & Row, Publishers, Inc.

Excerpts from *Go East, Young Man* by William O. Douglas, Copyright 1974 by William O. Douglas, Reprinted by permission of Random House, Publishers, Inc.

FIRST EDITION

Designer: Gloria Adelson

Library of Congress Cataloging in Publication Data

Simon, James F
  Independent journey.
  Includes index.
  1. Douglas, William Orville, 1898–1980. 2. Judges
—United States—Biography. I. Title.
KF8745.D6S55   347.73'2634   [B]   79-2637
ISBN 0-06-014042-9

80 81 82 83 84 10 9 8 7 6 5 4 3 2

CONTENTS

A section of photographs follows page 216.

INTRODUCTION

THE REVEREND WILLIAM DOUGLAS would have been proud. His son, Justice William O. Douglas, had asked to be remembered as a religious person, a Presbyterian, like his father and mother. He had left instructions that his memorial service include the old hymn "Shall We Gather at the River?" for he had recalled the Reverend and Mrs. Douglas joining in their own sweet rendition when he was a little boy. He would have preferred that "The Lord's Prayer" be sung by a cowboy he had known out West, but the cowboy had died before him and so the mourners heard the rich baritone voice of Master Sergeant William F. Kugel, a soloist with the U.S. Army Chorus.

During his long, productive life, William O. Douglas's religion had taken him along a very different path from that of his father. At the turn of the century, the Reverend Douglas had preached his rigid Presbyterianism from morning until late at night in the raw frontier hamlets of northern Minnesota. His son, however, had had little use for dogma, whether religious or political, and never needed a church pulpit from which to deliver his sermons. William O. Douglas preached his beliefs and hopes for mankind in tiny villages in Iran and Outer Mongolia, in his many books and on his treks through the wilderness, and most of all, from the bench of the U.S. Supreme Court.

The Reverend Douglas had been known as a gentle, humble minister who was loved and admired by all those who knew him. Though he was admired by millions, the Reverend Douglas's son was rarely seen as gentle and never seen as humble. His causes often thrust him into controversy and there was nothing, it seemed, that William O. Douglas liked better than a good, tough fight. The more formidable the adversary, the deeper Douglas dug in. He castigated McCarthyism in the fifties, U.S. involvement in Vietnam in the sixties and Richard Nixon's near successful attempt to undermine the foundation of our democratic government in the seventies. Four attempts to impeach Justice Douglas failed.

Throughout his thirty-six years on the Court, Justice Douglas promoted the causes of human dignity and enrichment, most often pinning his aspirations to the tangible guarantees of the Bill of Rights. His libertarian judicial opinions were calculated, by design, "to take the government off the backs of the people." For Douglas, that meant full constitutional protections for all Americans, including the despised, the defenseless and the penniless.

Douglas was not always true to his public image as the forthright humanitarian. Some of his colleagues knew the cold, often calculating, side of this man. And many of those who worked for him knew his callousness. He was easier to admire than to like.

His personal life was no more orthodox than his public one. He married four times, three more than the Reverend Douglas would have approved of. And he could be cruel or indifferent to his wives and children, traits that no member of the Reverend Douglas's family could recall in him.

But William O. Douglas served mankind, as his father had, in his own way and on a scale his father could not have dreamed of. He touched the hearts and minds of millions around the world. And those who came to the National Presbyterian Church in Washington, D.C., to mourn his death on January 23, 1980, including the President and Vice-President of the United States, the Secretary of State, leading members of both houses of Congress and every member of the U.S. Supreme Court, left celebrating his life. "Because of Bill Douglas," Clark Clifford, the former Secretary of Defense, said that day, "each one of us is freer, safer and stronger."

INTERVIEW

WILLIAM O. DOUGLAS lay motionless, his frail body warmed by a wool blanket and supported by a reclining leather chair. His hair was white and thick and long, hanging shaggily over his ears. His blue eyes still penetrated and his high cheekbones were more prominent than ever, due to the loss of weight that followed his severe stroke in 1974. He was dressed properly, in a brown tweed sport coat, a high-collared white shirt and tie. The formal dress and the weak body seemed incongruous, though in earlier, happier days, the formal dress and robust body would have seemed equally incongruous.

When I entered his chambers, Douglas stared noncommittally. After I sat down, he said nothing. To fill the void, I recounted quickly, too quickly, the members of his family I had seen and the old friends I had met. I risked an anecdote: When I visited the Double K Ranch in Goose Prairie, I had been advised by Kay Kershaw (a close friend of Douglas's) to take a "special" trail up a towering Cascade mountain. "The trail went straight up," I said. "I guess it was Kay's initiation rite for all Eastern slickers," I added, smiling. Douglas did not return the smile.

"On that same trip," I continued, "I met your son and daughter." I had already told Douglas that. "I also met two old hunting and fishing friends of yours in Oregon. Twin brothers. What were their names?" I scratched my memory but could not remember.

"Marsh." Douglas's voice was high-pitched and soft, but strikingly clear.

"Yes, Marsh, that was it," I said. It occurred to me that Douglas had been listening to every word, calculating, judging, controlling the situation. It was as if I were auditioning for a part in a play that he was directing. He seemed to know the script, but listened patiently as the tryout proceeded, interrupting only when I forgot my lines.

Once again, however, Douglas receded into silence. And once again I groped for a word, a phrase, an idea that would please— yes, please—him. And then I remembered that I had waited two years for the interview and it was, after all, to be an interview, not unlike the hundreds of interviews I had conducted in the past. That meant many questions and, with luck, many answers.

"What do you consider to have been your greatest achievement at the SEC?" I asked. It sounded too formal, too rigid, too predictable.

Douglas seemed to sense my nervousness and helped out. "Cleaning up the Street," he said, responding to my overly general question with a direct, concise answer.

And surely history would agree with William O. Douglas. As chairman of the Securities and Exchange Commission, he had forced the New York Stock Exchange to reform its trading practices, but not without a confrontation with the most powerful leaders of Wall Street. In that confrontation, as in so many others with powerful men in business and government, Douglas had not come out second best.

Encouraged by his answer, I tried another question. "What would you say was your most important decision on the Supreme Court?" This was also a broad question, better for a short magazine article or a TV interview than a biography. But it might stir Douglas to interesting observation.

It did not. He simply brushed aside the question with a shrug.

And then, to my chagrin and embarrassment, he closed his eyes. Was he bored? Or tired? In either case, the interview came to an abrupt and premature halt, only five minutes after it had begun.

I left the room and summoned Douglas's secretary. "Should I leave?" I asked.

"No," replied the secretary, a tall, stunningly beautiful young woman. "Why don't you wait here?" So I sat down, disappointed and deflated. The secretary returned shortly. "The Justice, unfortunately, has been very tired today," she said pleasantly. "Let him rest. Perhaps he'll see you a little later."

Then I fell into an easy, informal conversation with the secretary, her husband, who was Douglas's law clerk, and their two-and-a-half-month-old baby, propped up in an infant seat on the secretary's desk. Notes on new babies were exchanged; I spoke wisely and affectionately of my own eleven-month-old. The conversation eventually returned to Douglas, and I recounted the excruciatingly awkward five minutes I had spent with him.

The secretary laughed sympathetically. "That's the Justice. He controls every situation."

A few minutes later, the buzzer on the secretary's desk sounded and she walked into Douglas's chambers. When she returned, she said, "The Justice would like to see you."

This time he seemed more alert, though he still reclined in his leather chair. When he spoke, his voice was slightly reedy and weak, but the sentences came rapidly in his familiar clipped cadence. As he began to enjoy himself, telling stories of famous people he had known—FDR, Joe Kennedy, Frankfurter, Hugo Black—he seemed to want me to relax and enjoy the stories too. With the reminiscences he offered hot tea and later hard liquor. There were long pauses, for Douglas to collect either his strength or his thoughts. But the mind was clear and the adrenaline was flowing. He even returned to his old nervous habits, brushing his long fingers through his hair or drumming them on an armrest.

Between the stories, Douglas pressed the buzzer at his side to summon his secretary. This happened every two or three minutes. Each time, she walked into his chambers at an unhurried gait and asked calmly, "Mr. Justice Douglas, may I do something for you?" Sometimes Douglas simply stared into space for a few seconds or even a few minutes. Other times, he continued to talk to me, ignoring his secretary, who stood immediately beside him. In time, however, he made his wishes known. "Call my son [Bill junior, in Portland, Oregon]. . . . Call my wife. . . . Call Datcher [Douglas's messenger]. . . ." Or he asked for information. "Who was the man from St. Louis who wrote the book about Black?" Or he gave an order. "Get me that *Baylor Law Review* article. . . . Get me the *Attorney General's Report*. . . ." And then it began over again. "Call my son . . . call my wife . . . call Datcher . . . get me the law review article . . ." For the remainder of the afternoon, Mr. Justice Douglas, seventy-nine years old, kept his visitor, his secretary, his law clerk and his messenger fully occupied with his thoughts and commands. It was a remarkable performance.

Douglas began with some familiar tales, no less enjoyable to either speaker or listener because both had heard them before. "Joe Kennedy brought me down to Washington in 1934." (Kennedy, the first chairman of the SEC, had asked Douglas to direct a study of protective and reorganization committees, which were creating new scandals in their manipulations of bankruptcies and receiverships, and report the findings and recommendations to Congress.) "I came in September and went into his office. 'What do I do?' I asked. He said, 'Goddammit, I thought you knew. Maybe I've got the wrong man down here.' I told him he had the right man. Joe Kennedy had a tough exterior. Very able. He told me to get the bastards on the Street. And we worked [Douglas and his staff, including Abe Fortas, his former student at Yale and future associate justice of the U.S. Supreme Court] from nine to six. We took two hours out for dinner and then we worked until two in the morning."

Douglas and his staff produced an eight-volume report, which recounted in devastating detail the shenanigans of investment bankers and their lawyers who used bankruptcy proceedings for their personal and commercial gain, usually at the expense of corporations' stockholders. Among those interrogated by Douglas at his public hearings was his former boss Robert T. Swaine, of the prestigious Wall Street law firm of Cravath, Swaine and Moore.

"I understand you were pretty tough on Mr. Swaine," I said.

"We showed no favoritism," Douglas responded, with only a slight hint of a smile.

"After Joe Kennedy left the SEC, James Landis took over as chairman," I said. "What was he like?"

"He spent too much time in the library," said Douglas. "He didn't think we should attack the Street. He thought it would be the end of the SEC. He didn't really know what was going on in the Street."

Douglas was asked about his days as chairman of the SEC and the famous confrontation between Douglas and the governors of the New York Stock Exchange. Douglas had accused the governors of running the Exchange like a private club rather than as a public exchange responsible to individual security holders across the country. The struggle was played out in the press by Douglas and Charles Gay, then the president of the Exchange.

"What was Gay like?" Douglas was asked.

"He was a dumb son of a bitch."

Reforms on the Exchange did not take place, said Douglas, until Richard Whitney, the former president of the New York Stock Exchange, was indicted for the embezzlement of his clients' securities. "I told the President [Roosevelt] that one of his Groton and Harvard friends [Whitney and Roosevelt were classmates] was in big trouble unless he stopped it. 'Who is it?' the President asked. 'Dick Whitney,' I said. 'No, not Dickie Whitney!' Roosevelt said. But the President told me to press ahead. And we did. . . ."

Ultimately Whitney was convicted and sent to prison. More important from Douglas's point of view was the fact that the Whitney scandal enabled the SEC to conduct extensive public hearings on the loose financial practices that had enabled Whitney to go undetected for several years. And finally, it put pressure on Wall Street, at a critical time in Douglas's confrontation with Charles Gay and other members of the New York Stock Exchange, to introduce reforms that would make the Exchange a public institution, truly responsive to security holders.

The conversation turned to Douglas's years on the U.S. Supreme Court and his disagreements, both public and private, with Justice Felix Frankfurter.

"Felix belonged on this Court," said Douglas. "He knew constitutional history and he knew this Court. He was a brilliant advocate of his conservative philosophy. I put him on my list of the best members to serve on the Court."

This was very high praise for Frankfurter, who, in his diaries, wrote with bristling hostility of his relationship with Douglas.

"What was Frankfurter like?" It was a question, I suspected, that Douglas had been waiting for. With a perfect sense of balance and timing, he proceeded to undercut the lofty image of Frankfurter that he had just constructed.

"Felix always insisted that people be subservient to him. Even when he was at Harvard and I was at Yale, he treated everybody, even his colleagues, like his students. We used to kid about it when he came to New Haven." Douglas paused for a moment. "He was a divisive influence, even before he came to the Court. Everywhere he was, he was divisive. At Harvard. On the Court. He liked to see people argue. He was Machiavellian." Pause.

"He didn't like to be kidded," Douglas continued. "At judicial conferences, Hugo [Black] sat to Felix's left and I sat across the table from him. I told Felix that Hugo was the nutcracker and he was the nut. After Hugo got finished with him, I just picked up the pieces. He didn't think that was very funny. Once, after I read a story in the paper that Felix and I weren't speaking, I came into judicial conference and offered to shake his hand. Felix just stood there. I said, 'You'll have to hurry, Felix, I'm a busy man.' He didn't think that was funny either."

Frankfurter, I reminded Douglas, had written in his diaries that Douglas was fueled by political ambition while he was on the Court and that every opinion, it seemed to Frankfurter, was calculated to further that ambition.

"That's not true," Douglas replied. "I never had any political ambitions. I took my advice from Justice Brandeis. We spoke about it. He told me that a member of the Court could not have political ambitions because it would hurt the Court. I didn't. But Felix did. He tried to run Bob Jackson for the presidency."

When asked what the source for the last statement was, Douglas simply stated, "Letters." He did not elaborate.

"But you must have known that even if you yourself did not announce political plans, others were thinking of them on your behalf."

Douglas nodded agreement, but offered nothing more.

"As early as 1939, your name was mentioned as a possible

running mate with FDR," I said. "And it has since been documented that Roosevelt considered you as a vice-presidential candidate in 1940 and more seriously in 1944."

"I never talked to FDR about it," said Douglas.

"But you knew that he was considering you?"

"Yes," said Douglas.

"Weren't others, like Joe Kennedy, promoting you for political office?"

"He probably did. He was always promoting me for some office. Every high position that opened up he proposed me for."

"How do you explain the admiration that Kennedy held for you? Your political values could not have been more different."

"Kennedy once told me that he thought his son Jack and I were the two most able men in Washington. 'And I don't agree with one goddamn thing that either of you stand for!' he said. That was Joe Kennedy.

"During the early fifties," Douglas added, "I was with Joe Kennedy one day and I told him he was going to be embarrassed if he continued to be seen with me, because before long I thought I would be one of [Senator Joseph] McCarthy's targets. He just laughed. 'Don't worry,' he told me. 'You'd be surprised what ten thousand dollars can do in this town.' "

"Did you ever have any regrets about not holding elective office?" I asked Douglas.

He paused. "To be perfectly candid, I did have regrets after Truman ordered the dropping of the atomic bomb."

I pursued the point. "Running with FDR, a man you admired greatly, must have been tempting. You would have been an attractive running mate. Your experience had not been confined to the judiciary. You had proved yourself as an outstanding administrator at the SEC. . . ."

Douglas was enjoying the build-up. His blue eyes twinkled and the edges of his mouth lifted ever so slightly, forming a smile. Still, he said nothing. Then he reached for his buzzer. His secretary entered the chambers and was told to telephone Douglas's wife, Cathy.

"Your wife is on the phone, Mr. Justice Douglas," he was informed.

Douglas picked up the receiver. "Hello, sweetie. There's a man here who wants to run me for President. . . ." The telephone conversation was brief and when Douglas hung up, he returned to the interview.

"Tell me about some of your colleagues on the Supreme Court," I asked him. And then he distributed compliments and insults in one- and two-sentence spurts.

Chief Justice Charles Evans Hughes: "He was brilliant. He knew how to conduct a judicial conference. He had perfect command of the cases."

Chief Justice Harlan F. Stone: "He was not good as Chief Justice. We were always in conference. He couldn't move the cases along. When members of the Court would disagree with him, he would lean over to me and say, 'I can understand how the others might disagree, but not you. You, Bill, were my student at Columbia.' I'd lean back over to him and say, 'Mr. Chief Justice, I learned all the law I know from you.' "

Associate Justice James McReynolds: "When I played poker with FDR, I named a game 'McReynolds.' You were dealt five cards down. All were wild. I named it 'McReynolds' because the game was such a son of a bitch."

Associate Justice Hugo Black: "At heart, he was a Baptist preacher."

"There must have been a lot of tension on the Court in those early days," I suggested, "particularly after Black and you and [Justice Frank] Murphy split with Frankfurter."

"Not much," said Douglas, "except Monday through Saturday."

"When did the break between you and Frankfurter take place?"

"With *Barnette.*"*

"Why did you change your position in *Barnette?*"

"I don't think I had thought about all the implications of the first decision. Part of the problem was that Stone didn't circulate

*In 1940, a Court majority, which included Justices Douglas and Frankfurter, ruled that a school board could compel public school children to salute the American flag even if some of those children who were Jehovah's Witnesses said that the flag salute violated their religious principles. Three years later, in *West Virginia Board of Education* v. *Barnette*, the Court majority, including Douglas but not Frankfurter, reversed the earlier decision, ruling that a compulsory flag salute violated the First Amendment.

his dissent [in the 1940 decision] until the last minute. I didn't have a chance to fully consider it."

"After the *Barnette* decision, Frankfurter, according to his diaries, felt betrayed," I said. "He privately accused you and Justice Black of voting on the basis of political considerations. Apparently, Justice Jackson agreed with him. In 1946, as you know, while Jackson was in Nuremberg as the American prosecutor of the Nazi war criminals, the story appeared in the press to the effect that Truman wanted to appoint Jackson Chief Justice and that you and Black had sent word to the White House that you would resign if the appointment was made."

"Neither Hugo nor I told the President we would resign. That story sounds like a rumor that Felix would start. He was divisive. Machiavellian."

The mention of Frankfurter's name inspired another story. Douglas prefaced it with the accusation that Frankfurter had blocked Truman's nomination of Associate Justice Stanley Reed to the chief justiceship. "At dinner one night," Douglas recalled, "Mrs. Reed was seated between Felix and me. I told her that the man on the other side of her had kept her husband from being Chief Justice. Mrs. Reed spent the next three hours berating Felix. It drove him up a tree."

I reminded Douglas of his reputation on the Court for writing his opinions quickly and without the aid of his law clerks. "Felix could write quickly when he wanted to," said Douglas. Occasionally a draft of a Frankfurter opinion would be circulated, however, that Douglas suggested was not entirely the effort of the Justice. " 'Felix,' I said, 'this opinion doesn't have your footprints.' He didn't like that," Douglas said, with a chuckle.

There were more serious disagreements with Frankfurter. He accused Douglas of grandstanding when the legal appeal of Julius and Ethel Rosenberg reached the Court. Douglas, in 1953, had stayed the execution of the Rosenbergs—who had been convicted of conspiring to pass atomic bomb secrets to the Russians— pending a full Court ruling on new evidence presented by the Rosenbergs' lawyer. Chief Justice Fred Vinson had quickly reconvened the full Court and the majority overturned Douglas's decision. The Rosenbergs were executed within twenty-four hours after the Court decision. Douglas was a hero to supporters of the

Rosenbergs and to the liberal community generally.

Frankfurter later suggested that Douglas's public posture differed radically from his private votes. In his confidential memoranda, Frankfurter wrote that Douglas had voted against hearing constitutional issues raised by the Rosenbergs' case on five different occasions before he publicly issued the stay (while Frankfurter had voted to hear the issues on each occasion). It was a characteristically political maneuver by Douglas, Frankfurter contended. Frankfurter's view was recounted to Douglas.

"Felix never voted to grant certiorari [Supreme Court review]. Hugo and I and one other voted to grant cert. But it wasn't Felix."

Aware that Frankfurter's recollections differed from his own, Douglas was not upset by the contradiction. He seemed content to have historians weigh his word against Frankfurter's.

Douglas was asked about other high public officials, beginning with Harry Truman. It was suggested that, judging from his written comments, Douglas had not admired Truman and that his coolness seemed to begin in the summer of 1944, when Truman's name was placed ahead of Douglas's on FDR's list of vice-presidential candidates.

"You didn't seem to like Truman," I said. Douglas ignored the statement and all reference to the 1944 Democratic convention.

"I was angry with his Court appointments," Douglas said. "Vinson, Burton and Minton [Chief Justice Fred Vinson, Associate Justice Harold Burton and Associate Justice Sherman Minton] were all from the Truman Committee [when Truman was a U.S. senator].*

"When Minton and Truman were in the Senate, they would come into town. Minton would say to Truman, 'Should we check into the hotel or go straight to the whorehouse?' That was 'Shay' Minton."

Douglas was asked about Lyndon Johnson. "You were good friends, weren't you?"

Douglas did not respond to the question, but he did comment

---

*Actually, only Burton (but not Vinson or Minton) served on the Truman Committee, which investigated wartime profiteering and fraud by government contract during World War II.

on Johnson. "He used to keep a list of the girlfriends of congressmen. When he wanted a bill passed, he would have a little talk with the congressmen and suggest that their constituents back home might be very interested in their girlfriends. He did the same thing after he became President."

I asked about Chief Justice Earl Warren. "Under Warren, there was an openness of ideas in judicial conference," Douglas continued. "Under Burger [Chief Justice Warren Burger], there was pressure to join ranks."

Just before Chief Justice Warren resigned, and prior to Richard Nixon's election to the presidency in 1968, President Johnson sent Associate Justice Abe Fortas's name to the Senate for confirmation as Chief Justice. Fortas's nomination provoked a controversy that ultimately resulted in his resignation from the Court. I asked Douglas about the resignation.

"I was in Brazil giving a series of lectures at the time," Douglas recalled. He returned to Washington and went directly to Fortas's house, where he sat all night with his former student and Court colleague. "I told him that he should do what he thinks is right," said Douglas, "but he should not be influenced by political pressure."

I reminded Douglas that he had suggested that Nixon was behind the Fortas resignation and also the drive, publicly led by then Congressman Gerald R. Ford, to impeach Douglas himself.

Douglas nodded his head. "I thought Nixon was behind it and I was right."

Douglas pressed the buzzer for Datcher to take him home. The interview was over.

PART ONE: _____

THE ACHIEVER

CHAPTER ONE

TREASURE

THE FERGUS FALLS WEEKLY JOURNAL focused the attention of its readers in northwest Minnesota on the progress of the Paris Peace Commission. The news judgment was understandable. After all, Minnesota had been the first state in the Union to respond to President William McKinley's call for volunteers to wage war against a treacherous Spain, which, America's yellow press assured, had sunk the battleship *Maine*. Having won Lieutenant Colonel Theodore Roosevelt's bully war, United States negotiators at Paris in October 1898 determined to win the peace.

If news from Paris suggested that the United States was emerging from the Spanish-American War as a world power, other stories in the *Fergus Falls Weekly Journal* that October reminded readers that the dangerous frontier days of the nineteenth century were still with them. "HOSTILE REDS ON THE LEECH LAKE RESERVATION FIRE ON U.S. REGULARS," the *Journal* reported. The soldiers had been called to battle at Leech Lake, northwest of Fergus Falls, to help quell the Chippewa Indian uprising. Both sides had "suffered severely."

Even with peace negotiations abroad and Indian uprisings at home, the *Fergus Falls Weekly Journal* dutifully reported local activities on the newspaper's inside pages. The Reverend William Douglas, it was noted, attended the presbytery at Elbow Lake, fifteen miles south of Fergus Falls. More important to Reverend Douglas and to American history, however, was a less conspicuously placed item: from Maine, the tiny village ten miles northeast of Fergus Falls, the Reverend and Mrs. Douglas announced the birth, on October 16, of a son, William Orville Douglas.

When the township of Maine had been organized in 1871, the area claimed five lakes and a handful of farmers. The fishing was good then, as it is more than a century later, and the flat land yielded subsistence crops of wheat and corn, when the brutal winters permitted. The village of Maine became the population center of the township, boasting a general store, blacksmith shop and cemetery, all doing a thriving business.

Maine's settlers feared only God, and in time, churches dotted the landscape. One of them, the Maine Presbyterian Church, had been built in 1887 with five hundred dollars and the hard labor of the congregants. The first minister was an extraordinary man named Alfred C. Pettit, who was described by one congregant as "a gift of God to the community."

In 1895 the Reverend Pettit was joined by a tall, bearded, intense divinity student named William Douglas, who came to Maine to complete his field work for the Presbyterian ministry. Douglas had been born in Novia Scotia, where his family settled in 1773 after having sailed from Scotland. William's grandfather, Colin Douglas, cleared a stretch of rolling, rocky land on the east side of Middle River, Nova Scotia, and began a new life of farming and Presbyterian worship, a life that was carried on by William's father, Alexander.

As a youngster, William attended school in Alma and Pictou, Nova Scotia, but his primary interest was not in school or his father's farm. Rather, he spent most of his time in the Presbyterian church and earned a considerable reputation as a singing evangelist. His half brother, Lewis, remembered William's early performances. "When the hat was passed," Lewis recalled, "you could hear the silver dropping." Unfortunately, William was forced by throat trouble to stop his evangelical singing. Still devoted to religious work, he left Nova Scotia to study for the ministry in Chicago at Rush and Moody Bible Institute, before moving to Minnesota.

At the Maine Presbyterian Church, where he worked with the Reverend Pettit, Douglas met the church organist, Julia Fisk. She was a slight woman with clear blue eyes, reddish-brown hair and a firm, proud chin. Douglas quickly fell in love with Julia, and a year after they had been introduced, he proposed marriage.

Julia Fisk and her twin sister, Jennie, were born in 1872 in a log cabin in Maine, two of Orville and Salome Fisk's six children. Orville Fisk had come to Maine township from Vermont to farm, raise a family of devout Presbyterians and vote Republican. His vigorous life had been cut short by malaria, a disease he contracted while fighting with the Union forces in the Civil War. In 1885, at the age of forty-eight, Orville Fisk died, leaving his large family and farm to the care of his wife.

Though small and slight, Salome Fisk milked the cows, plowed and harvested the crops, cut the firewood, cooked for and raised eight children (two by a previous marriage). "My life at times seemed hard," Salome Fisk's grandson William O. Douglas wrote in his autobiography, "but whenever I started feeling sorry for myself, I thought of my grandmother and her burdens."

Salome Fisk's daughter Julia carried her own set of burdens. Julia weighed only two pounds at birth and was in such precarious health that she had to be carried around on a pillow for the first three months of her life. Like her own son William, Julia was sickly and weak as an infant. She could not walk until she was three, but with extraordinary determination, Julia learned to walk and then to run and, finally, to outrun her four sisters and her younger brother. Much of Julia's early life was spent taking care of other members of her family, helping with the chores on the family farm and worshiping at the Maine Presbyterian Church. "Mother resembled Grandma Fisk in many ways," Martha Douglas Bost, William O. Douglas's sister, recalled. "Grandma was a very fine woman—great strength of character and determination —just like Mother!"

After her marriage to the Reverend William Douglas in 1896,

Julia gave birth to a daughter, Martha, in 1897, and their first son, William Orville, in 1898. By this time, the Reverend Douglas had assumed his first regular pastorate at Maine, succeeding the Reverend Pettit. Douglas settled his young family into the church manse and began the active, hectic life of an itinerant preacher. He conducted three Sunday services, beginning at 10:30 A.M. in Maine, traveling by horse and buggy to nearby Maplewood for a three o'clock afternoon service, and delivering a final sermon at Elbow Lake or Friberg or Battle Lake in the evening.

The Douglas children's memories of home life in Maine were sketchy. William O. Douglas remembered only "sawdust pitched high around the foundation of our house for winter insulation, melting snow, the first new shoots of spring, an early yellow flower and a black cat." Martha's first memory "was watching the leaves of the trees from the cradle on our front porch."

For Martha, there were a few more vivid memories of her early childhood in Maine, most of which she would just as soon have forgotten. Martha showed her temper early and her tantrums were a source of concern to both her parents. Her mother and father differed, however, on how to deal with them. "Father would sit me down and talk to me for ten minutes," Martha has recalled, "and I would be in tears." Julia Douglas's method of dealing with a recalcitrant Martha was simply to lock her in the closet. That made Martha, whose quick temper equaled her mother's, even angrier. Fortunately for Martha, her mother was usually too busy caring for her ailing brother to concentrate on her. For William Orville Douglas was a sickly child almost from birth, requiring his mother's constant attention.

For the first five years of his life, William O. Douglas was called "Treasure" by his mother. She would not permit anyone in the family to call him "Bill," because she intensely disliked the nickname. "Orville" was rather cumbersome for so small a lad. It was "Treasure," suggesting his preciousness to the whole family, but most of all to Julia Fisk Douglas. He was her favorite child, very sensitive, high-strung, conscientious—in every way just like his mother.

When Douglas was still a toddler, both parents allowed him small indulgences. One Sunday, for example, the Reverend

Douglas was at the pulpit, his wife at the organ and Martha in a front pew. Suddenly "Treasure" walked up and sat in the extra chair by the pulpit. While a chagrined Martha looked on, her brother stuffed a handkerchief in his mouth, stood on his seat, turned to the audience and began to pull out the cloth, as a magician pulls colorful handkerchiefs out of a hat before a mesmerized audience.

But there were few such frivolous moments for the little boy in Maine, for he spent much of his time in bed, an early victim of infantile paralysis. After Douglas ran a high fever for several weeks, a country doctor came to the manse and told Julia that her son would soon lose the use of his legs. The doctor also predicted that he would die before he reached the age of forty.

Julia Douglas listened intently to the doctor's instructions to massage her son's legs frequently in salt water. For Julia, it was more than a country doctor's prescription; it became her obsession. While the Reverend Douglas took care of Martha and his church duties, Julia Douglas coached her son back to health with massages and prayers.

Douglas remembered his mother's determined vigil. "She soaked my legs in warm salt water and rubbed it into my pores, massaging each leg muscle every two hours, day after day, night after night. She did not go to bed for six weeks. The fever passed, but the massages continued for weeks thereafter. I vaguely recall the ordeal. I lay in bed too weak to move. My legs felt like pipestems; they seemed almost detached, the property of someone else. They were so small and thin that Mother's hands could go clear around them. She would knead them like bread; she would push her hands up them and then down, up and down, up and down, until my skin was red and raw. But she would not stop because of that. She said she wanted me to be strong, to be able to run. She told me that when she was a girl she could run like the wind; no one could catch her. She wondered if I would ever be able to do so. And then she'd laugh and rub my legs—rub and rub and rub—and two hours later, rub some more."

"Treasure" was not the only member of the family who fell ill in Maine. The Reverend Douglas began to have stomach pains, which became so intense that in 1901 the family moved west in search of warmer weather and the Reverend Douglas's improved health. "I was about three years old," William O. Douglas later wrote, "but I left Minnesota with great sadness. I was greatly attached to Grandmother Fisk and I cried when we left her. I cried most of the way across the country in a dirty, rickety Pullman car." When the family arrived in California, young Douglas "was desolate and I did not get over my sorrow for days." When she took her first look at the dry California countryside, Julia Douglas told Martha, she felt like crying for "Grandma" Fisk too.

The Douglases settled in Estrella, a small California town in the hot, arid county of San Luis Obispo. Shortly after the Reverend Douglas undertook the duties of his new pastorate, a second son, Arthur, was born. The family soon realized that they had traded one climatic extreme for another. Minnesota's paralyzing blizzards were only a memory, replaced by the fresh fear of tornadoes. Once a terrified Julia Douglas marched her family into their Estrella house and made them stand with their backs upright to the wall, waiting for the tornado that never came. What did appear, not only that day but almost every other, was the intense heat and glare of the sun. The Reverend Douglas complained less about stomach pains and more about the sun's rays, which were affecting his weak eyes. He began spending less and less time out of the house. Finally he set up his study in the basement of their house, totally protected from the sun. There he dictated his sermons and letters to his wife, who wrote out every spoken word in longhand. Although his elder son remembered fondly Estrella's fruit stands and the hills surrounding the town, the Reverend Douglas was not comfortable. A year and a half after they arrived in Estrella, the family was on the move, again searching for a more restful climate.

For his family's third home in less than two years, the Reverend Douglas picked Cleveland, Washington, a village nestled in a pine grove north of the Columbia River. A doctor promised that the new climate would invigorate the elder Douglas. Cleveland had many of the characteristics of Maine: a lively, friendly group of residents, a church, a school, a post office and several stores. The Douglases resumed a routine similar to the one they had left in Minnesota. The Reverend Douglas's pastorate included not only Cleveland, but also the nearby villages of Bickleton and Dot. He preached in two or three villages every Sunday and in one of them at least once more during the week.

It was an arduous schedule, but no more so than the one Julia Douglas maintained for herself and her three children. On Sundays she would dress the children in clean clothes and walk them to church at nine o'clock for Sunday school. They would return home briefly, then attend their father's regular service at eleven. By day's end, they had added a Christian Endeavor meeting and another regular church service. Every Thursday, the entire Douglas family again appeared at the little Cleveland Presbyterian Church for a prayer meeting.

Part of the family's dedication, no doubt, was motivated by the Reverend Douglas's position in the community. If the pastor could not inspire total devotion to God's word in his own family, others might understandably falter. And if the parishioners' enthusiasm waned, so, too, might the gifts of chickens and baskets of coal which were needed to supplement the minister's six-hundred-dollar annual salary. But it was not pragmatism alone that drove the Douglases to church so often. Fisks and Douglases had taught good old-fashioned Presbyterian ardor for three generations. Churchgoing would in fact be central to young William O. Douglas's weekly schedule even after his fervor for organized religion had cooled significantly. Julia Douglas insisted upon it and her elder son obeyed dutifully until he was an adult and more than 2,500 miles away from her.

In Cleveland, the Reverend Douglas again was plagued by stomach pains, but he refused to rest. Instead he went out preaching, not only through duty, but because of preference. It was unfortunate. Martha remembered seeing her father walking in a pine grove near their home in Cleveland. She could tell that he was still sick; was worse, in fact, than ever. A week later, the Reverend Douglas was taken to a hospital in Portland, Oregon, to be operated on for ulcers. The operation was successful, but doctors were not able to get food into the patient's stomach. In 1904, at the age of forty-seven, the Reverend William Douglas died.

"He knew me yesterday," Julia Douglas wrote her mother the day after her husband's death. "I asked him if he knew me. He tried to say 'yes.' I said to him, 'Do you know me, dear?' and he spoke so I could understand him. 'Yes.' Oh, it is so hard. You don't know how lonesome it is without him."

For William O. Douglas, five years old, the loss of his father was inexplicable, total desolation.

> He was present one day and then he was gone—forever. There would never be another to lift me high in the air, to squeeze my hand and give me masculine praise. There were no longer any pockets I could search for nuggets of maple sugar. The step in the hallway, the laugh, the jingle of coins in the pockets—these had gone as silently as the waters of the great Columbia. . . .
>
> As I stood by the edge of the grave, a wave of lonesomeness swept over me. Then in my lonesomeness I became afraid—afraid of being left alone, afraid because the grave held my defender and protector. These feelings were deepened by the realization that Mother was afraid and lonesome too. My throat choked up, and I started to cry. I remembered the words of the minister who had said to me, "You must now be a man, sonny." I tried to steel myself and control my emotions.

Douglas stopped crying, he wrote, only after he looked up from his father's grave to see Mount Adams, towering in the distance. "Adams stood cool and calm, unperturbed by an event that had stirred us so deeply that Mother was crushed for years. Adams suddenly seemed to be a friend. Adams subtly became a force for me to tie to, a symbol of stability and strength."

The primary source of stability and strength for Douglas in his formative years was not a towering peak, however, but a determined widow, Julia Fisk Douglas. She had been trained for her role as provider and catalyst for her family by her mother, Salome Fisk, who had been left in similar straits when her husband died. Grandmother Fisk had fought despair and financial desperation by the force of hard work. Julia would follow her mother's example.

Julia's Douglas's first decision was to present her children with a model by which to judge their own lives and achievements. "I want to bring them up so they will be good children," she wrote her mother immediately after her husband died, "and do as much good in the world as Mr. D. did." The late Reverend Douglas would become the Douglas family's symbol for all that was good and noble in life. Julia Douglas preserved his sermons, so the children could read them and be inspired. "Like St. Francis," William O. Douglas later wrote of his father, "he loved people and went humbly among them. Spiritual reward, not monetary gain, was his desire." He was, Douglas later concluded, "one of the truly good men I ever knew."

"Mother always felt she had married the only man in the world," Martha, William O. Douglas's sister, recalled. The Douglas children were brought up to strive to equal their father, a task that Julia Douglas considered impossible. When William O. Douglas was appointed to the U.S. Supreme Court, his mother noted the event with satisfaction. "Well, he's as smart as his father," Julia Douglas told Martha, "but not as handsome." Each of the three Douglas children realized extraordinary professional achievement—William as an associate justice of the U.S. Supreme Court, Martha as personnel director for large department stores and Arthur as president of the Statler Hotel chain. Still, none could equal their father, at least in their mother's eyes. "We were brought up to think we had to be as smart as Papa, but we could never be as good," Martha said. "At times, I thought this was particularly hard on the boys, because they had to compete with a phantom."

BORN FOR SUCCESS

AFTER HER HUSBAND'S DEATH, Julia Douglas moved her family to Yakima, Washington, only a few miles from Cleveland, where one of her sisters lived. By 1904, North Yakima (as it was named until the state legislature officially shortened it to Yakima in 1917) had become the state's seventh-largest city, with a population of seven thousand. The city's growth was directly attributable to two factors: irrigation and the railroads. The first assured farmers in the surrounding flatlands of bumper crops of apples, cherries, apricots and peaches. Farmers could anticipate 300 days of sunshine and, despite only eight inches of rain a year, a growing season of 195 days. The question, then, for Yakima valley farmers was not what fruits to grow or how much, but where to sell their produce. The Northern Pacific Railway soon helped them answer the question by locating its headquarters for central Washington in North Yakima and making the city a commercial-agricultural-industrial center.

"At times the congestion on the main thoroughfare is so great," noted the writer of a 1904 North Yakima Commercial Club promotion booklet, "that the question has been asked the writer on more than one occasion by strangers, 'if there were a circus in town and if people were waiting for a parade?' " He continued, describing one of Yakima's attractive residential sections: "Here are beautiful homes and lawns and gardens and fruit and shade on all sides. An unsightly ill kept place, an unpainted house is the exception. The wide streets with shade trees along each side of the borders of irrigating ditches give the portions of the residence district the appearance of parks. It is pre-eminently a city to live in, to make a home in."

With six hundred dollars from the proceeds of her husband's life insurance policy, Julia Douglas bought a small lot at 111 North Fifth Avenue and had a five-room clapboard house built for her family. She gave the rest of the insurance money to a local lawyer, James O. Cull, who invested it in an irrigation project in the Yakima valley, a project for which he was a promoter. The project failed, and with it the Douglas family's hopes for modest prosperity evaporated. William O. Douglas remembered Cull as "the devil incarnate," who forced his family to begin a financial struggle that would not end for Douglas until he had established himself as a promising young lawyer in New York more than two decades later.

The Douglas family lived, literally, on the "wrong" side of the Northern Pacific railroad tracks, if the "right" side was where most of Yakima's prospering businesses and beautiful homes were located. It was that side of the tracks which represented to William O. Douglas for the rest of his life the "establishment," where conformity and status seeking were as prevalent as shiny prosperity.

The Douglas children sometimes brooded about their status. "I think we all felt socially looked down upon," Martha recalled. "We were never invited to the parties. My brother Bill never talked about it, but we didn't invite people to our house."

But neither Orville (as he was called throughout his years in Yakima), Martha nor Arthur had much time to feel poor. Julia Douglas would not allow them the luxury of self-pity. There was too much work to be done. Martha summed up the Douglas attitude: "We never felt poor; we just didn't have money." Whenever self-pity seeped into the conversation, it was quickly overwhelmed by a burst of Douglas pride. Martha remembered the day that her brother Arthur came home from high school and said, "I'm so tired of being poor. All the other boys have more clothes and they have cars, too." Arthur then paused and added, "But I can lick the whole bunch." Martha replied, "That's all that counts."

Home life was rigidly structured for survival and cohesiveness. Julia Douglas was the head of the household; she cooked, cleaned, mended and, to earn a few extra dollars, washed some of the neighbors' laundry. Martha brought in the coal and was her mother's chief assistant in cleaning the house and taking care of the two boys. Orville chopped the wood, delivered the *Yakima Republic,* washed store windows, swept floors and mowed lawns. When he was old enough, Arthur joined his older brother, performing odd jobs and household chores.

When the children strayed from the narrow path that Julia Douglas had laid out for them, they instantly were advised of the error of their ways. Martha remembered, however, that most of her mother's anger was directed at herself and Arthur, not at Bill. "Mama never got mad at Bill," Martha said. Still, the lessons were learned by all three Douglas children. "When Mama was angry," Martha remembered, "she would say, 'If you children don't behave, I'll send you to Uncle Sam.' He was the husband of Mama's sister who lived across the street. He had black eyes and we were scared of him. She never did send us to him."

When the boys were in grade school, they broke a schoolhouse window nearby while playing ball. "Mama made them tell the principal they'd done it," Martha recalled, "and made them earn money to pay for it." One gentle expletive—"Gosh" would do— and Julia Douglas would fill her child's mouth with soapsuds at the kitchen sink. Whatever sin remained was carefully and regularly expiated at Yakima's First Presbyterian Church, where Martha, Orville and Arthur, scrubbed and constantly supervised by their mother, prayed three times a week. In church or at home, Julia Douglas raised her children by a single standard: would her husband have approved?

The Douglases exhibited the same intensity and purpose in play as in work. When chores were done, Julia Douglas sat down at an old pump organ in the living room and the family sang hymns and folk songs, led, of course, by Julia's rich contralto voice. There were also taffy pulls and regular games of Author and Pit after dinner. Although Julia's puritanical standards permeated her home, so did her humor, which was mischievous, and often tinged with a surprising hint of raucousness. One of her favorite stories was of a woman who finally rid herself of arthritis by taking generous gulps of a popular cathartic. Once cured, she offered a testimonial for the company peddling the cathartic. Before taking the medicine, she wrote, she had been bedridden. Since taking it, "I haven't been to bed for more than ten minutes at a time!" The story convulsed the Douglases, including Mama, in laughter each time it was told.

Storytelling—particularly tales with an irreverent or, better, a slightly off-color twist—delighted the young Orville Douglas. In time the boy became a master storyteller himself. As an adult, Douglas loved to tell anecdotes of his childhood or his latest fishing or mountain-climbing adventure. He also remained a sucker for the dirty joke or limerick, to the extent that the conversation during fishing trips with his close friend Fred Rodell was sometimes devoted entirely to the composition of bawdy rhymes.

Douglas satisfied his mischievous side by action as well as word, becoming an incorrigible practical joker. Martha was usually the target. His sister found alarm clocks in her bed, fish heads in her suitcases, salt or mothballs in her coffee. Once, Orville and Art built a merry-go-round by nailing together two wooden planks. Martha was pressed into service as the boys' first customer and, predictably, went tumbling off the planks into a neighbor's yard. She was also selected as the test pilot for her younger brothers' home-built glider. The maiden flight was short—from the gable of an old shed, with Newtonian directness, to the ground below. Both pilot and plane lay splintered and supine while the aerospace engineers planned anew. The playful harassment went on, unabated, even in church. With Mama sitting at the end of the pew, Orville would surreptitiously slip a straight pin out of the lapel of his coat and prick his sister, who was jolted by pain while Orville remained blissfully attentive to the service.

Once a year the Douglas family rushed downtown for the annual circus parade of six team horses, clowns and wild animals. Julia bought tickets for her family to both the circus and the midway rides. On the midway, she joined them at the top of the big chute, and then, face taut and skirt held snug, she slid down and out. If you were a Douglas, you worked hard—and you played with equal dedication.

Julia Fisk Douglas did not talk often to her children about her politics, but when she did, her views were not tainted by ambiguity. She was a Republican party worker in Yakima because the Republicans represented the Rich and the Rich employed the Poor. If you wanted jobs and security, you voted Republican. It was that simple for Julia Douglas.

It was not so simple or so obvious to her son William Orville Douglas. To be sure, the Republican party represented the Rich, and the Rich, when it suited them, employed the Poor. But Douglas watched the Rich—Yakima's establishment—and did not like what he saw: "I was hardly fourteen, but I knew the Rich who were pillars of Yakima. They treated labor as scum; they controlled the police; some of them even had investments in Yakima's brothels. They went to church and were 'godly' men but I had nothing in common with them."

Douglas bitterly recalled that he spent a few weeks as a teenager working as a "stool pigeon" for a member of Yakima's establishment who had decided to rid the town of all prostitutes and bootleggers. His job was to spend Saturday and Sunday nights strolling up and down South Front Street, the heart of the redlight district, inviting solicitation from the pleasure merchants. Douglas quit the job after a few weeks, ashamed by his part in the reformation con game. But anger quickly replaced shame, anger that a prominent member of the establishment would ask him, and not one of his own sons, to be the stool pigeon. According to Douglas, it was because no member of the establishment would allow his own family to be contaminated by society's outcasts.

The father of one of Douglas's best friends, Elon Gilbert, was a member of Yakima's establishment whom Douglas later accused of making him do the dirty work. A prominent fruit grower and shipper, Gilbert had three sons, but, according to Douglas, never asked them to patrol the brothels. Elon Gilbert was not aware of his friend's feelings until several decades later, when, sitting around a campfire and relaxed by a few drinks, Douglas revealed to Gilbert that his father had asked Douglas to do things on South

Front Street as a teen-ager that he shouldn't have.

Douglas attributed his later defense of minorities to his early days as a "stool pigeon" for the city's establishment in Yakima's red-light district.

> South Front Street in Yakima made me realize that there were those even in this free land who thought that some men were more equal than others, that their sons were to be preferred over the sons of other people less worthy. [There] was a residue of resentment of which I have never quite got rid—resentment against hypocrites in church clothes who raise their denunciations against petty criminals, while their own sins mount high. This feeling somehow aligned me emotionally with the miserable people who make up the chaff of society. I never sought their company, nor engaged in their tricks or traffic, nor spent my hours with them. I think, however, that I have always been quicker to defend them than I would have been but for the high churchmen of Yakima.

If Douglas resented the establishment, as he later stressed in his autobiography, it was a resentment that he kept very much to himself. During all their adolescent years together, Gilbert was unaware that Douglas was sensitive to being poor and that he hated the establishment, which included Gilbert's family. "Bill didn't resent having to work," Gilbert said. "He never mentioned his work. In those days, I don't think he had this antipathy for businessmen. That came later."

Some members of Yakima's present "establishment," such as W. H. (Ted) Robertson, who, like his father, published the *Yakima Herald-Republic,* believe that Douglas's recollections in his autobiography are so much revisionist sociology. "Douglas's view of division in Yakima between rich and poor is so much horseradish," said Robertson. "There were only three or four wealthy people in the whole town. I think Douglas in his autobiography was trying to prove why he was championing the underdog. This town was never divided into rich and poor."

Whether Yakima's rich numbered three or thirty was not so important to the Douglas family as the fact that they always felt like outsiders, regardless of the number of those who were "in." "While there were many children's parties in Yakima, we were never invited to a single one and we were far too poor to have one in our own home," Douglas wrote, recalling memories similar to those of his sister.

For someone with such an intense class consciousness, Douglas remained surprisingly aloof from formal political activity as a teen-ager. There is no record of a strong political commitment in school or outside. He sympathized with the prostitutes on South Front Street and with Yakima Susie, the Indian squaw who stood at the corner of Yakima Avenue and First Street, begging for money. He had been color-blind to the few blacks at North Yakima High School and caring toward the migrant farm workers he met in the summers of fruit picking in the Yakima valley. But it seemed to be a personal commitment between Douglas and another human being, not an endorsement of a broad ideology.

Douglas chided his mother for her rote Republicanism, but made no demonstrable commitment to the Democrats or Progressives. He remembered admiring William Jennings Bryan and even listening to his stump speeches at the age of fourteen. But he did not recall what Bryan said. Douglas also admired Hiram Johnson, William Borah and Gifford Pinchot, but he did not follow up his enthusiasm with local political activity. Yes, he admired Johnson's progressive reforms when he was governor of California. And he applauded Borah's defense of minorities when he was a U.S. Senator and Pinchot's protection of the nation's forests while he was Chief of the U.S. Forestry Service. But the interest came through newspaper reading and the applause, apparently, was kept to himself. Douglas did not talk to his family or friends about his political heroes, nor did he speak or organize publicly for their causes.

William O. Douglas, who as an associate justice of the U.S. Supreme Court would become the indefatigable champion of civil rights and liberties, was preoccupied with other matters when he was growing up in Yakima. His organizational preferences were nonpartisan; he was most active in Christian Endeavor and the North Yakima High School Debating Club. His acquaintances included American Indians and itinerant farm workers. But his closest friends covered the economic and social spectrum of Yakima, from Elon Gilbert, whose father was president of the Good Government League, a prominent church member and a prosperous fruit grower, to Al Egley, who left school at the age of thirteen to support his family with his earnings as a clothing salesman. Above all, Douglas shared his mother's view of what was most important to both of them: academic achievement.

When Julia Douglas had settled in Yakima, she selected a housing site facing the Columbia Grade School, where the three Douglas children were to receive the first eight years of their formal education. The proximity of the Douglas house to the school may have been more than coincidental. Julia Fisk Douglas, whose own education was meager, believed strongly that her children must have more. She often told her daughter that education meant freedom to do and be what you aspired to. In her last years, Julia sadly confessed her envy of Martha, who had by then become a successful businesswoman. She wished she could have worked in an office, she told her daughter, instead of having spent most of her life at home, raising a family.

Good grades in school were not accepted; they were demanded. When Arthur once brought home a report card with a single low mark, his older brother took him behind the woodshed and told him the grade was unacceptable. He was a Douglas, Orville told his younger brother, and a low mark in any category was un-Douglaslike. Julia Douglas never doubted that her children would succeed in school, as long as they were constantly reminded of her expectation. The syllogism was simple and to the point: They were Douglases; therefore they would excel. "And knowing she expected it of us," Martha remembered, "and having a lot of Douglas competitiveness, we tried very hard."

For her brother Orville, making good grades served an additional purpose. "We went to the same schools as the elite," he later wrote. "We competed for grades with them and usually won." In the competitive arena of the classroom, then, the distinctions of wealth meant nothing. It was every man for himself. William Orville Douglas liked the odds; after all, he was a Douglas.

In the classroom, Douglas pretended casualness. One of his classmates remembered him as a bluffer. "He'd come into class and say, 'Hey, kid, what's the English lesson? Hey, kid, what's a gerund? I didn't have time to study.' " And then, of course, he would receive the highest test mark in the class. "He had the fastest mind I ever saw," one of his classmates marveled.

The quickness of Douglas's mind dazzled those around him throughout his life. But in those early high school days, the achievement did not come as effortlessly for him as he liked to have his classmates believe. Orville, like his sister and brother, was required to devote the predinner hours to his studies. He sometimes became so anxious about his homework that Martha would be forced to help him before she could do her own. When Douglas entered school the next day, he was usually nervous and tense. But he performed flawlessly.

Douglas approached his favorite extracurricular activity in high school, debating, with the same intensity. He loved to pit his mind against the best the other schools could offer. The issue for debate did not matter—e.g., Resolved: That the Monroe Doctrine should be discontinued—so much as the intellectual process itself.

Before each debate, Douglas practiced his arguments on the back porch, with Martha as his captive audience. And the next day, there was Martha sitting uncomfortably in the front row of the auditorium, never taking her eyes off her brother. Usually Orville's outward signs of strain disappeared with the call to competition. But not always. In one of his early debates, Douglas's mind went blank on the platform. The frightened and frustrated boy kept repeating the first sentence of his argument, unable to remember what followed. Tears welled in his eyes. He left the stage in humiliation, and walked the Yakima streets for hours before gathering his courage to return to the proud Douglas home. The mental lapse, Douglas vowed, would not happen again. And it didn't.

His rare defeats were usually suffered on the basketball court, not on the stage or in the classroom. Douglas, whose legs had lengthened dramatically since the days when Julia Douglas had massaged them, more than a decade earlier, was the starting center for a North Yakima team that was remembered for its courage more than its ability. During Douglas's senior year, his team was beaten six times, while winning only two games.

Martha Douglas once overheard two high school teachers who had taught both her and her brother Orville speaking to Julia Douglas about her children. "Both Martha and Orville are good students," one of the teachers said, "but Orville has the more unusual mind." The remark disturbed Martha at the time. It shouldn't have. William Orville Douglas's mind, compared with almost every one else's, was awesome. It was not only extraordinarily quick, but probing and facile as well. That brilliant mind, combined with an intense desire to succeed, could only result in high achievement.

Douglas's reputation as a top student was so well known that some of his classmates suspected that teachers automatically gave him the top grade in the class, regardless of performance. Brad Emery suspected such favoritism after he and Douglas were paired for a chemistry experiment. "Our papers were identical copies of each other and Bill got a 95 and I got an 88," Emery recalled. "I never overcame my distrust for that instructor. Of course, Bill was valedictorian of our class and that may have accounted for the fact that the teacher thought he deserved higher marks."

In addition to being selected valedictorian, William Orville Douglas was named the student who most distinguished his class and his school. He shared with Lyndon Hassenmuller and Grace Lee the title of most brilliant member of the class. He was selected attorney to execute the class will and, in a one-act graduation play, Orville Douglas was cast in the role of President of the United States. The inscription next to the senior picture of the gaunt, confident Orville Douglas read: "Born for success he seemed, With grace to win, with heart to hold, With shining gifts that took all eyes."

"As a cork on a rolling, tossing sea," valedictorian Douglas began his graduation address, "I, as well as you, entered this high school in the fall of 1912, along with 100 other students, 59 of whom have survived. We were all as green as Ireland's shamrock and felt as independent as Mexican bandits." Douglas then recalled the first senior who spoke to him ("how big I felt"), the satisfaction of his first winning essay in a literary contest and the "concentration of mind and self-control" he had learned at North

Yakima High School. He concluded: "The past, full of pleasant memories, is not the time in which to live. Today, the present, is the time in which we should make our lives count. Now is the time for accomplishing things. We need not wait till our hair grows gray to live lives of service. We can start now and in daily life by doing deeds of kindness. And by making each day count for more than the one before, we can better appreciate the full meaning of that word—Love. Man loves God best by serving men."

It was a valedictory that would have pleased the Reverend William Douglas.

CHAPTER THREE ————————————————

ESCAPE

A SIGNIFICANT FACT of American history is that some of the most successful public leaders have been the first-born male children in their families. The mothers of these leaders have usually been highly intelligent, energetic women who have channeled their own strong drives for success into the careers of their oldest sons. For most of the mothers, religious observance has been central to their lives; sons have been expected to follow their example. Fathers rarely have played a significant role in the sons' upbringing, either because they have been weaker in character than their wives or because they have not been around. First-born sons like Lyndon B. Johnson and Jimmy Carter, for example, became their mothers' favorites. That was also true for Julia Douglas's elder son, William O. Douglas.

To be sure, Julia Fisk Douglas watched carefully as all three of her children strived mightily to please her and honor the memory of her late husband. But she watched the development of her first son with special care. He had been her "Treasure" since birth.

Julia's preference was not lost on her other children. Aware of her mother's early attention to her brother, Martha found herself more and more in the company of her father. When he died, she curried her mother's favor by helping her bring up her two younger brothers. Still, in Martha's eyes, Julia Douglas did everything for the boys. She laughed at their jokes and cheered at their basketball games. She took the boys to the circus and brought Martha along as an afterthought. Afraid that her boys would be sissies, Julia signed Orville and Arthur up for the Boy Scouts and the YMCA. Martha signed up for the YWCA herself.

In the family pecking order, the second son, Arthur, came before Martha but far behind his older brother. When Arthur or Martha did something wrong they were punished, but, somehow, Orville seemed to escape. "Mama said to me," Martha recalled, " 'He won't live past twelve so never cross him.' That meant always give in to him." When Douglas passed the age of twelve, his favored status was so well established that neither his brother nor his sister could challenge it.

Arthur appeared to be the very opposite of his brother. He was beefy and gregarious; Bill was slender and shy. Arthur's speech was tougher and his college girlfriends livelier. He shared his emotions, loving openly and laughing a lot. His older brother was more the loner who kept his feelings to himself.

The boys played together, worked together and camped together. But it was always Bill in the lead and Arthur following in his footsteps. Bill gave Arthur his newspaper route after he had graduated to a better job. When the two were camping, Bill set the pace and decided where they would rest. Arthur followed Bill to Whitman College and the Columbia Law School and inherited his brother's tutoring service. Arthur made the same top grades that Bill did and those who knew him said that his brain was equal to his brother's. But Bill was the family's first valedictorian and its first member of the *Columbia Law Review*.

For Arthur, who rarely had to be satisfied with second place in any competition, the rivalry with his older brother continued well into their adult years. Though the two brothers joked together throughout Arthur's life, the conviviality could be interrupted by flashes of anger and jealousy. Even when Arthur was president of the Statler Hotels and Bill an associate justice of the U.S. Supreme Court, the two sometimes fell into petty arguments, bickering just as they had as boys. Both Martha and Julia Douglas were relieved when Arthur was named general counsel of the Statler Hotels several years before his older brother achieved his high position in the Supreme Court. At least for that brief moment, Arthur did not have to share center stage. Later, with the increasing pressures of his job after he became president of the hotel chain, Arthur began to drink heavily. He died an alcoholic in 1956 at the age of fifty-four.

Favored sons have two choices: They can accept their preferred position and bow meekly to the wishes of their overbearing mothers. Or they can fight their mothers' pampering. William O. Douglas took the latter course. As a small boy, he had been aware of his mother's solicitous concern: "[Mother] set about to guard my health, to protect me against physical strains, to do all sorts of favors designed to save my energy. I was waited on, hand and foot. Worse than that, I began to hear what Mother was saying to others: 'He's not as strong as other boys; he has to be careful what he does—you know, his legs were almost paralyzed.' "

The words stung Douglas. "It seemed to me I was being publicly recognized as a puny person—a weakling. Gradually, there began to grow in me a great rebellion."

Douglas attacked his physical problem as he did all others, silently and with total concentration. He began to use the foothills outside Yakima as others used barbells in a gymnasium. At Selah Gap, the foothill nearest his home on North Fifth Avenue, Douglas tested his legs and lungs against the hillside. He pushed himself at the fastest pace his legs could endure, walking two miles a day up the hillside and down. When he returned to his home, he flopped into bed with every muscle in his legs aching. But he did it again the next day and the day after, for months, until the aches were gone and the muscles in his calves and thighs began to bulge. He had proved something then—as he did so often in his life. With will power and courage, he could compete with anyone, physically as well as mentally. He was no longer a weakling in his own mind or in that of his peers, or perhaps most importantly, in the eyes of his mother.

As he gained confidence, Douglas began to ask a few close friends to join him on his hikes. The two-mile walks grew to three miles and five, and eventually into week-long camping trips. In later years, Douglas gave the impression that his treks developed in him a total self-sufficiency. That was not entirely true. His sister prepared his backpacks, filling a large Indian blanket with baking powder and salt for bread, with beans and a bar of chocolate, and wrapping it all neatly in strips of sugar sacks.

Once out of the house, Douglas began his brutal calisthenics, which developed into a lifelong adventure with nature. From the mountains, Douglas playfully taunted his mother, who, he knew, always worried about him. Writing from a campsite deep in the Cascades in the summer of 1915, Douglas told Julia that he hoped he could finish his letter, that is, "if the mosquitoes don't chew me up before I get them." He was freezing without a coat, he wrote, but even if he had a coat and mackinaw (he didn't), he would still be shivering. And in a jest calculated to prick his mother's anxieties, Douglas wrote that he was "still looking for my bear, cougar and rattlesnake."

Douglas was aware that for all her strengths, Julia Fisk Douglas possessed more phobias than a three-year-old child. She feared electrical storms and the dark, the wilderness and cold weather, snakes and all wild animals, particularly bears. It was no wonder, then, that during her boy's camping trips Julia Douglas often woke her daughter in the middle of the night to ask: "Martha, do you think he's all right?" Douglas was not eager to allay her anxieties.

He began to thrive on the adversity that his mother so feared. The more miserable the conditions—rain, sleet, snow—the quicker Douglas's pace. The laughter usually came later, although Douglas's companions suspected that he secretly savored the challenge, even before the retelling. For his high school yearbook, Douglas wrote: "Try sleeping out under an open sky in an open stretch of woods, rolled up in regular blankets under a pouring rain. And lie there eight hours and get one hour of sleep. Then wake up in the morning and have all your clothes, which you left out in the rain uncovered, soaking wet and likewise your blankets." He also recalled mosquitoes as large as meadowlarks, lost trails, dinners eaten by his horse, soggy pancakes and sore throats.

When nature didn't provide the surprises that adventures were made of, Douglas supplied his own challenges. After he and his brother, Art, had camped for a week on the ridge of the Cascades known as the Pacific Crest Trail, Douglas decided that the days had slipped by without a proper physical feat. True, his legs had performed admirably for a week, carrying Douglas and his thirty-pound pack along the tortuous trails. But still, Douglas was not satisfied. After a ten-mile hike early one morning, he decided that the campsite that evening would be at Indian Flat, fifteen miles away. Without telling his brother of his plan to complete a twenty-five-mile hike with thirty-pound packs on their backs, Douglas simply urged Art on so that they could make the evening campsite.

Once on the trail, Douglas set a furious pace, for he wanted to make Indian Flat by sundown. A bewildered Art followed, wondering out loud where the fire was. His older brother did not respond, but kept up the pace, even when his shinbones began to protest. They walked until dusk without interruption, except for brief drinks of water along the river. There were no prolonged stops, no conversation. Halfway to Indian Flat, the two came to an open valley, a perfect campsite. Art suggested that they camp there. No, said his older brother, there was a better one down the trail.

As weariness overtook both boys, Art's questioning of the perfect campsite became more insistent and critical. Douglas ignored the complaints, though he knew how his brother felt. "The shin muscles of my legs were aching like a tooth with an exposed nerve," he later wrote. "A small pain commenced above my eyes and soon the pounding of my heels echoed in my head. I longed to stop and rest; I wanted to sleep and never move until tomorrow. But I pushed on."

Mile after mile, the two trudged on until they reached Indian Flat and collapsed. That night Douglas slept fitfully, aroused by nightmares and a splitting headache. When he tried to walk off his pain, he felt sick in his stomach. He lay down again. The next morning he was too ill to move. But though he was sick, he was satisfied. "Inwardly I felt a glow because of my achievement. I had walked 25 miles with a 30-pound pack in one day. My legs had stood up. I had conquered my doubts. So far as my legs were concerned, I knew that I was now free to roam these mountains at will, to go on foot where any man could go, to enter any forest without hesitation."

Testing his legs was one thing; testing his skills as a horseman quite another. One of his most painful adventures occurred when Douglas kept a rendezvous with Elon Gilbert, and Gilbert's brother and cousin, near the top of Darling Mountain. After a long hike on foot, Douglas had sat on a rock at the designated meeting place. Suddenly the silence was broken by the whoops of Douglas's friends on horseback.

Apprehensively, Douglas eyed the saddled horse his friends had brought for him. Though Douglas had ridden workhorses, he had always done so bareback. He put his foot in the stirrup and swung his lank body onto the saddle. It was not a comfortable fit, but before Douglas had time to think about it, his friends were whooping their horses wildly forward. Without warning, Douglas's mount lurched to the chase.

The next twenty minutes were among the most harrowing of Douglas's life. His horse galloped through willow and aspen and low-hanging fir. He took downhill slopes at a dead run and raced recklessly through rock fields. All the while, Douglas desperately clutched the reins and saddle horn. With stirrups bouncing freely, the rider's feet and legs flayed uncontrollably at the horse's body. Douglas's own body pounded incessantly against the saddle, not in cadence with the horse's steady gallop, but in jarring, painful challenge to it. Douglas's hips numbed and his knees and ankles radiated pain. At last a dazed Douglas glimpsed the lush Little Klickitat Meadow, where the group planned to camp.

After his horse halted, Douglas slipped down gingerly from the saddle. His legs trembled as he limped toward the others. He had decided that he would hide his pain behind the saucy banter that always followed an adventure. But his feigned nonchalance did not work. It did not work because Douglas's rear end was worn raw by the four-mile gallop. He needed medical attention and, grudgingly, admitted it to his friends. Elon Gilbert removed Douglas's pants and he was spread-eagled on a rock. Near the base of the spine, where there was no skin, Elon Gilbert applied ointment and bandages.

Later, when Douglas was lying down, Elon Gilbert came over and said, "Say, fella, you're okay. You sure can go it the hard way." It was Gilbert's way of saying, "We're proud to have you with us." The kind, admiring words soothed Douglas's pain and he fell asleep triumphant. Gilbert had other thoughts that evening, which he did not express. "The poor guy," Gilbert recalled. "What he should have done was stop his horse and come in at his own pace. But he would have thought that belittling."

Like his mother, Douglas rarely showed his true feelings to others. He felt pain and sadness, as his mother had so often during her life. But he, like her, struggled mightily to overcome those feelings or, at least, to hide them from others. Sharing his pain could be mistaken for weakness or self-pity, both intolerable to Douglas. He dealt with pain by silently persevering and then moving resolutely forward.

Douglas's adventures, of course, were more than proving grounds for his manhood. Throughout his lifetime, Douglas relished the horseplay and storytelling and chance encounters with strange travelers who crossed his mountain paths. One memorable encounter began after Brad Emery and Douglas had finished breakfast at their campsite at Dewey Lake in the Cascades and had just started out on their day's hike. An old sheepherder spotted the two teen-agers and motioned for them to come to his camp. The herder had argued with his packer six weeks ago, he told them, and the two hadn't spoken since. He needed company and promised to cook the boys an unforgettable meal if they would stick around for lunch. Emery and Douglas agreed and the sheepherder promptly sent the boys up the hillside to pick berries. When they returned, he was roasting bear meat over an open fire. Emery and Douglas dined on bear meat, fresh berries sprinkled on pan bread and the tall tales of a lonesome sheepherder.

Not surprisingly, Douglas, the conscientious student, often turned his hikes into intensive tutorials between himself and nature, learning the names of every rock formation and wild flower he saw. But the experiences were gently poetic as well. When the soft, balmy chinook breeze blew and the light rain began to fall, Douglas gloried in the fresh smell of dampened dust and the delicate yet pungent odor of sage. He stretched out, ear to the ground, to listen to the symphony of cheatgrass blowing in the wind and inhaled the smells of the exotic bitterroot, paintbrush and red mountain heath that guarded his mountain trails. And he looked below to gauge the slow, steady progress of the Yakima River as it wound through a valley of sumac, cottonwood and willow trees.

Douglas and his friend Elon Gilbert loved to stand on a peak of the Cascades with the wind in their faces and toast the short-sighted "city people" of Yakima. They were so busy, the boys noted smugly, that they never took the time to enjoy the spectacular natural beauty that surrounded them. But the city folk were missing more than an invaluable aesthetic experience, Douglas and Gilbert believed. There was also the powerful silence that nature could impose on the world below, which so often seemed petty and painful and unworthy.

Douglas began to think of God's work less in the pews at Yakima's First Presbyterian Church and more in the wilderness of the Cascades. "Dad told us the outdoors became his religion," his daughter, Millie, recalled. "He said he'd had enough of organized religion as a boy."

As a teen-ager, Douglas began to question the virtues of organized religion. "I realized that most members of the Establishment had received tickets to heaven merely for being pious on Sunday," he later wrote. "Heaven became in my mind a lovely pink cloud occupied by those who had made the greatest contributions to the church. I began to think how dreadful it would be to sit on a pink cloud with all those people who were not only a thieving lot, but hypocrites, and above all else, dull, pious and boring."

The wilderness became Douglas's place of worship. "When one stands on Darling Mountain, he is not remote and apart from the wilderness; he is an intimate part of it. The ridges run away at his feet and lead to friendly meadows. Every trail leads beyond the frontier. Every ridge, every valley, every peak offers a solitude deeper even than that of the sea. It offers the peace that comes only from solitude. It is in solitude that man can come to know both his heart and his mind."

After a hard day's trek in the Cascades, Douglas lay in his bedroll and gazed at the sky, his eyes transfixed by the distant stars. And his mind pushed back the centuries that the stars had witnessed the universe, from the earliest formations of the Cascade Mountains and the Yakima valley, through the coming of man and, finally, to civilization as he knew it then. He sensed the ineluctable power of time. With it, Douglas felt the basic compatibility of man with nature, the personal fulfillment that nature offered if man would only accept it. One night, Douglas wrote, "I felt at peace. I felt that I was a part of the universe, a companion to the friendly chinook that brought the promise of life and adventure. That night, I think, there first came to me the germ of a philosophy of life: that man's best measure of the universe is in his hopes and his dreams, not his fears; that man is a part of a plan, only a fraction of which he, perhaps, can ever comprehend."

Even with these inspirational thoughts, Douglas's escape from his mother's rigid Presbyterianism was slow and incomplete. As a teen-ager, he still attended church services three times a week and was treasurer of his church's youth group. At the same time, his questioning of basic tenets of Presbyterianism intensified. "Finally, I took the Apostles' Creed, a regular ritual in the Presbyterian church, and underlined in ink the parts—the only parts— in which I truly believed:

I BELIEVE in God the Father Almighty, Maker of heaven and earth; and in Jesus Christ his only Son
our Lord: who was conceived by the Holy Ghost, Born of the Virgin Mary; Suffered under Pontius Pilate, Was crucified, dead, and buried: He descended into hell: The third day he
rose again from the dead: He ascended into heaven, and sitteth on the right hand of God the Father Almighty: From thence he shall come to judge the quick and the dead.
I believe in the Holy Ghost: the holy Catholic Church; the Communion of Saints; The Forgiveness of sins: The Resurrection of the Body: And the Life everlasting."

At the same time that Douglas was rejecting much of Presbyterian ritual, he retained a private puritanical code. He refused to follow his peers who smoked or drank. He did not date. In those days, Douglas's glance at a pretty girl was usually taken covertly and sexual titillation was confined to the exchange of bawdy stories on camping trips. If he masturbated, his mother once told Douglas, his brains would blow up like oatmeal. Many of his later problems with women, Mercedes Douglas Eichholz, Douglas's second wife, has suggested, may have been rooted in his puritanical upbringing.

CHAPTER FOUR _____

RARE OPPORTUNITY

FOR WILLIAM ORVILLE DOUGLAS, the drums of World
War I were almost inaudible. It was a European war and any
bright Yakima schoolboy knew that Europe had for centuries
been convulsed by war. In the fall of 1916, Douglas's world centered on thirty acres of fine old trees and buildings that com-
prised the campus of Whitman College in Walla Walla. Douglas
had accepted Whitman's offer of a full-tuition scholarship, traditionally given to the valedictorian of each high school class in the
state.

Whitman had been named for Dr. Marcus Whitman, the first
medical missionary on the Pacific coast. Since its charter was
granted in 1859, the school had been dedicated to the twin goals
of quality education and community service. There were only 118
students in Douglas's class, but if prior classes were any guide, a
large proportion of the class of 1920 would choose a career in
high school teaching or missionary work. By 1916, 19 percent of
Whitman's male graduates and 41 percent of its female graduates
had become high school teachers, more than half of these settling

in the Northwest. Another 11 percent of the male graduates had entered the Christian ministry.

The college catalogue proudly boasted that "a spirit of reverence and of Christian life and thought permeates the College atmosphere." To remind Whitman undergraduates of this reverence, daily chapel service was required, made more attractive to the skeptics by a great pipe organ and a chapel choir. Outside the chapel, Whitman students were free to stroll along Mill Creek, which flowed through the campus, or to walk the streets of Walla Walla, a quiet, conservative community of 25,000 inhabitants.

Before he even met his freshman roommate, Douglas had divided his college days into tight, productive units. Earlier, he had been hired as an all-purpose handyman at Falkenberg's Jewelry Store in downtown Walla Walla. To accommodate his job, Douglas had arranged with the Whitman registrar to squeeze all his freshman classes into the morning hours, so that afternoons he was free to work at Falkenberg's. He had also signed on as an early-morning janitor in a candy store and as a dinner-hour waiter in a hash house, in an effort to provide the monthly twenty dollars that he had promised to send home.

At Falkenberg's, Douglas began in the stockroom as a delivery man at twenty cents an hour, but before long he had devised an intricate bookkeeping system for outside orders, which was still in use more than sixty years later. Gradually he was eased into sales at the jewelry store, with mixed success. Douglas's problems began when an elderly woman entered the store in search of a gold-handled umbrella. She approached the counter and asked to see a green umbrella. "Right away," Douglas replied, and he carefully unwrapped an umbrella and placed it on the counter. It was red. "Young man," the woman said impatiently, "I asked to see a green umbrella. This one is red." Douglas apologized and quickly replaced the red umbrella with another. It was blue. "Young man," the woman said, with more pity than anger in her voice, "I think you are color-blind." And indeed he was.

Although Douglas spent more time at Falkenberg's than anyplace else, the job was never pure drudgery, primarily because of three other young men who worked there—Jerry Cundiff, J. Howard Shubert and Philo Rounds. Actually, Douglas had become acquainted with them while he was still a senior in high school.

At that time, Rounds and Shubert, both members of Beta Theta Pi fraternity, had heard of Douglas's achievements at North Yakima High School. When they learned that Cundiff, who would later pledge Beta at Whitman, planned to attend the Walla Walla–North Yakima football game in Yakima, they asked him to look up Douglas and put in a good word for Whitman and the fraternity. Later in the year, Rounds and Shubert kept in touch with Douglas, urging him to choose Whitman and, implicitly, Beta Theta Pi.

Douglas chose Whitman primarily because the school offered him the full-tuition scholarship. He also chose to join Beta Theta Pi, and the explanation was not so simple. Why did Douglas, a poor boy with egalitarian values, choose to spend his carefully rationed time at a fraternity? It is a question that perplexed Douglas himself in later years: "In time, I came to regard college fraternities as a handicap, because they tend to create clannish attitudes at a time when one needs to break down all barriers and search to the outer limits for interesting people. I concluded that fraternities were a form of feudalism and that feudalism on a college campus paid few dividends."

In 1917, however, Douglas concluded that time at Beta Theta Pi was a good investment. After all, Beta did not fit the stereotypical fraternity image. It searched for achievers, like Douglas, and proudly displayed a fine choral group. So Douglas, who had never been invited to a private party in Yakima, was suddenly a member of a private club.

What went on in the Beta house, where Douglas soon resided, was not that different from the antics at fraternity houses across the country. Pledges were forced to eat raw hamburger flavored with asafetida, stand for hours in front of spotlights and steal milk bottles at dawn. Fraternity brothers were kidded mercilessly whenever nonconformist behavior was detected.

Douglas was no exception. His Beta brothers did not criticize "Doug," as he was called at Whitman, for his frenetic work schedule or superior grades, though both were conspicuous. Rather, it was Douglas's serious image that inspired the ridicule of his fraternity brothers. At Whitman, Douglas attended the Sunday school class for college men at Walla Walla's Presbyterian church and he was active in the YMCA, leading its campus fund drive in

1917. He did not smoke or drink or play around with fast women.

Douglas was elected to the fraternity "anti-cuss and fussing club." And he was criticized for spending too much time with his first serious girlfriend, the attractive brunette daughter of a Walla Walla minister.* The complaints came in Beta's weekly critique sessions, in which each member was criticized but given no opportunity to respond. Much to the fraternity brothers' relief, the minister and his family moved away the following year.

"Bill was against fraternities until he joined one," said former Whitman president Dr. Chester Maxey, himself a member of Beta a few years before Douglas. "He learned to deal with boys as equals, in a rough and tumble way. Later," Maxey said, "I think he intellectualized the experience. Then he began to criticize it."

Douglas's serious image provided a fine disguise for his incurable mischievousness. Every day, Douglas and his classmates marched into chapel and waited patiently until the president of the college, S. B. L. Penrose, had paraded to the podium. Penrose was a severe and stuffy man, so much so that Douglas could not resist an occasional deflating prank. One morning, minutes before Penrose was scheduled to make his ritual entrance into the chapel, Douglas tiptoed to the altar and placed an alarm clock on the podium. As Penrose approached the podium, the alarm went off, sending Douglas and his classmates into uncontrollable fits of laughter. Penrose was not amused. "Well, you've had your fun," he huffed. "Chapel is dismissed." When he left, the clock was still clanking disrespectfully.

Penrose, Douglas later wrote, "was a good Christian man, with a William McKinley type of political and economic philosophy, who would have fitted snugly into any sector of the Establishment. He was a pseudo-intellectual with the instincts of a stuffed shirt."

Douglas possessed the uncanny ability to poke fun at authority one minute and court that same authority the next. He was the master of inventing pranks to incense President Penrose. But when a task promised to serve Douglas's serious ambitions, such

---

*Douglas's family worried more about the money than the time Douglas spent with his girlfriend; during their courtship, he bought her a ring at Falkenberg's which, all agreed, he could not afford.

as writing an article for the college literary magazine to honor Penrose's twenty-five years at Whitman, Douglas was the intensely thoughtful honor student. He began his article, entitled "Souls Tempered with Fire," with a quotation from Matthew Arnold:

> Not like the men of the crowd . . .
> But souls tempered with fire,
> Fervent, heroic and good—
> Helpers and friends of mankind.

Today, when everyone connected with Whitman College is celebrating the twenty-fifth anniversary of President Penrose's administration, these words come with a peculiar fitness. Written by Matthew Arnold to describe his father, Rugby's famous Head Master, Thomas Arnold, and other members of that faculty, they express for us, students of Whitman, our appreciation of our own President and professors of the last quarter century.

Those more than commonplace virtues that our faculty possess have been to us during the last twenty-five years a continual source of inspiration and help. Their enthusiasms have helped us to cultivate a love of knowledge for its own sake. Their sincerity has helped to make us sincere. Their unselfish sacrifices have revealed to us a deeper significance of life. Through their personal friendships we have been made aware of the satisfactions that come to "helpers and friends of mankind."

There were priorities in Douglas's busy world, and at the top of his list was intellectual achievement. Achievement was the key. Douglas simply did not have much time for learning as its own reward. He rarely read unassigned books or participated in unscheduled bull sessions with the faculty. He did, however, make superior grades and did so with the same apparent ease that had impressed his classmates in high school. Nobody seemed to know when Douglas studied; actually, he squeezed in a feverish hour or two after completing his evening's waiter's duties. But Douglas's high grades and his friends' admiration followed the semester's examinations as regularly as one fruit-picking season followed another in the Yakima valley.

With the formal education, there was also inspiration. It did not come from the economics department faculty, though economics was Douglas's major, but from two professors with radically different personalities and areas of expertise. Dr. Benjamin H. Brown, or Daddy Brown as he was known to Whitman students, was a tall, broad-shouldered, painfully modest man, who approached the teaching of physics and geology with the awe and drama that he himself felt whenever he considered nature's wonders. Brown was also the pure skeptic, who taught his students that the accepted theories in science textbooks might be wrong. Whether measuring the speed of a rifle bullet, the candlepower of the moon or the weight of the earth, Brown insisted with his ingenious experiments that his students decide for themselves what was fact.

For Douglas, Brown's lessons transcended the findings of his remarkable experiments. The professor filled Douglas's mind with cosmic ideas that he had only begun to ponder as a teen-ager on the Cascade mountaintops. Man's politics and pettiness were momentary and of small consequence, Brown said, compared to nature's universal truths. In the spring of 1917, Brown was much more excited about Russia's fields of brilliant wild flowers than about her revolutionary turmoil. Brown offered his own special hope for an afterlife by telling his students of a skull he had dug up near an apple tree. The root of the tree had invaded the skull, sucking up the brain of the deceased. "How wonderful to become an apple tree," Brown exclaimed. "Can anyone think of anything more choice for an afterlife?"

Dr. William R. Davis, the other member of the faculty who inspired Douglas, taught English literature, making Shakespeare a part of his students' life. Whether reading the role of Falstaff or tracing the development of another Shakespearean character, Davis took Douglas and his classmates beyond the printed page and into the Elizabethan world, impressing upon them the foibles of humanity in literature—and life. In addition to his cherished readings and research, Davis took a deep interest in Walla Walla's First Congregational Church, Kiwanis Club and cultural activities. But most of all, Davis cared about his students.

"Davis was an inspirational man who had a way of worming his way into another's life," Douglas wrote in his autobiography. The English professor possessed such personal magnetism that Douglas, who hoarded his feelings as carefully as he did his free time, offered both to Davis. "He was, indeed, a second father," Douglas recalled. "If I had a speech to make, Davis heard me rehearse it at the crack of dawn in the outdoor amphitheatre. If I had a personal problem, he was my confessor."

At 8:30 P.M. on April 2, 1917, President Woodrow Wilson appeared before a joint session of Congress to tell the nation that Germany had resumed warfare against the commercial ships of neutral nations. It was "warfare against mankind," Wilson said, and it was now clear that the imperial government, like all autocracies, was a natural foe of liberty. Calling for a world "safe for democracy," Wilson requested a declaration of war against Germany, and Congress promptly acceded.

"WHITMAN SEES HER SONS OBEY THE CALL TO SERVICE," bannered the Whitman College *Pioneer*. In the spring of 1917, war fever swept the tiny campus. Students who only a few months before had worn little green beanies were now dressed smartly in military khaki. The young men at the Beta house and at men's dorms across the campus were full of bravado. Douglas and his friends were sure that "the Huns will be mighty sorry they started this fight." Recruiting lines swelled.

Douglas's loyalties were divided. He did not want to disappoint his family, who relied on him financially, or Uncle Sam, who pointed a finger at him in every recruiting poster. Finally loyalty to the nation, rather than to the Douglas family, won the day. Douglas applied for service in naval aviation and passed all the exams except the one testing color-blindness. The recruiting officer was more patient with Douglas than the elderly woman in Falkenberg's who had wanted to buy a green umbrella. But after Douglas consistently picked the wrong color yarn on the table in front of him, the officer's conclusion was as positive as the customer's. Douglas suffered from "green-red" color blindness; he was rejected.

Disappointed but not discouraged, Douglas again applied for service, this time for officer training school, and again he faced a physical exam. A nervous Douglas had undressed completely before the other prospective recruits had unbuckled their belts. His eagerness was quickly rewarded when the recruiting officer picked him to administer the color test. That was easy for a color-blind Douglas; he simply gave every recruit a passing grade. When the officer then asked Douglas to take the same test, Douglas quickly parried, "You mean the guy who gives it has to take it?" Logic overwhelmed judgment and the officer waived Douglas's exam. Finally, exultantly, Douglas was in the army!

His joy was short-lived. After he was sent to the Presidio in San Francisco for basic training, he was ordered back to Whitman's ROTC unit, not to a company bound for Europe's trenches. Douglas, restless and disappointed, dutifully performed his early-morning calisthentics on the Whitman campus and listened to his colonel's fiery "hate the Germans" exhortations. In the meantime, Whitman classmates were being killed abroad. Douglas waited in vain for his overseas orders. When the armistice was signed, he was still taking his orders from an ROTC colonel in Walla Walla. Douglas, whose patriotism flowed deep and steady throughout his life, was ashamed when he and the rest of his ROTC unit were welcomed as heroes as they paraded through the streets of Walla Walla to celebrate the armistice. When the genuine heroes of the war returned to Whitman, Douglas led the cheers as toastmaster at a college banquet in their honor.

While most Whitman students adjusted to a peacetime calm, Douglas churned forward with characteristic zeal. He resumed his work for the YMCA and was elected president of Beta Theta Pi. He attended church and wrote for the campus literary magazine. He delivered an occasional sermon at Sunday campus services and tutored slower students for his economics professor. And Douglas accomplished all this while working as a part-time janitor and waiter and spending five hours a day as a clerk at a Walla Walla jewelry store.

Above all other Whitman activities, debating offered the perfect stage for the Douglas will, intellect and competitiveness. By his junior year, Douglas was a star member of the Whitman debating team, whose triumphs captured as many college newspaper headlines as Whitman's athletic teams. When the team of Orville Douglas and Harold McGahey from tiny Whitman defeated the University of Washington team, the Whitman *Pioneer* reported the feat ecstatically. It did not matter that the subject of debate— Resolved: That a Federal Board of Arbitration should have compulsory powers to settle industrial disputes between capital and labor—might fail to quicken every Whitman student's heartbeat. "Orville Douglass showed that compulsory arbitration is an immediate method of sound principle for settling industrial disputes between capital and labor," the newspaper reported, and then abandoned objectivity altogether: "Let's give three cheers for Douglass!"* Douglas's roommate, Bill Wilson recalled the same debate with satisfaction: "He just knocked their ears down with two or three sentences in rebuttal."

When he was a senior, Douglas had become one of the biggest men on Whitman's quiet campus, having been elected president of the Student Congress and a charter member of the Whitman chapter of Phi Beta Kappa. He was chosen by the faculty to be one of his class's commencement speakers, although he did not stand at the very top of the class. The same week that he delivered his commencement address on "The American Today," Douglas paid his respects to five faculty members, including Daddy Brown, by speaking at a dinner in their honor.

Eighteen years later, Douglas delivered his second commencement address at Whitman, this time as the powerful chairman of the Securities and Exchange Commission. When he reminisced about his college days, Douglas paid homage to the faculty that had inspired and rewarded him. "Whitman to me means all of those who were on the faculty in 1920," Douglas said. "Those men still teach full time in the Whitman which is mine. In my Whitman there are no new appointments to the faculty; no alterations in curriculum." Later in the speech, Douglas turned to a favorite theme. "Whitman, like life, is exacting. Whitman means heartaches and struggles. But Whitman also means life and hope to those insistent on not being submerged by either social or economic limitations. It also means, to rich and poor alike, rare opportunity for individual development and growth."

As an undergraduate at Whitman, Douglas had combined energy, ambition and achievement to open the doors to many worlds. He found social acceptance in Beta Theta Pi and academic distinction in Phi Beta Kappa. He swept floors at dawn but

*Apparently, while at Whitman, Douglas preferred the Scottish spelling of his name, with a double *s* at the end.

read Shakespeare after dark. He supported union democracy and served the YMCA. He knocked down S. B. L. Penrose with a prank and picked him up with a hymn of praise. He was serious and irreverent, scholarly and childish. He was the supreme achiever, thrusting himself totally and successfully into every activity that captured his interest.

When Douglas's daughter, Millie, was a high school senior in Washington, D.C., and had begun to browse through college brochures, her father pledged total open-mindedness about her choice. "You can attend any college you want," Douglas said. "However," he added, "if you want me to pay the tuition, you'll go to Whitman."

FRUSTRATION

FOR THE FIRST twenty-one years of his life, William Orville Douglas's free choice had been severely limited by financial circumstance. As a Yakima schoolboy, he had taken odd jobs because his family needed the extra money. At Whitman, he worked before his morning classes and for long hours afterward, because he knew that his family depended on the twenty dollars a month that he mailed home. As Douglas's Whitman graduation approached, finances again circumscribed ambition. The old chains of responsibility were loosened, but not broken. True, brother Art, now at Whitman, had taken over the job at Falkenberg's. Still, Douglas carried part of the financial burden of supporting his mother. With this in mind, he attempted to decide what to do with the rest of his life.

Spurred by his high grades and conspicuous success as a debater, Douglas discussed a legal career with Grant Bond, the attorney for Falkenberg's. Through the years, Bond, who had no children, had helped a number of poor students at Whitman complete their education. Bond promised that he would help Douglas through law school if, in return, Douglas would join

Bond in his Walla Walla practice after graduation. It was a tempting offer for Douglas, who had no funds for law school tuition. But already showing an independence and confidence in himself that would only grow stronger, Douglas rejected the offer. He preferred to postpone a decision on law school until he could make a career choice free from heavy obligation.

Douglas's English teacher, Dr. Davis, inspired a second consideration, graduate school in English literature. But that posed the same obstacle as law—tuition money Douglas did not have.

A third possibility, high school teaching, had been selected by more than 40 percent of Douglas's Whitman classmates. Julia Douglas liked the idea, particularly since Douglas had never expressed an interest in the ministry, the preferred career for her first son. If Douglas taught high school in Yakima, he would have financial security, his mother would have his companionship and both could hope that he would someday rise to the respected position of high school principal.

In the summer of 1920, then, Douglas approached his old high school principal, A. C. Davis, and discussed openings on the Yakima High School faculty. Though Davis rarely hired teachers without experience, he rarely interviewed applicants with Douglas's credentials. Douglas was hired for the fall term to teach English and Latin and coach the Yakima High School debating team.

The next two years were filled with frustration for Douglas. He was never committed to a career in the Yakima school system, despite his mother's encouragement. He had taken the teaching job, in part, to bide time until he could save enough money to pay for graduate school or law school. Increasingly dissatisfied with teaching duties that did not absorb his prodigious intellectual energy, Douglas searched for a shortcut to graduate school.

He thought he had found it his very first fall in Yakima, when the committee to award Rhodes scholarships announced that it would be holding interviews in Seattle for worthy applicants. A Rhodes scholarship, Douglas thought, would enable him to study English literature at Oxford, laying the foundation for a career of college teaching and research. When he arrived in Seattle for his interview, Douglas was confident that he would soon be able to list the Rhodes scholarship with his other honors. After all, his academic credentials were outstanding. Moreover, Douglas had always impressed his elders, particularly teachers, with his intelligence and wide-ranging interests. The Rhodes committee would be no different.

Douglas sat nervously in the anteroom outside the office of the president of the University of Washington, where the interviews were being held. His twelve o'clock appointment time passed as other candidates shuttled in and out of the office. Finally, at six o'clock, Douglas was called in to face weary members of the Rhodes committee. They asked him only two questions: "What is the difference between a demagogue and a statesman?" and "What did Wordsworth mean by a 'feeling intellect'?" Douglas answered promptly and to his own complete satisfaction. He was not, however, awarded the scholarship.

Douglas did not fail often, and when he did he quickly looked for an explanation. If he found it and he had the power to change the results, he would. When his legs were weak from polio, Douglas prescribed the antidote—exercise—and doggedly took to the Yakima hills. When he was a high school sophomore, his mind had gone blank during a debate; Douglas was ashamed and wept, but for the next debate and those that came later, he prepared better and that humiliating moment on the North Yakima High School stage was never repeated. With the Rhodes rejection, however, there was failure with no possibility that Douglas could prescribe a remedy. That predicament, in which Douglas could not control his own destiny, frustrated and embittered him.

The Rhodes selection had been politically influenced to favor the elite, Douglas later concluded. The committee had been looking for a student to reflect its own conservative outlook. Forty years later, when Douglas met the man who had been selected that day in Seattle, he felt that his worst suspicions were confirmed. The Rhodes scholar had studied law at Oxford and had become a professor of government and, in Douglas's eye, "one of the most conservative influences I have known."

Soon after returning to Yakima from his Seattle interview, Douglas met O. E. Bailey, whose irreverent views of the town's establishment greatly appealed to Douglas. Bailey also sold insurance for the Sun Life Insurance Company, and when Bailey and Douglas were not discussing the low state of morality in Yakima, they sometimes talked about the lucrative life of an insurance agent. In a short time, Bailey, who was a persuasive talker on any subject, sold Douglas on the idea of representing the Sun Life Insurance Company in his spare time.

Douglas began calling on prospects in an old Dodge that he had bought in Walla Walla with forty dollars borrowed from Jerry Cundiff. The first policy that Douglas sold was to a man who tried to commit suicide a few days after Douglas had him sign on the dotted line. To add to his troubles, Douglas had advanced his customer the money for the first premium, which was never repaid. Experience did not seem to sharpen Douglas's technique or judgment. He lost most of his meager savings in a speculative insurance venture and soon abandoned the insurance business altogether.

Life in Yakima did offer some rewards to Douglas. He was a popular teacher at the high school, though he gave long assignments and insisted on high standards. His debating team won the Inland Empire Debate Championship, defeating competition from Walla Walla, Lewis and Clark, Wenatchee and Colville on the question "Resolved: That the principle of the sales tax law should be adopted and added to the general taxing system of the Federal Government." And in his spare time, Douglas, still in the tweed suit and Sherlock Holmes hat that he had worn to school, would often hang out in downtown Yakima, swapping stories with old friends like Al Egley.

Most important, Douglas met Mildred Riddle, a faculty colleague at the high school, whom he fell in love with, later married and lived with for twenty-nine years, until their divorce in 1953. Mildred was the youngest of three sisters who grew up near the small town of La Grande, Oregon. She was her father's favorite daughter, a petite brunette with uncommon good looks. Mildred was the first daughter to harness the family carriage, and after the Riddles purchased their first Model T, she was the first to be taught to drive, often leaving her sisters behind to fume. She loved to play tennis and to ride horses in the nearby Wallowa Mountains. But there was also a serious side. Her quiet intelligence was drawn irresistibly to good books, particularly the classics of ancient Greece and Rome. After graduation from the University of Oregon, Mildred taught classical literature and foreign languages at Yakima High School.

Mildred had been at Yakima High School for five years when young Orville Douglas assumed his teaching duties. Douglas was immediately attracted to Mildred's beauty, her zest for the out-doors and her intelligence. Mildred, though five years Douglas's senior, was captured by his rough, gangly good looks, his knowl-edge of the world and, most of all, his intensity. She sat in awe as her new friend spoke authoritatively about the world's prob-lems. Douglas could hold her in suspense as he discussed a com-plex intellectual problem or, eyes sparkling, make her laugh with a tall tale. Regardless of the subject, he had a knack for getting Mildred—or anybody else—to listen to him. Mildred was a good listener and soon the two were spending most of their spare time together, taking long walks, picnicking, talking of an uncertain future.

Douglas knew by this time that he could never be fully satisfied with high school teaching. But he still had not saved enough money for law school or graduate work in English literature. Moreover, he had not yet decided which of the two disciplines he would choose, even if he had the tuition money. Several events conspired to tilt Douglas's choice toward law. His close friend O. E. Bailey was an insurance salesman, not a lawyer, but he spoke to Douglas with passion about the power of the law and its poten-tial for righting society's wrongs. Bailey was the only man Doug-las had met who had actually seen the U.S. Supreme Court and he did not miss the opportunity to describe its glory in vivid detail.

After school, Douglas began to drift into the courtrooms of Yakima. His observations left him with two overriding impres-sions. First, Douglas concluded that even without a law degree, he would be a match for any of the practicing attorneys he had seen in action. Second, he watched Judge Frank H. Rudkin, then a state court judge with a full black beard and a sonorous voice, who looked and sounded like an Old Testament prophet. Rudkin was order and righteousness personified. Douglas had found his calling.

Only two questions remained: where to go to law school and

how to get there. Both questions were answered by a young attorney, James T. Donald, with whom Douglas fell into chance conversation in the reading room of the Yakima YMCA. It was May 1922, and Douglas had set his sights on an Ivy League law school, far away from Yakima and his mother. He had applied to Harvard and had been accepted. Donald, a Columbia Law graduate, congratulated him on his Harvard acceptance and, Donald assumed, the substantial funds necessary to sustain him for three years of study in Cambridge. Douglas hesitated. He had no savings, he told Donald. Forget Harvard, Donald advised, and apply to Columbia. Douglas could work his way through Columbia, as Donald had done. Donald promised to help with letters of introduction to Columbia's dean, Harlan F. Stone, and to the director of the law school's employment office. Douglas canceled his acceptance to Harvard and began to plan for three years in New York City and the Morningside Heights campus of the Columbia Law School.

Before he could begin his law studies, Douglas had to travel from Yakima to New York City, not an inconsiderable problem for a young man with seventy-five dollars to his name. Douglas knew that the seventy-five dollars would not cover his transportation expenses, so he arranged to take a herd of two thousand sheep from nearby Wenatchee to Minneapolis on the Great Northern Railroad. The Yakima firm that owned the sheep would pay Douglas's way to Minneapolis, just the financial boost he thought he needed to assure a successful trip to New York.

The day Douglas was scheduled to leave Yakima, he sat on the piano stool in his mother's house, surrounded by his family. Douglas was despondent as he contemplated his long trip. The separation from his family, from Mildred Riddle and from the Cascades might be for three years. His sister tried to console him and offered her help to pay for the trip. Douglas declined it. Columbia Law School was his idea, and he would pay for it, he declared. Just before he left, Douglas gave Martha his watch for safekeeping. "When I get to New York City," Douglas told her, "I'll let you know. Then you send the watch."

Accounts of Douglas's cross-country adventures have varied, the drama building with the passing years. Every version has begun in the caboose of a Great Northern freight in Wenatchee, and has taken Douglas and his two thousand sheep through the orchards of the Yakima valley, across the Rockies and the Great Plains and into the freight yards of Minneapolis. Along the way, Douglas sat with his herd through a pouring rain in Miles City, Montana, talked philosophy with a Harvard Ph.D. dropout, and endured several dust storms. For a brief period, famine caused him to live on the meager crumbs of a single piece of apple pie, and his sheep to search the feed pens of Minot, North Dakota. After delivering his sheep in Minnesota, Douglas paid his dues to the train crew. But when a replacement crew demanded another round of tips, Douglas balked and was forced to jump off the train on the outskirts of Chicago.

At this point, versions of Douglas's trip differ. In some accounts, Douglas met a kindly hobo, heading west, who advised him to buy a coach ticket for the remainder of the trip to New York City to avoid the hazards of "riding the rods." The hobo also told Douglas to stay away from flophouses and to sleep at the YMCA. Douglas took the advice. After his first bath and full night's sleep in two weeks at the YMCA, Douglas, in these versions, wired his brother for the money for a one-way coach fare to New York. When the money arrived, Douglas bought the ticket and had just enough left over to pay for sandwiches for the trip. Douglas's final and preferred version, recounted in his autobiography, has him riding the freights into New York City. In all versions, Douglas arrived in New York with his battered old suitcase and less than fifty cents in his pocket, although the exact amount of money has diminished over the years. In the autobiography, Douglas wrote that he arrived with six cents.

Weary and dirty from the long train ride, a bewildered Douglas asked directions to Columbia. He received hostile stares or studied evasions from passers-by, who were put off, he was certain, by his tattered clothes and disheveled appearance. Douglas concluded that in New York City "the stranger—especially the one with no badge of affluence—knew only the rough side of the hand."

The reception would be better at the New York headquarters of Beta Theta Pi, Douglas thought. He was wrong. The clerk at Beta gave Douglas the once-over, refused to believe that he could belong to any fraternity, certainly not Beta, and went about his business. Finally help arrived when Bill Wilson, Douglas's former roommate at Whitman who was staying overnight before heading for Johns Hopkins Medical School, passed through the lobby. Wilson quickly vouched for Douglas's Beta credentials, and the clerk reluctantly gave Douglas a room for the night. Douglas told Wilson he had one additional problem; he did not have the seventy-five dollars for law school registration. Wilson loaned Douglas the seventy-five dollars and Douglas went to sleep, confident that his days in New York could only get better.

The Columbia Law School was housed in Kent Hall, a four-story brick-and-limestone building in the neo-Renaissance style then fashionable. The first floor was devoted entirely to the law school's library and the second to classrooms and the offices of Dean Harlan F. Stone and his law school faculty. During his first day at the law school, Douglas saw nothing of the library or the faculty offices. Instead he spent several frantic hours shuttling between the university's employment and bursar's offices, pleading for work in the former and credit in the latter. Between trips, Douglas stopped in at Dean Stone's office.

He had put his last dollar toward law school registration, Douglas told Stone. If he did not receive a loan or scholarship, he could not afford his first year's tuition at the law school. Stone, combining a dean's sympathy with a Wall Street lawyer's caution, suggested that Douglas find a job and apply to Columbia again when he had the tuition money in hand.

A dejected Douglas searched the newspaper classified ads and found an opening for a high school Latin and English teacher in New Jersey. Had he traveled across the country to continue a career in high school teaching? Sad, but apparently true, Douglas concluded. Before leaving New York for his new position, Douglas decided to make a final stop at the Columbia employment office. Since his last visit, he discovered, a request had been sent in for a third-year law student to help draft a business-law correspondence course.

"I'll go," said Douglas.

"But you're not a third-year man," the director of the employment office reminded him.

"Let me try," Douglas pleaded.

Douglas's blind self-confidence in a desperate situation was irresistible. He was given the Columbus Avenue address of the correspondence school, and within hours was talking glibly to the school's proprietor about his plans for the business-law course. He would divide the course into fifty lessons, selecting a business-law problem for each lesson, based on New York court decisions. At the end of each case, Douglas would ask a question, which the student would answer and submit for a grade. The format was immediately agreed to by the owner. All that remained was Douglas's fee. He would take a flat payment of six hundred dollars for the course, two hundred dollars to be paid in advance. Douglas made two additional stops that day, first to the Columbia bursar's office to deposit the two hundred dollars for his first year's tuition and then, hastily, to the Kent Hall library to prepare the first lesson of his correspondence course.*

---

*Douglas's classmate and close friend Carrol Shanks later wrote that Douglas prepared the correspondence course the second semester of his first year in law school. It is an impressive feat and a good story, either semester.

CHAPTER SIX

KNUCKLES AND BONES

PROMINENT MEMBERS of the U.S. Senate chose to ignore the world across the Atlantic, but Columbia's undergraduates in the fall of 1922 refused to follow their isolationist lead. They listened intently as a Heidelberg student told of a deteriorating currency and rising nationalism in postwar Germany, and a foreign correspondent, recently returned from Russia, deplored the Bolshevists' takeover. Discussions in the Columbia Law School were more parochial. Kent Hall was a training ground for practicing attorneys,* not diplomats, and the energies of faculty and students were devoted primarily to that overriding purpose.

Roughly half of Columbia's law students were New Yorkers, many of them scrapping as desperately as Douglas to work their way through law school. Simon Rifkind, who later became a federal judge, rushed uptown to his morning law school classes and then hurried back home to his job on the Lower East Side. Classmate Thomas E. Dewey earned money singing at the Cathedral of St. John the Divine and Paul Robeson sang in Harlem's Cotton

*Men attorneys, that is. Women were not yet admitted to the Columbia Law School.

Club and played professional football on weekends for the Akron Indians.

Rifkind was vaguely aware of a lean and hungry fellow from Yakima ("all knuckles and bones"), but had neither the time nor the curiosity to get acquainted. Douglas, with his tales of sheep-herders and Cascade snowdrifts, could not have been more exotic to a ghetto boy like Rifkind "if he had been wearing antlers." Still, Rifkind and Douglas shared a singular objective: to learn how to think like lawyers.

For Dean Harlan F. Stone, there was one purpose in legal education. "It cannot be too often emphasized," he said, "that the professional law school with educational ideas has a definite and, of necessity, a relatively limited aim: it is to train men for the Bar in the best possible manner in the limited time at its command." Within that framework, Stone insisted on creative pedagogy. Columbia's law professors were not simply to drill mechanical rules into their students, but to force the students to master the legal principles on which the rules were based. That meant that Stone's teachers would, necessarily, draw on other disciplines—history, philosophy, economics, sociology—for support. But Stone was no radical. He never lost sight of his central task of training young men like Douglas and Rifkind for the bar. Columbia was not to become a graduate school of jurisprudence, though theoretical research was not discouraged. But inquiries into where the law had been or should be going were secondary. What is the law *now?* That was the compelling question for Stone. The other questions could, perhaps should, be pursued, preferably after the law school's main task of training practitioners had been accomplished.

The chosen technique for law school teaching was termed the "Socratic method" and demanded a highly structured dialogue between professor and student. At Columbia, the master of the Socratic method was Dean Stone. Stone, a portly man with twinkling blue eyes and a shock of light-brown hair hanging over his forehead, stood behind his desk, twirling his tortoise-shell glasses in his hands, peppering his students with questions. Always questions.

Stone's questions in Douglas's first-year personal property class rarely referred to the assigned cases. Rather, Stone, whose

voice never rose above a conversational pitch, narrated a hypothetical case which raised the legal issues discussed in the assigned reading. Stone never suggested the connection between
the assigned case and the hypothetical. But through his acute
questioning, Stone forced the student to make the connection
and arrive at the applicable rule of law. Just when a student had
grasped the connection, however, Stone pushed him forward
with a second hypothetical case, where the applicable legal rule
appeared to contradict the first. In fact, the second hypothetical
case would, Stone hoped, suggest a step in the development of
a broad legal doctrine.

Stone was resolute in his determination to make the student
come forward with the answer. He did not distinguish the cases
or tell the class what rule of law was under discussion or, when
two competing principles were introduced, say which rule he
favored. "Finally, one caught on," Douglas recalled, "at least
those who did well in the course, to the stages in the law's development by the intonation of Stone's voice. The way he would say,
'So you think, Mr. Douglas, that such and such is the governing
principle' was the only guidepost through the course, except the
voluminous materials he assigned for reading." At the end of the
course, the bright student—and Douglas was conspicuously quick
in class—had learned the habit of close analysis, skepticism of
absolutes and a sturdy belief in the vitality of the law.

In acquiring the analytical tools of his chosen profession,
Douglas showed an intellectual precociousness which had distinguished him in every classroom he had entered, from Yakima to
New York City. "He was unquestionably the smartest man in our
class," Simon Rifkind remembered. "Others may have been more
urbane and sophisticated, but for sheer intellectual talent, Douglas was at the top of the class."

At Columbia Law School, Douglas was introduced to the most
powerful mind that he had encountered in his life. It belonged to
Professor Underhill Moore, who taught courses in partnership
and sales, and exhibited a violent impatience with a student's
slightest intellectual fuzziness. When one of Moore's students
drifted into vague half thoughts, the professor brought him
abruptly back on target, hunching his massive shoulders, shout-
ing and pounding his desk with both fists in apoplectic fury. Time

and again, Moore turned scarlet with rage at a student's momentary mental lapse. His classes were, in a word, terrifying. But behind Moore's unbridled physical anger was a meticulously controlled mind that analyzed the law's technical minutiae with the precision of an expert jeweler.

Moore led a dual life in the law. He was, Douglas observed, the master of conventional legal analysis. He was also a relentless researcher into the relationship between law and community behavior. His restless, inquisitive mind was always exploring the edges of the law, dipping deeply into economics, sociology, anthropology, even experimental psychology and psychoanalysis, convinced that law could be fully and accurately understood only in the broader context of human behavior. A legal institution, Moore thought, was simply human behavior and its effects should be described in the same terms as the effects of other kinds of behavior. In studying banking transactions, for example, Moore did not focus exclusively on the facts as set out in a court decision. He looked behind the decision to probe the role of banks in the community where the case arose and then related the institutional behavior of the bank to the judicial decision.

Moore's speculative and open-ended research demanded increasingly large chunks of his time. When he needed help in his research and revisions of his commercial law casebook, he called upon one of his best students, Douglas. Moore was an exacting boss, Douglas learned, one who made incessant demands on himself and his assistant. Often Douglas was routed out of bed shortly after dawn. Would young Douglas, Moore demanded politely, like to take a walk near the professor's Englewood, New Jersey, home to listen to a new idea that had troubled Moore through a restless night? There were more invitations, for Sunday afternoons, when Moore and Douglas knelt in Moore's garden, discussing fresh possibilities in legal research.

During those many hours, the two explored scores of legal concepts together. In the process, Douglas recalled, "I came to respect his hard-edged mind more than any I had ever known. He was the master analyst in the law. He despised those of the facile school who manipulate legal concepts to serve their own purposes. His discipline was severe. He knew the ends served by the law. But in the role of which I now speak, he cared less for that than for orderly analysis and illuminating ratiocination. It was the synthesis that counted."

Aside from his expansive talks in Underhill Moore's garden, Douglas usually discussed law in a grimy basement room of Kent Hall, where the half-empty coffee cups strewn across the desks gave the appearance of a small-town newspaper office. In fact, it was the office of the *Columbia Law Review*.

Election to the law review was, and still is, the confirmation of superior academic achievement at Columbia, as at other law schools, and often the unwritten guarantee of placement in a prominent law firm upon graduation. Announcement of his selection to the law review's board of editors was, for Douglas, one of the happiest moments of his life. But once the work began—grueling, seven-day-a-week research into the law's most opaque technicalities—the euphoria quickly vanished. When they were not in class, law review editors usually worked in their basement headquarters, reading with meticulous care hundreds of court decisions, culling the most significant of them, and analyzing their meaning in lean, colorless prose. It was exacting, hard academic labor.

When at their weekly meetings the editors discussed the most recent court decisions, relief from the march of technicalities occasionally came in the form of a sexually titillating case. Automatically, whoever read the case first would tear it out and pass it over to Bill Douglas, whose taste for the raucous, off-color story was well known. "It was our way of kidding Bill," said a review colleague, Harold Seligson. Douglas accepted the teasing enthusiastically.

Those light moments, however, arose infrequently. Most of Douglas's and his colleagues' time was devoted to the glamourless legal fields, including Douglas's future specialty, commercial law. One student article explored "The Doctrine of Imputed Knowledge Applied to Corporations and Members Thereof"; another tersely described "The Power of a State Bank to Accept Time Bills of Exchange."

Occasionally a student editor would risk a public policy discussion. That occurred in the January 1924 issue when the writer, who, following law review tradition, remained anonymous, posed the question: How should prospective purchasers of stocks and bonds be protected from unscrupulous dealers peddling worthless securities? One answer was legislation that imposed specific regulation of corporate financing and granted broad powers to governmental administrative officials to supervise dealers. An alternative approach was to require corporations to publish detailed prospectuses, thus providing prospective stockholders with the critical information on which to base an investment decision.

The writer favored the latter approach, quoting approvingly from the book, *Other People's Money and How the Bankers Use It* written by Louis D. Brandeis before his appointment to the U.S. Supreme Court. "Compel bankers when issuing securities to make public the commissions and profits they are receiving," Brandeis wrote. "Let every circular, letter, prospectus or advertisement of a bond or stock show clearly what the banker received for his middleman services, and what the bonds and stocks net the issuing corporation. That is knowledge to which both the existing security holder and the prospective purchaser is fairly entitled." Demanding full disclosure by the private corporation, Brandeis concluded, was the best guarantee of corporate responsibility to the public. It was a theme that would more than a decade later be repeated often and with uncompromising force by the third chairman of the Securities and Exchange Commission, William O. Douglas.

Academic success, of course, was a Douglas staple. During his years at law school, Douglas experienced another kind of triumph. He learned how to make money—not just hand-to-mouth dollars, but big money. Six weeks after his first semester at Columbia began, Douglas had completed his business-law correspondence course and, with the proceeds, assured himself that he could complete the school year. But with money still tight, Douglas had hunted for additional income, and hit upon the idea of tutoring high school seniors preparing applications for Ivy League schools.

"To obtain my services," Douglas wrote in his autobiography, "students needed to be both stupid and rich. My boast was that I never failed to get even a dumb student into Princeton." The tutoring service was enormously successful, fattening both Douglas's wallet and his ego. The first students paid five dollars an hour. As demand rose, Douglas, applying the lessons of capitalist market theory, raised his prices, pushing his fee to a twenty-five-dollar-an-hour top.* For the first time in his life, Douglas could bank his earnings.

As important, perhaps, Douglas had shown once again that he was equal—no, superior—to those he perceived to be the "establishment." The "establishment" label was no longer confined to the prospering families of Yakima; Douglas could now point to the true captains of America's industry, who wanted the best education for their slow sons and were willing to pay a poor boy from North Fifth Avenue to guarantee it. It was sweet satisfaction indeed. Douglas could not only control the destiny of the sons of the "establishment," but be paid handsomely for the service.

By June 1924, Douglas had accumulated, as a result of his tutoring, one thousand dollars over bills and expenses. At the same time, he had continued to receive superior grades. His present and future had never looked brighter, and with justified satisfaction, Douglas bought a train ticket west, a coach ticket for the entire trip this time. He celebrated his success in La Grande, Oregon, where he married Mildred Riddle.

Mildred and Bill Douglas† were married in a simple wedding in the Riddle home. Afterward the couple headed for the nearby Wallowa mountain range for a honeymoon carefully planned to accommodate their outdoor interests. For weeks they rode horseback across the high uplands and fished for trout in clear mountain lakes. At the end of summer, the Douglases were happy —and broke.

"We blew my thousand bucks," Douglas later recalled proudly. His seat-of-the-pants financing provided more than a juicy conversation piece. It pointed to a trait that deeply concerned Douglas's family: he was improvident with money. They had worried when he bought a ring he could not afford for his girlfriend in Walla Walla, and they were again concerned when he took on the responsibilities of marriage, apparently with no change in attitude. When he and Mildred stepped off the train at Grand Central

*It was $7.50 tops in an earlier version.
†At Columbia, Douglas abandoned the name Orville for good.

Station in 1924, it would not be the last time they would face financial problems. In 1948, for example, after Douglas had already served nine years as an associate justice of the U.S. Supreme Court, Mildred wrote from Walla Walla (where their daughter, Millie, was a Whitman freshman): "I never felt so low and discouraged over bills in my life, and I thought I had reached the bottom many times before."

Although newly married in 1924 and reduced to a familiar state of poverty, Douglas was not desperate. Solving financial problems presented a formidable challenge and Douglas thrived on challenge. After all, if he had had the money for a cross-country coach ticket in 1922, he would have missed the adventure of herding two thousand sheep to Minneapolis. And if he could have paid the two-hundred-dollar law school tuition, he might not have had the courage to write a business-law correspondence course before he had even completed his first year in law school.

A week after he and Mildred arrived in New York with less than a dollar between them, Douglas had pocketed ninety dollars, the result of a furious tutoring spasm. In a short time, the couple had settled in a rented house in Bernardsville, New Jersey, close to the high school where Mildred taught Latin and within commuting distance of Columbia.

When Douglas was the chairman of the Securities and Exchange Commission and, later, an associate justice of the U.S. Supreme Court, his friends became accustomed to his complaints of impending bankruptcy. He was always searching for additional funds. And he usually found them, but not by borrowing or by investing his small savings in the stock market. Douglas, in fact, avoided the market on principle; it was, he thought, too much of a risk.

Douglas preferred to invest in only one stock: William O. Douglas. In his middle years on the Court, for example, Douglas sometimes planned his trips to Asia and Africa with his itinerary and travel party set, but funds lacking. A friend, like Elon Gilbert, might not know until the very last minute whether Douglas could pay for the trip. He did not borrow money from Gilbert, who could easily have afforded the loan. Instead he waited for a book proposal to be accepted by a publisher. When it was, and the publisher had sent Douglas the advance, he then used the money to cover expenses for the trip he later wrote about.

Throughout his life, Douglas prided himself on his self-sufficiency, sometimes slighting those who helped him along the way. He never credited his sister, Martha, with moral support during his insecure years as a Yakima schoolboy nor even acknowledged her preparations for his many camping trips. And later, in stories of his seat-of-the-pants financing while studying at Columbia, Douglas never mentioned the substantial financial support he received from his wife, Mildred, whose high school teacher's salary paid more bills than his tutoring service fees.

"Remember," cautioned Martha, "he wants you to think he did it all himself." Apparently, in Douglas's mind, admitting that he did not do *everything* by himself not only spoiled a good story but detracted from his indomitable image.

There is an old law school axiom that the student is scared to death his first year, worked to death his second year and bored to death his third. Although Douglas might have agreed with the axiom's conclusions for the first two years, he would have taken exception to the final observation, and would have owed his demur to Professor Underhill Moore. He had already helped Moore with the revision of his commercial law casebook and, gratefully, listened while Moore mined new fields of knowledge. In Douglas's third year, Moore asked him to join on a different kind of venture, neither as cumbersome as casebook revision nor as provocative as those Sunday afternoon discussions in Moore's garden. But helping Moore with his investigation of the sales practices of the Portland cement industry had its own, unique rewards.

The assignment came shortly after the Justice Department in 1924 had begun a study of the operations of large trade associations, searching for monopolistic practices that might have violated federal antitrust laws. Although the cement associations' practices had not yet been challenged, they nervously concluded that they might be next to come under the Justice Department's scrutiny. To bolster their arguments and credibility, the cement industry had hired Moore.

Moore and his student assistant, Douglas, performed traditional research tasks for the industry with quiet dedication. But the expense account possibilities of doing work for a rich and anxious trade association did not escape them either. Moore and Douglas periodically jumped into an automobile and toured the eastern seaboard in search of cement plants. It was Douglas's introduction to expense account living, and it did not take him long to decide that he liked it.

At graduation, Douglas stood second in his class at Columbia and set his sights very high indeed. He wanted to work as the law clerk to the former law school dean recently appointed associate justice of the U.S. Supreme Court, Harlan F. Stone. But Stone skipped past Douglas's application, to choose, instead, the only man whose academic record surpassed Douglas's, Albert McCormack. When he later spoke of his disappointment, Douglas never openly blamed Stone or McCormack, but there was always the nagging question of the justice of the McCormack selection. In short, Douglas thought that he should have been chosen. When he wasn't, he remembered, "The world was black. I was unspeakably depressed that for all those years and all that work, I had so little to show for it. The one opportunity I had wanted had passed me by."

In the years to follow, however, few opportunities would pass by William O. Douglas.

PART TWO: _____

THE OPPORTUNIST

CHAPTER SEVEN

DUCKS IN A ROW

Aɫᴛʜᴏᴜɢʜ Dᴏᴜɢʟᴀs had been denied the Stone clerkship, his future was still extraordinarily bright. Grant Bond, the attorney who had offered to help Douglas through law school, renewed his invitation to take him into his Walla Walla firm. Practice in Yakima, Douglas's hometown, an idea that he had discussed with friends before his first year at Columbia, was also open to him. Douglas rejected both opportunities to practice in the shadow of his beloved Cascades. Instead he decided to join one of the most prestigious Wall Street law firms, Cravath, Henderson & de Gersdorff.

Why did this poor boy from Yakima, who claimed an early and intense hatred of the establishment, want to join lawyers who represented some of the most powerful business interests in the nation? It is a question that Douglas never, even in later years, fully answered. One of Douglas's closest friends, Abe Fortas, the former Associate Justice of the U.S. Supreme Court, has suggested that Douglas was too insecure at that early stage in his career to reject the first opportunity to step across the tracks to the establishment's side. Practice in a large Wall Street firm also made sound professional sense. Douglas had spent much of his classroom and research time in law school studying the intricacies of corporate law. No practice in Walla Walla or Yakima could offer the opportunities to use his newly acquired skills that a large Wall Street firm could provide. Finally, Douglas had to contend with his own relentless ambition. The pungent smell of lupine was strong and the sight of the snowy peak of Mount Adams awesome; but Douglas, like his sister and brother, was driven by a desire to succeed. For the moment, Wall Street practice seemed to offer the best professional arena for achievement.

Before he joined the Cravath firm in June 1925, Douglas made the rounds of other large Wall Street firms. He later wrote about the experience as if he had interviewed the firms' partners, rather than the reverse. He gave one firm a low mark because, he said, he could smell liquor on the breath of one of the partners. At a second firm, he was interviewed by John Foster Dulles, the future Secretary of State. In a story he loved to repeat, Douglas claimed he deflated the pompous Dulles by tipping him a quarter when he helped Douglas with his coat after the interview.* Finally Douglas chose the Cravath firm because, Douglas later wrote, the attorneys there were "earnest and frank and not at all pretentious." By Wall Street standards that may have been so, but the Cravath lawyers were decidedly not "just folks."

Between 1923 and 1928, the Cravath firm grew from thirty-three associates serving eight partners to forty-six associates—including Douglas, John J. McCloy (who would become High Commissioner of West Germany and chairman of the board of the Ford Foundation) and Douglas's law school rival, Albert McCormack—serving thirteen partners. The nonlegal staff grew from seventy to 104 employees and the firm, to accommodate the expanding staff, took over three and a half floors at 52 William Street. The Cravath firm was divided into trial and corporate departments, with those in the corporate department responsible for a variety of tasks for the firm's corporate clients and those in the trial department concentrating exclusively on litigation of the

---

*Dulles's version was different. He recalled the interview but not the tipping incident. According to Dulles, Douglas was not offered a job because he did not meet the firm's high standards.

clients' interests. Cravath's clients in those years included the Radio Corporation of America, Bethlehem Steel and Kuhn, Loeb & Co.

The authoritative head of the firm was Paul D. Cravath, a commanding figure with bushy eyebrows and slightly stooped shoulders, who hurled his prodigious energy forcefully into the causes of the firm's corporate clients. Cravath expected no less of the other partners and the young associates in his firm.

To assure that everyone in the firm would meet his standards, Cravath personally recruited young lawyers from the nation's top law schools. Cravath's partner Robert T. Swaine wrote of the Cravath model: "For a poor law school record Cravath never had tolerance. He believed that a man who had not attained at least the equivalent of a Harvard Law School 'B' either had a mind not adapted to the law or lacked purpose and ambition; in either case, the man was not for the Cravath office. The scholastic standards of the Cravath system thus made a Phi Beta Kappa from a good college who had become a law review editor at Harvard, Columbia or Yale the first choice. . . . Cravath did not, however, want colorless, narrow-minded bookworms. From applicants who met his standards of scholarship, he wanted those who also had warmth and force of personality and physical stamina adequate to the pressure to which they would often be subject because of the rugged character of the work."*

"Douglas was not on our list of those we were trying to get," recalled John J. McCloy, then a young associate with the firm. "Since most of our young lawyers came from the good colleges in the East, he was a little off the beaten track. And when he came in, he looked like he had come off a hike. He was not one of the usual Brooks Brothers set. In fact, he looked like a singed cat. But then he told me what he had done to get a legal education and I was interested because I had worked my way through law school, too. He talked about his background and how hard life had been. I told Bob Swaine, 'I think this fellow's got something.' "

---

*It also helped if an applicant was a white Anglo-Saxon Protestant; Simon Rifkind, a Jewish classmate of Douglas's with high grades, did not even bother to interview leading firms, like Cravath, because he assumed he would not be hired.

Douglas impressed another of Cravath's rising young attorneys, Bruce Bromley, who found Douglas "alert, vigorous and a good talker." Douglas asked Bromley, who was then working in the firm's trial department, if he could begin in the trial department and switch to the corporate department. Bromley said that he could. Bromley, like McCloy, sent Douglas to the Cravath senior partners with his high recommendation. Douglas accepted the offer of a job at a starting salary of $1,800 a year, which in two years time was raised to $3,000.*

The sixteen-hour workdays at Cravath were well known; Bromley was then putting in over three hundred hours a month of time billable to the firm's clients. Douglas was undaunted. While he was a Cravath associate, he even accepted a part-time job as lecturer in law at Columbia. He taught one class each in Bankruptcy, Damages and Partnership, although he had studied only one, Partnership, while he was a law student. Douglas prepared and taught his Columbia classes at 8:00 A.M., then rushed to Cravath for a full day and night of duty, sometimes not returning to his wife—the Douglases now lived in Pelham, New York—before four in the morning. It was an inhuman work schedule by other people's standards, but not by Douglas's. At least, not at first. Eventually the pace and substance of the work seriously impaired his health.

At Cravath, Henderson & de Gersdorff, young associates were immediately introduced to the Cravath system, the only approach to the practice of law tolerated by Paul Cravath. The system was explained with paternalistic simplicity by senior partner Robert Swaine: "At the outset of their practice, Cravath men are not thrown into deep water and told to swim; rather, they are taken into shallow water and carefully taught strokes. The Cravath office does not follow the practice of many other offices of leaving small routine matters entirely to young men fresh from law school without supervision, on the theory that a man best learns how to handle cases by actually handling them. Under the 'Cravath system,' a young man watches his senior break a large problem down into its component parts and does thoroughly and

---

*Douglas has written that his salary was raised from $1,800 to $3,600 in one year, but Cravath records show that he was wrong.

exhaustively the part assigned to him—a process impracticable in the handling of small routine matters. Cravath believed that the man who learns to analyze the component parts of a large problem involving complicated facts, and to do each detailed part well, becomes a better lawyer faster than the man who is not taught in such detail."

Douglas and John McCloy shared a cubicle that had just enough room for two desks, one by the window, the other by the door. Under the "Cravath system" both men worked under Donald C. Swatland, himself only thirty years old, but a driving young associate who would make partner a year later. Swatland, a Phi Beta Kappa graduate of Princeton and *Harvard Law Review* editor, attacked each assignment with fierce dedication, leaving no detail to chance or a junior associate's carelessness.

Douglas learned of Swatland's perfectionist ways with thudding abruptness. Late one night, after Swatland and Douglas had drafted a document transferring title of a vast railroad empire to a newly formed corporation, Swatland sent Douglas to the printer's to proofread the final copy. The next morning, Douglas was told, he was to pick up fifty copies of the document and deliver them to Swatland's office at nine-thirty sharp. Douglas followed orders well, he thought. He meticulously proofread the document and left the printer's at 4:00 A.M., returning after a few hours so that he could deposit the copies on Swatland's desk at the appointed time. But seconds after Douglas had placed the papers on his young boss's desk, the fifty copies came flying back at him, accompanied by Swatland's raging voice.

"My name is Donald *C.* Swatland," Swatland screamed, "not Donald Swatland."

A bewildered Douglas gathered the copies. Sure enough, in one segment of the document, the middle initial had been dropped from Swatland's name. Douglas apologized and said that he would quickly correct the omission, putting in the missing initial in ink.

"Not in this office," Swatland roared, ordering Douglas back to the printer's to have the fifty copies reprinted, this time perfectly.

Swatland was understandably nervous. The document that he and Douglas had been working on would transfer title of the financially troubled Chicago, Milwaukee & St. Paul Railroad (known as the St. Paul) to a new corporation. It was all part of a series of intricate legal and financial maneuvers which had placed the ailing St. Paul into the largest receivership in U.S. history.

"Bill Douglas and I worked on the details of the St. Paul reorganization under Swatland's supervision," McCloy recalled. "Supervising the logistics of the massive reorganization was late-night drudgery. There was some looking up of the law, but not too much, because there was not too much law on the books. It was mostly organizing a very big job. We prepared titles and deeds of transfer. There were trips to Chicago and leg work for the investment banks. It didn't require legal genius to do it; it did require a lot of hard work. Bill Douglas worked under Swatland and me. He fulfilled all the potential I thought he had. He was a producer."

The Cravath firm had been hired in 1925 by Kuhn, Loeb & Co., an investment banking firm with large financial interests in the St. Paul, to study the legal problems created by the railroad's desperate financial condition. The railroad's deficit in 1924 had been nearly $2 million. To add to the St. Paul's woes, $50 million worth of refunding bonds were due to mature in 1925, the year the railroad hired Cravath. The railroad had no cash in its treasury to meet its financial obligations and no possibility of borrowing. The St. Paul prepared for receivership.

By the time the St. Paul had collapsed and been fully reorganized, not only Cravath but twenty-nine other law firms had become involved. Cravath, representing Kuhn, Loeb & Co., and the law firm of Shearman & Sterling, representing the National City Bank, the other major underwriter of the St. Paul, assumed responsibility for the brunt of the work. Paul Cravath decided all questions of major policy and conducted all important negotiations for his firm. His partner Robert Swaine was responsible for keeping all reorganization proceedings moving and supervising all drafting of legal documents. Donald Swatland, aided by associates McCloy, Douglas and others, drafted all the legal papers and attended to the endless detail of the receivership.

In writing a history of the Cravath firm, Robert Swaine discussed the St. Paul reorganization in fourteen dry pages, largely devoted to the intricate financial and legal problems that confronted Kuhn, Loeb and its counsel, Cravath. At the end of the

discussion, however, Swaine admitted that the St. Paul reorganization became a "cause célèbre," drawing "adverse criticism,"
from investigators of the Interstate Commerce Commission and
several congressional committees. The criticisms of the reorganization were "full of inconsistencies," Swaine wrote, but "upon
one criticism all the malcontents were in accord: Wall Street
bankers and their lawyers had too much to do with the whole
matter and should never again be permitted to profit from a
railroad reorganization."

One "malcontent" stood above all the rest in his outspoken
denunciation of the St. Paul reorganization. He was Max Lowenthal, a New York attorney who wrote a book, *The Investor Pays,*
depicting the St. Paul reorganization as an orgy of greed and
plunder by Wall Street bankers and lawyers. Lowenthal* pictured
the bankers (Kuhn, Loeb and National City Bank) and their legion of lawyers (primarily, Cravath and Shearman & Sterling) as
vultures, hovering over a sickly St. Paul, waiting for the proper
moment to swoop down and pick the bones of the railway dry.
The collapse of the railroad was, in fact, a financial bonanza for
both the bankers and the lawyers. Kuhn, Loeb and the National
City Bank received $1,044,000 for their services. The Cravath
firm submitted bills for more than $450,000.

Unfortunately, the St. Paul reorganization was a disaster for the
bond- and shareholders, Lowenthal wrote. They were, in effect,
paying for all the bright young lawyers on the Street—including
William O. Douglas—to churn out legal papers. From the beginning, the security holders were shut out of any effective role in
the reorganization. Kuhn, Loeb and Cravath, Lowenthal wrote,
opposed "intervention in receivership by any security holders
except those connected with and supporting the bankers."

One of the key documents in the process of reorganization, and
the one that, according to Lowenthal, was responsible for the
stock and bond committees relinquishing their legal powers to
the bankers, was the reorganization document prepared by the
Cravath firm. Lowenthal wrote that "the language by which the
committees were made to surrender themselves into the bankers'
hands was scattered throughout the almost endless document

---

*Swaine later referred to Lowenthal as a "cynical New Deal iconoclast."

and had to be pieced together." That document provided, among other things, that the bankers would manage the reorganization and that they "could determine when there was sufficient support for the reorganization plan 'in their sole and unrestricted discretion.'" The carte blanche given the bankers was the shrewd handiwork of the Cravath lawyers who, Lowenthal charged, "rubberized the words" of the document so that the bankers could do whatever they pleased.

Douglas did not question the propriety of what he and his superiors at Cravath were doing. He later wrote: "One of my duties in those days was to attend stockholders' meetings in Hoboken, New Jersey, or in Wilmington, Delaware. I would go with a briefcase filled with proxies. A secretary of the corporation was also present, another officer and myself. Motions were put and I would cast all 900,000 votes or all 1,900,000 votes for those motions. Once in a while a minority interest would appear— perhaps two or three people, plus their lawyer. I still cast my briefcase of proxies for the management and against the dissenters, for I was only a courier, a ministerial agent." Douglas added that he wondered "what injustices, if any, were being perpetrated." Still, he accepted the situation passively.

After less than a year at Cravath, Douglas thought that he had had enough of big-time corporate law practice in New York. But his objections were not directed at Kuhn, Loeb & Co. or the work he did at Cravath on their behalf. Douglas's complaints were personal rather than ideological.

"I don't think he ever had his heart wholly in his work," McCloy recalled. "The work at Cravath was pretty much of a grind. Wouldn't it be more fun, Douglas would ask, to practice for yourself? Partnership at Cravath didn't appeal to him. He seemed restive under the controls at Cravath. I don't think he liked the exactions. It lacked the expression of his own talents. I don't think he had the chance to show his brilliance."

At the same time that Douglas was questioning the personal satisfactions of Wall Street practice, the back-breaking hours and enormous mental pressures of the Cravath practice were jeopardizing his health. When he began to have severe stomach problems, Douglas wrote to his old Whitman roommate, Bill Wilson, then serving his residency at Women's Hospital, Baltimore, and asked his advice. Douglas told Wilson that he had gone to a chiropractor in Brooklyn but that the pains continued. He was also running a fever. Wilson invited Douglas to come down to Baltimore for diagnostic tests. The results showed that Douglas was suffering from nervous tension.

He was not physically set up for the competitive practice of law, Wilson told Douglas, and suggested that he teach full-time. Douglas was not certain that he should make that career change. There were, however, several conclusions he *had* arrived at. First, he could never devote his life to Wall Street law practice; the hours were too long and the work too confining. Second, he missed the natural beauty of the Northwest. When he dropped into his bed after another sixteen-hour day at Cravath, Douglas rolled and tossed, unable to sleep. Instead of counting sheep, he drifted into pleasant reverie, his mind pushing him up Darling Mountain and down into the Klickitat Meadows. He would catch cutthroat trout in the Little Klickitat and roast them on a stick over a willow fire. And then he snapped out of it and realized that he was almost three thousand miles and a whole professional life away from his fantasy.

Reality, Douglas decided, was not only unpleasant but un-necessary. Bill and Mildred Douglas headed west, stopping first in Seattle for job interviews. Douglas hoped to affiliate with a Seattle law firm whose pace would accommodate his sensitive nervous system but whose legal problems would challenge his extraordinary mind. What he found were Northwest versions of Cravath, with the corporate work piled high. Only the substan-tially lower associates' salaries seemed to distinguish the Seattle firms.

Douglas returned to Yakima, where he met James O. Cull, the lawyer who more than two decades earlier had spent the proceeds from his father's insurance policy on a doomed irrigation project. Cull had recently declared bankruptcy and was trying to make a fresh start. What better way to begin than to wipe away his guilt at having taken advantage of a poor widow twenty-two years before? Cull hired the widow's son as his associate, and promised to pay him fifty dollars a month if business was good. Cull and Douglas then opened an office in downtown Yakima.

Instead of transferring titles for multimillion-dollar railroads, Douglas was drafting mortgages on Yakima valley chicken coops. He worked as assiduously in Yakima as he had in New York City, but his hours and craftsmanship were not reflected in his billing. In a good month, he could expect to make twenty-five dollars. Douglas quickly calculated that it would take him several years before he could make a down payment on a home for Mildred and himself and, in time, a family. And that calculation assumed that his law business would remain steady. With sixty-five lawyers to service the legal needs of a population of twenty thousand, the competition was certain to be keen. It was not a comforting prospect.

After only eight months in the Northwest, Douglas returned to the Cravath firm. "I don't know why he came back," said McCloy. The Cravath partners did not question Douglas's decision. They welcomed him back with a raise of four hundred dollars over his previous salary of two thousand dollars. Douglas resumed work on the St. Paul reorganization and, three months later, received another raise, this time to three thousand dollars. It would be his last at Cravath; he left the firm for good in June 1927.

Cravath's work on the St. Paul reorganization continued until 1931, much of it an involuntary defense of its practices and fees before the Interstate Commerce Commission and in the federal courts. Cravath and its client Kuhn, Loeb were forced to justify their work because members of the Interstate Commerce Commission viewed the St. Paul reorganization critically. Like Max Lowenthal, they charged that the reorganization plan had ignored the public interest and rewarded the bankers and lawyers with exorbitant power and fees. The security holders were peripheral to the entire reorganization, members of the ICC concluded, and through the efforts of Kuhn, Loeb and Cravath, as well as the other bankers and lawyers involved, they were prevented from having any say in how their money was being spent or how the company *they owned* was being managed and reorganized. The security holders seemed to be responsible for only one thing: paying the astronomical fees of the bankers and lawyers.

When the Interstate Commerce Commission attempted to investigate the reasonableness of their practices, the bankers and lawyers argued that this was a purely private matter which was off limits to the ICC and the federal courts. A six-man conservative majority of the U.S. Supreme Court agreed with the Wall Street bankers and lawyers.

But those same practices and fees were attacked as "wasteful and extravagant" by Justice Harlan F. Stone, joined in dissent by Justices Louis D. Brandeis and Oliver Wendell Holmes. The St. Paul shareholders paid the bills, Stone noted, but enjoyed no effective voice in the railroad's management. That might not have been harmful to the public interest if the federal agency that possessed official supervisory powers over railroad reorganizations, the Interstate Commerce Commission, could have exercised those powers in the St. Paul case. But the ICC was carefully blocked out of any meaningful supervision by the shrewdly evasive manuevers of Kuhn, Loeb, Cravath and others. The firms in charge of the reorganization had shown, said Stone, "a failure to conform to those elementary standards of fairness and good conscience which equity may always demand." Stone said that the practices did not serve the public interest and would, ultimately, undermine the public's confidence in the nation's railroads.

That focus on the public interest would characterize Douglas's philosophy when he later served at the SEC and on the U.S. Supreme Court. But not in the mid-1920s, when Douglas was a struggling young associate at the Cravath firm. Douglas's interest was not in broad public policy then, but in the endless research and detailed paper work necessary to satisfy the legal needs of the firm's corporate client, Kuhn, Loeb & Co. "I don't remember any ideological interchange between Douglas and me at Cravath," McCloy said. "We just talked about how to get the day's business done. How do we get our ducks in a row? What consents do we have to get? Who on the bondholders' committee is important? Who should we talk to at the banks? Bill Douglas wasn't the passionate crusader then."

While Douglas was putting "ducks in a row" for Kuhn, Loeb & Co., another brilliant lawyer, Professor Felix Frankfurter of the Harvard Law School, was a leading advocate for the cause of two Italian immigrants, Nicola Sacco and Bartolomeo Vanzetti, who then faced murder charges and mob hysteria. It is ironic that Douglas, the great libertarian of a future Supreme Court, was

involved in commercial law at Cravath and, later, at the Columbia
and Yale law schools, while his chief adversary on that future
Court, Frankfurter, was at the barricades, defending the have-
nots.

In retrospect, Douglas claimed a firm loyalty to the cause of
Sacco and Vanzetti, having written in his autobiography that he
had supported Frankfurter's position and "had written letters,
spoken at meetings and circulated petitions—all to no avail."
Still, no Douglas colleague interviewed who served with him at
Cravath or, later, at Columbia or Yale could recall Douglas's
strong support for Sacco and Vanzetti. Indeed, none could remember Douglas's support for any liberal cause. They did recall
that Douglas was an intense young man who, above all, seemed
interested in his professional career.

In pursuing that career at Cravath, Douglas never questioned
his firm's practices or that of their client, Kuhn, Loeb, in the
controversial St. Paul reorganization, even after he had left
Cravath and was well established as a national authority on corporate bankruptcy and reorganization. In the years that followed his
work for Cravath, Douglas published law review articles, delivered speeches and wrote judicial opinions on the subjects. Frequently he attacked selfish Wall Street bankers and corrupt corporate lawyers. He defended the little shareholder and the public
interest. But nowhere is there a Douglas criticism or a careful
analysis of the St. Paul reorganization.

In fact, in a law review article written in 1934, in which he
discussed railroad reorganizations, Douglas arrived at some conclusions that seemed sympathetic to the power wielded by Kuhn,
Loeb in the St. Paul reorganization. Douglas's article was produced in response to criticism of a new section of the Bankruptcy
Act by Max Lowenthal, the same New York attorney who had
written the book attacking the St. Paul reorganization and, specifically, the roles of Kuhn, Loeb and Cravath in that reorganization. In his article, Lowenthal had criticized the new section of the
Bankruptcy Act, which dealt solely with railroad reorganizations,
because, he said, it left too much power in the hands of large
institutional investors. The small security holders would continue
to be powerless, victimized again and again by the same Wall
Street bankers who had always controlled protective reorganiza-

tion committees. "Protective committee racketeering is not only possible but probable under the new legislation," Lowenthal concluded.

Amazingly enough, in light of his later public positions, Douglas staunchly defended the protective committees that were dominated by institutional investors. The real problem was that the committees had not too much power under the new legislation, Douglas wrote, but too little. A protective committee controlled by the small shareholders and closely supervised by the federal government was a nice ideal, according to Douglas, but could never be effective. A more realistic and a better idea, Douglas suggested, would be to have powerful executive control without the restraints that heavy government regulation would bring. He brushed aside Lowenthal's fears of abuse that such concentrated power could bring. "Abuses could arise in any system," Douglas wrote. Given a choice of filling committee slots with institutional investors or small-town shareholders, Douglas voted for the investors. He concluded: "In view of their substantial investments, their positions of prestige, their organization and technical equipment, and their real capacity to serve investors, the problem is not one of making it more difficult to act. Rather it is one of perpetuating and making more certain the continuance of that control."

CHAPTER EIGHT

THE BATTLE OF 1928

NEITHER THE PACE at Cravath nor Douglas's nervous tension slackened in the winter of 1927 and Douglas began once again to think of leaving Wall Street law practice. He was still teaching his early-morning courses at the Columbia Law School, and the idea of making law school teaching a career, as his ex-roommate Bill Wilson had suggested, became more attractive. Not that law school teaching was anxiety-free. Douglas knew better. He had felt paroxysms of nervousness whenever he entered his Columbia classroom. But that only happened for a few moments before class, not relentlessly, morning to early the next morning, every day of the working week, as at the Cravath firm.

The opportunity to switch careers arose in the spring of 1927, when the Columbia Law School faculty offered Douglas a full-time position as assistant professor of law, to teach courses in his specialty, commercial law. He accepted Columbia's invitation and began attending faculty meetings even before he officially left the Cravath firm in June.

Since Douglas would not begin full-time teaching until September, he and Mildred decided to leave New York's summer heat for the cool serenity of New Hampshire's countryside. They rented a cottage and invited Bill Wilson, still a medical resident in Baltimore, to visit. Although Douglas had begun to smoke and drink, he still impressed his old friend as the serious type of his Whitman days. So did Mildred, whom Wilson remembered as "a demure, quiet and very pretty little housewife." She didn't drink or swear, and took a dim view, as Wilson discovered, of her husband and his friends when they did.

"We fished all day," Wilson remembered. "I had brought a bottle of rum and brought it out one evening. I offered some to Bill but he wouldn't take it. Finally he drank some and got very sick. Mildred got very mad at us. She didn't like it at all."

When Douglas returned to Columbia, he found a law school tormented by an identity crisis and an internal struggle that would profoundly affect his future. Like Harvard and Yale, Columbia for decades had expertly trained the nation's best law students for the lucrative practice of law. In the early twentieth century that legal training had been based on the case method, in which students learned legal principles and rules by studying actual appellate court cases. The classroom training could be intellectually exciting under masters of the Socratic method, such as Stone at Columbia. But even Stone occasionally worried that the exclusive study of cases threatened to cut the student off from the realities surrounding the courthouses.

As early as 1922, members of the Columbia faculty, led by Professor Herman Oliphant, who had taught Douglas contracts, had argued that the law school curriculum was far too narrow. Court decisions alone could not give students a clear understanding of the underlying economic, political and social problems. More important, a rigid adherence to the case method, Oliphant had argued, deprived students of the intellectual tools to gauge the significance of law in the larger society. For those who opposed the broader approach as an idle intellectual exercise, Oliphant offered a practical argument: besides receiving a firmer understanding of legal phenomena, students would be better equipped to handle intelligently their professional business, which, as every practitioner knew, regularly spilled over the boundaries of casebook law.

With characteristic caution, Dean Stone had allowed two new courses, organized along functional rather than traditional legal lines, to be introduced into the Columbia curriculum in 1922. One was a course in Industrial Relations, which dealt with the legal problems that arose from employer-employee relationships and considered legal solutions to those problems. The other, taught by Professor Oliphant, had been a course in Illegal Contracts and Combinations, later named Trade Regulation, in which Oliphant scrutinized illegal business practices and their consequences for society.

The introduction of these two courses did not excite many Columbia educators. Even Columbia president Nicholas Murray Butler, not noted for his revolutionary zeal, grew restless. In his annual report in 1922, Butler had criticized the law school directly and its dean by implication: "That legal education has fallen into ruts and that it has never been subjected to critical examination from the standpoint of educational principle, is generally admitted. In fact, legal education has been treated too largely as a matter of law and too little as a matter of education."

Stone, who had feuded with Butler for years, was stung by the criticism and asked for a year's leave of absence. Butler's criticism of Stone was not lost on another member of the law school faculty, Herman Oliphant. Oliphant, too, had grown restless with the dean's foot-dragging. On November 1, 1923, Oliphant had written to Butler, outlining his ambitious ideas for a total reorganization of the law school curriculum. Further productivity at the law school was impossible, Oliphant told Butler, without concentrated research on the interrelation of law to the other social sciences. That research would have to be so intensive, Oliphant stated, that it should be the single concern of the law school. In other words, the Columbia Law School, as it was then known, would cease to exist. In its place, Columbia would offer the nation's foremost center for legal research. In response to Oliphant, President Butler wrote that Oliphant should "go hammer and tongs at the question you raise" until the full law faculty was willing and able to make a final decision. At the same time, other faculty members, led by Professor Young B. Smith, quietly urged more modest changes than Oliphant, but changes that would nonetheless place the law in the broader context of social, economic and political realities.

Nothing had been resolved in 1924, when Stone resigned the deanship to return to private practice. He was replaced by Huger W. Jervey, a New York attorney who came to the law school with a reputation for mastering complex sets of facts and finding a common ground of agreement among adversaries. It was a talent that would be tested time and again in the next three years at Columbia. For while many members of the Columbia faculty were convinced of the importance of legal research, and were open-minded, if wary, about the introduction of nonlegal materials into the law school classroom, they were unwilling to abandon the casebook and the view that the law school's primary purpose was to train practitioners. In 1926, Jervey developed an ulcer and soon resigned, leaving the Columbia faculty hopelessly splintered and, now, leaderless. By this time, Professor Leon Marshall had divided the law faculty into small groups to study every aspect of the curriculum. The faculty, with a surge of inspired verbosity, produced one hundred reports covering eight hundred typewritten pages. And in a move that was intellectually sound but politically disastrous, Professor Herman Oliphant was asked by Professor Young B. Smith, who had been appointed acting dean by President Butler, to write a summary of the faculty's findings. Smith relieved Oliphant of all classroom duties so that he could devote full time to the project.

Even before Oliphant submitted his final report, his conclusions were anticipated. It was well known through endless faculty discussions that Oliphant, Underhill Moore and Leon Marshall were persuaded that Columbia should become a genuine community of scholars, devoted primarily to the nonprofessional study of law. Only with this clearly defined mission, they believed, could Columbia's faculty study the law in its broader and more meaningful context, evaluate the impact of law on society and plot its future development in modern life.

The idea sent tremors through the law faculty offices. "It seemed to me as though those fellows were going to wreck the school," Harold Medina, then an adjunct professor of law and later a federal judge, recalled. "It would have pleased Oliphant to have a law school with forty students and two hundred professors," said Medina. "It was a matter of indifference to him where you got the money to maintain the school." Professor Richard Powell also opposed Oliphant, but he took a calmer view of the feud. "I was indoctrinated with the belief that a law school's objective and task was to train practicing lawyers to do a competent job," Powell said. The other side "had different views, perhaps more sophisticated, more philosophically oriented."

Pro- and anti-Oliphant forces focused their energies on a single issue: Who would succeed Jervey as dean? Both Oliphant and Young B. Smith openly campaigned for the deanship. Those who wanted Columbia to become a legal research center naturally supported Oliphant for the deanship. Those, like Medina and Powell, who feared that Columbia's reputation and funds would be frittered away on esoteric research backed Young B. Smith, who had long since parted ideological ways with Oliphant. Smith still wanted change in the Columbia curriculum, but not at the expense of traditional legal education.

"I was for Smith," Medina recalled. "He was my classmate and I liked him. I thought if we let the others get their way, it would have ruined the law school."

Douglas entered the political contest at the law school in 1927 believing implicitly in the functional approach advocated by Oliphant and Underhill Moore. As his student assistant, Douglas had admired the quality of Moore's mind above all others and marveled at the research results that Moore's creative intellect could produce. But Douglas's position was not entirely dependent on Moore's influence. Since law school graduation, Douglas had worked in a large, prosperous Wall Street law firm whose practice, as Douglas knew firsthand, involved high corporate finance as well as legal theory. He was convinced that law could not be practiced, or taught, in a vacuum. In his field of commercial law, Douglas wanted to teach the anatomy of finance as well as the rules of law. The intellectual cross-fertilization should not, Douglas believed, be confined to the commercial law field. He urged law professors in every area to trade their expertise with that of other departments—economists, sociologists, political scientists —to better understand the law in modern life.

In 1927, the idea was not revolutionary. In fact, leaders of both Columbia factions, Oliphant and Smith, could and did agree on that point for years. It was surprising, then, that in his autobiography Douglas totally condemned the position of those who supported Smith and, indeed, Smith himself. "I had nothing against

Smith," Douglas wrote. "He was a fine man but he was the antithesis of what we wanted: he represented the past. Under him our educational venture was doomed."

Legal historian Julius Goebel, Jr., whom Douglas counted as an ally in the faculty controversy, has documented Young B. Smith's considerable role in urging reforms in the law school curriculum. Douglas's total condemnation of Smith and his exaggerated account of the controversy seem to confirm Goebel's conclusion. "The atmosphere of intellectual debate," Goebel wrote, "became, on occasion, dimmed by the smoke of a political contest between two groups of dominating personalities." The leading antagonists were Oliphant and Smith. Interestingly, participants say that Douglas, who later claimed ferocious allegiance to the Oliphant forces, rarely ventured an opinion in the heat of the controversy.

In meeting after exhausting meeting, the two factions fought like politicians deadlocked in a national party convention. "There was a great deal of electioneering and intrigue," Goebel wrote. "There was certainly a mounting feeling of bitterness."

Impatient with the law faculty's inability to decide on a successor to Jervey, President Butler, in the spring of 1928, finally made the decision for them. But before he did, Butler consulted with former Dean Stone, Benjamin Cardozo (the future Associate Justice of the U.S. Supreme Court and then a trustee of Columbia) and other law school alumni about the candidates for the deanship. Then, without consulting the law faculty's special committee on the deanship, Butler announced that he would recommend to the university's trustees that Smith be appointed dean.

Butler's announcement touched off a fire storm of protest among the law faculty. Many members of the faculty, particularly those who backed the losing candidate, Oliphant, charged that Butler's action was autocratic and in flagrant violation of the faculty's traditional prerogatives. A meeting in the Columbia faculty club was promptly called to protest the action and professors were summoned from as far away as Virginia. But Butler was unmoved, and on May 7, with Butler's recommendation, the trustees formally announced Smith's appointment.

Douglas wrote of the dispute in dramatic terms, suggesting that the law school's revolutionaries, including himself, Oliphant,

Moore and Goebel, had frightened Butler into taking his action. "He [Butler] was so terrified at the prospect of Columbia being dominated by 'sociological jurisprudence' that he appointed a dean, Young B. Smith, without consulting the Law faculty." It was a disastrous decision, Douglas added, because Smith "was utterly opposed to what we were trying to do."

Goebel's history of the dispute suggests that Douglas was not only wrong in his characterization of Butler's and Smith's views on legal education, but misguided in his outrage at Butler's appointment of Smith. "Although the statutory power of appointing a dean lay entirely with the trustees on the recommendation of the president, some members of the faculty conceived that there existed a tradition that no dean should be appointed without its concurrence," Goebel wrote. "Apart from the fact that as lawyers, they should have known better than to argue that an alleged usage should prevail over the explicit mandate of a statute designed to end faculty election, they should have realized as participants in the embroilment that nothing remotely approaching general agreement on a candidate could be secured."

After the Smith appointment, Douglas claimed, he alone resigned in protest. That was not true. On the same day that Douglas's resignation became effective, June 30, 1928, so did that of Professor Hessel Yntema; the next year, Yntema and Professor Leon Marshall accepted appointments to a new legal research center at Johns Hopkins. Herman Oliphant also resigned in 1928, but his resignation became effective a year later so that he could benefit from his sabbatical leave. Oliphant afterward became counsel to the Department of the Treasury, in what both sides considered a tragic loss to future law students, who would be denied his classroom brilliance. Underhill Moore, though invited to Johns Hopkins, remained at Columbia until January 1, 1930, when he went to Yale's Institute of Human Relations. For his last year and a half at Columbia, Moore spoke to no one at the law school, not even to say good morning.

The Columbia Law School did not become the intellectual wasteland under Smith that Douglas later suggested. Declaring the need for a "university law school," Smith began to revamp the curriculum. The first-year course in Personal Property was dropped and a new one introduced, showing how English and

American property law had reflected and influenced social change over the centuries. A second course, Legislation, was offered, tracing the relationship between common law and statute law, the factual basis of the legislation, problems of legislative drafting and judicial interpretation of the statutes. In the commercial law area, Adolf A. Berle, Jr., and Roswell Magill shared responsibility for combining courses in Agency, Partnership and Corporations. Berle's approach, not unlike that of another professor in the commercial law area, named Douglas, was to view business associations in the light of economic and legal materials relating principally to problems of corporate finance.

Douglas distorted not only the facts in dispute at the Columbia Law School, but also the circumstances surrounding his resignation. According to Douglas, he resigned from Columbia in a fit of anger and principle after Smith's appointment was announced on May 7, 1928. But on June 1, 1928, according to the faculty minutes of the law school, Assistant Professor Douglas attended a meeting of the Columbia Law School faculty. Moreover, at that same meeting, Douglas was appointed to the faculty scholarship committee for the academic year 1928–1929. It is not clear why Douglas would have been asked to sit on a faculty committee, and accepted the invitation, if he had resigned so dramatically from that same faculty several weeks earlier.

In fact, Douglas's resignation from Columbia was not announced until a faculty meeting the following fall. By that time Douglas had accepted an offer by Dean Robert Hutchins to join the faculty of the Yale Law School.

In his autobiography, Douglas's version of the Battle of 1928 revealed more about the author than about his role in the Columbia dispute. Though he certainly did support the Oliphant forces, he was not the outspoken Young Turk that he later claimed. His exaggerated account of his role and the forces he opposed suggest a strong desire on Douglas's part to link his early professional career with his later progressive record at the SEC and the U.S. Supreme Court. Because he played a major role in so many important struggles for reform in his later life, Douglas seems to have reasoned backward that this was always so. It was not.

——————————————————————

CHAPTER NINE

THE NATION'S OUTSTANDING LAW PROFESSOR

THERE WERE DIFFERENCES between Douglas and Yale's
Dean Robert Hutchins. Bill Douglas craved exercise, particularly
outdoor exercise, and would go out of town, across the country
or around the world to sate that craving. Exercise for Bob Hutchins was an idea whose time never came. Whenever the temptation to exercise threatened, Hutchins would lie down and wait
patiently for the impulse to go away.

But the similarities between the two men—in background, ambition and intellectual energy—were even more striking. Hutchins had been born four months after Douglas, the son of William James Hutchins, pastor of the Bedford Presbyterian Church
in Brooklyn. Although Hutchins had considered following his
father into the Presbyterian ministry, the church's appeal to emo-
tionalism ultimately turned his ambition to secular pursuits. Even
so, his father imbued in Hutchins an ascetic spirit that conditioned him to arise every morning of his life at 5:30 A.M.

At sixteen, Hutchins entered tiny Oberlin College; he interrupted his college education to serve in the Army Ambulance Corps in World War I, and then transferred to Yale for his junior year. To pay for his education, Hutchins worked nights at an ice cream spoon factory, raked grass and tutored students less gifted than himself. At Yale, he demonstrated a dazzling intelligence and extraordinary oratorical skill. He graduated with honors in 1921, having been elected to Phi Beta Kappa. After a brief stint teaching at an upstate New York prep school, Hutchins became the secretary of Yale University, at twenty-four the youngest person ever to fill the position. While serving as secretary of Yale, Hutchins enrolled in the Yale Law School and three years later graduated magna cum laude. In 1927, at the age of twenty-eight, he was appointed acting dean of the law school.

Over the objections of his senior faculty, Dean Hutchins introduced courses in economics, the social sciences, history and philosophy into the Yale Law School curriculum. The new dean anticipated the resistance of law students, who felt more secure with traditional law courses. "Naturally," Hutchins said, "the courses had to be made compulsory; otherwise, nobody would have taken them." Although his methods may have been autocratic, his goals were pure. "The object of a law school education," Hutchins said, "was to produce educated lawyers and not merely lawyers who knew the rules and how to manipulate them."

One May evening, when the Battle of 1928 was being fought at the Columbia Law School, Hutchins was speaking at a Pelham, New York, country club. In the audience was the young Columbia law professor William O. Douglas, a guest of Richard Walsh, the head of the John Day Publishing Co. Douglas was instantly attracted to the young Yale dean's ideas and pursued the speaker into the country club's locker room after the talk. There, drinking bootleg liquor, Douglas traded ideas, witticisms and addresses with Hutchins.

Three days after Young B. Smith was officially named dean at Columbia, Hutchins called a meeting of the Yale faculty to discuss the controversy at Columbia and the opportunities it might present to Yale. Because of the Columbia shootout, several members of the Columbia faculty might be interested in coming to New Haven for the next academic year, Hutchins said, and specified Douglas, Underhill Moore and Hessel Yntema. Hutchins asked for and was given authority "to proceed to negotiate for any one or more of the men suggested." Yntema went to Johns Hopkins, Moore postponed the move to Yale for a year and a half, but Douglas accepted Hutchins's offer.

In 1928, America was enjoying a boom economy. Industry's captains were prospering spectacularly and they expected the good fortune to go on and on. To perpetuate their good fortune, the nation's economic elite believed in sending their sons to schools where laissez-faire capitalism was not questioned and those from the correct social backgrounds could get their gentlemen's C's and pass smoothly into high economic and social strata.

Yale College was a preferred choice. The faculty offered an excellent education and the student body represented a fair cross-section of the better Eastern prep schools. Unpopular ideas were not welcomed. Petitions for Sacco and Vanzetti had been returned with only a few signatures; the signers were perceived by the college majority to be radicals. The college admissions office did not often select members of religious or racial minorities. But for the chosen, Yale was an interesting place to spend four years.

On the surface, the law school did not appear to be much different. It pulled a disproportionately large number of "white shoe" graduates from the college. Law students' enthusiasm for civil liberties was not much greater than at the undergraduate level. Most law students aspired to become partners in the big Wall Street firms, like Cravath, which defended the interests of big business. Although Hutchins had hired Lee Tulin and Harry Shulman, both Jews, for his faculty, it was rumored that the law school's selection process was weighted against minorities. And students suspected that Corbey Court, the private dining club for law students, was subtly discriminatory. The corridors of Hendrie Hall, which housed the law school, were populated with young men wearing three-piece suits, silk ties and gold watch chains.

But the differences from the college were there, not in Hendrie Hall's corridors but in its classrooms. Hutchins had begun his deanship with a question to himself and the faculty: What is the purpose of the Yale Law School, apart from being a trade school? His answers thoroughly upset the existing order. Hutchins drove hard to make Yale a "school of Government," and a place where law was studied, not just memorized. The faculty was expanded to include an economist, a political scientist and a psychiatrist (who taught Evidence with Hutchins). The new dean encouraged new courses and cut out old ones that clung to outdated legal doctrines. Hutchins welcomed field studies that took his faculty outside their classrooms. "At Yale," said Hutchins, "we were taking a new look at everything."

Douglas impressed Hutchins with his ideas for reorganizing the business law courses. Douglas rejected the old approach to corporate law, which confined the study to what judges wrote in their judicial opinions. He wanted students to learn how corporations worked—how they were formed, financed, managed, merged, reorganized and, occasionally, dissolved. His approach was to look at the vital facts and principles that determined what courts *did,* not just what courts *said* in judicial opinions. He was more interested then, as he would be later when he was on the U.S. Supreme Court, in results, not in abstract legal reasoning.

Teaching, for Douglas, was only one aspect—and not the most attractive one—of his new job. Privately he was disdainful of many of his students, particularly those he thought were in his classroom because of their family wealth. Yale College men in his law classes, Douglas believed, were "spoon-fed, coddled, pampered." He added: "I early discovered that they were unused to intellectual discipline, for the Yale College men in my law school classes were waiting for someone to fill their heads with knowledge."

All Yale College men were not so neatly stereotyped. One, Professor Thomas I. Emerson, the eminent civil liberties scholar, graduated from Yale College, class of 1928, and was in one of Douglas's early law school classes. He suggested that Douglas's students carried an equally unflattering image of their professor. "Douglas came to Yale with the reputation of a very expensive star," Emerson recalled. "He gave the impression of somebody from New York who had been bought away from Columbia at a high price by Hutchins. Money was thought to be significant. It never occurred to us that Douglas was a country boy who came to New York with six cents in his pocket. We looked at him as an up-and-coming big-city lawyer from Cravath."

Douglas attempted to introduce the Socratic method which he had learned under Dean Stone at Columbia. But he was not patient with his students as Stone had been. Douglas characterized his own style as uncompromisingly brutal: "In retrospect, it was a rather hard-bitten approach, fashioned on the Socratic method, and based on the premise that in the forums of the law, the soft-spoken, philosophical advocate had no place. So I bore down hard, treating each student as if it were irrelevant that his father or grandfather was a 'great man.' I tended to treat the class as the lion tamer in the circus treats his wards."

His students remembered him differently. "Douglas was a pretty dull teacher," recalled Emerson, who said that Douglas was highly competent but "without any spark or flair." Douglas, in fact, did not waste time with his students in prolonged Socratic dialogue, but pushed steadily through his materials. In class he was very reserved, speaking in clipped, nervous phrases that explained no more than he thought necessary. Occasionally he would offer a sarcastic, usually an ironic, remark about some deplorable appellate court decision. He was no lion tamer. "He didn't try to put students down," said Emerson, "but he had a tough mind and he held you to high intellectual standards."

The view of Douglas as a competent but not outstanding classroom teacher was confirmed by another of Douglas's brightest students, Fred Rodell, later a Yale law professor and a lifelong friend of Douglas's. "His large classes were fairly stiff," Rodell recalled. "He didn't waste time on any student, but just kept going. He wanted to cover a lot of material, sometimes at the expense of his students. He didn't wait to get the answers he wanted. He was always moving ahead. I don't think he enjoyed teaching a large class."

To be sure, Douglas suffered by comparison with his competition. Wesley Sturgis, one of Douglas's close friends, taught Credit Transactions and was, according to Emerson, a master of the Socratic method. "He jumped around the class, getting students into impossible logical positions. Sturgis was not cruel, just spectacular. Douglas was not in the same class. He just didn't shine."

Douglas's effectiveness in large classes did not seem to improve with experience. Myres McDougal, a graduate student at the law school in 1930 and later Sterling Professor of Law at Yale, said that Douglas, at that time, was still not a popular teacher. "He made the students do all the work," said McDougal. "In large classes he didn't seem to be putting out. He asked a few questions, but let students do the rest." Having observed Douglas's indifferent classroom performance, McDougal was surprised to discover, a few years later, that Douglas's lecture notes were superior. McDougal made that discovery as a young professor at the law school after he was asked, on short notice, to teach a class in Business Units. He borrowed Douglas's materials. "In terms of structure, I have never seen a better set of notes," McDougal said. "He just couldn't communicate well; he seemed to freeze before a large audience because he was shy."

Douglas was more effective in small seminars, where his students took an intensive look into selected legal problems of corporate law. In the small group, when Douglas focused on a problem his analysis was dazzling. "The precision of his mind was fantastic," said Abe Fortas, a Douglas student who later joined him as an associate justice of the U.S. Supreme Court. "When he chose to, he could turn a searchlight on a problem better than any teacher I ever had."

Douglas made no effort to court student favor. He did not linger after class or often join students for a beer at Mory's. He was indeed shy; he was also very busy. In his first year at Yale, Douglas wrote two major law review articles, a book review, and began first drafts of his own casebooks on corporate law (ultimately, with Carrol Shanks, Douglas published four casebooks). Douglas also participated in two field studies on business failures and planned a third. "He was always doing twenty things at once," said Rodell. It was hardly an exaggeration. Douglas was already exhibiting the incredible intellectual energy that would awe his colleagues throughout his professional life.

No ideological pattern emerged from Douglas's work at Yale. His early writings were neither pro-business nor anti-business. His conclusions did not advocate more government regulation or less. His book reviews scored authors on intellectual, not moral or political, grounds. Did the casebook Douglas was reviewing include the latest cases and provide enough materials on compli-

cated technical problems? His intellect was as restless on paper
as it was in the classroom. As in his classes, Douglas threw out
questions in his law review articles without waiting around to
provide the answers. But if a reader paid attention to Douglas's
questions alone, he could gain insights into the field of corporate
law.

"For a young man, he did quite a thing," Myres McDougal said.
"He asked the right questions. He was innovative. In later years
I used his notes and books well. He came up to the policy issues
without being able to solve them. But anybody who could do that
was close to a genius."

Douglas made his, and McDougal's, point effectively in his first
signed article, with the formidable title "Vicarious Liability and
the Administration of Risk." Who should pay the bills, asked
Douglas, when a driver of a delivery truck has had an accident?
Suppose the owner of a retail coal business has hired a delivery
service to take coal to his customers, Douglas hypothesized. On
a detour from the established delivery route, the truckdriver
crashes into a passenger car. Assuming the truckdriver's modest
salary could not cover the damages resulting from the accident,
courts had traditionally looked to the owner of the driver's delivery service or the coal business for payment. Which one should
pay?

Traditionally, courts had constructed elaborate rules to answer
Douglas's question. Judges had assigned liability according to
stiff legal rules that determined which employer was more responsible for the accident. Courts had drawn a "zone of risk" in
some cases so that a delivery service might have been held responsible for any accident, say, within a fifty-mile range of the
delivery route. But the judicial rules could differ if the truckdriver
had detoured for a personal reason that the delivery service
owner could not have anticipated. Douglas termed such judicial
distinctions "meaningless and purely arbitrary."

The error that several generations of judges had made, wrote
twenty-nine-year-old William O. Douglas, was in asking the
wrong question. Scratch the inquiry: Who was theoretically responsible? Substitute: Who was actually better prepared to pay
damages? In this way, wrote Douglas, courts would be dealing

with the broad social and economic problems behind the legal rules.

If both the coal company president and the head of the delivery service knew, for example, that the delivery man might detour and have an accident, and both agreed to do business nonetheless, then Douglas suggested both might be liable to the accident victim. But absent that express agreement, Douglas might stick the delivery service with the hospital bills. The delivery service agreed to deliver the goods, Douglas reasoned, and perhaps should have anticipated the risks involved. Another consideration would be whether the delivery service hired the drivers and could have screened out those who might stray from the assigned route.

Douglas urged courts to consider, ultimately, which employer was better able to absorb the costs of accidents. Had the delivery service taken out thousands of dollars' worth of accident insurance, anticipating the accidents of its drivers? Did the insurance cover accidents on detours? Could the delivery service pass on the expense of insurance to its customers? Questions, questions, prickly questions, which, Douglas insisted, courts had never asked, much less answered.

Douglas did not say who should pay, the delivery service or the coal company. In every situation it would depend on the facts, not on abstract rules, and on a determination of which party could better absorb the losses. Douglas was not promoting independent contractors (the delivery service) or manufacturers (the retail coal company). Nor was he coming to the rescue of defenseless victims; even before he wrote his article, courts found *someone* liable. Instead he was attempting to spread the judicial net over a larger area, trying to relate the narrow legal problem to the larger economic and social environment.

"Gentlemen: The conclusion of the year 1928–29 finds the Yale Law School in the best condition in its history," declared Dean Robert Hutchins. Hutchins boasted of substantial additions to the school's endowment, a student body selected from an impressive number of applicants, and a "materially strengthened" faculty. But the dean took special pride in a fourth item, the establishment of the Institute of Human Relations. The institute would be the research center that Herman Oliphant and Underhill Moore had lobbied for unsuccessfully at Columbia. Law professors would work with economists and sociologists and psychologists to make those connections between the law and the social sciences that were essential to a full understanding of the law's role in modern society.

No sooner had the institute been established than Douglas was planning a massive study with a sociologist, Dorothy Thomas, into the causes of small-business failures in Newark, New Jersey. The institute soon died a quiet death (autopsy report: lack of funds and interest). But Douglas, with characteristic energy, made certain that his work would survive. He and Thomas later published two exhaustive articles on the Newark study and conducted a law school seminar based on the study. In addition, Douglas either wrote or was the coauthor of four more law review articles, published over a four-year period, that made repeated reference to the Newark study.

Douglas's field studies were not focused exclusively on small-business failures; he also studied large corporations that had failed. What makes corporations die, asked Douglas, and what happens to them when they do? While still in his first year at Yale, Douglas directed a study of corporate failures for the U.S. Department of Commerce in Philadelphia, examining the causes of the failures and the effectiveness of legal and nonlegal solutions. The work for the Department of Commerce was followed only a few months later by another field study, investigating failed businesses in New York City.

In print and in the field, Douglas's work reflected a highly disciplined mind that approached each problem with intellectual detachment. Were Douglas's value-neutral evaluations out of character? For the Douglas who later headed the Securities and Exchange Commission, the answer is yes. For Douglas the outspoken future Associate Justice of the U.S. Supreme Court, again the answer must be yes. But for Douglas the ambitious young assistant professor of law at Yale, pushing hard for promotion and recognition in his field of commercial law, the restraint was not surprising.

Douglas had mastered the rules of the academic community early. He prepared carefully and well for his classes, but did not seem to care that his performance was not given a top rating by his students. He wrote provocative law review articles and here he took greater care, knowing that academic reputations were made in print, not in the classroom. At the same time, he attempted in his field studies to expand the parameters of legal research. The overriding goal in all Douglas's endeavors was to impress the academic community with the quality of his mind. In later years, his goal would be different: to remind a nation of its fundamental values.

In two years in the deanship, Robert Hutchins had established Yale's reputation as the most innovative law school in the country. At a meeting of law educators in Chicago in 1928, trustees of the University of Chicago, intrigued with Hutchins's razzle-dazzle reputation, asked him to come by for an interview. They were looking for a new university president, they told him, and cautiously probed his interest. When asked about his ideas for building a faculty, Hutchins told the trustees that he believed all professors should be paid at least $15,000 a year. The incredulous trustees recovered from the shock of Hutchins's statement and hired him anyway. At thirty, Hutchins became the youngest university president in the country.

Hutchins's resignation from Yale was a personal blow to Douglas. The two had become close friends, sharing common backgrounds of poverty, hard work and high achievement. They admired each other's minds and the results those minds could produce with their extraordinary energies. And despite their willingness to experiment intellectually, the two held fast to the old-fashioned Puritan work ethic.

Hutchins's defection to Chicago could have stunted Douglas's academic career. Instead it was instrumental in allowing him to leapfrog over his colleagues in both rank and salary. The extraordinary chain of events that led, ultimately, to Douglas's being named Sterling Professor of Law at Yale, with a salary of $15,000, began with a single sentence. "Bill Douglas is the outstanding professor of law in the nation," Hutchins said, shortly after assuming the presidency of the University of Chicago. Hutchins meant what he said and was prepared to put the University of Chicago's money where its president's mouth was. He offered

Douglas a professorship at Chicago at the unheard-of salary of $20,000.*

If Hutchins had early shown that he was a wheeler-dealer in a world of aloof academics, the object of his latest professional affection, Douglas, seemed to be a match for him. For Douglas knew a good thing when he saw it, and the University of Chicago offer was very definitely a good thing. But Douglas did not accept the offer and be done with it. Nor did he reject it. He did both, in time, and in the process helped promote himself to the top of his profession.

After prolonged and well-known soul-searching, Douglas accepted Hutchins's offer in 1930. But he remained on the Yale faculty nonetheless. The new dean at Yale, Charles E. Clark, provided the official explanation for Douglas's unusual position. "Last winter Associate Professor William O. Douglas [he had been promoted the year Hutchins left for Chicago], who has deservedly achieved a reputation in teaching and research unequalled for one of his age, received a wholly unusual offer, financially and intellectually, from his former chief, President Hutchins of Chicago, by whom he was originally brought to Yale. Under the circumstances, it was not surprising that he felt he could not refuse. Later his unwillingness to leave various projects at Yale in an unfinished state led him to postpone his going for at least another year. He remains with us this year as Visiting Professor of Law and we are hoping as time passes, he will find his Yale entanglements too many to sever."

What Clark presented as Douglas's laudable drive to complete his work at Yale appeared to others as nothing more lofty than a young professor trying to play two institutions off against each other for his personal and professional advantage. Whatever the explanation, Douglas's position at Yale was substantially advanced. A year after Clark had reported Yale's precarious hold on Douglas, the dean triumphantly announced that "Professor William O. Douglas becomes Sterling Professor of Law and will remain on permanent appointment at Yale."

"I never understood why he didn't come to Chicago," Hut-

*Douglas's version put the offer at $25,000.

chins later recalled. "He just said he couldn't come. I don't remember his giving any reasons."

Throughout the twenties, traders on the New York Stock Exchange were selling American business to the public with astonishing ease. But on October 29, 1929, the trading tilted ominously. Some 16,419,000 shares of stock were dumped and there were depressingly few buyers. In this boom time, disaster was impossible, wasn't it? "Wall Street may sell stocks," the *Saturday Evening Post* bravely reported, "but Main Street is buying goods." It was wishful thinking and soon even the wishes were devalued. Businesses folded, banks closed and bread lines formed. America had dived into its Great Depression.

Yale girded for the smaller contributions that it knew would come from Old Blues who had played too heavily in the market. But under the steady hand of President James Rowland Angell, the university survived and, eventually, prospered once again. The law school tightened its belt as well, but still was determined to forge ahead with new courses and research. "It is still possible for a student to obtain a more or less orthodox legal education," wrote Dean Clark. "The activities are, however, so many and so varied that he is not likely to choose such a course."

Not even the Depression, Clark insisted, could dampen the law school's innovative spirit. In fact, the Depression lent special significance to some of the work, including the pioneering studies of business failures by William O. Douglas, who attempted to impose intellectual order on the financial chaos. After October 29, 1929, business failures were no longer merely the professional concern of a young commercial law professor. Bankruptcies were not isolated financial pockmarks, but spreading scars of a national disease. Douglas dissected defunct businesses by the hundreds and became a recognized authority on the diseases that afflicted them. His files were a vast business morgue; he conducted the autopsies with careful intellectual detachment.

Beginning in October 1929, Douglas woke up before dawn every Monday morning, dressed quickly and hurried to the New Haven railroad station, where he boarded, with sociologist Dorothy Thomas, the five-fifteen train for New York. By eight o'clock, after scrambling for connections in Penn Station, the two had arrived in Newark. An hour later, they were in the U.S. district court of Judge William Clark, who had agreed to let Douglas and Thomas interview bankrupts in his court. From morning until late afternoon, every Monday for nine months, Douglas and Thomas interviewed distraught owners of small grocery stores, restaurants and retail clothing stores who had, for one or several reasons, realized that they could no longer pay all their bills. In all, Douglas and Thomas interviewed several hundred "bankrupts," as they were referred to in articles published later.

The young law professor and the sociologist were not content to limit their study to the immediate causes of the business failures, though they were interested in those causes. After they discovered that a man's business failed because of competition or the general sorry state of the economy, Douglas and Thomas insisted on probing deeper. They wanted to know every available detail about the owner of the failed business—his education, age and nationality, how he kept his books and where he sold his goods, when he paid his creditors and what illnesses he reported to his doctor during the bad times.

Obviously, such investigations required more than a single interview with the bankrupt. Without asking the bankrupt's permission, Douglas and Thomas talked to the man's accountant, employees and creditors. They talked to the Better Business Bureau and relevant trade associations that might give them clues to the character of the debtor and the quality of his management. And they sought confidential exchanges with social agencies that had dealt with the debtor and his family. If he had been ill, they sought out the doctor who treated him to find out if the debtor had been telling the court the truth about his medical problems. They even considered grading the debtor's intelligence, though the idea was eventually dropped because Douglas and Thomas felt that the "facilities for giving intelligence tests are not adequate, nor has a practical method for securing necessary observations by a mental hygienist yet been devised."

It did not seem to occur to Douglas that there were values at stake that might have transcended the practical problems of a researcher. The privacy of the debtor, for instance. But the man who later wrote of every citizen's fundamental right to privacy did not seem to care. As a researcher interested in scientific truth,

Douglas was concerned only with facts about the debtor, not with his rights. He and Thomas devised several methods of eliciting those facts. The questions—136 for the bankrupt, fifty for others —were posed by Douglas and Thomas after consulting with lawyers, economists, psychiatrists, sociologists and physicians. At first, eight investigators conducted the interviews with the debtors. If that didn't work, Douglas and Thomas sent out questionnaires by mail, asking the debtors' cooperation. At other times, they sent their questionnaires at the court's direction, no longer asking, but demanding cooperation of the debtor.

The methods were sometimes heavy-handed and, surely, would have been onerous to the future Justice Douglas, who defined the constitutional right of privacy. At that time, however, Douglas was more interested in social and economic data that could help him understand the causes of business failures than in any broad claims of privacy. Douglas and Thomas were searching for answers in coldly scientific ways that had never been tried before. The results, they hoped, could be used for social reform. Legislators, with the new data, could enact more enlightened bankruptcy legislation. Businessmen could study the practices of the bankrupt and avoid similar problems. Creditors and consumers and laborers, always losers in a bankruptcy, could be winners once again if the information could help avoid future failures.

Their results fell far below their expectations, as Douglas and Thomas were quick to admit. The problem was that the human beings, particularly the debtors, who responded to their inquiries did so in a frustratingly nonscientific manner. When the debtors agreed to fill out the questionnaires that had been mailed, for example, Douglas and Thomas often received incomplete or evasive answers. Sometimes there were no answers at all. Those problems were avoided with the personal interview, but that presented other difficulties. "It was expensive and time consuming," reported Douglas and Thomas, "and few bankrupts would consent to an examination without approval of counsel." When the debtors' attorneys did approve, they were usually at their clients' sides, casting a very suspicious eye at the investigators. It was not, Douglas the future libertarian concluded, an atmosphere conducive to objective data gathering.

CHAPTER TEN

OUTWARD CALM, INNER TURMOIL

F OR MILDRED, the days in New Haven were the happiest she spent as Bill Douglas's wife. The Douglases were not struggling for the few extra dollars to meet the month's bills, as they had been when both were working to send Bill through law school. Nor was Douglas dragging into their Pelham apartment after a sixteen-hour day at Cravath, questioning whether the status and salary at a Wall Street law firm were worth the drudgery and exhaustion. Even when Douglas had switched to the academic life at Columbia, the faculty was so torn by strife that no one, certainly not a first-year assistant professor, could feel secure.

New Haven was different. Douglas came to Yale at a good salary and with the strong endorsement of the school's dean, Robert Hutchins. For the first time, Douglas felt both financially secure and intellectually satisfied with his work. The rewards for Mildred were no less significant. For the first time since they were married, Douglas introduced his wife to a settled small-town community. Mildred no longer sat in Bernardsville, New Jersey, or Pelham, New York, waiting for her husband to return from his daily commute to the city. Now he lived and worked in New Haven, a pleasant, tree-filled college town with a town green and churches that dated back to the Revolutionary War. The couple celebrated their good fortune by moving into a house on Willow Street, a brisk walk from the Yale campus.

A year after the Douglases had settled in New Haven, their first child, Millie, was born, followed in two years by a son, Bill junior. Mildred's life now seemed complete. She was married to a brilliant and successful law professor whom she loved deeply. They lived in a pleasant neighborhood where she made friends easily and her gentle personality could thrive. At the small dinner parties or bridge games that her husband arranged, she served impeccably and listened attentively as Douglas and his friends spoke of Yale and the world. And she cared for her small children, Millie and Bill junior. They were the only audience that Mildred held captive and she did so with such intelligence and sensitivity that those loving conversations continued for a lifetime. Mildred could even bring her one academic passion, the classics, to her children's bedrooms, reading them as bedtime stories, translating from the original Latin as she went along.

Life on Willow Street was only a small part of Bill Douglas's world. From the time he first arrived at Yale, he was engaged in dozens of intellectual activities. But when he did enter the domestic world of his wife, he did so with characteristic vivacity. He was a fun-loving father, joking and kidding Millie and Bill junior, and riding them on his knee when he came home. Sometimes he would take his son for a ride around the town in their old Dodge, showing Bill junior his office and walking with him on the New Haven green.

But even in those days, Douglas was always in a hurry. There was never enough time for Millie and Bill junior; at least, that was the way it seemed to them. Their father was never totally relaxed with them, though the moments of play were invariably fun-filled and spirited. Uncle Art, on the other hand, seemed to have all the time in the world for them when he visited. For hours, it seemed, he would crawl on the floor with his nephew. "He was the perfect uncle," Bill junior remembered. "He was all love. He would give each member of the family his undivided attention."

Mildred was more familiar with Douglas's preoccupations. She had lived with them while he was a law student and a young associate at Cravath. In New Haven, at least, she had her own life and now a family she adored. And her life with Douglas was interesting, centering on social activities with Douglas's colleagues at the law school.

Occasionally the parties got out of hand. When Douglas drank a little too much applejack (fermented cider), for example, he would organize a game of Murder, blindfolding a guest and inviting others to hit him over the head with a newspaper. But the parties were not so frequent or so intense as those in their later days in Washington and Mildred happily tolerated her husband's boisterousness.

Mercifully, Douglas spared his wife some of his most outrageous antics. Douglas once showed up at a *Yale Law Journal* banquet, correct in tuxedo, but with his collar painted red and turned backward. He was drunk and so were his student companions. When they began throwing biscuits at each other, the university president, James Rowland Angell, who was sitting at the head table with Dean Charles Clark, demanded that Clark dismiss the rowdy "students." The next day, Clark dutifully called Douglas into his office and cheerfully accepted his apology, between guffaws, instead of his resignation.

Douglas was also capable of enjoying more subdued pleasures. He played poker with favored students, like Fred Rodell and Abe Fortas, and colleagues, like Walton Hamilton, Carrol Shanks and Thurman Arnold. There was a round or two of dirty jokes before and after the game, but while the game was in progress, Douglas was all business. It was the one form of gambling he risked. It paid off later, not in winnings, for Douglas never played for big stakes, but in the company that he kept. During the New Deal, FDR admired Douglas almost as much for his skills in five-card draw as for his analysis of corporate wrongdoing.

For fun, sheer, unadulterated Western fun, Douglas preferred the company of Professor Thurman Arnold to any game, party or other companion. Arnold came to Yale in 1930 from the University of Wyoming. In the classroom, his incisive mind could cut through the law's small print to discover its basic meaning and promise for the future. When off duty, that same mind could conjure up outrageous jokes and inspire outlandish behavior. Whether in a bar or in a classroom (he was equally at home in both), Arnold would naturally attract a crowd. His cigar ashes would be sprinkled generously over his suit and nobody, least of all Arnold, seemed to care. For he would be laughing or storytelling or loudly defending a previously indefensible point of view. He was charming and boorish and brilliant, and he broke Douglas up.

Douglas returned the favor, usually in the form of practical jokes. Once, Arnold received a mysterious note in his mailbox from an "admirer" who signed her name Yvonne. "She told me that she had met me at a party in San Francisco," Arnold recalled in his inimitable style, "and admired me extravagantly. She thought I was one of the coming leaders in the intellectual world. She was bold enough to suggest that it would be a tremendous privilege if I would call up a number which she gave and arrange to have cocktails with her. Of course, I hesitated, being a man with strict regard for the proprieties. But I thought this would be unfair to the little girl. I would seem aloof and unresponsive and priggish. I therefore called the number she gave. I asked for Yvonne; the voice on the other end said 'Who?' and I said 'Yvonne,' giving her last name. He said, 'What the hell are you talking about? This is the morgue.' " Douglas was always too modest, Arnold added, to claim credit for these little "favors" for his friends.

Arnold remembered another mysterious communication, this time a telegram that was delivered to him immediately preceding a speech he was to deliver at Yale College. "Please mention me in your speech tonight if you can do so," Arnold read. The telegram was signed by his colleague Wesley Sturgis. Arnold thought it was a slightly improper way of boosting Sturgis's score in the celebrity game that Arnold had invented for himself, Sturgis and Douglas: if one of them got his name in *The New York Times,* he received ten points; in a local paper, five points; and in a speech, one point. Nonetheless, Arnold obliged and mentioned Sturgis in his speech. At the same time, Sturgis had received an identical telegram as he was about to address the Bridgeport Bar Association. But his telegram was signed "Thurman Arnold." Like Arnold, he silently brooded over his colleague's foul play, but also abided by the telegram's request.

The more Arnold and Sturgis thought of the telegrams, the angrier they got. The next day, Arnold marched into Sturgis's office and demanded an explanation. "I mentioned your name, Wes," said Arnold, "but what the hell were you up to?" Sturgis looked strangely at Arnold, then reached in his desk drawer and pulled out the telegram he had received in Bridgeport. It suddenly occurred to them that the third member of the triumvirate, Douglas, had greeted them that morning with a special twinkle in his eye.

Douglas savored his Thurman Arnold stories. There was the night that Frances Arnold seized her drunken husband and threw him out the front door. When Arnold recovered, he advised his companion, Douglas, that they must seek friendlier people. And so they stepped into Arnold's car and spent the rest of the evening driving on New Haven sidewalks and streets, stopping every so often for Arnold to deliver an impassioned plea for better human relations in the city. Another high moment began when Arnold put the warning of the New Haven Railroad that "Passengers will please refrain from flushing toilets while the train is standing in or passing through a station" into verse, to the cadence of "Humoresque." Then Arnold lustily led parlor car passengers in a lively rendition of the ballad. Douglas also loved to recall Arnold's and Wesley Sturgis's conversation in a New Haven barbershop. "Don't put any of that smelly stuff on my hair," Sturgis told the barber, "or my wife will think I've been in a whorehouse." When Arnold's turn came, he said, "Put as much of that smelly stuff as you want on my hair; my wife has never been in a whorehouse."

Arnold gleefully recalled the report that he and Douglas wrote in 1930 for the National Commission on Law Observance and Enforcement, commonly known as the Wickersham Commission. Douglas and Arnold had collected judicial statistics that, it was hoped, would shed much needed light on the inner workings of the courts. Arnold remembered: "We counted everything that was capable of being counted in and about the courtrooms under observation. By dint of our industry and the consumption of midnight oil and prewar beverages, we got hundreds of thousands of figures. These figures were transferred to cards which could be run through computing machines which would sort them out and tell us how many there was of anything that we wanted to know how many there was of. Then we proceeded to write our report. The only trouble was that we never could think of any intelligible thing to say about the figures or what to do with them. They are still around somewhere, probably in the government archives, waiting for someone who can think of a purpose to which they can be put.''

Douglas's version was even better: "Thurman and I were brought in [by the Wickersham Commission] to make a report on criminal statistics. We got ourselves a Hollerith machine and made some wondrous computations. The commission printed our report, and we were so mesmerized by what we had produced that each of us ordered a hundred copies of the reprint, making sure we could supply the insatiable demand. Thirty years passed and I refreshed Thurman's mind, telling him that recently I had counted my copies and I still had ninety-nine. "Ninety-nine?" he exploded. "You must have given one away. I still have my original hundred."

In New Haven, Douglas seemed to have everything. For the first time, he was financially secure and professionally prominent. He worked and played with the best students and the most innovative members of the law school faculty. He filled leisure time with new research projects and outside reading, poker games and prankish antics. At home, his pretty wife was settled and happy. Millie and Bill junior gave Mildred the daily problems that all young children give their mothers, but for Douglas, they were delightful new companions and playmates.

With it all, Douglas could not shake persistent migraine headaches which, he later discovered, signaled deep-seated psychological scars. The headaches, like the stomach cramps that preceded them, seemed to be a product of nervous tension. But they stalked Douglas through his long nights at Cravath, his brief teaching career at Columbia and his outwardly successful days in New Haven. Douglas had consulted several New York specialists, as well as his friend Bill Wilson, while he was working in New York. But neither their advice nor his switching to full-time teaching seemed to have any effect. When the headaches continued in New Haven, Douglas decided to pay a return visit to a New York psychoanalyst, Dr. George Draper, whom he had first talked to while at Columbia.

Before he began his practice, Dr. Draper, Professor of Clinical Medicine at Columbia, had been a patient of Jung's and an avid student of Freud's theories. "It is the imponderable that causes much illness," Draper had told Douglas when he was teaching at Columbia. But it took Douglas several years to make the connection between Draper's statement and his migraine headaches. After he was at Yale and had agreed to undergo intense psychoanalysis with Draper, Douglas began to understand the emotional strains that produced the headaches.

Draper's clinical conversation with Douglas focused, almost immediately, on Julia Fisk Douglas. Douglas was reminded once again that he had been overly dependent emotionally on his mother and that that dependence was at the root of many of his adult problems. Once again he fought his bout with polio and his mother's prolonged physical and emotional pampering; Douglas realized that many of his early decisions had been motivated by a desire to rebel against his mother's domination. He hiked the Cascades and, eventually, rode the freights East to get away. But physical distance from Julia did not solve Douglas's problems.

Douglas carried with him to the Klickitat Meadows and New York City and, finally, New Haven some of the debilitating phobias that he had learned from his mother when he was a child. Through Draper's careful probing, Douglas remembered stories of Julia Fisk's younger brother, Milo, who had died of peritonitis as a teen-ager. Douglas's Uncle Sam, his mother's half brother who lived across the street in Yakima, had told Douglas that Milo died because he ate a green plum and tomato. No, said Douglas's mother, Milo died either because he had sinned or because God had willed that someone close to Milo should suffer for their sins. Those horror stories of his mother's and uncle's combined to develop Douglas's phobia about intestinal disorders. Whenever he experienced stomach pains, Douglas subconsciously believed that Jehovah was working his will. And always hovering in the background was Milo and his stomach problems and his fate.

Draper and Douglas explored another fear, of water, that

Douglas shared with his mother. Beware of the Yakima River, Julia Douglas had told her young son. To emphasize the point, she kept current on drownings in the river and reported each local drowning in lugubrious detail to her son. Not surprisingly, Douglas grew up fearing water. That fear was intensified at Yakima's YMCA when Douglas was still a skinny kid trying to overcome his fear at the shallow end of the pool. Suddenly a muscular teen-ager had picked Douglas up, carried him to the deep end and thrown him in. Douglas's body had plummeted nine feet to the bottom, but with great effort he battled to the surface. And then he had gone down again, lungs aching, head throbbing, completely seized by stark terror: "I went down, down, endlessly. I opened my eyes. Nothing but water with a yellow glow—dark water that one could not see through. And then sheer, stark terror seized me, terror that knows no understanding, terror that knows no control, terror that no one can understand who has not experienced it."

Still, Douglas had found the strength to spring from the bottom a second time. But it had done no good. "I tried to call for help, to call for Mother. Nothing happened." He went down a third time and now all effort ceased. "I relaxed. Even my legs felt limp; a blackness swept over my brain. It wiped out fear; it wiped out terror. There was no more panic. It was quiet and peaceful. Nothing to be afraid of. This is nice . . . to be drowsy . . . to go to sleep . . . no need to jump . . . too tired to jump . . . it's nice to be carried gently . . . to float along in space . . . tender arms around me . . . tender arms like Mother's . . . now I must go to sleep."

Douglas had lost consciousness. His next memory was of lying on his stomach beside the pool, vomiting. He had never returned to the YMCA pool, but his memories and his fears persisted. Afterward, whenever he entered a swimming pool or lake, he was possessed of that same icy terror that had victimized him as a child. With typical feistiness, Douglas challenged his fear at every opportunity, daring each new pool or lake to terrify him. But unlike his response to so many other challenges, Douglas could not control his adversary or himself. He remained a prisoner of his phobia.

Draper listened to his patient's dilemma. If he had the will power and courage, Douglas asked, why couldn't he overcome his fear? Draper suggested that will power could not always overwhelm the fears that worked through the sympathetic nervous system. Douglas now knew why he was having such difficulties. Invigorated by this knowledge, he set out anew to conquer his old fear.

After returning from a session in New York with Draper, Douglas arranged with Yale swimming coach Bob Kiphuth to swim at the Olympic-size Yale pool five days a week. His laps were somewhat unorthodox, however. Each day a swimming instructor would tie a belt around Douglas, slide a rope through the belt and attach it to an overhead pulley cable. Douglas went back and forth across the pool, the instructor relaxing the rope gradually until Douglas was fully immersed in the water. At first the old terror returned, but in several months time, Douglas's panic slowly disappeared. After this unusual therapy, Douglas still took to the water gingerly, but he did so without the fear that had haunted him all his life.

Douglas's proud telling in his autobiography of his victory over his fear of water revealed one of his great strengths. If he, or anyone else, could force an obstacle into open combat, that obstacle, whether irrational fear or towering mountain, could be conquered. Douglas lived by that creed. He climbed mountains to build his body and, with Draper's help, he reached back into his childhood to subdue his worst fears. He faced down his fear not only of water but of lightning, cougars and falling trees as well, and later, with FDR, whom he quoted approvingly, he realized that "The only thing we have to fear is fear itself."

But Douglas's strength was also, paradoxically, his greatest weakness and the source of much of his later unhappiness. Since he was successful in overcoming obstacles, Douglas advised others to take the same path. But others—his son, for instance—were not so strong physically, nor did they see the world in quite the same terms of "Papa" Hemingway courage. Douglas took his son to the top of Mount Adams when Bill junior was fourteen years old, and the father's response to his son's faltering steps was to push forward resolutely. "Dad's idea of climbing a mountain was to go straight up and straight down," Bill junior said. "It wasn't mine." Douglas did not seem to notice.

Because strength was so important to Douglas, he rarely discussed his weaknesses, except after he had overcome them. He could write of his dramatic battles with polio and poverty and migraine headaches, for once he had presented the obstacle, he could happily report his final victories. There was always a moral: keep fighting and you will conquer.

But Douglas was reluctant to share anxieties and failures that were not so tidily resolved. With Dr. Draper, Douglas discussed his sense of guilt at having left his mother in Yakima. She had wanted him to stay near her as a high school teacher in Yakima, and aspire to become a high school principal. She had, of course, also instilled in him a prodigious ambition to succeed, and that ambition, once unleashed, was not easily confined to the city limits of Yakima. Even so, Douglas, then Sterling Professor of Law at Yale, experienced ambivalent feelings. Should he have returned to Yakima so that he could have cared for his mother and played out the career of her choosing? It was too late for that, but the guilt feelings persisted, heightened by the knowledge that his sister had been left with the responsibility of caring for their mother in her old age.

Julia Douglas's dominating presence may have also been at the root of her elder son's later problems with women. She was his inspiration but also his judge. She offered him love but also demanded achievement.

In later life, Douglas was very demanding of the women he married. He insisted on both the affection and the admiration that his mother had provided. He wanted their love but also required their adulation, and somehow the two became synonymous. When that adulation seemed to wane, Douglas drifted away. The more he achieved, the more he demanded and, inevitably, the less his hopes could be fulfilled. "He is a great man," said Douglas's second wife, Mercedes Douglas Eichholz, "but an unhappy one."

CHAPTER ELEVEN

THE ROAD TO WASHINGTON

In 1931, Americans laughed nervously when Amos asked Andy: "Did you hear about the fellow who registered at the hotel and the clerk said, 'For sleeping or jumping, sir?' " By 1932, no one was laughing anymore. The bottom had fallen out of the American economy.

Unemployment had climbed to thirteen million. Idle West Virginia coal miners, evicted in midwinter from their homes, watched their families shiver in tents. With their gas and electricity cut off, the unemployed in Los Angeles cooked over wooden fires in back lots. When the trucks pulled away from the Chicago garbage dump, men, women and children dug in with sticks and hands, grabbing bits of spoiled fruits and vegetables. Millions just wandered, roaming the waterfronts, riding cattle cars, sleeping in makeshift shacks of boxes and scrap metal, named Hoovervilles, for the President whom they blamed for it all.

Throughout the crisis, President Herbert Hoover had held tenaciously to the traditional American notion that government and private enterprise had to deal warily with each other. When the federal government responded to the Depression in the private sector, it did so grudgingly and with mincing steps. That the federal government would have to help and, sometimes, goad the private sector was a fact that only the Republican administration seemed reluctant to accept.

Dean Charles Clark of the Yale Law School anticipated the partnership of government and private enterprise and gauged its consequences for the legal profession. "Only a short time ago the cry, in which lawyers joined, was that government should be kept out of business," Clark wrote in 1932. "Pressure of events has caused a complete reversal of this point of view, and business in dire need has begged for government aid. The result has been the formation of connections between private industry and the public which can never be broken and which will require skill and statesmanship to disentangle and adjust. The corporation lawyer of the past decade must give way to the public counsel of the next."

In the same report, Clark announced with special urgency the need for the law school to meet the changed needs of the profession with a broad and more realistic approach to law. Yale would begin to emphasize statutory and administrative regulation of economic activities in the curriculum. Students would be offered courses on regulatory agencies and small seminars in which such modern problems as "Property in a Crisis Society" would be minutely dissected.

Months before Clark's report, Douglas and Carroll Shanks had published their new casebook on business units, which promised an integrated approach to the study of business by the use of economic and sociological materials as well as court decisions. "Experience has shown that [the student] spends a more intelligent classroom hour if the materials give him this wider horizon," Douglas and Shanks wrote in their introduction. The authors promised considerably more than they delivered; after the upbeat introduction, Douglas and Shanks proceeded to cram their text with the traditional high quota of court decisions and offered only references to nonlegal materials. Despite their essentially traditional approach, Douglas and Shanks could take credit for tracking the new trend in legal education. In short order, Douglas, as coauthor, had published three more casebooks in the field, each pledged to a more realistic analysis of the law.

Still in his early thirties, Douglas had already produced studies on failed businesses, crowded courtrooms, and social trends in the law. He sent his best students, like Abe Fortas, to Chicago to gather facts and conclusions about loan sharks and consumer credit. He also persuaded Dean Clark and the faculty of the Harvard Business School that a joint law–business administration program could effect a worthy intellectual cross-fertilization. As a result, Douglas taught courses at the Harvard Business School and wrote several articles with Harvard's George Bates on securities regulation from the dual perspective of business administration and law.

And Douglas did all this without incurring the hostility of older and more conservative members of the Yale faculty. When, for example, a senior member of the faculty, Professor Arthur L. Corbin, the nation's leading authority on contract law, objected to Douglas's proposal for a more liberal independent research program for students, Douglas tactfully disagreed with him. Then, at the next faculty meeting, Douglas returned with nine carefully articulated reasons why his proposal should be adopted. It was.

"Douglas was a diplomat," said Fred Rodell. "He didn't kowtow to senior faculty members, but when he disagreed, he did so quietly." Myres McDougal offered a different appraisal: "I think he was quiet, partly because he was shy, partly because he was self-disciplined and partly because he was politically ambitious."

During the Depression, Americans searched for a leader who could give them hope; instead they found Herbert Hoover, a humorless man who approached the nation's problems with a relentless pessimism. "If you put a rose in Hoover's hand," said the sculptor Gutzon Borglum, "it would wilt." Although he came to office with impressive accomplishments and worked longer hours than any of his predecessors, Hoover could not shake the image of a loser. As his troubles mounted, Hoover attempted to insulate himself from the demands of popular government. He forgot that governing involved human contact as well as statistical studies, empathy as much as enterprise. "Hoover can calculate wave lengths, but cannot see color," observed Willmott Lewis,

Washington correspondent for the London *Times.* "He can understand vibrations, but cannot hear tone."

The contrast with Franklin D. Roosevelt, Hoover's political opponent in 1932, was startling. Roosevelt's voice was warm and assuring, his smile infectious and his enthusiasm for large crowds obvious. During the campaign, Roosevelt buried any new ideas he might have had under his happy-warrior image. His campaign speeches were stuffed with meaningless generalities that drove sophisticated commentators to sarcastic despair. Roosevelt was the master of the "balanced antithesis," wrote Walter Lippmann, "a pleasant man who, without important qualifications for the office, would very much like to be President."

Not surprisingly, however, the American people wanted a change and they wanted hope, and they elected FDR by a landslide. And by the end of the famous "One Hundred Days" after Roosevelt's inauguration, Americans began to realize that there was toughness behind the jaunty grin, a passion to act after the campaign rhetoric had served its political purpose. The country needed bold, persistent experimentation, Roosevelt said in one of his first speeches as President. "It is common sense to take a method and try it: if it fails, admit it frankly and try another. But above all, try something."

It was an approach calculated to appeal to bright young men across the country. And they responded, packing their bags and ideals, and heading for Washington. Many of them seemed to possess only two qualifications: boundless enthusiasm and a law degree. "A plague of young lawyers settled on Washington," groused one veteran bureaucrat. "They all claimed to be friends of somebody or other and mostly of Felix Frankfurter and Jerome Frank. They floated airily into offices, took desks, asked for papers and found no end of things to be busy about."

Felix Frankfurter, whose name was dropped most frequently around Washington in the spring of 1933, was already well known for his defense of liberal causes, and maintained impeccable credentials as a scholar at the Harvard Law School. But his intellectual energy and ambition could not be contained in a narrow academic environment. He was an effervescent intellectual who had been introducing provocative ideas to public men, including FDR, for more than a decade. Frankfurter's "hot dogs," the legions of young Harvard Law graduates he sent to Washington in the early days of the New Deal, became a symbol of the intellectual in government. Frankfurter's ideas and protégés were so plentiful, in fact, that at least one high-ranking member of the Roosevelt administration labeled Frankfurter "the most influential single individual in the United States."

While Frankfurter was happy to pump ideas into the new administration, either directly or through his former students, Jerome Frank accepted an official position as general counsel to the Agricultural Adjustment Administration. Frank, an attorney who later taught at Yale and wrote the innovative book *Law and the Modern Mind,* used his position in the New Deal to try to push through long-needed reforms to relieve the poverty of sharecroppers, tenant farmers and farm laborers and to crack down on unscrupulous packers, millers and big milk distributors. It was a strange ambition for Frank, an urban lawyer whose specialties were jurisprudence and corporate law. But this was the New Deal, and all the old rules and expectations had been tossed out with the Republicans.

Men with ambition and talent usually create their own opportunities, and William O. Douglas—vigorous, brilliant and shrewd —was no exception. By 1933, his reputation as an expert in the field of corporation law was built on the solid foundation of impressive law review articles, fresh teaching materials and original field studies. Now Douglas was eager to share his expertise with influential people in the New Deal, like Jerome Frank, and outside it, like Felix Frankfurter.

Douglas and Frank had become friends when Frank was practicing corporate law in New York City and Douglas consulted with him on a technical problem in his field. Later Frank became a research associate at the Yale Law School, and only a few months before Frank's New Deal appointment, he and Douglas collaborated on a law review article on corporate reorganizations. After Frank's appointment was announced, Douglas sent his former colleague a congratulatory letter. But Douglas did not let the occasion pass without a few more comments. In the same letter, he informed Frank that Ferdinand Pecora, who, as counsel to the Senate Committee on Banking and Currency, had gained national attention with his investigation of the New York Stock Exchange,* wanted some help from Douglas. Douglas invited Frank to join him, Pecora and Judge William Clark (who had sponsored Douglas's Newark business-failure project) for lunch in New York. "It might be hot dope," Douglas wrote enticingly, "and again it might be a dud." Douglas ended the letter with friendly advice for Frank and the big boss, FDR: "For God's sake convince FDR that there is something more to the depression than currency. The big job is credit and the only way out is government guaranty. Yours, Bill."

The same week that Douglas wrote his letter to Frank, FDR sent to Congress the first piece of legislation that would bring the securities market under direct federal regulation. In proposing the Securities Act of 1933, Roosevelt added "to the ancient rule of caveat emptor, the further doctrine 'let the seller also beware.'" The Securities Act, modeled on the British Companies Act, gave the Federal Trade Commission power to supervise issues of new securities, required each new stock issue to be accompanied by a statement of relevant financial information, and made company directors civilly and criminally liable for misrepresentation.

Three weeks later, Douglas commented to Frank on the new securities bill that had been sent to Congress. "I haven't seen the final draft," wrote Douglas. "I only hope that they have not taken all the teeth out of it." In the next few sentences, however, Douglas began to drop hints that he not only had a lot of ideas for the New Deal but might want to come to Washington personally, to try them out. "The dope is that Judge [Robert] Healy will head up the corporation division of the Federal Trade Commission. I think there is a splendid opportunity for adventurous thinking and planning in that field. I was thinking the other day that it would be a grand thing to go down there for the first year or two of that division's existence and help organize it in an intelligent

---

*In a year of intensive research and questioning, Pecora had shattered forever the image of the investment banker as a man of probity, fairness and public spirit. Wall Street's finest, Pecora revealed, had rigged pools, profited by pegging bond prices artificially high and lined their pockets with huge bonuses. Pecora spared no one. When J. P. Morgan appeared before the committee, Pecora jabbed his stubby finger at him and suddenly even that titan seemed life-size. "Pecora has the manner and the manners of a prosecuting attorney who is trying to convict a horse thief," complained Morgan.

and efficient way. I was talking to Felix [Frankfurter]* the other night about it and he seemed quite enthusiastic. Some time I would like to get your views on it."

Frank responded enthusiastically, "I can think of nothing better for the U.S.A. than for you to take charge of the Corporation Division of the Federal Trade Commission," he wrote to Douglas. "I am going to pass the idea on to [Rexford] Tugwell [who had been a member of FDR'S campaign brain trust and was then Assistant Secretary of Agriculture]." Although the FTC appointment never materialized, Douglas continued to throw ideas and invitations at Frank. Would Frank be interested in participating in a Yale seminar on corporate reorganization? Wouldn't the new securities bill be a nice subject to throw into a seminar?

Clearly, Douglas was doing more than renewing an old friendship. Like so many other ambitious young men of the time, he was excited by the drama beginning to unfold in Washington. And he was determined to be more than a member of the audience. He would either be an actor on stage or be directing some important scenes from a few paces away. In any event, he wanted to be part of the production, though the details of his role were not clear to him. For the moment, he would keep in close touch with the most influential players that he knew, notably Frank and Frankfurter, letting them know what he was thinking.

At about the same time, Douglas wrote a letter to *The New York Times* proclaiming his allegiance to the basic philosophy of the new securities legislation. In his letter to the *Times,* Douglas defended the bill against the charge that it would give the federal government "the power of a dictator over American business." Douglas characterized the attack on the legislation as reflecting "a typically conservative philosophy" which always put the interests of the bankers and large corporations ahead of the public investors. "There is a need for some agency to step in between the persons who get the money and those who supply it and to fulfill the role of protector of the latter," wrote Douglas. "The bankers and the issuing corporations can take care of themselves. But the investors cannot. The ideal of rugged individualism when

---

*Douglas had become friendly with Frankfurter in 1930 when Frankfurter delivered the Dodge lectures at Yale and taught a seminar on administrative law.

applied to investors has no longer any place in the program for American high finance. If we are to avoid the blowing of financial bubbles which burst with disastrous consequences, we need exactly some such restraint."

Defending the basic philosophy of the Securities Act did not, however, mean that Douglas accepted every technical provision of the bill. Indeed, Douglas flailed away at the new Securities Act as if it had been submitted to him by a mediocre student in a legislative drafting seminar. In a six-month period, Douglas wrote alone or coauthored three articles on the new legislation, each more outspokenly critical than the preceding one.

The first article, curiously, took the drafters to task for not providing enough protection for *investment bankers.* The problem, wrote Douglas, with Harvard Business School assistant professor George Bates, was that the legislative language was too broad. It appeared to make investment bankers liable to any investor who purchased a security, whether the bankers were in fact responsible or not. Douglas and Bates worried that such vague and ambiguous language might discourage many banking houses from participating as underwriters of securities issues. "If the Act is as revolutionary as some think, the raising of capital will be seriously hindered and the methods employed will take quite different forms," Douglas and Bates concluded. "In such processes, investment bankers as they are known today may have little or no place."

A month later, Douglas and Bates published a second article, this one denouncing the act in more sweeping terms. Their major criticism was that the act could not possibly do what it purported to. "There is nothing in the Act which would eliminate wholly unsound capital structures," wrote Douglas and Bates. They complained, further, that nothing in the act "would prevent a tyrannical management from playing wide and loose with scattered minorities, or . . . would prevent a new pyramiding of holding companies violative of the public interest and all canons of sound finance." Douglas and Bates foresaw problems in interpreting the measure of civil damages and criminal conduct, and even in defining the term "security."

Up to this point, Douglas had analyzed the legislation with the academic detachment that had characterized his law review articles on other subjects. In those articles, the problems of the bankruptcy process and corporate receiverships had been dissected without any noticeable ideological preferences. Douglas had criticized lawyers who had profited excessively from receiverships. On the other hand, he had supported a large role for institutional investors on protective committees, fearing that the dominance of small shareholders would turn the committees into unproductive debating societies. In his first law review article on the Securities Act, Douglas again seemed content to raise provocative questions about technical legal matters.

But in the second article, there was a critical difference. After pointing to the technical weaknesses of the legislation, Douglas recommended that an agency be established to deal with violations of the act in a flexible but stern way which would protect both the investor and the public interest. With that recommendation, Douglas began to carve out a new position with far-reaching political implications. He was advocating an even larger role for a federal agency in regulating securities than the Securities Act provided.

It was a position that Douglas knew his friend Felix Frankfurter did not totally share. Frankfurter, whose Brandeisian philosophy of promoting economic competition had carried considerable influence in the drafting of the Securities Act, believed that solutions to Wall Street's undisciplined power over the economy came through strict enforcement of the regulations in the new law in the courts, not through a watchdog agency in Washington. Frankfurter placed his faith in statutory regulation rather than administrative direction; he urged corporate responsibility through full disclosure, not coercion.

"I would have liked very much to have had you available, before I went to press, on various aspects of the Securities Act," Douglas wrote to Jerome Frank in December 1933. "I have been spending an enormous amount of time on it and I fear that some of my observations will not be particularly pleasing to my good friend, Felix Frankfurter. While I think a securities act is very essential, it is, in a total program of social control over high finance, quite secondary."

Soon one of Douglas's scholarly articles contained the distinct outlines of a political philosophy, not just the familiar language of the cool academic. In an article for the *Yale Review*'s Spring 1934 issue, Douglas viewed the Securities Act as a potential weapon to be used by the small investor against the powerful interests of Wall Street. The Securities Act, Douglas wrote for the *Yale Review,* is "significant politically. It is symbolic of a shift of power. That shift is from the bankers to the masses; from the promoter to the investor. It means that the government is taking the side of the helpless, the suckers, the underdogs. It signifies that the money-changers are being driven from the temples."

Douglas followed up his stump-speech rhetoric with his more familiar technical analysis of the legislation's weaknesses. He criticized the narrow reach of the new regulation, suggesting that its requirements did not provide effective protection for the investor. The act, wrote Douglas, was basically a "nineteenth century piece of legislation" which attempted to return to simpler days, when strong regulation was not needed. Douglas wanted more effective control over Wall Street. That required "constructive planning and organization conditioned by requirements of the public good." For Douglas, it meant a federal agency that would protect the capitalist system, but not at the expense of the public interest.

In both style and content, Douglas's *Yale Review* article signaled a radical departure from the past. He was no longer the cautious academic. He could and did justify his position to academics, but now he was appealing to a different audience—influential members of the New Deal. And he was doing so with an unmistakable rhetorical flourish which would, he hoped, capture that audience for his broad message: the time had arrived for bold initiatives from the Roosevelt administration, instead of the mild palliatives that were being offered in the Securities Act.

Both Frankfurter and Frank reacted sharply to Douglas's new aggressiveness, each sending him letters critical of his position. Douglas fired off return letters to both. "If you would read my goddam articles instead of believing what someone says about them, you would not have these screwy ideas as to what I think," Douglas wrote Frank. "We are much closer to a National Investment Board (to use the phrase of the Labour Party in England) than most realize. Felix and his common law are not going to pull us out of this hole."

In his letter to Frankfurter on April 6, 1934, Douglas wrote: "My dear Felix, Your letters are a joy even though each one takes me for a buggy ride. I am sure of but one thing and that is that you are making a Red out of me, and I do not think you will like the brilliant hue. I started to dictate a reply to your last letter. But after I had dictated ten pages, I found I had barely started, so I thought I better save you the pain until I could get you in person (under any circumstances and handicaps—alcoholic or otherwise —whichever you prefer) and go into the points of difference between us—which I am sure are not so much differences in diagnosis as in therapeutics."

After that cheerful introduction, Douglas ticked off his arguments in staccato bursts that outlined his criticism of the Securities Act and the need for a supervising administrative agency. Douglas did not miss the opportunity to chide Frankfurter for his patronizing references to Douglas's inexperience, either, pointing to "the need for us youngsters (whom you dismiss as inexperienced) getting the administrative experience and training for the tasks ahead—you see we have only moved a few rods off the base of laissez-faire and we have miles and miles to go." Douglas also wrote that "the Securities Act is propagating and accentuating some of the most vicious evils in the old system. By God, Felix, I lose my composure at this point—and so would you if you had seen the stark realities I have. Say, must a fellow have Wall St. in his blood and bones to have experience?" He concluded by again teasing Frankfurter: ". . . you are not only making but have made a Red out of me. So you see why my letter was abandoned. I hope I can see you soon so I can get all of these things off my chest. Until then, and only until then, will you be permitted to feign confusion. Yours faithfully, Bill."

Exactly three months after Douglas sealed his letter to Frankfurter, Congress passed the Securities Exchange Act, which required registration and full disclosure on all securities traded on the exchange. More important, the legislation created the Securities and Exchange Commission and gave it the power to enforce the provisions of the new act as well as those of the Securities Act of 1933. The new SEC promised to fulfill precisely the supervisory role that Douglas had been advocating.

Douglas was elated. He saw the new legislation not only as a vindication of his intellectual position but also as an opportunity for him to join the New Deal. In short, he wanted to become a member of the new Securities and Exchange Commission. Within a week of the bill's passage, Douglas had conferred with members of Congress from Connecticut, who supported his candidacy, and had written Jerome Frank for additional support. "The Connecticut crowd in Congress has placed before the President my name for the new stock exchange commission and desires some outside letters to the President in support of me," Douglas wrote Frank. "I would appreciate anything you might be able to do."

In the same letter to Frank, Douglas expressed his satisfaction with the new legislation. "I think the Stock Exchange Act is a vast improvement over the type of regulation envisaged in the Securities Act," Douglas wrote. "It has a broad grant of administrative power—at least broad enough for a starter. As you know, my only objection to the Securities Act was its insistence on the common law to pull us out of the hole. That can never be done. It's a tragedy that the Securities Act is not geared up with the N.R.A. [National Recovery Administration]."

Despite Douglas's conspicuous knowledge in the field and enthusiasm for the Securities and Exchange Commission, he was not appointed an SEC commissioner in 1934. But neither Douglas's expertise nor his ambition was wasted. Shortly after Roosevelt had named Joseph P. Kennedy, a financier who had made a fortune in the stock market, to be the first chairman of the SEC in 1934, one of Kennedy's associates, James M. Landis, placed a call to Douglas in New Haven. Would Douglas be interested in directing an SEC study of unethical and illegal manipulations of bankruptcies and receiverships by protective and reorganization committees? Douglas said that he would.

It was not Douglas's first choice for serving the Roosevelt administration, or even his second, but it was a promising position nonetheless. Certainly it was a rare opportunity to use his experience and knowledge. He had worked for almost two years at Cravath on the largest railroad reorganization in the nation's history. At Yale, he had led pilot studies into the causes of bankruptcies. And his law review articles and casebooks attested to his mastery of the existing law on corporate bankruptcies and receiverships.

More significantly, the SEC study would give Douglas a power base where he could put his experience and academic knowledge to practical use. He would no longer have to be satisfied to raise provocative questions in learned journals. Now Douglas could hale bankers and lawyers and securities dealers before his staff and demand answers to these questions. With the new power, Douglas would project a more aggressive image, which had only begun to surface. He now identified with the New Deal and claimed its cause, the public interest, as his own. When that cause was threatened by financial and legal skulduggery, he attacked with the full force of his intellect and power. Douglas had seized his role on the national stage, small at the beginning, but one that would expand spectacularly in a very few years.

PART THREE

THE SEC

LIGHTING THE MATCHES

WHEN PROFESSOR WILLIAM O. DOUGLAS of the Yale Law School arrived in Washington in the fall of 1934 to begin his assignment as director of the SEC's study on reorganization and protective committees, he anticipated that SEC Chairman Joseph P. Kennedy would have a warm welcome and a generous budget to offer him.

"Your budget is fifty thousand dollars," snapped Kennedy.

"Fifty thousand," gasped Douglas. "You mean five hundred thousand, Mr. Chairman."

"You heard me," said Kennedy. Douglas was stunned. "Well, what in hell are you waiting for?" barked Kennedy. "Get going."

That was the gruff beginning of an enduring friendship between the two men. Shortly after Douglas began work at the SEC, he received invitations to join the Kennedy family on their rented estate outside Washington. "It was a family that was very close knit," Douglas remembered. "At the dinner table conversation was built around the family: they were all participants in the conversation. It wasn't two elderly people with an older guest or two conducting the table conversation. It was the youngsters actively participating, and the mother or father, usually the father, asking some question like, 'Jack [John F. Kennedy], what do you think about this?' and so on. It was that kind of family. They were highly competitive with each other. The father particularly laid it on pretty hard, trying to make the boys and girls excellent in something, whether it was touch football or tennis or boating or something else.''

Long after those weekend visits, years after Kennedy and Douglas had each left the SEC, the two remained close friends, surprising admirers of both men since, in terms of experience and philosophy, the two could not have been more different.

In the twenties, Kennedy had moved successfully within the intense, secretive circles of operators during the wildest stock market in history. Supremely self-confident, Kennedy had matched strategies and a smell for a bull market with other operators of similar temperament and ambition, and he had become a multimillionaire. While Kennedy was engaging in plots and lucrative pools, William O. Douglas was a struggling Wall Street lawyer and, later, law professor, who had dropped out of the market after a single venture.

Although Kennedy had pledged his support for Roosevelt in 1932, he was no reformer. As late as 1933, he was active in a manipulative pool operation, just the sort of activity that Professor Douglas was condemning in his law school classroom. What, then, accounted for this strange mutual attraction between the market operator and the economic reformer?

Neither Kennedy nor Douglas ever provided an adequate explanation. But there are hints. Both men exhibited tough exteriors, but that toughness was peeled away when a colleague or underling held to Kennedy's and Douglas's high standards of performance. Both were men of action, not philosophical brooding. Both were fiercely competitive and ambitious.

Finally, Joe Kennedy possessed one talent that Douglas admired but could not emulate: the ability to meld a close-knit family despite increasing public demands on his time. Recalling the evenings spent with the Kennedys, Douglas wrote: "Each evening was a seminar. I could not help contrasting those evenings with my own in Yakima, where food was gulped, everyone too busy for dinner-table conversation." Douglas could also have found the comparison with his days at the SEC and, later, on the Court to be equally troubling. The more prominent Douglas became in the federal government, the more he seemed to grow apart from his family.

Douglas's first task at the SEC was to hire a staff to help with his investigation of corporations whose financial difficulties had led them into bankruptcy. At the top of Douglas's list of candidates was Abe Fortas, his prize student at the Yale Law School. Unfortunately, Fortas was already employed as assistant to Jerome Frank in the general counsel's office of the Agricultural Adjustment Administration. Douglas was undaunted. What soon transpired was an extraordinary exchange of letters between Douglas and Frank, in which Douglas, with an impressive combination of audacity, good humor and persistence, wrenched Fortas away from his protesting employer.

After Douglas had initially approached Frank about Fortas's transferring to the SEC, Frank conferred with Fortas and wrote Douglas that Fortas had decided to stay with him. "This was his own conclusion," Frank wrote, "and he did not act under any compulsion from me."

A skeptical Douglas replied in verse that he said he had lifted from a judicial opinion: "I sent a letter to the fish:/It told them 'This is what I wish.'/ The little fishes of the sea,/ They sent a message back to me/ The little fishes' answer was/ 'We cannot do it, sir, because-'/ I sent to them again to say,/ 'It will be better to obey.' "

Frank parried. "Dear Bill: Gosh! If it has come to this, that the Yale School of Law doesn't know its Alice in Wonderland, if you have to get your fish stories out of judicial opinions, it is not surprising that you don't know a true story when you see it."

In a return letter, Douglas appeared to give up the battle over Fortas, though not without one last needling of Frank, whose "finesse & high-powered tactics" were too much for a "country lawyer" like Douglas. Still, that was not the end of the matter as far as Douglas was concerned. Yale Professor Wesley Sturgis became Douglas's emissary. "I am venturing to write to you with regard to Abe and his continued desires to be associated with Bill Douglas," Sturgis wrote Frank. "As I see the situation on their side, it is not entirely dissimilar from that of the children who wish to marry but are afraid of what the old man will say and do; not that they do not have affection for the old man but because they want to do what they want to do and make him like it. . . ."

Frank capitulated. "Dear Bill," he wrote Douglas, enclosing a copy of Sturgis's letter. "Apparently you and Abe think I am like old man Barrett in the Barretts of Wimpole Street. . . . Nonsense! Bless you my children. You needn't elope. You can be married at the old homestead. . . . The only thing that disturbs me is that you felt it necessary to communicate with me through Wes. . . . I told Abe to prepare his trousseau but to stay with papa for a brief time until I can get a hired girl to take his place."

In wresting Fortas away, Douglas had successfully challenged Frank, not only a good friend but a New Dealer, who in 1934 ranked higher and possessed more influence than Douglas. Despite the frayed feelings, both men emerged with their friendship and respect for each other intact. "You are a swell old man—none better," Douglas wrote Frank. Only a few years later, when Douglas's name was mentioned as a likely successor to Justice Brandeis, Frank spearheaded the drive for endorsements of the Douglas nomination. For his part, Douglas told President Roosevelt that Frank possessed "the best legal mind in the country," recommended him as a commissioner on the SEC and, later, as his successor as SEC chairman.

Once his staff had been selected, Douglas devised a questionnaire to be sent out to corporations that had been involved with problems of bankruptcy and reorganization. The questionnaire, though carefully drafted, was somewhat more thorough—and intimidating—than certain members of the SEC, notably Commissioner James Landis, believed was necessary. When Landis raised objections, however, Chairman Kennedy backed Douglas.

After the questionnaires had been returned, Douglas began to build his investigation on the devices used by corporate officers, investment bankers and corporation lawyers to maintain control of the bankrupt corporations during reorganization. In case after case, Douglas and his staff discovered a trail of deceit, manipulation and outright illegal conduct. It usually began when officers and bankers of the old corporation (who, by their decisions, were largely responsible for the corporation's financial problems) shrewdly placed themselves in key positions on the protective committees and in the newly organized corporations. This was done by having their lawyers so manipulate the terms and timing of the election of protective committee officers that the old managers and bankers could emerge victorious with only a small percentage of the shareholders voting.

Once in power again, the managers and bankers could carry on a very profitable enterprise, at least for themselves, by running the protective committees and reorganized corporations for their immediate financial advantage and long-term control of the corporate assets. Investment bankers who underwrote corporate securities were, for example, made officers of the new corporations and promptly voted for the issuance of new securities through their investment banking houses. The legal structure of the new corporate enterprise was drawn up in such a manner as to immunize those same corporate officers from suits by ordinary security holders charging conflict of interest or outright fraud.

Behind all the double-dealing was the corporation's counsel, usually the very same lawyer who advised the company before the bankruptcy. The lawyer earned his generous fees the second time around by advising corporate trustees of the reorganized company to assume conflicting financial positions, or at least, not advising his clients *not* to assume them. Protective committee members were advised that they could trade with impunity in the property of their trust by virtue of the protective features of their deposit agreement. Stockholders were allowed to serve on protective committees to protect bondholders against the very same stockholders. Members of the protective committees were made the sole and exclusive judges of the reasonableness of committee expenses, which, when fees for the managers, bankers and lawyers were finally tallied, could run into millions of dollars. Protective committees were frequently used, not to protect the investment of the security holders, but to protect themselves from liability.

With the power of the subpoena and the force of Congress's endorsement behind his protective committee study, Douglas prepared for public hearings with the same thoroughness that he expected of his adversaries, the corporation lawyers and their clients, so familiar to Douglas when he was at the Cravath firm. Abe Fortas, who was Douglas's lieutenant at the SEC, remembered: "Douglas was surgical in his interrogation. He was thoroughly prepared and knew exactly where he wanted to go. He went to the jugular but he did so with questions that were precise, sharp and surgical."

A prime target of the Douglas investigation was the corporation lawyer himself. "He is not only the director of the play," Douglas had said earlier, "he is in charge of stage settings, he writes the dialogue, he selects and trains the actors. He is responsible for the tone, the quality, the finish of the play. It is his production and so it is that you cannot study reorganization without studying him."

One of the first witnesses before Douglas was Robert Swaine, senior partner in Douglas's old Wall Street law firm. From his own experience in the Cravath firm, Douglas knew that corporate reorganizations represented one of the most lucrative fields of law. Large fees for legal services to the bankrupt corporation, such as the $450,000 submitted by the Cravath firm in the St. Paul Railroad reorganization, were commonplace. But that fee, Douglas's staff discovered, was frequently only the beginning of the process that brought Wall Street firms such as Cravath stupendous profits and considerable influence over the reorganization.

"The earmark of Douglas in those days," said a former assistant, David Ginsburg, "was total preparation. During the public hearings, Douglas was always polite, but tough and unyielding. He remembered the ties with previous aspects of the testimony and kept testing the witnesses. By the end of the day, the witnesses were exhausted from the rigorous examination. Then Douglas and his staff would go back and prepare for the next day. It was all work and no play in those days."

The preparation paid off. "You stood me on my head and shook all of the fillings out," Swaine told Douglas after he had completed his testimony. In later years, Swaine criticized Douglas for conducting his hearings with "preconceived conclusions," but admitted that his interrogation was fair, or at least fairer than most Swaine experienced before government agencies. For

Douglas, the rough interrogation of Swaine, whose legal talents he continued to respect, only showed that he did not play favorites.

Douglas found that detached attitude more difficult to maintain when he faced John Foster Dulles, whose unctuous manner had roiled Douglas in their first meeting in 1925, when Douglas was interviewing for a job at Dulles's Wall Street law firm. As with Swaine, the roles were virtually reversed, Douglas now asking the questions and Dulles on the defense.

The focus of this aspect of Douglas's investigation was the collapse of the Kreuger and Toll empire after Ivar Kreuger, known as the Swedish match king, had committed suicide in 1931. Protective committees had been formed to represent debenture holders, with Dulles as counsel for bankers who had sold the securities. Another attorney, Samuel Untermyer, represented a second committee, formed to oppose the bankers, which planned to sue the bankers for fraud in the sale of the securities. Although Dulles's clients' investment represented thirty times that of Untermyer's, Untermyer began fighting every Dulles legal move as if the clients' financial interests were equal. Later, however, Douglas discovered that Dulles and Untermyer had made a "treaty" (unknown to their clients) so that both would be able to collect handsome fees without engaging in difficult litigation.

In questioning Dulles, Douglas suggested that besides a fee-splitting arrangement, one of the concessions that Dulles made to Untermyer was his agreement to accompany Untermyer to the chambers of U.S. District Judge Julian Mack to urge the appointment of Untermyer as counsel to the American trustee in bankruptcy for the Kreuger and Toll empire. After Douglas established that Dulles had accompanied Untermyer to Judge Mack's chambers, he pressed for an explanation.

Douglas: "You are going to chambers with an old enemy so to speak. It seems to be more than just a coincidence. . . ."

Dulles: "Well, you know how things are. They get very bad—the storm gets more intense just before the quiet comes. The very intenseness of the controversy we have been carrying on was such that that itself carried the germ of a subsequent peace between us. It was just impossible to go on at the rate we were going on, and I can't see—I mean I can see that a suspicious mind might look for improper influences here, but I can also see, and I assert that on actual analysis of the facts, there was nothing done here that reasonable and honorable people would not do. . . ."

Douglas: "Did you fear that if you refused this request of his [Untermyer had asked to become counsel to the trustee in bankruptcy], his attacks might be renewed?"

Dulles: "I did not. I knew they would not be renewed. I knew they would not be renewed because Mr. Untermyer, despite all I said about him, is a fine, honorable gentleman and we had agreed to try to cooperate together and if I had felt that there was any impropriety in going up with him to see Judge Mack and had told him that I thought there was an impropriety about it, he would have accepted. . . ."

Although Dulles saw nothing improper in the appointment of Untermyer, Judge Mack, after consultation with the senior U.S. district judge, did and rejected Dulles and Untermyer's request. Douglas also found Dulles's explanation less than persuasive: "Dulles posed as one wise enough, generous enough, and good enough to be able conscientiously to represent any number of conflicting interests. He was so unctuous and self-righteous that from then on we at the SEC called him a 'Christer.' "

After Dulles had testified, Douglas's committee immediately subpoenaed Untermyer. Just as quickly, Untermyer's doctor sent back a response, saying that Untermyer's failing health prevented his coming to Washington at that time. Douglas conferred with Joe Kennedy, who authorized a hearing at Untermyer's country home at Hastings-on-Hudson, New York. Certain that Untermyer would feign illness, Douglas took the precaution of hiring Dr. George Draper, his former psychoanalyst, as his "medical adviser" for the day.

At 9:00 A.M. on the appointed day, Douglas began his examination of Untermyer, reading from the Dulles transcript describing the fee-splitting arrangement. It was all too much for Untermyer, whose head tilted to one side and eyes closed. Douglas motioned to Dr. Draper, who examined Untermyer and pronounced him fit and faking. Draper winked at Douglas, signaling that he could continue the examination. Once again Douglas read from the Dulles testimony describing the fee-splitting arrangement and once again Untermyer "passed out." Draper repeated his examination and again winked at Douglas. Untermyer collapsed several more times during the day and Draper, each time, examined him and gave Douglas the signal to continue.

Before the day's hearing was completed, Douglas had elicited from Untermyer the fact that he and Dulles had, indeed, agreed on a fee-splitting arrangement; the Dulles firm received $540,000 and Untermyer's firm $272,500. "Their arrangement," Douglas later wrote, "reflects the struggle not for fair treatment of security holders but for division of spoils among the lawyers."

Despite his work at the SEC, Douglas continued to teach at Yale. That meant innumerable train rides between Washington and New Haven and weekend glimpses of his family. The train rides were enervating but not unfamiliar to Douglas, who had been commuting as early as 1929, when he undertook his first bankruptcy studies in Newark. The time with his family became increasingly short and took its inevitable toll. Douglas's son, Bill, remembered that his father didn't seem to be around much. "He treated us like toys," his daughter, Millie, recalled; "he showed us off. But he didn't have much to do with us."

Douglas's tight schedule also cut into his writing time at the law school. One day he called Professor Myres McDougal into his office and asked his younger colleague if he would write an article on bankruptcy for the *Encyclopaedia Britannica.* "Douglas told me," McDougal recalled, "that he didn't have the time to write the article and asked if I wanted to do it and we would share the honorarium. I remember trying to rework a few sentences to make them more eloquent. I asked Douglas for advice. He said, 'Does it say what you want?' 'Yes,' I replied. 'Then, the hell with it,' he said, and he put the article in an envelope and sealed it. I was surprised."

But the shuttling between Washington and New Haven did have advantages, at least for students. Gerhard Gesell, who was later appointed to the federal bench, found Douglas's split professional life a boon to his seminars. "Douglas was always in and out of law school," Gesell recalled. "He would come into his seminar all worked up. He gave us practical problems. 'Let me tell you what it's really like,' he would say, often running his hand nervously through his hair. He brought to the school what the real world was about. I found it terribly stimulating."

Douglas's protective and reorganization committees investigation resulted in an eight-volume report to Congress, representing a study of 200,000 protective committees and an investment of $36 billion by public security holders. In the report, Douglas and his staff catalogued the spectacular abuses of financial power and privilege. The offenders included not only some of the most powerful Wall Street law firms but also some of the nation's largest and most prestigious financial institutions. Chase National Bank and Manufacturers Trust Co., Douglas charged, routinely performed at least two institutional functions that presented obvious conflicts of interest, frequently at the expense of security holders. The banks served as indenture trustee and underwriter of the securities of the same corporation. The problem was that as trustee, the banker was supposed to be protecting the interest of the security holder (before and after bankruptcy). In fact, the banker invariably protected his bank's investment, pushing the security holder's interest aside. In criticizing the practices, which he said were both unethical and unprofessional, Douglas noted that "the corporate trustee had been sitting idly by while bondholders had been exploited."

Douglas's criticism of Chase National and Manufacturers Trust was mild compared to his attack on the financial institutions that issued real estate bonds, such as American Bond and Mortgage Co. and S. W. Straus & Co. The study of the operations of the bond houses, said Douglas, "revealed one of the greatest tragedies in the history of finance." It also presented a microcosm of the pervasive problems of those investors who had the misfortune of sinking their savings into financially troubled securities in the early thirties.

During that time, real estate bonds were largely held by ordinary wage earners who, rather than putting their modest savings into a savings bank, invested in what they assumed were safe long-term real estate bonds. It was a mistake. In 1931, 60 percent of the outstanding real estate bonds (representing an investment of $3.6 billion) were in default or distress. The bond houses that originally issued the securities were largely to blame for the financial problems; once in trouble, the bond houses usually compounded the difficulties.

Douglas's committee carefully documented the debacle: After the bond houses received payment for the bonds from the investors, they often engaged in speculative business ventures (ventures in which the bond houses frequently already had an interest), without telling investors of the new and risky policy. When the investments turned sour, the bond houses kept the bad news to themselves. Rather than informing investors that the principal or interest of the bonds was in default as a result of the speculation, the bond houses kept the value of the bonds at an artificially high level. At times, when there had actually been a default on the real estate bonds, the houses of issue pretended that there was no default and marketed the securities anyway.

When the inevitable default was finally announced, the bond houses moved quickly to control the reorganization. The ordinary bondholder watched helplessly since his "defender" by law, the indenture trustee, was usually an officer or employee of the bond house. Once in control of the protective committees, the bond houses spent much of their time protecting themselves from claims of fraud in the issuance and sale of bonds. And when not insulating themselves from legal liability, members of the protective committees frequently used their inside information to trade in securities.

The report on real estate bond defaults alone was based on five thousand pages of testimony. Douglas once speculated that only one man had ever read the entire eight volumes, Professor Vern Countryman of Harvard, and he did not do so for bedtime reading but to prepare for his judicial clerkship with Douglas. Despite its technical nature and formidable volume, the report did bring tangible results.

Congress in 1938 inserted into a revised bankruptcy act a provision making the SEC the courts' adviser in corporate reorganizations. The purpose was to provide federal judges, most of whom had little background in business and financial matters, with advice from a public-interest-oriented federal agency with the requisite expertise. Douglas's study also contributed to the passage of the Trust Indenture Act, which raised the fiduciary standards for trustees who acted under deeds of trusts created when the securities were issued. The new standards, Congress hoped, would eliminate the skulduggery that Douglas's committee had reported.

With the completion of the public hearings and the publication of the report, Douglas not only enhanced his reputation as a master of the technical detail of securities law, but became identified with the mainstream of the New Deal, exposing corrupt business practices, speaking for the public interest and defending regulatory legislation. Among those who recognized Douglas's prodigious feat was Professor Felix Frankfurter of Harvard. "And now has come part two of your report on reorganization," Frankfurter wrote Douglas. "And while I have only sniffed it—paged it here and there—one does not have to strike all the matches on the box to know that they light. Having a little familiarity with the field, I think I appreciate the thorough preliminary analysis, the indefatigable industry, and resourcefulness in examination and, above all, the fearless clarity that followed trails, wheresoever they led. And your report makes luminous what your examination revealed."

CHAPTER THIRTEEN

CRUSADER AND IRRITANT

W<small>HEN</small> J<small>OE</small> K<small>ENNEDY</small> accepted the SEC chairmanship, his primary purpose was to renew investors' confidence in the capital market. He had promised himself and the President that once that goal was achieved, he would step down. By September 1935, there were more than three times as many new securities issues as when Kennedy had taken office fifteen months earlier. Kennedy succeeded in bringing wary members of the Wall Street investing community and the New Deal together, assuring each of the good intentions of the other. Besides helping to break the capital logjam, Kennedy's diplomacy had facilitated the registration of all national security exchanges with the SEC.

Having made the SEC "a going concern," Kennedy resigned only 431 days after Roosevelt had appointed him. With the SEC firmly established and the lines to Wall Street reopened, Roosevelt could appoint a very different sort of SEC chairman. What appeared to be needed in 1935 was a man who knew the intricacies of the securities acts and could supervise the technical research necessary to provide an unassailable foundation for any rules that the commission promulgated. SEC Commissioner James M. Landis, a former Harvard law professor and a drafter of the 1933 Securities Act, was the obvious choice.

With Landis's appointment as SEC chairman, attention shifted to Landis's replacement as a member of the five-member commission. Reporters began to speculate on Landis's successor; one name mentioned was Wendell Willkie, president of the Commonwealth & Southern Corporation. Willkie, however, was angered by the very thought of the appointment. In a letter to Chairman Landis, he wrote that "this fool rumor about my going on the Commission has been embarrassing to me. . . . I have enough trouble on my hands without occupying public office and my ambitions, if any, are one hundred per cent in the opposite direction. . . ."*

William O. Douglas's ambitions in 1935 blew just the other way from Willkie's. He wanted a commissionership in 1935, as he had wanted one in 1934. After the Landis vacancy occurred, Douglas's friend Senator Francis Maloney of Connecticut tried to help by sending a telegram to Roosevelt recommending Douglas for the commission. In the fall of 1935, Douglas carried more impressive credentials for the job than he had in 1934, when Maloney had first tried to swing a commissionership for him. His protective and reorganization committee hearings were almost complete, and while the report had not been written, Douglas's extraordinary work was well known in Washington.

In addition to Maloney's support, Douglas could count on two new sponsors who carried considerable weight with Roosevelt. They were Benjamin V. Cohen and Thomas G. Corcoran, the New Deal team from the Harvard Law School that had drafted the Securities Exchange Act. Corcoran and Cohen formed as improbable a partnership as ever wielded power in behind-the-scenes Washington. Cohen was a shy, modest Jew from Muncie, Indiana, while Corcoran, nicknamed "Tommy the Cork," was an Irishman from Rhode Island who could sing a bawdy ballad or quote Dante with equal ebullience. Both agreed that Douglas would make an

---

*Willkie changed his mind only five years later, when he accepted the Republican party's nomination for the presidency.

outstanding addition to the SEC. "Ben and I chose Bill," Corcoran said. It would not be the last time that Corcoran and Cohen would recommend Douglas for high public office.

SEC chairman James Landis did not favor Douglas for the vacancy at first, preferring John J. Burns, the SEC's general counsel, for the opening. "John didn't want it," Landis recalled. "So the choice, from the commission's standpoint, narrowed down to Douglas, and I went over to the President to recommend Douglas for appointment to that vacancy."

Douglas's version of his appointment differed from that of both Corcoran and Landis. He wrote in his autobiography that Joe Kennedy's endorsement was decisive and that Kennedy personally escorted him to the White House, where FDR told him, "You're my man." A Douglas letter suggests, however, that Douglas did not meet Roosevelt for at least six months after his appointment to the SEC. The Douglas explanation of his appointment is even more puzzling in view of a letter Douglas wrote to Felix Frankfurter giving *Frankfurter* primary credit for his selection.

With the announcement of his appointment on January 21, 1936, Douglas was suddenly "discovered" by the national press; it was love at first sight. Rhapsodized *Time* magazine: "Sent to the Senate for confirmation was the name of William Orville "Bill" Douglas, 37, as brilliant a professor as the New Deal has attracted to Washington." *Time* told the tale of Douglas's rise, from the days when "this remarkable young man turned up in the East on the brake rods of a transcontinental freight train" to Douglas's role in the protective committee study. "Having since ploughed through the mire of 200,000 committees which, in varying degrees, were ostensibly protecting an investor's stake of $36,000,-000,000," *Time* reported, "he will soon report the findings to Congress, probably with recommendations for toothy legislation."

Although reporters agreed that Douglas was a "remarkable young man," they differed on what his appointment would mean to the financial community. *Newsweek* attached no policy significance to the appointment. Douglas "is not looked upon by financial interests as a zealot in any political cause." *Fortune* disagreed: "Washington thinks that his skeptical, disrespectful attitude toward Wall Street will stiffen the SEC's attitude and actions in that direction."

The New York Times reported that the Douglas appointment had the enthusiastic backing of Chairman Landis, whose policies, the *Times* was certain, would be just as enthusiastically endorsed by Douglas. The *Times* was wrong. Even before the story of Douglas's appointment was published, there were rumblings that Douglas did not approve of Landis's policy. In an off-the-record interview, Douglas was reported to remain "frankly illusionless about Wall Street today and probably will remain so because, unlike Chairman Jim Landis, he refuses to be dazzled by friendship of the Street's great minds and the luncheon invitations from George Whitney [a partner in J. P. Morgan & Co.]." A reporter was told of Landis's attempt to soften Douglas's protective committee questionnaire, an indication, it was suggested, that "Landis tends to relax vigilance."

Shortly after he was made head of the SEC's Trading and Exchange Division, Douglas began to put philosophical distance between himself and Landis. He told a group of investment bankers in Washington that the SEC was interested in preventing unfair competition, which, according to Douglas, included the withholding from the public of necessary information on a security or the "vicious" trading in a security—i.e., insiders' manipulation of a stock. Either would be harmful to the general public and "it would be the clear duty of the commission in such a case to intervene to correct the situation."

By the summer of 1936, Douglas had stepped up his speaking schedule and begun publicly to criticize the financial community. After Charles R. Gay, the new president of the New York Stock Exchange, had defended speculation in the market, Douglas attacked. "The SEC's primary concern is the investor," said Douglas, "not the speculator. The objective is neither creation of 'thin' markets nor 'thick' markets,* but with the curbing of speculative excesses which are so dangerous to our national economy and with the injection into these market places of higher standards of fiduciary relationships. . . ."

---

*The reference was to Gay's position that if speculation was stopped, the market would be too "thin" and, therefore, unhealthy.

The reaction on the Street to Douglas's remarks was swift and sour. "Floor traders, as well as many other members of the Exchange, were nettled by the remarks of William O. Douglas," *The New York Times* reported. "Some regarded his approach to the problem of stock market management as pedagogic rather than practical, and many felt that the commissioner sought to annihilate the speculator's reason for being."

In the speech attacking market speculators, Douglas also defended New Deal spending policies, which had been under intensive attack by the financial community. He produced figures to show that the national economy had recovered impressively from the Depression "at a surprisingly low cost." While the net increase in national debt amounted to $7.5 million since 1932, Douglas pointed out that national income had increased by $20 million. "These simple facts," Douglas concluded, "demonstrate very clearly that we have spent surprisingly little for what we got in return."

The two themes—attacking the financial community and defending large-scale federal spending—could have been taken out of the notebook of a presidential speechwriter. They were also favorite Roosevelt themes. Rumors circulated on the Street that Roosevelt would soon replace Chairman Landis, said to be headed back to Harvard, with Douglas.

In fact, Douglas had not even met Roosevelt when the rumors began to circulate. Only four days before his outspoken speech attacking market speculators and defending the New Deal, Douglas wrote the President to ask for a personal introduction. "When you honored me by appointing me to this Commission," Douglas wrote, "Chairman Landis assured me that he would shortly arrange for me to meet you on one of his trips to your office so that I could have the privilege of thanking you in person for the opportunity for public service which you have afforded me. Hence I deferred writing you and expressing to you my deep appreciation of the honor which you had bestowed on me, thinking that I would have the opportunity to do it in person."

Did Chairman Landis purposely keep the bright young Commissioner Douglas away from the White House? Douglas, of course, was suggesting no such thing. He did, however, want "to express to you [Roosevelt] my deep appreciation of this opportunity to serve you and the nation in your great constructive reform program." Douglas noted in passing that he was "especially happy to report that the reorganization study and investigation which I headed under Joe Kennedy is now culminating in a comprehensive legislative program which should go far towards carrying into the reorganization field the high standards for finance which you have sponsored." Douglas concluded with a pledge of total loyalty to Roosevelt and the New Deal: "I want you to know that I am ever at your service in the high cause which you are serving."

A day later, Douglas wrote to Roosevelt's assistant Steve Early, enclosing portions of his speech. "In view of the fact that it involves some campaign material on pages 3 & 4" (Douglas's discussion of "the surprising low cost of national recovery"), Douglas wrote Early, "I thought you might like a copy for your files."

In a space of two days, Douglas had put the White House on notice that: (1) Chairman Landis, for some unexplained reason, had not invited Douglas to accompany him to the White House, an invitation that Landis had promised; (2) Douglas's reorganization study was an integral part of the New Deal's policy of demanding high standards for finance and would soon produce important New Deal legislation; (3) the new man at the SEC, Douglas, was willing and able to trade punches with the financial establishment; and (4) Douglas was a devoted soldier of the New Deal, eager to defend New Deal policy.

On July 9, two days after Roosevelt received Douglas's letter of introduction, the President sent a memorandum to his appointments secretary, M. H. McIntyre: "Call him [Douglas] on the telephone and say I was delighted to have his letter and I hope very much that he will come in and see me sometime in August on my return" (from vacation).

In October 1936, Douglas again appeared to appoint himself a spokesman for the administration, as he had in his earlier speech, and again he sent a copy of his speech to the White House. The speech, entitled "The Forces of Disorder" and delivered at the University of Chicago, was a spirited defense of New Deal economic planning. He also lamented the problems of "irresponsible, laissez faire democracy." Douglas took dead aim at the established financial community; "The financial and industrial world has been afflicted with termites as insidious and destructive as the insect termites. Instead of feeding on wood, they feed and thrive on other people's money. . . . These financial termites are those who practice the art of predatory or high finance. . . . In the eyes of high finance, business becomes pieces of paper—mere conglomerations of stocks, bonds, notes, debentures. . . . High finance is interested solely in the immediate profit. Its organizations are not interested in whether our natural resources are wasted, whether we are overbuilding in one direction and under-building in another, whether our economic machinery is getting out of balance. Finance moves into the zone of exploitation whenever it becomes the master rather than the loyal servant of investors and business. . . ."

Douglas's University of Chicago speech brought together, for the first time, several disparate influences which would now constitute the basis for a Douglas economic philosophy. First, the attack on "financial termites" reflected Douglas's deep-seated distrust of the business "establishment," a distrust formed in his childhood days in Yakima and confirmed by the scandals that Douglas uncovered in his protective committee investigation. Second, both the language and the philosophy underlying Douglas's words borrowed generously from the works of Louis D. Brandeis. Douglas gratefully acknowledged his debt to Brandeis, who, more than two decades earlier, had spoken of financiers who profited unnecessarily and irresponsibly with "other people's money."

Finally, Douglas's approach was remarkably similar to that expressed by Franklin D. Roosevelt, who, in advocating an industrial democracy based on competition, showed his own debt to Brandeis. In fact, Douglas's Chicago speech tracked closely with a Roosevelt campaign speech in the fall of 1936 that lashed out at "economic royalists who take other people's money to impose a new industrial dictatorship."

While Roosevelt and Douglas were lambasting the financial community, SEC Chairman Landis continued quietly to go about the business of putting the technical SEC machinery into working order. What critics, like Douglas, took to be an unnecessarily diffident, sometimes obtuse attitude by Landis toward members of the financial community, Landis's admirers read as the cautious policy of a meticulous administrator. Landis, it was said, approached every problem faced by the SEC as if it would eventually wind up in the U.S. Supreme Court. As a result, every issue was painstakingly researched and exhaustively discussed before action was taken. Dramatic confrontation was not the Landis style, nor was it consistent with his objectives.

Roosevelt respected Landis's abilities but seemed to sense that his SEC chairman was a conscientious administrator with limited objectives for his agency. As a result, FDR did not try to push Landis into aggressive policies. The approach was best described by Landis himself, who recalled a meeting with the President: "At most, you had fifteen minutes. Ten minutes of that would be gone while he [Roosevelt] told you what Jesse [Jesse Jones, chairman of the Reconstruction Finance Corporation] had had the previous appointment] had been telling him. Then he'd relate some of his experiences in Dutchess County. By that time, a lot of the time would be gone. So you had five minutes, and you started. After your fifteen minutes was up, McIntyre would come in the door and say, 'Time's up.' The President would say, 'Oh, look, Mac,' and give you three more minutes and you'd go out of there. He might not have helped you at all. He might have just thrown the problem right back at you. But you went out of there as if you were walking on air. . . . Then you'd go back and solve the damn problem yourself."

Chairman Landis's self-effacing manner presented an increasingly conspicuous contrast to Commissioner Douglas's. Two Douglas speeches, in particular, emphasized the contrast. In November 1936, Douglas spoke to an audience of "customers' men" (stockbrokers) and immediately suggested that they were glorified salesmen whose middleman services (between corporation and investor) were probably unnecessary. "The institution of customers' men has at present an unestablished value," Douglas told the customers' men. He suggested that the brokers too often emulated money-hungry market operators and were solely interested in churning up their customers' portfolios for quick commission profit. "It was all part of a familiar pattern on Wall

Street," Douglas charged, "where men were immunized from a feeling of social responsibility, trained in the art of plunder in gentlemanly ways, imbued with the false ideal that the American way means exploitation."

The Douglas speech was one part Presbyterian Sunday school sermon and one part Brandeisian primer; Wall Street did not like either ingredient. Partners in member New York Stock Exchange firms in the audience grumbled that the Douglas speech showed "the cynical attitude of the speaker and his failure to credit the Exchange with efforts in the last five years to elevate customers' men's standards." A week later, the Exchange's public relations chairman attempted to rebut Douglas. "The customers' man was not as predatory and conscienceless as he has sometimes been painted," he harumphed, deploring the "unpleasant publicity" that the Douglas speech had inspired.

Four months later, Douglas returned to Wall Street to deliver a speech that made his message to "customer's men" a valentine by comparison. The scene was the Bond Club of New York and every important investment banker on Wall Street was in the audience. Between the "spontaneous round of applause" that greeted Douglas upon his introduction and "the spattering of hand clapping" at the conclusion of his remarks, Douglas suggested that:

1. investment bankers be ousted from their "entrenched position" on the directorates or in control of industrial companies;

2. competitive bids be taken from banks for all new issues of securities;

3. "financial royalism," promoted by the investment banks, be ended and the rights of investors who had been reduced by financiers to the position of "orphans in our financial economy" be protected.

Douglas might just as well have told the College of Cardinals that the Catholic Church was outdated or lectured a cattleman's association on the virtues of vegetarianism. In short, Douglas's message was not calculated to win the hearts and minds of his Wall Street audience. When it was over, the head of one of the nation's largest banks leaned across to his neighbor, another prosperous banker, and remarked in a stage whisper: "Do you suppose he really is God?"

Word that the SEC chairman would be returning to Harvard, for months an active rumor, became fact when the university announced that Landis had accepted the deanship of the Harvard Law School and would begin his duties after Labor Day 1937. While financial reporters busily made lists of candidates to succeed Landis, Wall Street bankers and brokers offered their own preferences. Douglas was not on their lists. At first, members of the Wall Street community were unwilling to condemn Douglas openly, hoping that word of their preferences for another man would suffice. When the names of Douglas and fellow commissioner Robert Healy were prominently mentioned, Wall Street quickly lined up behind Healy. Meanwhile financial leaders, like W. Averell Harriman, who was chief of the business advisory counsel for the Department of Commerce, were telling high government officials that Landis's successor must have the confidence of the business community.

Healy's name was dropped from the list of candidates and replaced by still another SEC commissioner, George C. Mathews. Douglas remained a possibility. Now a nervous Wall Street community, through the press, advised the President openly: "Since Mr. Douglas is reported to be unpopular with Wall Street because of alleged 'reforming' tendencies," *The New York Times* reported, "his selection is believed to depend largely upon whether President Roosevelt is inclined at this time to make a gracious gesture to the financial community. If the President feels so disposed, it is believed he would lend his support to George C. Mathews, also a member of the commission, who is said to have the backing of Wall Street. He was one of the original commissioners and while he has made a record for advancing the safeguards for the investing public, he is regarded as less radical than Mr. Douglas."

Douglas's hometown newspaper, the *Yakima Republic,* did not rush to his defense. When the staunchly Republican *Republic* picked up the rumor that Douglas might be appointed SEC chairman, an editorial headlined "YAKIMA NOT AT FAULT" explained: "The Yakima school system should not be held responsible for the career of the infant prodigy who seems destined to become chairman of the Security and Exchange Commission. It is true that William O. Douglas . . . acquired the rudiments of his education in the public schools of this city, but that does not account for the vagaries of his later life. . . . No, it must have been in the halls of Yale and Columbia that he acquired the idea of becoming a crusader and an irritant to all dealers in stocks and bonds. . . ."

CHAPTER FOURTEEN

NO MONKEY BUSINESS

Charles Gay could not enjoy his own party. The problem was not the July heat or the company, close relatives whom Gay usually found good, relaxing companions. That night Gay was preoccupied with business and his thoughts so agitated the president of the New York Stock Exchange that he excused himself early so that he could put them on paper. He lugged his typewriter to the screen porch, and when he returned to his party later in the evening, he was satisfied that he had written a complete and well-deserved denunciation of the Securities and Exchange Commission.

The next day Gay showed his work to a few officials and lawyers of the Exchange, and with minor modifications, he incorporated it into his 1937 annual report as Exchange president. In the published report, Gay dolefully reported the dramatic decline in stock market prices since spring and held the SEC singularly responsible. The volume of the Exchange's daily stock and bond auction was reduced to a trickle, Gay suggested, because traders couldn't do a proper job with SEC officials looking suspiciously over their shoulders. SEC trading rules and regulators were more than bureaucratic irritants; they were, quite simply, destroying the stock market.

The blast by Gay took most of Wall Street as well as the SEC by surprise. Good old Charley Gay had never seemed to irritate or be irritated by anyone or anything. He always did his job well and quietly, and that had been the secret of his considerable success. Gay was a Brooklyn boy who had gone to work, at three dollars a week, as a runner in a Brooklyn textile commission house. He learned business through wholesale coal and insurance and as secretary to a bank. Business success led to an invitation to join Whitehouse & Co., the oldest firm in the Street. At thirty-six, Gay obtained a seat on the New York Stock Exchange, where he quickly built a reputation for cautious, conscientious service to his clients. For twenty-six years he faithfully executed orders for customers, and never by stock manipulation or price juggling. "Neither I nor my firm has ever had an interest in any syndicate, pool or option," Gay said proudly.

To Gay, the stock market was not just a business; it was a way of life, and a very good one at that. An appreciative Gay treated the market as a doting parent would pamper a delicate, favored child. One of Gay's proudest accomplishments was to sell half a million shares of Baldwin Locomotive for one customer without breaking the market. He did it over a period of months, not days or weeks, patiently, carefully lining up buyers for his customer without causing so much as a tiny ripple in the market. That was not just Charley Gay's style; it was his deepest conviction.

Richard Whitney, Gay's predecessor as Exchange president, was different. Tall and imperious in manner, Whitney was the leader of the Exchange's old guard. The floor traders and specialists,* Whitney's constituency, considered themselves direct descendants of the intimate community of beaver-hatted bulls and bears who first gathered under Wall Street's buttonwood tree. They thought of the Exchange as being the intimate family affair that it had been in the beginning, when trading "in the stocks" was confined to a small group of experts in New York's financial community.

*The floor traders and specialists bought and sold stock on the Exchange floor for themselves; commission house brokers, such as Gay, executed orders for their clients.

Whitney did not defend the old guard's control of the Exchange on historical or elitist grounds alone, though those considerations were never far from his mind. No, Whitney's commitment to self-regulation of the Exchange, according to the old guard's rules, went deeper. He was convinced, quite simply, that the Exchange operation was beyond reproach. "You gentlemen are making a great mistake," he warned government officials who began to question the Street's practices. "The Exchange is a perfect institution."

To avoid what seemed to be an inevitable confrontation with the SEC over trading regulations, Exchange officials in 1935 had begun searching for an alternative to the obstinate Whitney. They naturally looked in Charley Gay's direction. Gay was never of the "Bourbon dynasty," like Richard Whitney, who demanded respect on the Street as a birthright. Gay could talk to commission house officials, who respected his hard work and reverence for the market. It was also hoped that Gay could assuage the feelings of diehard Whitney followers, who would, had they been asked by Whitney, have been perfectly content to ride with their man to the final confrontation between the Street and the SEC.

Whitney himself only grudgingly had consented to the succession. In fact, he had rallied his men, intensified his proselytizing on the Exchange floor and set out to show Gay and his sponsors that Richard Whitney could collect more votes as a member of the Exchange's board of governors than Charley Gay could win as president of the entire Exchange. And Whitney had made his point impressively, not only receiving more votes than Gay in the election but sweeping his friends into the governorship of the Exchange. The result had assured Whitney's continued reign on the Exchange, despite Gay's election as president.

In a short time, even Gay had accepted Whitney's dominance. One of Gay's early supporters—and Whitney's archenemies— Paul Shields, had invited Gay to his club for dinner so that he could confront him with his betrayal. Gay's only answer had been: "What else can I do? My hands are tied." That had surely been true, but it was not the whole story. In fact, Gay had been easily persuaded by Whitney that the government, particularly the SEC, was the enemy. And that conviction had been accompanied by noticeable foot-dragging when the SEC demanded compliance with its regulations. When SEC officials, notably William O. Douglas, did not relent in their criticism of the Street's failure to reform itself, Charley Gay thought he knew what to do. Attack.

William O. Douglas lay on a Cape Cod beach in early September 1937, but he could not relax. The problem he had hoped to leave at the SEC would not go away. He had been troubled for months by the unwillingness of the New York Stock Exchange to make a significant effort to comply with SEC regulations. Now Charles Gay's 1937 annual report was an effort, Douglas believed, to destroy the SEC.

Two weeks later, Douglas's view took on considerably more importance. On September 21, 1937, Douglas was appointed the new chairman of the SEC, despite the unanimous opposition of Wall Street's establishment. He owed his appointment, primarily, to the friends he had made in the New Deal, particularly Joe Kennedy, Ben Cohen and Tommy Corcoran, and also to his enemies. For his attacks on the Wall Street establishment, whether shrewdly calculated or not, had endeared him to Roosevelt.

The *New York Herald Tribune* compared Douglas to a younger Jim Landis, who had joined the SEC as "a militant idealist fresh from the classroom of Harvard, inclined to take lightly the importance of the Stock Exchange." Yet, the *Trib* noted, Mr. Landis "quickly reoriented himself once he assumed responsibility. This was not in any sense because his idealism became blunted; it was that his mind mellowed, his sense of values adjusted itself to the new atmosphere in which he lived and worked." That pattern, the *Trib* hoped, would be repeated by Douglas, who "in the recent past has given Wall Street moments of apprehension with some of his unorthodox observations on finance."

When Chairman Douglas called his first news conference the day after his appointment was announced, the financial community listened for reassurance. "What kind of bird am I?" Douglas asked himself, displaying the combination of offhand humor and straight talk that would make him a press corps favorite for his entire tenure as chairman. "To tell you the truth, I think that I am really a pretty conservative sort of a fellow from the old school, a school perhaps too old to be remembered. I think that from the point of view of investors, the one safe, controlling and guiding stand should be conservative standards of finance—no monkey business. I am the kind of conservative who can't get away from the idea that simple honesty ought to prevail in the financial world. I am the kind of a fellow who can't see why stockholders shouldn't get the same kind of fair treatment they would get if they were big partners instead of little partners in industry. I can't see eye to eye with those whose conscience lets them deal themselves two or three hands to the investor's one, or perhaps deal themselves two and even three without giving the investor any deal at all. I don't see why it isn't possible to have a completely honest relationship between finance, industry and the investors."

Douglas declared that the SEC was the investor's advocate, since, he assured reporters, the brokers, the bankers and the stock exchange itself had more than adequate representation. That didn't mean that the SEC was there to "save a fool from his folly" in the marketplace. But the SEC did exist to see that the innocent investor had only his own stupidity to blame—and not others' cunning—for losses in the market. If the SEC detected illegal pools or manipulations, Douglas promised, "there will be direct, aggressive prosecution of any and every case we can discover."

A *Herald Tribune* editorial found Douglas's remarks encouraging. After all, Douglas had said that the SEC was not there to "protect a fool from his folly," hadn't he? That must mean that he believed in the capitalist system and was not the radical "left-wing" economist that some of his more vociferous detractors had claimed. And who could fault Douglas's call for simple honesty on the Street? That was no radical demand. Perhaps this man Douglas was a conservative fellow, and with proper tutoring from wise Wall Street heads, he might work out, as had his predecessor, Jim Landis.

But there were disconcerting signals as well. Douglas had told reporters that under Kennedy, the SEC had consolidated the gains provided by New Deal legislation in the securities field. Under Landis, Douglas said diplomatically, "we were taught how to get things done." And under his leadership, Douglas declared, "we're now going to go ahead and get them done."

Douglas did not specify in what area he was going to get things done, but both he and the Wall Street community knew where he wanted to begin: with the reorganization of the Exchange. Dick Whitney had run the Exchange much as a private club for his kind, the floor traders, specialists and bond brokers, since 1930 and Whitney's successor, Charles Gay, had neither the power nor the conviction to change things. Whitney's club, like most club establishments, took care of its own nicely, allowing floor traders to make quick profits in in-and-out trading. Thus the major activity of the club was a form of financial poker, with the floor traders holding all the winning cards. Those engaged in the brokerage business—that is, in handling customers' accounts for fees—were usually excluded from the largesse and so were their customers, the investing public.

Under the earlier SEC administrations, the machinery had been put in place for eliminating favoritism and fraud at the Exchange. The trouble was that every time the SEC suggested significant reforms to the Exchange's governing law committee, it had been met, in Douglas's view, by legal objections, petty obstruction and insincere blandishment.

The only way to shake the status quo, Douglas believed, was to directly challenge the Exchange's governing members. Douglas proposed three measures: First, he wanted to reduce membership of the Exchange so that there would be fewer members who could speculate on the Exchange floor. Second, he proposed that the partners of members would have to comply with SEC regulations. As it then stood, nonmember partners could engage in illegal or irregular trading practices without fear of SEC sanctions.

Finally, and most importantly, Douglas advocated a radical revision in the management of the Exchange. Douglas thought that the Exchange, in recognition of its importance to investors across the country, should be run by a paid nonmember president and paid nonmember officers, who would represent the public interest. The clear intent of Douglas's last proposal was to break the hold that the Whitney faction had had on the Exchange management for years.* And not surprisingly, it was on Douglas's

*An SEC study had shown that though the Whitney faction (floor traders, specialists,

third proposal that the SEC chairman and the Whitney-led Exchange establishment reached an impasse.

The behind-the-scenes battle over the Exchange began only a few weeks after Douglas had taken office as SEC chairman. On October 16, 1937, Paul Shields and E. A. Pierce, two outspoken members of the Exchange who had always opposed Whitney's rule, came to Washington to meet Douglas. At the meeting, Shields and Pierce said that the Exchange should be reorganized.

"Would you mind saying that again?" said Douglas, grinning mischievously.

"Why, we believe the Exchange ought to be reorganized. You can't get anywhere so long as the Exchange is a sort of private club. We wonder whether the SEC would back us in a fight for reorganization."

"Why, damn it," shouted Douglas, "that's just what I want!"

Two days later, however, Douglas's attention was diverted by a disastrous stock market plunge. Prices dropped so abruptly and dramatically that everybody at the SEC and on the Street was thinking what they dared not say: this could be the beginning of a crash as devastating as that of 1929. Now Charles Gay's charge in his annual report that the SEC was responsible for the crash in the market made New Deal officials squirm. Something had to be done. The suggestion to close the Exchange was rejected by Douglas. Instead he renewed his call for reorganization. At this point, Joe Kennedy, who was still FDR's chief adviser on Wall Street problems even though he had left the SEC more than two years earlier, reentered the picture. The President met with Kennedy and approved the reorganization idea. A meeting to discuss details of the reorganization plan was set up between Kennedy and Paul Shields.

In characteristically blunt language, Kennedy told Shields that he was ". . . **$#$% sick and tired" of the Exchange's resistance to every move of the SEC and demanded that Shields and his minority faction do something about it. Shields eagerly agreed to comply, returned to New York and arranged a meeting of major-

bond brokers) held only 45 percent of the seats on the Exchange, they had a two-thirds control of the governing board.

ity and minority governing representatives of the Exchange which included Shields, Pierce, Whitney and Gay. It was not a congenial discussion. Shields, a big man with a tempestuous nature to match, marched into the room and repeated Kennedy's lecture, complete with a few bombastic flourishes of his own. Reorganize, Shields said, or else the SEC will do it for you. That message stunned Whitney and his group. When Shields revealed that he and Pierce had discussed the reorganization with Douglas previously, Whitney exploded. He called Shields a traitor and worse.

After calm was restored to the meeting, all agreed that they must make some gesture of compliance with the President's will, as communicated through Kennedy. Several meetings later, the group composed a memorandum for Shields to present to the President. Whitney's intransigence, however, made the agreed-upon memorandum a very tepid document indeed. It was limited to one brief paragraph, in which the group stated that plans for a new Exchange management, perhaps including a paid president, were "under consideration."

Shields took the memorandum to Hyde Park on October 26 and discussed it with the President and Douglas. Roosevelt tossed off the memorandum as a meaningless piece of paper, a typical ploy by his traditional enemies in the financial community. Douglas reacted differently. He had always felt that it would be far better for the Exchange to reform itself than for the SEC to govern from Washington. He saw the germ of reform in the gesture. Douglas, backed by Shields, persuaded the President that peaceful negotiations with the Exchange should be continued.

On October 29, five representatives from the Exchange (but not Richard Whitney, who Exchange officials decided would be too infuriating to the SEC) were received in Douglas's office by the SEC chairman and Joe Kennedy, who was present at Douglas's request. The fireworks began immediately with another Kennedy tirade, this time warning that the market's crash would surely be investigated by a congressional committee, and just as surely, Kennedy threatened, the SEC would blame a recalcitrant Exchange for the whole economic debacle.

Douglas, angry but calculating, focused on the critical issue: "The job of regulation's got to be done. It isn't being done now and, damn it, you're going to do it or we are. All you've been doing is giving us the run-around. The Exchange calls it co-operation, but the SEC calls it the run-around. If you'll produce a program of reorganization, I'll let you run the Exchange. But if you just go on horse-trading, I'll step in and run it myself."

The Exchange delegation, shaken by Kennedy's tirade and Douglas's bluntness, agreed to a Douglas suggestion that the Exchange write a letter to the SEC promising to reorganize. Douglas would reply by letter that he approved of the plan and the two letters would be made public simultaneously. It seemed simple enough and showed, ironically, that Douglas, whom the Wall Street establishment had branded a radical, was not so rigid or so determined to destroy the Exchange as the Whitney faction had supposed.

Three weeks and a fistful of drafts later, however, it was clear that Douglas and the Exchange could not come to an agreement. Meetings between the two sides merely underscored the distrust of each for the other. At the New York Yale Club in early November, Douglas met with Gay and composed a letter to his liking. It included a reference to a paid Exchange president. Gay carefully penciled out the reference. Douglas, believing that a paid presidency was the cornerstone to reform, insisted that it stay in. The meeting broke up disagreeably. Later, Kennedy's insistence that the Exchange exonerate the SEC from all blame for the market slump further complicated negotiations. The Exchange did not want a paid president and it did not want to take the SEC off the hook for the crash. No amount of urgent phone calls between the Exchange and the SEC could patch things up.

On November 22, an official of the Exchange submitted a final draft letter to the SEC. Douglas convened a meeting of the SEC; the commission unanimously rejected the draft. That afternoon, William H. Jackson, an attorney for the Exchange, met with Douglas to discuss the letter.

Jackson: "Have you read the last draft of our proposed statement?"

Douglas: "The SEC has read it and it is not satisfactory. The negotiations are off."

Jackson: "Well, I suppose you'll go ahead with your program?"

Douglas: "You're damn right I will."

Jackson: "When you take over the Exchange, I hope you'll remember we've been in business for 150 years. There may be some things you will like to ask us."

Douglas: "There is one thing I'd like to ask."

Jackson: "What is it?"

Douglas: "Where do you keep the paper and pencils?"

The feud went public. On Tuesday morning, November 23, the *New York Herald Tribune* carried a front-page story that negotiations between the SEC and the Exchange had broken down because the SEC had tried to wheedle the Exchange into taking the blame for the market slump. A Dow Jones news ticker item at noon confirmed the *Herald Tribune* story, which was based "on a source generally considered reliable." Standing on sturdy principle, the Exchange, the stories reported, had refused to take the rap.

Douglas was furious. He called a press conference for Tuesday afternoon for the avowed purpose of issuing a statement about the true nature of the SEC-Exchange dispute. There was nothing in the statement about the *Herald Tribune* story, but as Douglas expected, one of the reporters asked about the authenticity of the *Trib*'s report anyway. "Bullshit,"* shouted Douglas, who stood up and swung his arms downward for emphasis.

In his statement, Douglas made public what he had thought privately for months. The New York Stock Exchange, vested with a broad public purpose, could no longer be run as a private club for the benefit of floor traders, as it had in the past. "I have always regarded the Exchange as the scales upon which that great national resource, invested capital, is weighed and evalued," Douglas said. "Scales of such importance must be tamper-proof, with no concealed springs—and there must be no laying on of hands. Such scales must not be utilized by the inside few to the detriment of the outside many."

Professional traders on the Exchange floor frequently tipped the scales for their personal profit, Douglas charged. Citing statistics that the SEC had collected since the market began to decline in August 1937, Douglas accused floor specialists of selling active

*Earlier versions substituted the euphemism "Hooey."

stocks as they were going down, for speculative profit, totally oblivious to the demoralizing effect such short selling had on the investing public. In sum, the floor trader was looking out for himself alone, and in his headlong pursuit of profit, was irresponsibly tampering with the market. To balance the scales or, at least, to assure the public that the market scales were tamper-proof, Douglas suggested firmer Exchange self-regulation, beginning with a nonmember paid president and a reduction in Exchange membership.

Wall Street cried "foul." The only reason that Douglas was now talking reform, Street spokesmen suggested, was that he couldn't exact the Exchange's promise to shoulder the blame for the stock market decline. Talk of stricter self-regulation was merely a screen to cover the SEC's blatant political motive. Besides, the Exchange had been considering reforms for months, and without the harassment from Washington, perhaps they could get on with it.

Joining the Exchange's counterattack, Charles Gay issued a statement which again suggested that SEC regulations were primarily responsible for the dismal state of the market and that further government regulations could only make matters worse. Of course, his comments were offered "in the friendliest spirit and in the firm belief that cooperation between the Exchange and the commission is essential." But the Exchange had operated efficiently and fairly for many years without Mr. Douglas's advice and would continue to do so.

Despite the studied bravado, Gay gave the first hint that the pressure from Douglas was having an effect. To further assure effective Exchange management, Gay said, he would appoint a special committee to study the proper administration of the Exchange. Without admitting it publicly, Gay was ready for Exchange reorganization. More important, most members of the Exchange—fearful of a SEC takeover and also tired of Whitney's rule—were ready to follow Gay. Significantly, the study committee that Gay selected included no member of Whitney's old guard. And when the Whitney group protested and insisted on the removal of one of Gay's choices, the Exchange president held firm.

Douglas, in the meantime, had made it clear that he was not

bluffing in his threat to govern the Exchange. As soon as the breakdown in negotiations between the SEC and the Exchange was announced, Douglas ordered his staff to prepare a tough set of trading rules. The first, a rule restricting short selling, was ready by late January. The SEC chairman did not, however, wish to discourage the work of the Gay-appointed study committee. Before announcing the new short-selling rule, Douglas talked to the chairman of the study committee, Carle C. Conway, and promised not to release his rule if the Conway committee was finished with its study and could announce its findings. Conway told Douglas that the conclusion of the study was near but that he needed more time. Douglas promptly announced the short-selling rule, which Exchange president Gay found infuriating but ominously suggestive of worse things to come if the Exchange did not act quickly.

Less than a week later, the Conway report was completed and published, and it read as if Douglas had written it himself. The committee recommended a paid president, a technical staff and increased influence by anti-Whitney Exchange members on the governing board. The report was enthusiastically endorsed by a unanimous board of governors, save Richard Whitney, who, firmly resisting change to the last, abstained.

Richard Whitney's problems cut deeper, tragically deeper, than a single vote of no confidence by the Exchange's governing board. The financial empire of Richard Whitney and Co. was crumbling, and Whitney had begun a desperate search for funds to bolster it. Among his many other Exchange offices, Whitney was a trustee of the Exchange gratuity fund, which paid members' death benefits. In 1937, Whitney had kept part of the fund's bonds and cash, and unknown to anyone, had channeled those funds into Richard Whitney and Co. He had been asked to return $375,000 of the funds to the Exchange vaults and had not done so. Only George W. Lutes, an Exchange employee who quaked at Whitney's very presence, knew that Whitney had not returned the funds and he told no one. On November 22, however, Lutes could hold back no longer. He told the gratuity fund trustees of the missing funds; the trustees voted at once for the return of the entire $1,121,000 that had been entrusted to Whitney. The order was telephoned to Richard Whitney and Co. that afternoon.

When Whitney learned of the order, he made a private visit to his brother, George, a partner in J. P. Morgan and Co. and one of the most respected members of the Wall Street community. George Whitney was "completely thunderstruck" by his brother's request for the huge sum. He felt, however, that he had no alternative to covering for his brother, so he pledged the money. Richard Whitney stalled for time, informing E. H. H. Simmons, a fund trustee, that his office was too "short-handed" to send someone to the vault for the bonds and cash. Whitney added that he had talked to his brother about the matter, which made Simmons suspicious. Simmons decided to pay a visit to George Whitney, who assured him the bonds and cash would be delivered on time.

On Thanksgiving Day, the Whitney brothers were together at George Whitney's estate on Long Island, but it was not a day of celebration. George Whitney instructed his brother to liquidate his business and leave the Exchange. Richard Whitney made preparations as his brother had ordered, all the while going about his public business calmly, as if he had nothing to think about except the SEC's threat to the Exchange's autonomy.

By early January, however, reports of the true state of Whitney's affairs were beginning to circulate at the Exchange. On January 10, a floor specialist took an Exchange governor aside and quietly told him that he believed the Whitney firm was engaged in distress selling. The word was passed to Howland Davis, the chairman of the Exchange's business conduct committee. A few days later, when Davis was composing a mailing list for firms expected to answer questionnaires on their financial condition, he put Whitney's firm at the top.

In the first weeks in February, Whitney frantically searched for new loans and tried desperately to juggle the accounts of his firm to avoid detection. On February 21, he completed the Exchange questionnaire. On the same day, the Exchange comptroller, John Dassau, examined it and detected signs of a shortage of working capital. Two days later Dassau sent Exchange accountants to Whitney's firm. Shortly, Dassau returned to Davis with the report that the investigation would "have to go up some dirty alleys." He was told to proceed, and in the next two weeks, accountants uncovered case after case of Whitney defalcation.

Richard Whitney was proud and stubborn to the end. Believing that if he could raise enough money to cover his defalcations the Exchange would let him off, Whitney continued to seek loans. He was so busy in his quest, in fact, that he could not attend Exchange committee meetings. For each absence Whitney would send a formal note, regretting his "unavoidable absence." On March 5, when the extent of Whitney's defalcations was fully known, Whitney faced Charles Gay. "I'm Richard Whitney," he told Gay. "I mean the Stock Exchange to millions of people. The Exchange can't afford to let me go under." Mild-mannered Charley Gay finally lost his temper. He bluntly told Whitney, the man who had once dominated his thinking at the Exchange, that the Exchange had every intention of pressing charges.

At precisely 10:05 A.M. on Tuesday, March 8, Charles Gay stepped to the rostrum on the Exchange floor. The secretary of the Exchange rang the gong that suspended trading. In a voice cracking with emotion, Gay announced that all trading for Richard Whitney and Co. was suspended because of "conduct inconsistent with just and equitable principles of trade."

Richard Whitney would later go to prison. But that final humiliation was anticlimactic; on March 8, Richard Whitney had been found both bankrupt and dishonest by his peers on the floor of the New York Stock Exchange, *his* New York Stock Exchange. On the same day that Whitney was expelled, the Exchange membership unanimously accepted the reforms proposed by the Conway committee. The battle between the Exchange and the SEC was over.

CHAPTER FIFTEEN

IN BRANDEIS'S FOOTSTEPS

DURING HIS EARLY MONTHS as SEC chairman, Douglas was locked in a second debate, this one far removed from the issue of reform of the New York Stock Exchange. It took place behind closed doors at the White House and dealt with the direction of the administration's economic policy. The discussion among FDR's circle of key economic advisers, which now included Douglas, centered on what the federal government should do to bring the nation out of the recession that had begun in August 1937 and was getting progressively worse. Industrial activity had fallen off with the most precipitous drop in the nation's history; by the end of the year, two million people had been thrown out of work.

The "prosperity" of the first months of 1937, FDR's advisers knew, had been achieved largely by government deficit spending. Worried that the spending had caused debilitating inflation, Roosevelt had cut the WPA (Works Progress Administration) rolls drastically and turned off the PWA (Public Works Administration) pump priming. With the collection of two billion dollars in new social security taxes, the administration had not only stopped "pump priming," but was even "taking some water out of the spout." Big business, still lacking confidence in the economy and showing increasing hostility to the administration, had refused to recharge the private sector left slack by Roosevelt's actions. The recession had continued.

At the White House, Henry Morgenthau, Roosevelt's Secretary of the Treasury, argued for a balanced budget even though "the patient might scream a bit when he was taken off narcotics." But FDR's "liberal" advisers, including Douglas, Harry Hopkins, Harold Ickes, Marriner Eccles, Jerome Frank and Robert Jackson, opposed Morgenthau's austerity approach. They argued that since private investment had declined, the federal government would have to spend more. Douglas, Hopkins and the other liberals took the Keynesian view that the federal government must be the compensatory agent in the economy. Faced with conflicting advice, Roosevelt at first hesitated to embrace either side. By April 1938, however, he had made the decision to back the Douglas group, asking Congress for a huge fund for public works.

Douglas's prominent role in the liberals' victory did not escape press notice. *The New York Times*'s Arthur Krock reported the administration's decision to pour more funds into the public sector and said that Roosevelt's closest advisers, including Douglas, "are taking particular pains to be sure what they are doing and to estimate on as sound a basis as possible the chance of their plan and its corollaries to succeed." A week later, Douglas was singled out as one of Roosevelt's advisers "who have expressed approval of government spending to get business going again on a higher level—a step which Douglas feels is necessary to create a situation where the capital markets will again become active in supplying funds to private interests."

The more conspicuous Douglas's public prominence, the more stubbornly Douglas and his family clung to their informal ways. True, Douglas had rented a handsome two-story stucco house on the outskirts of Washington and had even hired two black servants. But life was casual in suburban Maryland, where Millie, now seven, and Bill junior, five, roamed freely. Mildred ran the household, but still had ample time to play tennis, read—she preferred biographies—and most of all, lovingly attend to the needs of her children.

Douglas drove a 1926 Studebaker and wore comparably venerable clothes. The Douglases did not entertain often, but when an invitation was extended, Douglas could mix mint juleps or offer traveling-salesman stories, as the occasion required. He still stirred at the sight of a bird with unusual plumage or a splendid sunset, but his pleasures in the outdoors were more domesticated than in the past. In the nation's capital, his exercise was usually confined to an occasional round of golf at the Manor Club. He wrote to his old friend Jerry Cundiff, asking whether the crap game was still alive in the back room of Falkenberg's Jewelry Store. But he had new friends now, not swell pals from Whitman days or Cascade companions, but busy New Dealers, like Willis Ballinger of the Federal Trade Commission or Carroll Reese, a young congressman from Tennessee.

Although home life held its attractions, Douglas was rarely there to enjoy them. The center of Douglas's universe was not the stucco house in suburban Maryland—or the White House, at which he now served as a key Roosevelt adviser—but the office at 1778 Pennsylvania Avenue, where he presided as chairman of the Securities and Exchange Commission. Here Douglas was still the unpretentious Westerner, draping his long legs over his desk, scratching his hair incessantly, or lighting a match on the seat of his pants as he had done in his cherry-picking days in western Washington. His suits were no better tailored than his work clothes and no one seemed to care, least of all Douglas. He could dine at the poshest clubs in Washington or on Wall Street, but was just as happy to slip off for a hamburger at a nearby diner, munching with the same purposefulness as the truckdrivers and clerical personnel who sat next to him at the counter.

A sixteen-hour day at the SEC was routine for Douglas, and during those long hours he rarely mentioned his private life. The work at the SEC seemed so important to Douglas and his staff that their conversations took on a crusading urgency.* When Douglas

*Douglas did relax. After hours, he, Fortas and others would go to the top of the Roger Smith Hotel to drink and trade tales. He also retained his sense of fun. In the wee hours

talked to his former students, like Tom Emerson, and tried to lure
them to the SEC, his words danced with the excitement of a true
believer. Like so many New Dealers, he was certain, Emerson
recalled, that all the world's problems could be solved. He was
working on new corporate frontiers, willing to experiment, eager
to challenge old ways with new ideas. "He was very committed,"
Emerson remembered, "and he wasn't at all concerned that he
was attacking the power structure."

The word "tough" was often used in conversations at the SEC,
and it was most often used to describe the boss. Douglas's coolness under pressure was legendary. "When most men would turn
on the heat," they said of Douglas, "he turns on the cold." Douglas was tough on his staff, demanding long hours and high-quality
work. And he was tough on the opposition, insisting that Wall
Street bankers and lawyers give straight answers to disconcert-
ingly straight questions. But most of all, Douglas was tough on
himself, outworking even the most dedicated of his staff. "I don't
think he ever slept," said one staffer, Gerhard Gesell.

Although it may have appeared to the public that Douglas
spent all his time in acerbic dialogue with the New York Stock
Exchange governors, this was far from accurate. In fact, Douglas
concentrated most of his energies on enforcing the three major
pieces of New Deal legislation that dealt with the capital markets.
The first was the Securities Act of 1933, which required the registration of new issues. Here Douglas's agency served a watchdog
function: to make sure that investors were given complete information on new securities. Beyond that, however, it was Douglas's
job to convince the financial community that the act would not
discourage new issues. Month after month, Douglas would receive mail and speeches accusing the SEC, through the Securities
Act, of freezing capital markets. And month after month, by letter
and speech, Douglas would bombard the act's critics with statistics showing that the charge was baseless. "The issuance of over
fifteen billion in securities issues through the machinery of this
statute," Douglas would note by the end of his term, "is ample
evidence that the machinery is neither unworkable nor exces-

---

of the morning, he and Thurman Arnold, then the Assistant Attorney General in charge
of the Antitrust Division, played an antic version of hide and seek in East Prospect Park.

sively burdensome. Stoppage of at least a quarter of a billion dollars of fraudulent issues demonstrates its protection to investors."

The Public Utility Holding Company Act, a second statute under Douglas's domain, was passed in an effort to control the gargantuan holding companies. Those companies frequently held just enough stock in operating companies, particularly retail utilities, to control and drain them for the holding companies' considerable financial profit. Security holders in the smaller companies had no voice in the holding company's decisions, even though those decisions affected (usually detrimentally) their own investment. Moreover, the states, which could regulate the utility companies, could not touch the octopus-like holding companies. The Holding Company Act imposed pervasive controls over the holding companies, including restrictions on the sale of securities, simplification of corporate structures, the screening of intercompany contracts and the reduction of holding company empires through geographical integration. The last provision was immediately labeled the "death sentence" by holding company lobbyists, which, for the propagandists, meant the death of the pure capitalist system as they had known and exploited it.

For Douglas, the Holding Company Act fit neatly into the Brandeisian philosophy of curbing giant monopolies that posed a threat to the genuine capitalist system (not the specious one held out by the holding company lobbyists). After the U.S. Court of Appeals for the Second Circuit delivered an opinion upholding the constitutionality of the act,* Douglas accepted it with the quiet confidence of an SEC chairman who would now expect— and welcome—the cooperation of the business community. In his public statement, Douglas assured holding company executives that "we do not harbor resentment or grudges and, furthermore, . . . we are not out looking for scalps."

It was this message of cooperation between the financial community and the government that was the cornerstone of Douglas's SEC policy. For he knew that, realistically, the 1,800 employees of the SEC had no chance to effectively enforce the provisions of the New Deal legislation if they were to meet con-

*The act was later held constitutional by the U.S. Supreme Court.

stant open or covert resistance. That did not mean that Douglas would stand passively by and watch his agency be hoodwinked or ignored by the facile minds in the business community. "Government will keep the shotgun, so to speak, behind the door, loaded, well-oiled, cleaned and ready for use," Douglas warned, "but with the hope it will never have to be used."

That policy was never more in evidence than in Douglas's enforcement of the third statute that was his responsibility, the Securities Exchange Act, and most notably as it applied to the New York Stock Exchange. When Richard Whitney and Charles Gay had balked at the SEC suggestion to reorganize the Exchange, Douglas had increased the pressure until reformers at the Exchange broke ranks with Whitney. But once reforms had been promised, Douglas openly pledged cooperation with the Exchange. Douglas held frequent meetings with the new paid president of the Exchange, William McChesney Martin, and the Exchange president emerged smiling and confident that the new spirit of cooperation was no public relations ploy. After one such meeting with President Roosevelt and Douglas, Martin told reporters: "if we can get together on these problems [of reorganization], we can make the New York Stock Exchange the national public institution it ought to be."

Douglas permitted himself a slight private chortle over the series of events that had promoted this era of good feeling: "It looks as if the reorganization of the Exchange which you and I started last October," he wrote Joe Kennedy, then U.S. Ambassador to Great Britain, "is going through with a bang and I must say that Dick Whitney did not make the task more difficult."

Under Douglas, the SEC built the reputation of a no-nonsense outfit of bright, aggressive young men who feared no one. "We were doing what had to be done," said Abe Fortas, "and we weren't afraid. Nobody worried what Douglas would say if we went after somebody big. He'd say, 'Piss on 'em.' "

The primary targets were on Wall Street, but when the SEC staff's suspicions led them elsewhere, as with Transamerica, the California-based giant holding company, they pursued zealously and with the full support of Douglas. For years, Transamerica had gone about its profitable activities, immune from state regulation and, seemingly, serenely above the suspicions of the federal government as well. Cynics suggested that the explanation lay in the special relationship between Roosevelt and A. P. Giannini, the head of Transamerica and a generous contributor to the Democratic party. The SEC had monitored Transamerica's activities in 1936 and 1937 and become convinced that Transamerica housed an illegal investment trust, among other suspicious practices. Before moving in on Giannini, Douglas made a precautionary visit to the President.

"Is the front door to the White House closed when I move in on Transamerica?" Douglas asked.

"Absolutely," Roosevelt replied.

"Mr. President, how about the back door?"

Roosevelt laughed and said, "The back door, too, is closed."

Despite tenacious resistance from Giannini, the SEC investigation continued. In the end, Douglas was completely satisfied. "We finished the job on Giannini," wrote Douglas, "and eventually cleaned up an unwholesome situation."

On rare occasions, however, the zealousness of SEC investigators was misplaced—and embarrassing. The great *New Yorker* magazine investigation was such an instance. Two of Douglas's investigators in New York thought they had spotted tricky jumps in the stock of Cuneo Press and decided to interrogate Cuneo's buyers. One was Harold Ross, editor of *The New Yorker* magazine, who had bought one hundred shares of Cuneo stock. The intrepid SEC investigators telephoned Ross and asked him to come to the SEC's New York office for some questions. Ross said he was very busy and couldn't make it. Even under threat of subpoena, Ross would not budge. The investigators, by this time, sniffed a scandal and raided *The New Yorker* offices, armed with subpoenas for Ross and his secretary. They did not find Ross or his secretary, but did corner the magazine's receptionist. With stenographer at their side, the investigators interrogated the perplexed receptionist in the best Clarence Darrow tradition. They wanted to know Ross's height ("medium"), age ("somewhere in the thirties but I don't know where"), work habits ("he hasn't any regular hours") and more:

Q: "Does he habitually wear a soft hat or a derby or what?"

A: "Good gosh, I think he wears a soft felt hat, but I'm not sure."

Q: "Does he lean toward grays or tans in his clothes?"

A: "I think tans, but I'm not sure."

Q: "Does he carry a cane?"

A: "No, I haven't noticed."

Q: "Does he carry an umbrella?"

A: "I don't think so. Isn't that awful?"

When told of the interrogation, Ross found it only slightly amusing. "My receptionist was prostrate the next day with the excitement of it all," Ross wrote attorney D. H. Silberberg. "I presume the SEC Johnnies took it in their stride, triumphantly. Technicians and bureaucrats (as I told them on the phone) are swamping the country and have it almost ruined." Ross closed drolly: "I am now wearing a derby hat and going around with a cane in one hand and an umbrella in the other, so if you see me you'll know who I am."

When he heard about *The New Yorker* investigation, Douglas made one of his infrequent concessions to a potential adversary, sending a member of the commission to New York to assuage Ross's feelings. But that was an exception. Douglas seldom apologized for the conduct of his staff. "I was proud of all of them," he later wrote. The pride was reciprocated. "He gave loyalty and he commanded it of us," Fortas said. "It was the respect one gives to a boss who knows what he's doing."

For Douglas, loyalty at the highest level of the SEC—the commission itself—was equally important. There was never a problem with Robert Healy, the quick-tempered Vermonter whose skepticism of big business matched Douglas's. George Mathews, the other original commissioner, though a Wisconsin Republican, had solid progressive instincts and worked well with Douglas (though Douglas often found himself refereeing heated debates between the temperamental Healy and the stubborn Mathews). When Landis returned to Harvard and J. D. Ross, the fifth commissioner, resigned late in 1937, the chairman made certain that their replacements were Douglas team players.

The President and his son Jimmy had urged Douglas to take at least one man from the financial world, but Douglas refused to reserve a seat on the SEC for the New York Stock Exchange or "any other such special interest." When he talked to John W. Hanes, a partner in Charles D. Barney & Co., however, Douglas found a man from the Street whom he could recommend enthusiastically. Hanes possessed a "fund of technical knowledge" that would be helpful to the commission, Douglas wrote the President. More important, Hanes had assured Douglas that he was "one hundred per cent back of us in our struggle for reorganization of the New York Stock Exchange." Yes, Douglas believed, Hanes could contribute to the "compact, loyal group which will work in unison and harmony in carrying out the important program that you and Congress have entrusted to us."

Although Douglas trusted Hanes to carry out the policies of the SEC, he insisted that his old friend Jerome Frank be appointed with Hanes. Frank would not only be "a very distinguished appointment" but he would serve as a "liberal" counterbalance to Hanes, whom Douglas still suspected of latent Street sympathies. "I think the two of them will pretty well distribute the weight in the boat," Douglas wrote FDR. Roosevelt took his SEC chairman's advice.

Although Richard Whitney's expulsion had ended the most vitriolic period in SEC–New York Stock Exchange relations, it had not caused Chairman Douglas to relax pressures for reform. The watchword between the SEC and the Exchange was now "cooperation," but Douglas was persistently vigilant and his "shotgun" was never out of reach. Within minutes of receiving word of the Whitney scandal, Douglas had, in fact, dispatched Commissioner John Hanes to New York on the 2:00 A.M. train. Hanes arrived at the Exchange at nine-thirty the next morning, the precise time that Douglas had convened a meeting of the other four commissioners to ask for, and receive, permission to initiate a full-scale investigation of the Whitney scandal.

To head the SEC investigation Douglas chose Gerhard Gesell, twenty-eight years old and only recently graduated from the Yale Law School. "Once Douglas was satisfied that I knew what I was doing," Gesell recalled, "he let me alone. I've always thought what a tremendous thing it was for him to let me have my head." Of course, Douglas's way of letting Gesell alone was slightly different from most bosses'. Though newly married, Gesell quickly became accustomed to phone calls at one o'clock in the morning. At the other end of the telephone was Douglas, popping questions or suggestions at his young investigator.

Both Gesell and Douglas knew that the stakes were high, with far-reaching implications for both the Street and the nation. How could Whitney have covered his trail of defalcation when he was doing it, literally, under the nose of every reputable banker and lawyer in New York? What did Whitney's success say about Wall Street's own detective machinery? If Whitney could embezzle for almost a year without being caught, how many others in sober three-piece suits were still skipping outside the law?

The Whitney scandal was Wall Street's Watergate and Gesell was the SEC's special prosecutor. He did not miss his opportunity. For what Gesell uncovered was not a simple case of embezzlement by Whitney, but a more ominous trail of dishonesty leading to the top of Wall Street's most prominent banking house, J. P. Morgan and Co. Two partners of J. P. Morgan and Co., George Whitney (Richard's brother) and Thomas Lamont, knew of Whitney's embezzlement months before it was made public. Neither felt an obligation to report the crime to law enforcement authorities or even to suggest that Whitney resign his position on the Exchange's board of governors. When J. P. Morgan himself was asked if he would have reported the crime had he known about it, the president of J. P. Morgan and Co. did not hesitate to support his partners. Like Whitney and Lamont, J. P. Morgan would not have felt an obligation to report Richard Whitney.*

The SEC's Whitney Report fully documented Douglas's early charge that the Exchange had been run like a private club, that members did not consider themselves vested with a public interest and that the most prominent member of the club, Richard Whitney, could steal from thousands without so much as a twitter from his colleagues. The report also contained the program for Exchange reorganization which had already partly been implemented. Douglas termed the Whitney Report "a honey" and boasted to his old friend Joe Kennedy about the success of the Exchange reorganization. "The program is really a swell one," Douglas wrote Kennedy. "It shows what can be done when the

---

*Morgan did not, however, approve of Whitney's conduct. Indeed, Morgan refused to lend Whitney the money that would have rescued him.

real guys in the Street put their shoulders to the wheel with us
10¢ an hour birds down here in Washington."

With the completion of the reorganization of the New York
Stock Exchange and the Exchange's acceptance without a fight,
of new trading rules for brokers, the SEC was giddy with confidence. That attitude was well reflected in song by an anonymous
SEC composer, "The Wall Street Wail or the Unholy Five":

Verse

One dark afternoon down in Wall Street
Some financiers stood round a bar,
Bidding farewell to a comrade
Soon leaving in his private car.
Their eyes dimmed with whiskey and sorrow—
They knew he'd not come back the same.
They placed gentle hands on his shoulder,
But 'twas elsewhere that they placed the blame!
They begged a few words of their hero—
This man was their government's choice!
The martyr to Capital rose in their midst
And said with a catch in his voice:
"So long, fellows. Shed a tear for me.
I'm off to be investigated—by the SEC."

Refrain

"All of you boys know how it is
When that crowd is conducting a quiz.
They want to know where you were on the date
Steel jumped from seven to seventy-eight—
They beg to inquire where you got the stocks
They found in your safe in that little black box—
You've all been through it. You know whom to thank—
DOUGLAS, HANES, HEALY, MATHEWS AND FRANK.

The announcement of the SEC's invincibility was premature, as
events following the Exchange reorganization quickly showed. In
an effort to better protect the investing public, the Exchange had
restructured its board of governors to include "public" representatives who were not from the Street. Douglas's old friend

University of Chicago President Robert Hutchins was one of the first "public" governors. With Exchange president Martin pledging cooperation and public-spirited men like Hutchins on the board, Douglas, understandably, anticipated that the new board would transfer reformist talk into action.

The opportunity arose almost immediately when the Board considered what action, if any, should be taken against those investment bankers, like Thomas Lamont, who had knowingly covered up Richard Whitney's crimes. He did not want to meddle in Exchange affairs, Douglas wrote Martin, but he did want to call to the attention of the Exchange president the undeniable transgressions committed by members of the Exchange as exposed in the Whitney Report. At the very least, Douglas reasoned, bankers, such as Lamont, violated the Exchange bylaws, which forbid conduct "detrimental to the interest or welfare of the Exchange."

Twenty-eight governors disagreed with Douglas's interpretation of the phrase "detrimental to the interest or welfare of the Exchange." Ten governors felt that "it would have been much more to the interest of the Exchange if the persons involved had been more successful in their attempts at secrecy and the whole matter had been kept from the public and quietly hushed up." The remaining majority believed that "the whole matter had been given such publicity through the Commission's proceedings as to require no further inquisition or discipline."

Robert Hutchins, alone, dissented. "In the hearings before the Securities and Exchange Commission," Hutchins wrote Martin the day after the vote had been taken, "there was evidence tending to show that members of the Exchange or their partners knew of Richard Whitney's criminal conduct or of the condition of his firm some months before the failure. The public interest, the good name of the Exchange, and the good name of the members referred to all require the Board of Governors to institute proceedings in which the question of the responsibility of these members may finally be disposed of. The decision of the Board yesterday to take no action compels me to present my resignation."

Douglas sent a one-line telegram to Hutchins: "IT IS NOT AS LONESOME IN THE FRONT TRENCHES AS IT MAY NOW SEEM. BILL." Two days later, Jerome Frank wrote Hutchins that "your decision was apparently compelled by the logic of the situation, but, as the conduct of other members of the Board shows, not all men have the guts to act upon such logic."

Despite the private outrage of Douglas and Frank, the SEC's public reaction to the board's vote was conciliatory. In public, Douglas said that the vote would not affect the cooperative effort that would continue between him and Martin. He did suggest, however, that the vote underlined some "unfinished business," namely, "the problem of better coordination and allocation of the policing and disciplinary functions between the Exchange and the Commission."

Conversations on the matter between Martin and Douglas continued, though they were more strained than before. At the end of Douglas's term as chairman, little progress had been made. Douglas concluded privately, in a letter to Roosevelt, that nothing short of new legislation was needed "to take off the hands of the stock exchanges cases which they have found 'too hot to handle.' "

This final confrontation with the Exchange, as the first, showed a side of Douglas that Douglas himself, particularly as his reputation for uncompromising devotion to principle built through the years, rarely acknowledged. Throughout his years at the SEC, Douglas was a man who was willing to compromise if the realities demanded it. In the first and most dramatic confrontation with the Exchange, over Douglas's insistence on reorganization, the chairman did not dictate terms. Instead he consciously left the door open for Exchange mobility. Only when it was clear that *the Exchange would not compromise* did Douglas break off negotiations. And Douglas still could have been deprived of his hero's image if Richard Whitney had not helped out, as Douglas was the first to recognize.

Douglas's sense of reality was also evident when he sent Martin the stern letter reminding him of the bylaws of the Exchange and the clear evidence that Exchange members had violated them. He did not say that the SEC would move in if the Exchange didn't take action. Rather, he strongly urged the board to take action. When the board refused, Douglas repeated his pledge of cooperation with the Exchange, and only suggested that more had to be done in the area of Exchange discipline.

Douglas did not expect to win every battle at the SEC. He had told reporters early in his term that he would be satisfied with a 50 percent success rate. He surely surpassed that goal; his bloody skirmishes with Wall Street were no exception. To be sure, the board of governors balked at disciplining several of the Exchange's most powerful members in the aftermath of the Whitney scandal. Although disappointed, Douglas realized that this may have been a case that was "too hot to handle" for the Exchange.

In less politically sensitive cases, however, the Exchange cracked down on Street corruption—and Douglas led the applause. Less than two weeks after the board had refused to censure members Lamont and Whitney, the Exchange expelled Joseph A. Sisto, head of the brokerage firm of J. A. Sisto & Co. Sisto was found guilty of violating Exchange rules, including the selling of his own stock in the Sisto Financial Corporation (which he controlled) at an arbitrary markup price.

"A bang up job," said Douglas in praising the Exchange action in the Sisto case. He gave full credit to the Street. "This Sisto matter is a case that was initiated by the Exchange," said Douglas, "and one which they handled entirely under their own power." That, of course, was the way Douglas had wanted it all along. But it took Douglas's pressure to shake the Exchange out of its clubby complacency to do a "bang up job."

The long-term effect of Douglas's work could not be accurately gauged until the end of World War II, when economic conditions returned to normal for the first time in years. The reforms that had been urged by Douglas resulted in a more efficient New York Stock Exchange. More important, the reforms once again instilled public confidence, so that investors felt safe in participating in the capital markets. With some minor scandals, many of which were resolved by the Exchange itself, Wall Street has, since that time, proved to be a major factor in providing funds for capital investment, fueling the great expansion of the U.S. economy which has essentially continued to this day.

When word of Justice Louis Brandeis's retirement from the U.S. Supreme Court reached a Georgetown cocktail party on February 13, 1939, one guest, *The New York Times* columnist Arthur Krock, toasted a second guest, SEC Chairman William O.

Douglas, as Brandeis's successor. Douglas later recalled that the Krock toast made him consider for the first time—and not very seriously—the possibility of his sitting on the U.S. Supreme Court.

"I had never cast my eyes its [the Court's] way, never dreamed, let alone wished, that I would sit there," Douglas wrote. He also wrote that when Roosevelt later told him that he would succeed Brandeis on the Court, he was "dumbfounded," since he had never given the Court a covetous glance. Events following the announcement of Brandeis's retirement suggest, however, that Douglas was very much aware that he was in contention for the Court seat and, in fact, shrewdly worked in his own behalf.

No one can plan on a Court appointment, Douglas wrote in his autobiography. "The important thing is to stay in the stream of history, be in the forefront of events—and carve out a career that will be satisfying in all other respects." Douglas followed perfectly his own prescription for a Court appointment.

As a young member of the SEC, Douglas had introduced himself to the President and sent him his speeches so that Roosevelt could know his thoughts and loyalty. After he was appointed SEC chairman, Douglas proved himself to be a tough, exceptionally competent administrator, and for the first time, he began to enter the stream of New Deal history. Both in his capacity as SEC chairman and as presidential economic adviser, Douglas emerged as a prominent member of the Roosevelt administration.

By February 1939, the month that Brandeis retired, Douglas was very much in "the forefront of events." In addition to serving as SEC chairman and Roosevelt economic brain truster, he had chaired a special committee to study possible legislative remedies for the nation's troubled railroads, conferred with other New Deal insiders on ways to stimulate the electric utilities industry, and served on a presidential committee to study the electric power supply in the event of war.

At the same time, Douglas's allegiance to the Brandeis philosophy was well publicized. He promised U.S. Senator Joseph O'Mahoney's Temporary National Economic Committee (of which Douglas was a member) that the SEC would investigate the vast investment funds controlled by insurance companies and study the impact of that power on the national economy. Three days before Brandeis retired, Douglas, in a speech at Fordham University, castigated big corporations as exemplars of materialism which "degrade moral values in this country and are a menace to the ideals of democracy." Brandeis himself was aware of Douglas's espousal of Brandeisian principles and, Douglas later wrote, told Roosevelt that he wanted Douglas to succeed him.

There were two obstacles to Douglas's appointment to the Brandeis seat on the Court. At forty, he was very young to sit on the Court; only one justice in history, Joseph Story of Massachusetts, had been appointed at an earlier age (thirty-two). But Douglas's youth hardly seemed to disqualify him; the New Deal, after all, had been a young man's administration from the beginning.

The second obstacle was more serious. It was well known among New Deal insiders, including Douglas, that Roosevelt wanted to appoint a Westerner to the Brandeis seat, since that area was not then represented on the Court. Though raised in the West, Douglas had spent his entire adult life in the East and maintained his voting residence in Connecticut. The early favorite for the appointment was U.S. Senator Lewis Schwellenbach, of Washington State. Schwellenbach appeared to have the two essential credentials: he was a Westerner and he was a loyal New Dealer, who supported to the end FDR's ill-fated Court-packing plan.*

When Harold Ickes, Roosevelt's Secretary of the Interior, had lunch with the President in early March 1939, the two discussed the Brandeis vacancy and Roosevelt made it clear that he was leaning toward Schwellenbach and that Schwellenbach's hailing from the West was a critical factor in his preference. Douglas's name was mentioned, but he was seen as an Easterner. "The President was not particularly inclined to appoint Douglas," Ickes recalled.

Meanwhile Jerome Frank had organized a campaign to make Douglas a Westerner, or at least to show that he had strong support from the West. Frank and Tommy Corcoran, who

---

*Douglas was curiously discreet after Roosevelt's Court-packing plan was introduced. Though he said that he privately opposed the plan, he never mentioned his opposition to FDR because, he later wrote, he did not offer "unasked for advice."

jumped on the Douglas bandwagon early, decided that it was crucial to gain the support of a prominent Westerner. William Borah, Republican senator from Idaho, was the chosen target.

Douglas himself was not idle. On February 14, one day after the Brandeis resignation was announced, Douglas wrote letters to three influential New Deal Democrats: Attorney General Frank Murphy, Speaker of the House of Representatives Sam Rayburn, and Postmaster General (and Roosevelt political strategist) James Farley. The letters were identical: "Dear Frank [Sam/Jim], The only additional adornment which my office needs is an auto-graphed photograph of you. Then it will be perfect. Yours faith-fully." Six days after he had sent the letters to Murphy (who soon was promoting the Douglas candidacy), Rayburn and Farley, Douglas wrote a brief note to Justice Brandeis, enclosing his Fordham speech and a letter from the secretary of the Indepen-dent Bankers Association, which praised the speech.

Douglas also wrote flattering letters to two other influential Americans, one identified with the liberal intelligentsia and the other with the Wall Street establishment. Douglas told columnist Walter Lippmann that he "was delighted to have had an opportu-nity to chat with you" and that a Douglas speech, which he en-closed, undoubtedly could be traced to a Lippmann column. The other letter was addressed to John Foster Dulles, senior partner in the New York law firm of Sullivan and Cromwell, the same J. F. Dulles Douglas attacked in his autobiography as pompous, dishonest, wrong-thinking and self-righteous. "In all candor," Douglas wrote Dulles, "your address of January 14, 1939 [on administrative law], is one of the most sensible and enjoyable discussions that I've seen in recent months." The Dulles ap-proach and attitude toward administrative law, Douglas said, "is almost unique among practicing lawyers and really cheering to one engaged in the business of government." Only a month earlier, Douglas had written Dulles a letter praising his book, *War, Peace and Change,* as "stimulating, absorbing and constructive."

While Douglas was carrying on a busy private correspondence, his supporters were soliciting endorsements from Douglas's old friends in Washington and Oregon. Douglas himself, reportedly, wrote Herbert Ringhoffer, a fellow Whitman graduate, a Beta, and a member of the Walla Walla County Bar Association, urging

Ringhoffer and other Whitman graduates to secure Douglas endorsements from lawyers and bar associations in Oregon, Washington and Idaho. Ringhoffer, Cameron Sherwood, Chester Maxey and other Whitman alumni (mostly Betas) lined up Washington State bar association support for Douglas in Spokane, Walla Walla, Yakima, Columbia and Garfield counties. Word that the Washington State legislature was about to endorse Schwellenbach brought a barrage of phone calls from Douglas supporters. The result was that the state legislature adopted a resolution stating that both Douglas and Schwellenbach were suitable Court appointees. After Borah held a press conference saying that William O. Douglas would make a fine representative from the West on the U.S. Supreme Court, Douglas's candidacy caught fire.

As Douglas gained supporters, Schwellenbach followers began to cast doubt on Douglas's loyalty to fundamental New Dealism, disputing his claim to being a "liberal" and asserting that he had been a "pawn of Wall Street." Douglas had cooperated with the conservative business community, Schwellenbach boosters pointed out, while their man had earned a reputation as one of the foremost antibusiness radicals of the New Deal.

At the height of the dispute over Douglas's New Deal loyalty, Douglas captured newspaper headlines with his most outspoken attack on the financial community since he had broken off negotiations with the New York Stock Exchange sixteen months earlier. Responding to proposals by seventeen stock exchanges to modify government security regulations, Douglas blasted the plan as a "phoney." The SEC chairman added that "Opening things up so that the boys in the Street can have another party isn't going to help recovery."

The attack caught the financial community by surprise. It shouldn't have. No one, wrote the *Times*'s Arthur Krock, should have expected Douglas to give exchange proposals to water down New Deal legislation "impersonal, non-political consideration." Douglas was now a leading candidate for the Court vacancy as well as the SEC chairman that the financial community had come to respect, if not love. "This correspondent," wrote Krock, "happens to believe that Douglas was wholly sincere in disapproving the proposals though the use of the word 'phoney' and of certain other expressions suggested a wish to prove his loyalty to the acts he is administering." In short, Douglas pounced on the Exchange proposals as a means to prove his New Deal loyalty, and effectively squelched rumors, spread by Schwellenbach supporters, that he had become a prisoner of Wall Street.

March 19, 1939, was a bright, springlike day in Washington and Douglas decided to celebrate with a game of golf at the Manor Country Club. The game was interrupted, however, by a summons to the White House. As Douglas told the story, he entered the Oval Office to speak to the President, certain that he would be offered another administrative job, this time as chairman of the Federal Communications Commission. He dreaded the meeting and the anticipated offer, Douglas later wrote, because he had already decided to accept the deanship at the Yale Law School.

"I have a new job for you," Roosevelt told Douglas. "It's a mean job, a dirty job, a thankless job."

Douglas wrote that at that moment his heart sank, as, in his mind, the President had described the FCC chairmanship perfectly. After continuing the tease for a few moments more, Roosevelt finally said, "Tomorrow I am sending your name to the Senate as Louis Brandeis' successor."

In the U.S. Senate, only Lynn T. Frazier of North Dakota took the Senate floor to oppose the nomination. A somewhat eccentric populist, Senator Frazier worried about Douglas's "intimate connections with the Stock Exchanges and with Wall Street." Frazier also was troubled by the absence of any public record by the nominee on the subjects of progressive farm and labor legislation. Most important, Frazier was not persuaded that Douglas was dedicated to the cause of civil rights and liberties.

PART FOUR:

MR. JUSTICE DOUGLAS
—THE EARLY YEARS

CHAPTER SIXTEEN

THE SHORT REIGN OF FELIX FRANKFURTER

THE GREAT CHIEF JUSTICE John Marshall established in 1803 the U.S. Supreme Court's authority to review an act of Congress. Since that time, the Court's essential role in guiding the Republic has been seriously challenged several times, but never for very long or with permanently debilitating results. The Court's success can be attributed to wisdom and luck and, perhaps most of all, to the justices' sensitivity to the dominant political currents at work in the nation.

On the few occasions that the justices entered the political arena, bloated with the image of their own importance, they were quickly reminded of their place. That happened in 1857, for example, when the Court attempted, by the force of a single judicial opinion, to solve the slavery issue once and for all. It did not work. Abolitionists railed against the so-called wise men of the Court, who could perpetuate the moral and constitutional wrong that blacks were chattel. "Accustomed to trample on the rights of others," said Abraham Lincoln, addressing the Court rhetorically, "you have lost the genius of your own independence."

And indeed, the Court did lose a large measure of independence with its *Dred Scott* decision. For the decision was, in Chief Justice Charles Evans Hughes's phrase, a "self-inflicted wound," so blatantly political that for several years few took the Court very seriously. In time, by force of hard work and careful, rational judicial opinions, the Court once again built its reputation for responsible decision-making in the constitutional scheme. It did so by working the fringes of the political arena, advising and even prodding the executive and legislative branches of government, but rarely openly challenging their authority.

In 1935 and 1936, the conservative Court majority forgot the lesson of history. Infuriated by what they perceived as the creeping socialism of the New Deal, the justices struck several reverberating blows for the old order. In the process, the Court tore great chunks out of the New Deal program of recovery legislation. The National Industrial Recovery Act, the Bituminous Coal Act and the Agricultural Adjustment Act fell. The Court also took aim at a state law, New York's statute providing minimum wages for women, and, again, lectured a legislature; the minimum wage legislation, the Court declared, interfered with the freedom of contract between an employer and women employees.

The Court's assault on the New Deal and similar attempts at social and economic reform at the state level naturally produced a fusillade of criticism. How could a handful of old men in black robes thwart the majoritarian will? It was a question asked throughout the country, but most importantly, at the White House. For Franklin D. Roosevelt, braced by the greatest landslide victory in modern American political history, decided that he could challenge the Court's work as they had his. The President's Court-packing plan followed. FDR proposed that he appoint one new justice for every sitting justice over seventy; that would have given him six appointments and effective control of the Court. The justices looked on uncomfortably while the political debate over the Court's fate raged. In the spring of 1937, one member of the Court majority, Justice Owen Roberts, changed his attitude and vote in several critical cases involving reform legislation. The Court was asked to rule on a state minimum wage law, not unlike the New York statute that it had knocked down only nine months earlier. This time, however, Justice Roberts voted with Justices Louis D. Brandeis, Benjamin N. Cardozo, Harlan F. Stone and Chief Justice Hughes to uphold the law. Two weeks later, an astonished nation learned that the same majority of five justices had upheld the constitutionality of the National Labor Relations Act. Finally, on May 24, 1937, the Court retreated further from its previously defiant posture, this time finding the Social Security Act constitutional.

And so the New Deal survived and, perhaps even more significantly, so did the U.S. Supreme Court. The Court-packing plan was defeated shortly after the Court's dramatic turnabout. That defeat suggested that Americans cherished the Court as an institution, no matter how wrong-headed they thought those who populated that institution might be.

But there was another inescapable lesson of the internecine war. The modern Supreme Court, like its wiser predecessors, would have to announce its constitutional principles clearly but never without considerable respect for the political process. For the post-1937 Court, that meant that the justices would leave social and economic legislation—no matter how unwise they thought it to be—to the policy-makers in the other branches of government. The primary constitutional mission after William O. Douglas took his place on the Court would be of a different sort —not to favor one economic or social philosophy over another, but rather to define the constitutional dimensions of civil rights and liberties.

By the time Douglas was sworn in by Chief Justice Hughes on April 17, 1939, it was clear that Roosevelt had lost the Court-packing plan but won the Court. At first Justice Roberts's switch had been responsible. Later FDR owed a debt to the justices' mortality; in the next five years, Justices Willis Van Devanter, George Sutherland, Benjamin Cardozo, Louis Brandeis, Pierce Butler, James McReynolds and Chief Justice Charles Evans Hughes either retired or died in office.

When he first had the opportunity to appoint a man to the Court, Roosevelt thought long and carefully about his selection. Having struggled with a hostile Court majority for his first four years in office, FDR wanted to be absolutely certain that he put men on the Court who were loyal New Dealers. For his first appointment, the President chose an unquestioned Roosevelt loyalist, Senator Hugo Black of Alabama. His second appointee was equally safe, FDR's Solicitor General, Stanley Reed. New Dealers and constitutionalists alike applauded Roosevelt's third choice, Professor Felix Frankfurter of the Harvard Law School. SEC Chairman William O. Douglas and Attorney General Frank Murphy soon followed, and a New Deal majority was a reality. Who would lead the new Roosevelt majority away from an assault on the New Deal and toward a sturdy protection of individual rights? Civil libertarians had no doubt of their man. It would be Felix Frankfurter.

At the time of his Court appointment, Felix Frankfurter was not only the nation's preeminent constitutional scholar but so eloquent a defender of unpopular causes that Justice Brandeis had said he was "the most useful lawyer in the United States." The Frankfurter civil liberties record began in 1917, after he had been appointed by President Woodrow Wilson as counsel to a commission investigating the case of Tom Mooney. Mooney, a labor leader, had been convicted and sentenced to death for alleged complicity in a bomb explosion that killed many people in a San Francisco Preparedness Day parade in 1916. The presidential commission filed a report, written by Frankfurter, charging that Mooney's conviction had been obtained by perjured testimony and recommending that Mooney be given a new trial. President Wilson made the request of the California governor, but the governor limited his response to commuting Mooney's sentence to life imprisonment. "Free Tom Mooney" became a libertarian rallying cry for two decades.

Shortly after he had filed his report on Mooney, Frankfurter was again asked by President Wilson to investigate an alleged injustice, this time involving a thousand striking miners in Bisbee, Arizona. The miners had been rounded up by a local vigilante group in 1917 and put on a train to New Mexico, where they were dumped without food and water. Frankfurter concluded that the treatment of the miners was "brutality and injustice in the raw." By this time, Frankfurter's investigations had scandalized American conservatives and inspired Teddy Roosevelt to suggest that Frankfurter's attitude was suspiciously similar to "Trotsky and the other Bolshevik leaders in Russia."

The attacks hardly discouraged Frankfurter. He fought the Palmer "Red" deportations of the early twenties and joined in a *Report Upon the Illegal Practices of the United States Department of Justice,* which attacked such actions as arrests without warrants, illegal searches and seizures and the use of provocative agents. He assisted Roger Baldwin in organizing the American Civil Liberties Union and headed the legal defense of the Amalgamated Clothing Workers against an injunction that would have destroyed the union. And his 1927 article in the *Atlantic Monthly* cataloguing the injustices in the Sacco-Vanzetti case touched the conscience of the nation.

No wonder that civil libertarians across the country rejoiced with the announcement of Frankfurter's appointment to the Court. There was no room for doubt, as there was with Hugo Black, who had once been a member of the Ku Klux Klan, or Bill Douglas, who had spent his entire professional life in the field of commercial law. *The Nation* magazine, which later expressed misgivings about Douglas's dedication to civil liberties after Roosevelt announced his appointment to the Court, hailed Frankfurter: "From the time he was instrumental in saving Mooney from execution to his defense of Sacco and Vanzetti, Frankfurter has shown his devotion to justice and his courage."

There was still another reason for libertarians to celebrate. A Frankfurter on the Court would mean more than one solid vote in civil liberties cases. By force of his knowledge, experience and personality, it was thought, Frankfurter would forge a new liberal majority on the Court, which, liberals suspected, had been frustrated in the past by Chief Justice Hughes. "What is urgently needed at this time," Solicitor General Robert Jackson wrote Roosevelt shortly before the Frankfurter appointment, "is someone who can interpret the Constitution with the scholarship and with sufficient assurance to face Chief Justice Hughes in conference and hold his own in discussion." Jackson's choice was Frankfurter.

When word of Frankfurter's Court appointment had spread through New Deal Washington, Tom Corcoran burst into Harold

Ickes's office at the Department of the Interior with two magnums of champagne. Soon a small group, including Douglas, Jackson, Harry Hopkins and Frank Murphy, had gathered to celebrate. "We were all very happy," Ickes wrote. "All of us regard this as the most significant and worthwhile thing that the President has done. He has solidified his Supreme Court victory, and regardless of who may be President during the next few years, there will be on the bench of the Supreme Court a group of liberals under aggressive, forthright and intelligent leadership."

Frankfurter had accepted his leadership assignment enthusiastically. In fact, he had been advising one Roosevelt appointee, even before his own appointment. "Do you know Black well?" a worried Justice Stone had asked Frankfurter while he was still at Harvard. "You might be able to render him great assistance. He needs guidance from someone who is more familiar with the workings of the judicial process than he. . . . There are enough present-day battles to be won without wasting our efforts to re-make the Constitution *ab initio,* or using the judicial power as a political tract."

Frankfurter happily had obliged Stone. "Judges cannot escape the responsibility of filling in gaps which the finitude of even the most imaginative legislation renders inevitable," he wrote Black. "So the problem is not whether the judges make the law, but when and how much. . . . I used to say to my students that legislatures make law wholesale, judges retail. In other words they cannot decide things by invoking a new major premise out of whole cloth; they must make the law that they do make out of the existing materials with due deference to the presuppositions of the legal system of which they have been made a part. . . ."

It was a role that had been familiar to Frankfurter for twenty-five years at the Harvard Law School, where he had introduced two generations of students to the complexities of constitutional law. That he was now "introducing" a new member of the U.S. Supreme Court to the same complexities did not cause Frankfurter to alter the lecture, though his tone was more respectful than it would have been with a law student.

After he had been sworn in as a member of the Court, Frankfurter went about his tasks as if he had trained for the job for a professional lifetime, which he had. No one revered the Court more or knew its history so intimately as Frankfurter. In a world filled with stupid, often irrational, acts by governments and individuals, the Court, for Felix Frankfurter, remained sacred—at least, as sacred as his incessantly questioning mind would permit. The Constitution was the holy writ and the Justices the secular priests, interpreting the meaning of the document with the tool that Frankfurter most respected: reason.

At oral argument, he peppered counsel with tough, probing constitutional questions. When the lawyer's responses to the former Harvard professor's questions were disappointing or worse, Frankfurter did not hide his disdain. He was conducting a seminar, no longer at the Harvard Law School, to be sure, but a seminar nonetheless. He led the sessions with professorial certainty and his students, now counsel appearing before the Court, jumped to his every intellectual command.

In judicial conference, where the nine justices discussed the pending cases, Frankfurter's knowledge of the Court and the Constitution, his strong analytical powers, his energy and insatiable intellectual curiosity, were on impressive display six days a week. But the sheer bulk of his learning and his incurable habit of communicating it endlessly to his colleagues soon began to irritate. Justice Stone, for example, privately chafed at Frankfurter's "zeal for self expression." And Frankfurter's close friend Judge Learned Hand, of the U.S. Court of Appeals for the Second Circuit, made the same point another way: "He's too discursive. . . . If you're discursive, people get lost."

When the justices were not in formal session, Frankfurter continued to conduct his business with zeal. At Harvard, Frankfurter had been the inveterate communicator who, through letter or lecture or informal chat, sought and usually found a grateful audience. It would be no different on the Court. Frankfurter walked the corridors when the Court was not in session as if it were his private estate, dropping in on his colleagues at will for serious conversation about cases and the Constitution. When he returned to his office, Frankfurter dashed off memoranda, just to clear up a point or two.

As long as his colleagues appreciated his position, Frankfurter could be soothingly accommodating. Almost humble. But when there was a clash of wills, Frankfurter jumped into the intellectual brawl ferociously. He used every weapon in his arsenal—history, logic and rhetoric, flattery, guile and sarcasm. This was Frankfurter's battleground and he did not often lose a skirmish. When he did, he did not lose it gracefully.

"I am bound to say," Frankfurter wrote Douglas about an early Douglas court opinion, "that it is bad for both of us that we are no longer professors. Because if you were still a professor, you would have written a different elaboration and if I were still a professor, I would get several lectures out of what you have written." In another case, Douglas, according to Frankfurter, did not "disclose what you are really doing. As you know, I am no poker player and naturally, therefore, I do not believe in poker playing in the disposition of cases. Or has professoring for twenty five years disabled me from understanding the need for these involutions?"

Frankfurter's needling particularly irritated Justices Douglas, Black and Murphy. They could not claim Frankfurter's background in constitutional law, but they were hardly callow law students ready to sit at the professor's feet. Despite their growing irritation, they deferred to Frankfurter's leadership in the early months of their collective judicial tenure. A dramatic test of that leadership came little more than a year after Frankfurter's appointment, in a case that presented a constitutional challenge to a school board's requirement that all students salute the American flag. The Court decision would prove to be the high-water mark of solidarity among the Roosevelt appointees. It would also sow the seed for their discontent, and in a very short time, result in the total disintegration of the alliance.

Lillian Gobitis, twelve years old, and her brother, William, ten, had attended the Minersville, Pennsylvania, public schools for years without incident. They were not troublemakers, and even after they were expelled by school superintendent Charles Roudbush, they did not think they had done anything wrong. True, they did not join their classmates, who were obeying an order of the Minersville school board, in saluting the American flag at the opening of their school exercises.

But Lillian and William Gobitis believed they were obeying a higher order, from the God Jehovah. For it was written in the twentieth chapter of Exodus that "Thou shall not make unto thee any graven image, or any likeness of any thing that is in the heaven above, or that is in the earth beneath, or that is in the water under the earth:/Thou shalt not bow down thyself to them, nor serve them." Saluting the American flag, their Jehovah's Witness training had taught them, was a form of worship forbidden by Chapter 20. If they disobeyed the God Jehovah, they believed, they would be punished by eternal annihilation.

At first, Lillian and William's father, Walter Gobitis, accepted the school board's edict and enrolled his children in private school. But as the costs mounted, so did Walter Gobitis's indignation. He decided to challenge in court the board's right to make all public school children salute the flag. Walter Gobitis had been tutored not only on Jehovah's Witness doctrine but also on the constitutional right provided by the First Amendment to freely exercise the beliefs of one's religion.

Judge Albert B. Maris, in the U.S. District Court for the Eastern District of Pennsylvania, ruled in favor of Walter Gobitis. "Our beloved flag, the emblem of religious liberty," Judge Maris wrote, "apparently has been used as an instrument to impose a religious test as a condition of receiving the benefits of public education. And this has been done without any compelling necessity of public safety or welfare." The Minersville school board appealed, but the U.S. Court of Appeals for the Third Circuit unanimously sustained Judge Maris's opinion. On three previous occasions, the U.S. Supreme Court had refused to grant certiorari* in cases in which the issues raised by the *Gobitis* case were argued. This time, however, the Court agreed to hear the appeal by the Minersville board of education.

No one outside the U.S. Supreme Court knows exactly why the justices agree to grant a cert petition, but there was ample material for speculation in the case of *Minersville School District* v. *Gobitis.* The time was 1940, and most thoughtful Americans believed that the United States could not, for long, resist the Allies' call

---

*Most cases come to the Court by petition for writ of certiorari. In these cases, the Court exercises discretionary jurisdiction. Four justices must vote to grant the certiorari petition before a case is put on the Court calendar for argument.

for help against Hitler. It seemed a ripe moment for the justices
to consider the extent to which a government could insist upon
a show of patriotism among its citizens. What better place to
decide this vital issue than in the sanctuary of reason, the U.S.
Supreme Court?

Chief Justice Charles Evans Hughes opened the discussion on
the *Gobitis* case at judicial conference. "I come up to this case like
a skittish horse to a brass band," he began. "There is nothing that
I have more profound belief in than religious freedom, so I must
bring myself to view this case on the question of state power." For
the Chief Justice, then, the debate would have to focus on a
balance between two important constitutional rights: religious
freedom and a state's authority to curb that freedom in the name
of a higher calling to patriotism among its young citizens. "As I
see it," Hughes concluded, "the state can insist on inculcation of
loyalty. It would be extraordinary if in this country the state could
not provide for respect for the flag of our land. . . ."

Would Felix Frankfurter take the side of individual liberty
against the Chief Justice, as so many libertarians had expected?
As an immigrant Jew, Frankfurter was particularly sensitive to the
agonies suffered by minorities. As a student of world history and
politics, he was acutely aware of the tyrannies of Adolf Hitler. The
Führer had his own way of dealing with troublesome minorities,
including the very minorities involved in the *Gobitis* case. In Germany, the Jehovah's Witnesses were called Earnest Bible Students, and in 1935 Hitler had called them "quacks," destroyed all
their literature and confiscated their property.

Although sympathetic to the Witnesses' problem, Frankfurter
was a complicated man with complex allegiances. He believed in
civil liberties but also in judicial restraint where the Court was
asked to second-guess the wisdom of decisions of other branches
of government. He was a member of a minority but he was also
an American and no one could have been prouder of that fact. "I
can express with very limited adequacy," he once said, "the passionate devotion to this land that possesses millions of our people, born like myself under other skies, for the privilege this
country has bestowed in allowing them to partake of its fellowship." And so, with passion, tempered by the reason he so revered, Felix Frankfurter told his colleagues that the Court must

not strike down the school board's flag-salute requirement. To do otherwise, said Frankfurter, would show a disrespect for state authorities, who were more responsive to the popular will than were the nine insulated members of the Court. Besides, the salute was inspired by the highest public purpose: inculcation of loyalty in the young citizens of the country.

The vote in judicial conference was eight to one in favor of the Minersville school board regulation. Frankfurter's argument had persuaded every Roosevelt appointee, not just Stanley Reed, but Frank Murphy and Hugo Black and William O. Douglas. Only Justice Harlan F. Stone dissented. Both Frankfurter and Justice Owen Roberts suggested that the Chief Justice write the majority opinion himself. No, said Hughes, the opinion was properly Frankfurter's to write "because of his moving statement at conference on the role of the public school in instilling love of country in our pluralistic society."

Frankfurter was mindful of the importance of his opinion not only to those who would agree with him but to libertarians who would not. He began by admitting the constitutional conflict in the *Gobitis* case between liberty and authority, heightened because "the liberty invoked is liberty of conscience and the authority is the authority to safeguard the nation's fellowship." Having posed the judicial dilemma, Frankfurter proceeded to resolve it. A salute to the American flag ("the emblem of freedom in its truest, best sense") was no violation of an individual's conscience nor an invitation to government tyranny. "It mocks reason and denies our whole history," Frankfurter wrote, "to find in the allowance of a requirement to salute our flag on fitting occasions the seeds of sanction for obeisance to a leader." Frankfurter concluded with a reminder that "to the legislature no less than to courts is committed the guardianship of deeply-cherished liberties." The wisdom of the flag-salute requirement, then, should be argued "in the forum of public opinion and before legislative assemblies rather than to transfer such a contest to the judicial arena."

On the day the *Gobitis* decision was announced, Frankfurter disappointed those who attended the Court session by merely declaring the result in the case, leaving to the printed record his full analysis. The drama immediately followed Frankfurter's announcement. While Justices Frankfurter, Reed, Black, Douglas and Murphy—Roosevelt's "liberal" appointees—sat in silence, Justice Harlan F. Stone, a Republican appointed by President Calvin Coolidge, leaned forward in his chair to read, in a deep, impassioned voice, the single dissenting opinion, defending the Gobitis children. Stone conceded that certain government obligations outweighed the objections of individuals' religious beliefs. The government could make war and raise armies, for example, even though some draftees might object that military training conflicted with their religious beliefs. But that government power did not include forcing "these children to express a sentiment which, as they interpret it, they do not entertain, and which violates their deepest religious convictions." For Stone, "The Constitution expresses more than the conviction of the people that democratic processes must be preserved at all costs. It is also an expression of faith and a command that freedom of mind and spirit must be preserved, which *government* must obey, if it is to adhere to that justice and moderation without which no free government can exist."

Stone was alone on the Court, but he won a larger majority. One hundred and seventy-one newspapers and almost every law review in the country supported his dissent. "We think this decision of the United States Supreme Court is dead wrong," an editorial in the *St. Louis Post-Dispatch* declared. "If patriotism depends upon such things as this—upon violation of a fundamental right of religious freedom,—then it becomes not a noble emotion of love for country, but something to be rammed down our throat by the law." Benjamin V. Cohen wrote to only one justice after the *Gobitis* decision, and it was to neither of his close friends Frankfurter and Douglas. "When a liberal judge holds out alone against his liberal brethren," Cohen wrote Justice Stone, "I think he ought to know when he has spoken not for himself alone, but has superbly articulated the thoughts of his contemporaries who believe with him in an effective but tolerant democracy."

Perhaps Eleanor Roosevelt best expressed the disappointment among libertarians in the Frankfurter opinion. She did not question Frankfurter's reasoning or legal scholarship, but suggested that "there seemed to be something wrong with an opinion that forced little children to salute a flag when such a ceremony was repugnant to their conscience." The decision, Eleanor Roosevelt feared, would generate intolerance, particularly in a period of rising war hysteria. In the months following the *Gobitis* decision, her fear became prophecy. The meeting hall of Jehovah's Witnesses was burned in Kennebunkport, Maine, their automobiles were overturned in Litchfield, Illinois, and they were banned entirely from the city of Jackson, Mississippi.

Neither the wave of intolerance against the Jehovah's Witnesses nor the condemnation of his *Gobitis* opinion by scholars and respected friends shook Frankfurter's belief that he was correct. He would, in years to come, rethink the issue, but he would not change his mind. Justices Douglas, Black and Murphy, however, did not share Frankfurter's certainty and they would, in a short time, take the other side of the argument.

The defection of Black, Douglas and Murphy from Frankfurter's leadership began only seven months after *Gobitis,* with a First Amendment challenge that brought together in companion cases two improbable bedfellows, the conservative *Los Angeles Times* and the militant leftist West Coast labor leader Harry Bridges. The issue was "trial by newspaper." Both the *Times* and Bridges had been found in contempt by state courts for trying to intimidate the judiciary. In angry editorials, the *Times* had urged a judge, while sentence was pending, to commit two convicted members of a labor "goon squad" to state prison. Bridges had sent a telegram, later published, threatening the Secretary of Labor with a longshoremen's strike if a state court enforced what he termed an "outrageous" decision in a labor dispute.

The cases presented a confrontation between the First Amendment's guarantee of free speech and press and the Sixth Amendment's equally explicit guarantee of a fair trial. More important, perhaps, they presented the Roosevelt appointees with an opportunity to give further thought and expression to their views on civil liberties.

The Court majority, including Justices Black, Douglas, Murphy, Reed and newly appointed Justice Robert Jackson, overturned the contempt citations in *Bridges* v. *California.* The state courts had no right to inhibit speech, said Justice Black, speaking for the majority, unless it could be shown that there was a "clear and present danger"* to the judicial process. To prove this, the state would have to show that the threat was extremely serious and the likelihood of its taking place was imminent. A genuine threat to a fair trial would be beyond the pale, Black admitted, but the *Times*'s acerbic editorials and the publication of Bridges's telegram did not even come close to meeting the standard. That judges might find such criticism disrespectful and, perhaps, intimidating did not bother Black. "The assumption that respect for the judiciary can be won by shielding judges from published criticism wrongly appraises the character of American public opinion. For it is a prized American privilege to speak one's mind, although not always with perfect good taste, on all public institutions."

At first blush, it seemed as if the Court majority was accepting a balancing test, between state authority and individual liberties, not unlike the process by which Frankfurter had sanctioned the compulsory flag salute in *Gobitis*. The majority had, after all, recognized that a state court might issue a contempt citation if the fairness of a trial was seriously and immediately threatened by speech. But on closer analysis, it was clear that the majority gave considerably more weight to the civil liberties guarantees of the First Amendment than Frankfurter had done in *Gobitis*. It was difficult to conceive of an actual situation that would have satisfied the majority that a "clear and present danger" existed. An exhortation to "get the judge" delivered in the courtroom or in the courthouse lobby, perhaps. But short of that, the majority seemed to say that the First Amendment freedom would prevail, its protection bordering on absolute immunity from government interference.

Sensing the potency of the majority's view, Justice Frankfurter, in dissent, argued that the "clear and present danger" test was a useless label for judging complicated issues of clashing constitutional doctrines. The editorials and telegram presented a "real and substantial threat" to an impartial judicial decision, and for Frankfurter, that was the decisive fact. "To be sure, the majority do not in so many words hold that trial by newspaper has consti-

---

*The "clear and present danger" test was first articulated by Justice Oliver Wendell Holmes in 1919.

tutional sanction," he wrote. "But the atmosphere of their opinion and several of its phrases mean that or they mean nothing."

Protection of free speech was not limitless, Frankfurter said, and here the potential threat to the judicial process was enough to stop it. Could a court in Washington, D.C. be so certain that the telegram or the editorial published in California presented no threat to the state judicial system? Frankfurter wouldn't risk that judgment and he did not think the majority should have, either.

With *Bridges,* Frankfurter lost his hold on the Roosevelt appointees. Black no longer accepted the Harvard don's counsel and, to Frankfurter's chagrin, neither did Douglas, Murphy and Stanley Reed. Reed's defection was temporary, but for Black, Douglas and Murphy, *Bridges* marked a constitutional turning point. There would still be talk of balancing state interests against those of the First Amendment, but for Black, Douglas and Murphy, now the scales were emphatically tipped toward the First Amendment guarantees.

A second case, decided by the U.S. Supreme Court only six months after *Bridges,* would present Black, Douglas and Murphy with yet another opportunity to declare their philosophical independence from Frankfurter. It involved a forty-three-year-old unemployed farm hand named Smith Betts, who was accused of committing an armed robbery near a country store in Carroll County, Maryland. According to the indictment and the testimony of prosecution witnesses, Betts had approached the car of a country store employee, drawn a pistol from his overcoat and demanded the money the employee held in a brown bag in his hand. When the employee, a young man named Norman Bollinger, hesitated, the holdup man cocked the pistol hammer. Bollinger then handed over the bag, containing fifty dollars in coin which he had taken from the store register only minutes before. Betts, who had already served time for larceny, was known in the neighborhood and was quickly picked up by police as their prime suspect.

At his arraignment, Betts had pleaded not guilty, told the judge that he had no money, and asked the court to appoint an attorney to represent him. The judge said that the practice in Carroll County was to appoint counsel for indigent defendants only if they were charged with capital crimes, such as murder or rape, for which they could be given the death penalty. Betts, though too poor to hire his own attorney, would have to represent himself since he was accused only of armed robbery.

At the trial, the prosecutor had begun with a list of witnesses from the country store who placed Betts near the store at dusk (the time of the robbery) and described the overcoat, dark glasses and "rough voice" of the robber. The victim, Norman Bollinger, then gave a similar description of the robber, pointed to Betts and said he was the man who had demanded, at pistol point, the brown bag containing fifty dollars. Betts's cross-examination was brief and ineffective. His defense consisted of the testimony of a few witnesses, including his common-law wife, who presented vague and not always consistent statements that placed Betts far from the country store at the time of the robbery. The judge found Betts guilty and sentenced him to eight years in the Maryland penitentiary.

Had Betts been represented by professional counsel, his defense surely would have been conducted differently. A trained defense counsel could, for example, have given the prosecution's key witness, Norman Bollinger, a very hard time on the witness stand. The armed robbery occurred at dusk and Bollinger admitted that he could not see the robber's face. He identified the robber only as wearing an overcoat and amber dark glasses and as speaking in a "rough voice." That is the kind of vague identification that makes aggressive defense attorneys salivate. Betts had been identified at the police station only after police forced him to wear an overcoat and amber dark glasses and speak to Norman Bollinger, not in a line-up, but alone. An attorney, had Betts had one, would have challenged that station house identification (on which the prosecution's case hung) as too contrived to have been used as evidence against Betts.

These challenges were not made by Smith Betts. From his prison cell, however, Betts had second thoughts about his defense and sought a writ of habeas corpus against the warden of the Maryland penitentiary, charging that he had been denied his constitutional right to the assistance of counsel. His petition was heard by the chief judge of the Court of Appeals of Maryland, who rejected Betts's claim because the defendant seemed to be a man with "an ordinary amount of intelligence and the ability to take care of his own interests on a trial of this narrow issue" (the identity of the robber).

The U.S. Supreme Court, in *Betts* v. *Brady,* upheld the state court ruling by a six to three vote, with Black, Douglas and Murphy dissenting. Although recognizing that a *federal* court was obligated to appoint counsel in a felony trial if a defendant was too poor to hire one, the Court majority said the same rule did not apply to the states. In state court trials, the court majority insisted only that the process conform to its notion of "fundamental fairness." Smith Betts's trial did not violate that standard, the Court majority said. The defendant, a man of "ordinary" intelligence, had cross-examined prosecution witnesses and presented witnesses in his own behalf; he had, in short, defended himself adequately.

That was not good enough for Black, Douglas and Murphy, who preferred to anchor Betts's constitutional rights at trial to the right to counsel guaranteed in federal courts by the Sixth Amendment. Black, writing for the three dissenters, said that right, which applied to *federal* trials, had been extended to the states when the framers wrote the Fourteenth Amendment.* But even if the Court majority would not accept his theory that the right to counsel was guaranteed by the Fourteenth Amendment, Black said Smith Betts should have received a new trial. To be deprived of counsel merely because of poverty, Black declared, was a violation of "fundamental fairness." Without counsel, Black concluded, a defendant was denied "the promise of our democratic society to provide equal justice under the law."

Unlike *Bridges,* the second wedge between Frankfurter and fellow Roosevelt appointees Black, Douglas and Murphy did not center on the issue of balancing governmental interests against those of the individual. In *Betts,* Frankfurter embraced the traditional notion of federalism, allowing the states to set their own rules for criminal trials within broad limits. Black, Douglas and Murphy wanted to enlarge the protections given individual defendants—in state as well as federal trials—by applying the spe-

---

*Black believed that the Fourteenth Amendment "incorporated" the privileges and protections of the Bill of Rights and applied them to the states.

cific guarantees of the Bill of Rights to the states through the
Fourteenth Amendment. Implicit in the dissenter's view was the
belief that a criminal defendant was usually poor and relatively
defenseless against the power of the state. The guarantees of the
Bill of Rights, they believed, provided essential protections for
the accused in state as well as federal trials. This basic difference
in philosophical approach would lock the two factions in taut
intellectual debate for two decades. In 1942 the debate focused
on the Sixth Amendment guarantees, but later the argument
would spread both up and down the Bill of Rights.

If Frankfurter harbored any doubts that his influence over
Black, Douglas and Murphy, so impressive only two years before,
was gone, that shattering fact was communicated formally and
with finality in *Jones* v. *Opelika,* another decision in which the
Court grappled with the constitutional claims of Jehovah's Witnesses. Members of the Witnesses had been convicted for not
paying a municipal licensing fee required to sell their religious
publications. The issue was essentially the same as that raised in
Gobitis: what are the limits of government interference with the
free exercise of religion? As in *Gobitis,* the Court majority ruled
that the government restraint (the licensing fee) on religious
practice was constitutional. But for Felix Frankfurter, there was
an ominous difference. Black, Douglas and Murphy no longer
voted with him in the majority. Even more remarkable than the
complete turnabout by three justices in so short a time (barely
two years) was the manner in which they repented for their earlier
Gobitis votes. In addition to joining a dissent by Chief Justice
Stone (who, since *Gobitis,* had replaced Hughes as Chief Justice),
the three issued a statement confessing their error in *Gobitis:*

> The opinion of the Court sanctions a device which in our opinion
> suppresses or tends to suppress the free exercise of religion
> practiced by a minority group. This is but another step in the
> direction which *Minersville School District v. Gobitis* took against the
> same religious minority and is a logical extension of the princi-
> ples upon which that decision rested. Since we joined in the
> opinion in the *Gobitis* case, we think this is an appropriate occa-
> sion to state that we now believe it was also wrongly decided.
> Certainly our democratic form of government functioning under
> the historic Bill of Rights has a high responsibility to accommo-

date itself to the religious views of minorities, however unpopular and unorthodox those views may be. The First Amendment does not put the right freely to exercise religion in a subordinate position. We fear, however, that the opinions in this and in the *Gobitis* case do exactly that.

The reign of Felix Frankfurter had been short. The revolt of Black, Douglas and Murphy was now an irrevocable fact. Frankfurter would go his philosophical way and Black, Douglas and Murphy, theirs. The parting, however, would not be an amicable one, but would be followed by vicious personal attacks as well as bitter public disagreement.

CHAPTER SEVENTEEN

AN UNCLUTTERED MIND

FELIX FRANKFURTER took his loss of leadership over his fellow Roosevelt appointees bitterly. He began to refer to Douglas, Black and Murphy scathingly as "the Axis"* and angrily denounced each of them in his diary. Frank Murphy was the easiest target since he clearly could not compete intellectually with the others. Frankfurter found Murphy's opinions hopelessly result-oriented: "We are not sitting as Santa Clauses," he once wrote Murphy. But Frankfurter's contempt for Murphy was not confined to his judicial opinions. He spoke disparagingly of Murphy's love of night life, repeating a quote attributed to a chorus girl: "Us girls call him 'Murph.' "

Frankfurter's displeasure with Hugo Black was based on very different grounds. Black had rejected Frankfurter's philosophy of judicial restraint, preferring a literal interpretation of the Bill of Rights more suitable to his activist temperament. There was,

---

*Frankfurter included a fourth member of the Court, Associate Justice Wiley Rutledge, after he was appointed in 1943 and often joined Black, Douglas and Murphy in dissent.

William O. Douglas and family at the turn of the century. Left to right: W.O.D., Julia, Arthur and Martha.

Douglas as an undergraduate at Whitman College, 1919.
(Mildred Douglas Read)

Douglas (center) holds his first news conference as Chairman of the Securities and Exchange Commission, September 22, 1937. (*Bettmann Archive*)

Douglas relaxes after tellin reporters of his appointment to the U.S. Supreme Court, 1939.
(*Bettmann Archive*)

Douglas in his chambers at the Court with his son, Bill Junior, shortly before he took the oath of office on April 17, 1939. *(Wide World)*

At home with the Douglas family, 1946. W.O.D. and Mildred with their children, Millie and Bill Junior, and spaniel, Colonial. *(Culver Pictures)*

Honorary pallbearers at the funeral of Chief Justice Harlan F. Stone, 1946. Left to right: Associate Justice Hugo L. Black, former Chief Justice Charles Evans Hughes, Associate Justices Stanley F. Reed, William O. Douglas and Wiley Rutledge. *(UPI)*

Members of the Supreme Court sit for the official group photo, January, 1947. Front row, left to right: Felix Frankfurter, Hugo Black, Fred Vinson, Stanley Reed, William O. Douglas. Back row, left to right: Wiley Rutledge, Frank Murphy, Robert H. Jackson, Harold Burton. *(Curator's Office, U.S. Supreme Court)*

...ouglas poses on horse in January ...50, in Arizona where he was re...perating from a serious horseback ...ing accident suffered in the ...scades. *(Wide World)*

Fred Rodell (left) and W.O.D. at the Douglas cabin, Lostine, Oregon, 1951. *(Michael Rodell)*

...cretary of the Interior Douglas McKay (left) waves to W.O.D. and his group of ...kers as they completed their 180-mile hike along the C & O Canal from Cumber-...d, Maryland to Washington, D.C. in 1954. *(UPI)*

Robert F. Kennedy (left) and Douglas pose in ceremonial robes during their tour of the Soviet Union in 1955. *(Wide World)*

Queen Elizabeth and Prince Philip greet Douglas and his second wife, Mercedes, at a reception given in the Queen's honor at the British Embassy in Washington, D.C., 1957. *(UPI)*

Douglas and his third wife, Joan, at a White House reception in 1963 for the Supreme Court Justices. *(UPI)*

Douglas and his fourth wife, Cathy, drink a toast after their wedding in Encino, California, July 15, 1966. *(UPI)*

Chief Justice Warren E. Burger and
Douglas at a dinner in 1973 honoring
Douglas for serving longer than any
other justice in Supreme Court history.
(Wide World)

On his 77th birthday, October 16, 1975,
Douglas is wheeled down the walk of his
home by his aide, Harry Datcher. *(UPI)*

Cathy Douglas unveils a bust of her husband on the C & O Canal, 1977.
(Washington Post)

however, considerably more behind the conflict than philosophical abstractions. Black's powerful mind was a match for Frankfurter's, though Frankfurter only grudgingly accepted that fact. "Felix thought he was smarter than everybody else," said Philip Elman, one of Frankfurter's earliest and most devoted law clerks, and later assistant to the U.S. Solicitor General.

As infuriating to Frankfurter as Black's refusal to bow to Frankfurter's reason was the moral passion that lay behind Black's position. "Every time we have that which should be merely an intellectual difference," wrote Frankfurter, "it gets into a championship by Black of justice and right and decency and everything and those who take the other view are impliedly always made out to be the oppressors of the people and the supporters of some exploiting interest." What made matters worse for Frankfurter was Black's ability to persuade his colleagues, notably Douglas, Murphy and Rutledge, as Frankfurter could not, that his position was not only morally correct but constitutionally sound.

Frankfurter's relationship with Black fluctuated between love and hate throughout their twenty-three tumultuous years together on the Court. With Douglas, Frankfurter's annoyance quickly turned to unmitigated hatred of such intensity that the two justices did not speak to each other for extended periods of time. Frankfurter once called Douglas one of the "two completely evil men I have ever met." Douglas, alone among members of the Court, did not attend Frankfurter's funeral.

To Frankfurter, Douglas was an unprincipled opportunist who was forever running for political office from his Court seat. Douglas was, according to Frankfurter, "the most systematic exploiter of flattery I have ever known." His judicial opinions, Frankfurter was convinced, were singularly calculated to advance his political ambitions.

Douglas was no less suspicious of Frankfurter. Though he did not accuse Frankfurter of seeking political office for himself, Douglas believed, with considerable justification, that Frankfurter went to extraordinary lengths to perpetuate his political and judicial philosophies. Frankfurter's role as political adviser to Roosevelt was well known among Washington insiders; not so well known was Frankfurter's quiet lobbying with the Truman administration for the state of Israel. Douglas believed that

Frankfurter had also promoted his friend and colleague, Associate Justice Robert Jackson, for Secretary of State under Truman.

But that wasn't the end of it. Before and even after Frankfurter's death, Douglas suspected a cabal of Frankfurter admirers, including Professor Paul Freund of the Harvard Law School and Professor Alexander Bickel of the Yale Law School, of systematically promoting the Frankfurterian philosophy of judicial restraint in the law schools and the media (from the *New Republic* to *The New York Times*).

The Douglas-Frankfurter antipathy often extended to Frankfurter and Douglas law clerks and close friends. Yale Law Professor Fred Rodell, a former Douglas student and a lifelong friend, lashed out at Frankfurter's judicial restraint, which, Rodell believed, was an excuse to duck the tough constitutional questions. Professor Bickel, also at Yale but a former Frankfurter clerk and close friend, rarely missed an opportunity to criticize Douglas's opinions for sloppiness and logical incoherence. In time, even Rodell and Bickel did not speak to each other.

In Frankfurter's and Douglas's pre-Court days, there was no hint of the acrimonious split to come. When Douglas was the younger, appreciative academic colleague at Yale, Frankfurter accepted his respect and friendship with good grace and generosity. The mutual admiration continued through Douglas's SEC years, Frankfurter offering effusive congratulations on Douglas's SEC studies and Douglas gratefully accepting the praise.

Douglas's appointment to the Court changed the relationship; the junior colleague was now an equal. Moreover, Douglas and Frankfurter were poles apart temperamentally and their forced collegiality made the personality differences more pronounced. Douglas possessed a mischievous comic streak that Frankfurter did not appreciate. So, for example, when Douglas, straight-faced, told Frankfurter that he and Justice Black viewed him as a nut to be cracked, Frankfurter did not laugh. Douglas's humor was totally alien to the Austrian immigrant. "Douglas was a Westerner," said Abe Fortas. "He either worked or played. Felix never played and he never understood Douglas, who did. It caused him to underestimate Douglas."

Douglas was no better at appreciating Frankfurter. He did not approach his judicial task with Frankfurter's reverence, nor did he find Frankfurter's insistent discursiveness beneficial. At times, Douglas rudely showed his displeasure. Bored with an extensive Frankfurter presentation at judicial conference, Douglas would leave the conference table and plop down in a nearby easy chair.

A further source of irritation for Frankfurter was that Douglas had taken the seat of Frankfurter's mentor, Louis Brandeis. When the press played up Douglas as Brandeis's logical successor, and Douglas concurred in the commentary, it further rankled. In his diary, Frankfurter recalled a conversation he had had with Associate Justice Robert Jackson about Brandeis's successor. Jackson had told Frankfurter "that the line that is going round about Douglas is that he is the great successor and follower of Brandeis. As Jackson said, 'He has about as much in common with him as black has with white, but since his death, Douglas sees a great deal of Mrs. Brandeis so as to absorb Brandeis' philosophy through her.' Admirable woman that Alice Brandeis is," wrote Frankfurter, "to regard her as the spring at which one refreshes oneself on Brandeis' philosophy, is egregiously funny."

Even stripped of sarcasm, Frankfurter's (and Jackson's) charge that Douglas had nothing philosophically in common with Brandeis was totally unfounded,* particularly in the economic sphere. Throughout his years at the SEC, Douglas had shown that he understood Brandeisian economic theory and was willing and able to put it into practice. It was no different on the Court.

When major oil companies were charged with fixing gasoline prices in violation of the Sherman Anti-Trust Act, the stage was perfectly set for Douglas to demonstrate that the Brandeisian economic philosophy would continue to have a spokesman on the Court. Dismissing a series of earlier Court decisions which sanctioned prices set by monopolies so long as they were reasonable, Douglas said *any* monopolistic combination to fix prices was illegal under the Sherman Anti-Trust Act. Period. "Those who fixed reasonable prices today would perpetuate unreasonable prices tomorrow," Douglas wrote. "Those who controlled the prices would control or effectively dominate the market. And those who were in that strategic position would have it in their

---

*Brandeis's biographer, Alpheus Thomas Mason, wrote that Brandeis was pleased that Douglas was his successor.

power to destroy or drastically imperil the competitive system."

Besides Brandeis, Frankfurter's and Douglas's hagiology included a second public servant, President Franklin D. Roosevelt. Both Douglas and Frankfurter had been appointed to the Court with reputations as loyal New Dealers and confidants of Roosevelt. Though neither admitted it, Frankfurter and Douglas competed for influence with FDR after their appointments. Both eagerly maintained their contacts with the White House, discussing domestic politics and foreign affairs with the President. The personal friendship was equally important. When, for example, FDR sent flowers to Julia Douglas's funeral in 1941, Douglas was deeply touched.

Douglas offered the President two gifts that FDR cherished—and that Frankfurter could not match: an irreverent sense of humor and a very good game of poker. Shortly after Douglas's appointment to the Court, Douglas and the President exchanged a series of letters in which they planned an imaginary baseball game between the executive and judicial branches of government.* FDR used the "game" idea to poke fun at the nine "old men" on the anti–New Deal Court, who had undercut his New Deal program. The President suggested that Chief Justice Hughes pitch and Justice McReynolds catch for the Court team, which, FDR pointed out, "gives some advantage to the Supreme Court because an experienced battery counts and yours will be about ten years older than ours." Not to be outdone, Douglas replied with a dig of his own—aimed at Roosevelt's Court-packing plan: "Pitching and catching are quite strenuous," wrote Douglas. "We have no substitutes or replacements. *Suppose one— or even both—of our battery gave out completely!!* You could, of course, replace them. Yet some of the 'Yes, but' group will say, 'Why take the chance? If, instead, younger men constituted the battery, that risk would be avoided. By using your candidates for pitcher and catcher in the outfield, they could be preserved for *many, many* years!!' That will be the argument against your proposal. And I thought I ought to call it to your attention now, lest, having

---

*The game idea was inspired by the *Washington Post*'s political cartoonist, Herblock, who depicted the "Nine Young Men" of the Supreme Court in a huddle, suggesting a ball game with Roosevelt's cabinet.

started with a nice, friendly ball game, we be charged with concocting (or we unwittingly end up with) a court plan.''

Douglas's sense of humor made him a regular at FDR's poker parties. When Harold Ickes first invited Douglas to the President's poker party, "he [Douglas] was lots of fun with his inimitable wit, and I think that it was the best party we have had. . . .'' And at a later gathering: "Bill Douglas is lots of fun at these parties. He is bright and quick and plays good poker. He is always introducing some new hand. One he calls 'Bushy' [meaning Chief Justice Hughes], and he has a particularly mean one that he calls 'McReynolds' [after Associate Justice James McReynolds].''

On the Court, Frankfurter expected to collect acolytes, as he had at Harvard. But with Douglas (as with Black), Frankfurter confronted a man whose intellect was as powerful as his own. And so, though Frankfurter held himself out as Douglas's mentor, Douglas accepted him as a peer and did not need nor solicit Frankfurter's approval of his every opinion.

Most infuriating to Frankfurter, Douglas and Black were robbing the former Harvard professor of the reputation as the Court's most devoted civil libertarian. Here was Douglas, a former corporate law professor, of all people, claiming a deeper allegiance to the cause of individual rights than the man who had defended Sacco and Vanzetti. And despite the thoroughness with which Frankfurter explained his judicial decisions and elaborated on his philosophy of judicial restraint, his liberal friends did not seem to understand. Douglas received credit for being a libertarian purist, even though Frankfurter's positions in certain areas, notably on Fourth Amendment issues of government eavesdropping, were considerably more sensitive to individual liberties than Douglas's. In 1942, Frankfurter, for example, condemned the use by federal agents of a detectaphone placed against the wall to overhear conversations in an adjoining room as an illegal search prohibited by the Fourth Amendment. At that time, Douglas found no constitutional violation in the government's conduct, though he would change his mind on the issue ten years later.

Despite his inconsistencies, Douglas was usually presented in the press as an intrepid protector of civil liberties. Frankfurter was on the other side too many times to suit libertarians. Frankfurter could blame Douglas's split with him in *Bridges, Betts* and *Opelika* on Black's influence, which, Frankfurter was convinced, increasingly dominated Douglas's thinking. But Frankfurter had more difficulty explaining Douglas's votes in cases where Douglas, not Black, carved out new civil liberties ground. This happened in 1941 in a case challenging California's "Okie" law. Anticipating the influx of migrant farmers from the Dust Bowl, California had passed a law that made it a misdemeanor to bring an impoverished person into the state. The Court majority found the law an unconstitutional burden on commerce, since no state could "isolate itself from difficulties common to all of them by restraining the transportation of persons and property across its borders."

Justice Douglas, who as a boy had heard stories of discrimination and violence from his migrant worker friends in the fruit orchards of Washington, saw it differently. For Douglas, to be poor was bad enough; to be poor and not be given an opportunity to change that condition was intolerable. The right was so basic to the spirit of the country, Douglas wrote, that "it occupies a more protected position in our constitutional system than does the movement of cattle, fruit, steel and coal across state lines" (protected by the commerce clause). Douglas declared that the right to travel was a guarantee of citizenship under the Fourteenth Amendment's privileges and immunities clause. A Court majority would recognize the right to travel as "fundamental" under the Fourteenth Amendment*—twenty-seven years after Douglas had written his opinion.

A second early Douglas opinion that would have enduring constitutional significance involved a challenge to an Oklahoma law that provided compulsory sterilization of criminals after the third conviction for a felony of "moral turpitude." The statute, however, exempted several crimes, including embezzlement. Why, asked Douglas in his opinion for the Court, should a clerk who appropriated over twenty dollars from his employer's till be exempt from the statute while a stranger who stole the same amount

---

*The majority would use the Fourteenth Amendment's equal protection clause as the basis for the decision rather than the privileges and immunities clause, as Douglas had earlier suggested.

was not? Douglas noted that the state statute fell more heavily on common larcenists (drawn predominantly from the lower class) than on embezzlers (who stole while working on white-collar jobs). The Fourteenth Amendment's equal protection clause, said Douglas, forbids such discrimination.

If Douglas had stopped there, the opinion would have been recorded as an interesting constitutional curio of the time, since the Court had rarely relied on the equal protection clause to overturn state legislation. But Douglas went further. "We are dealing here with legislation which involves one of the basic civil rights of man," Douglas wrote. "Marriage and procreation are fundamental to the very existence and survival of the race." Since the Oklahoma statute could irrevocably deprive a citizen of that basic civil right, said Douglas, the Court was obligated to view the statute with "strict scrutiny." In other words, where basic human rights were involved, Douglas would hold a state to an extraordinary high standard in justifying its statutes. It was a constitutional approach which would claim a judicial majority more than two decades later.

Douglas continued to write innovative opinions, but sometimes his creativity seemed to jump ahead of constitutional justification. The problem was demonstrated in yet another case involving Jehovah's Witnesses. The Witnesses had challenged several municipal ordinances that required the payment of a licensing fee for door-to-door solicitation, much like the ordinance upheld in *Opelika*. This time, however, there was a new Court majority, ready to strike down the ordinances as violations of the Witnesses' First Amendment rights.

Douglas, perhaps remembering his father's riding religious circuit in Otter Tail County, Minnesota, found the Witnesses' evangelism occupying "the same high estate under the First Amendment as do worship in the churches and preaching from the pulpits." Douglas added that it "has the same claim as the others to the guarantees of freedom of speech and freedom of the press." Reading the religion and speech guarantees together, Douglas seemed to make the Witnesses' mission ("Go ye into all the world, and preach the gospel to every creature") virtually untouchable by government officials.

The Douglas opinion raised as many questions as it answered, a fact that did not escape the Court dissenters, including Justice Frankfurter. One problem was that Douglas did not draw the line between constitutionally protected religious activity and un-protected commercial activity very clearly. His opinion did not explain, moreover, why it was permissible for a city to impose a tax on a local newspaper, though its contents were presumably protected by the free press guarantee of the First Amendment, and not on the literature of a religious sect, unless religious expression was more important than secular speech. But neither constitutional history nor precedent gave priority to religious speech over other protected expression.

Douglas might have been helped if the ordinances had imposed a prohibitive licensing fee on the Witnesses. But, as Frankfurter noted, even the Witnesses did not argue that the twenty-five-cent pamphlet fee would have suppressed their activity. What was left, then, was a blanket prohibition against any licensing fee imposed upon a religious group—though other solicitors would have to pay. And that, argued Frankfurter, amounted to a government subsidy of religion, which violated the most fundamental princi-ple of religious freedom in this country—the separation of church and state.

The disagreement between Douglas and Frankfurter in the Jehovah's Witnesses case typified their differing philosophical approaches. For Douglas, protection of individual liberties was his goal and the route he traveled to reach his destination seemed to his critics to assume secondary importance. For Frankfurter, the path (that is, the reasoning process itself) was critical and taking problematic shortcuts to reach a destination was a viola-tion of the basic judicial function.

In private relationships with their law clerks, Douglas and Frankfurter switched roles. Frankfurter's clerks felt that Frank-furter, the intense, bitingly critical Justice, offered them compas-sion, wisdom and love in equal doses. Frankfurter, who had no children of his own, treated his clerks as members of his family and, sometimes, as his confidants. Douglas, the expansive liber-tarian in public, was the driven introvert in his chambers, at times ordering around his clerks and staff like servants. Douglas's early clerks discovered that their boss was intellectually self-contained, personally shy and often insensitive to those around him.

"Justice Douglas was someone to be approached with a feeling of terror," one Douglas clerk remembered. "He didn't see that much of his clerks. If he had a question, he would press a buzzer. You responded and if you didn't hear from him again, you were doing well."

Douglas worked his clerks from morning until late at night, with no time out for small talk. On those rare occasions when the clerk was called in to discuss a legal point with Douglas, it was clear, as one clerk remembered, "which one of us was appointed by the President and confirmed by the Senate." In short, Douglas expected his clerks to work the same long hours that he did, but he never gave them the impression, as Frankfurter often did his clerks, that their contribution was indispensable or that the Justice and his clerk were working in a spirit of professional camaraderie.

The Douglas clerks were there to do a job and that was the end of the matter. Douglas did not want to know their personal problems, nor would he think of sharing his with them. David Ginsburg, who had begun working for Douglas at the SEC in 1935, did not even meet Mildred Douglas and the Douglas children until 1939. One clerk asked for time off to get married and Justice Douglas gave him exactly twenty-four hours.

If the clerks accepted the limits of the Douglas clerkship, however, it could be rewarding. "I thought the clerkship was the way it ought to be," said Professor Vern Countryman of the Harvard Law School, who clerked for Douglas during the 1942 term. "He worked your ass off but he worked his ass off, too, so it was acceptable."

Douglas asked his clerks to perform three tasks. First, they were responsible for reviewing petitions for Court review and summarizing their contents in one-page memos so that Douglas could decide which petitions should be granted. Second, Douglas clerks checked the first drafts of his opinions for mistakes in style, logic and research. Third, Douglas frequently asked a clerk to research a monumental legal question—to identify and analyze every case handed down by the Court in which the Court had reversed itself or every decision based on the Federal Employers' Liability Act.

Those jobs, obviously, were challenging and a clerk's thorough performance of the task could be its own reward. But for those who expected excessive praise or a full-dress intellectual engagement with the Justice over a point on which the clerk had struggled for hours, perhaps days, disappointment was sure to follow. "He didn't create the atmosphere that 'we're both judges, so let's hash it out,'" one clerk said. "He would always listen but he never gave the impression that he was playing the game of what ought to be done." A clerk's argument rarely changed Douglas's mind on a subject, whether on a pivotal constitutional issue in a decision or on a historical footnote. Sometimes that lesson came slowly. Countryman once bravely rewrote an entire first draft of a Douglas opinion, with the result that Douglas included a one-sentence footnote in his final draft. "But that footnote was mine," said Countryman, "all mine."

Countryman was not disturbed by Douglas's certainty of his own conclusions, "I wasn't appointed to the Supreme Court," said Countryman, "he was." Another clerk said Douglas's manner reflected his mind: "He wasn't a man of enormous doubts. He had a very uncluttered mind which didn't get him off on the byways like some of the others on the Court." David Ginsburg put it differently: "I doubt that he ever changed his mind on a case. He was not retrospective. His mind had a laser-like quality. He could focus himself in ways that only athletes parallel. Douglas was like the best professional tennis players, who are oblivious to the distractions in the stands, and who concentrate exclusively on the ball."

Even the most devoted Douglas clerks admitted that Douglas did not invite intimacy. "His conversation was often hesitant," David Ginsburg recalled. "Rarely was it easy, spontaneous, free and open." Another remembered that Douglas "expected you to work hard and he gave the impression that you were pretty damn lucky to be his clerk. He was not a particularly gentle spirit in that respect."

This formal, rather remote relationship contrasted so dramatically with the experiences of other clerks that some Douglas clerks brooded or complained openly (to other clerks, never to Douglas). The clerks' displeasure was understandable after they heard of Frankfurter engaging in animated debate with his clerks or Black cooking a sumptuous dinner for his clerks in his eight-eenth-century Alexandria house. To be sure, Douglas would duti-fully extend dinner invitations for Thanksgiving and Christmas, but those invitations were often given on such short notice that the clerk did not know whether Douglas wanted him to come or was simply making a half-hearted gesture of hospitality. On rare occasions, a clerk would be honored by an invitation for a hike and Douglas, on the trail, would be the salty storyteller the clerk had read about in the newspapers. But once Douglas and his clerk returned to the Court and the elevator doors closed, one clerk recalled, "we were back to the master-slave relation-ship."

CHAPTER EIGHTEEN

ILLUSION AND REALITY

Wartime Washington epitomized the soberness with which the nation set to the task of defeating the Axis powers. High officials worked six days and nights a week. Full-time mothers became part-time mothers and substituted in the schools, hospitals and libraries to take the place of those on the war production lines. There were few leisurely strolls and even fewer rides around the capital's monuments. Gas was rationed and so were nylons and beef. War was serious business and Americans knew both the stakes and the sacrifices required.

To relieve the pressure and monotony, the press offered readers sunshine items, nostalgic looks at the America that had been left behind with the sunken battleships at Pearl Harbor. Between the grim war news items, there were reminders of what the struggle and sacrifice were all about. Apple pie and mom and model airplanes would become tired clichés to later generations of cynics, but during World War II, Americans embraced them with unabashed pleasure.

Justice William O. Douglas and his family were an irresistible subject for media adulation. Here was one of America's brightest young leaders at home, and the environment could not have been more perfectly Americana. The reporters and their photographers introduced readers slowly, titillatingly, to the Douglases, beginning with the panoramic view of the red-brick colonial house, set serenely on a rising crest of hillside in suburban Maryland. Visitors entered by the central hallway, admiring the decorations, which one reporter found to be "a pleasant melange of Eighteenth Century English and Colonial American which gives the whole a distinctive personal quality."

They met Bill junior, called "Bumble," who ran in from school, chunky and properly grass-stained from a busy day of classes and football. He was ten years old and already a striking replica of his father, with the same firm chin, fine, slightly upturned nose, and pale-blue eyes. He tended the big coal furnace in the basement for thirty cents a week, but wanted a raise so that he could devour more ice cream sodas at the neighborhood drugstore. He was always hungry and always looking for a game of catch with his father, who, according to the articles, happily accommodated him —that is, when he was not helping his son build model airplanes. Bill junior's ambition, naturally, was to be his father's law clerk.

Young Mildred, twelve, "the living image of her mother," raised Plymouth Rock chickens with names like Dracula and Draculette and waited patiently for their combined output of one egg a day. Millie, as she was called by everybody, was pictured watching Bumble build model airplanes and holding the bat in preparation for a family game of baseball. When her parents went out at night, which happened frequently since they were busy and famous and charming, Millie was the house proctor, seeing that all doors and windows were locked and that Colonial, the family spaniel, was snugly stowed in his basket under the stairs.

The children were lovingly cared for by their mother, Mildred, who was pretty, cheerful, unpretentious and the perfect homemaker. She had pared the household staff by half (from two servants to one) and helped lighten the load by sending most of the laundry out and tidying the downstairs rooms herself. Since the Douglases had only an A gas card, Mildred and the children took the bus everywhere. When she entertained, as she did frequently, Mildred did so informally. The style was less important than the substance—that is, the conversation with the Thurman Arnolds, the Hugo Blacks, Senator Francis Maloney, to name a few of the Douglases' closest friends.

At half-past seven, the brisk footsteps of "the boss" were heard on the concrete steps of the portico. Justice Douglas, with the usual sheaf of legal papers under his arm, gave a cheerful greeting to his family and his dog, who, naturally, wagged his tail with approval. After dinner, Dad slipped into scuffed old moccasins and a checkered wool shirt and retreated for a night's work to his small upstairs study, which was also the family blackout room, its windows taped in V-for-Victory patterns by Bumble and Millie.

Sundays were family days for the Douglases, with the Justice kicking a football or rooting for the Washington Redskins, playing a vigorous game of badminton in the yard or a quiet game of parcheesi on the cool side porch. In the summer months, when the Court was not in session, the Douglases had more free time together and spent it far from Washington, D.C., in their log cabin retreat in the Wallowa Mountains of Oregon. There, the four Douglases took family pack trips through the mountains, fished for trout in the mountain streams and rode horseback over the narrow mountain trails.

The reality of the Douglas family life was as remote from the media picture as their log cabin was from their two-story colonial in suburban Silver Spring. Begin with the pictures: a smiling Bumble tending the big coal furnace or tossing a football with his dad or working through his geography lesson with the Justice at his side. All the while the photographers were putting Bumble through his paces, the boy was seething inside.

"I hated it," Bill junior remembered. It seemed as if his father was always surrounded by photographers and reporters and that he thrived on the attention. Bumble did not, but he was forced into the celebrity parade anyway. "Let's get a picture of you and your son playing football," a photographer would say to the Justice, and he would happily oblige. "Now let's go out and spade in the garden." Bumble trailed along obediently but suffered silently. The artificiality bothered him, and the more his father seemed to enjoy the poses, the more bitterly his son resented it.

Bumble's feelings of bitterness ran much deeper. For it wasn't merely that the pictures were posed; the wholesome togetherness was as well. Bill junior remembered the days in New Haven when his father would greet him with a bear hug and let him ride on one leg, while his sister rode the other. Now that simple, uninhibited fun was gone, not only because Father seemed to have so little time for his family but because Bumble himself was growing up painfully, neither the cheerful tot of his memories nor the happy soda-sipping, football-playing boy of the magazine spreads.

Being the son of a famous man began to grate. The pats on the head and the inevitable question—Do you want to be a lawyer like your dad?—were constant and intolerable. Bill junior had told a reporter that his one ambition was to be his father's law clerk, but inside, his ambitions were very much different, for himself and his family. He wanted to be away from the busy Washington scene, from the reporters and the parties and the very proper Quaker private school where he was called William and voices were never raised.

He also wanted more time with his dad, not for picture-taking with a football or a garden spade, but for the two of them to give unphotographed, unreported love to each other. The big bear hugs were still offered, but now Bumble wanted more. And his father, still the joking, kind authority figure of the family, did not respond. It seemed as if his father's major contribution to the family was to give orders. Do this, do that. When you're famous, Bumble concluded, there were dozens of people who would answer every time you pressed a buzzer. "Yes, sir, what can I do for you, Justice Douglas. Right away, Justice Douglas." When he came home to Silver Spring, it seemed as if Justice Douglas was still pressing the buzzer and demanding that people—his family —wait on him. But the Justice could not organize the home as he did his office schedule and he could not dictate the family emotions as he did a business letter.

Inevitably there was trouble in the Douglas household. Bumble recorded his displeasure with his family and his life in quiet ways, doing poorly, for example, at private school. Later, when he was transferred to a public school, he discovered that the new environment brought new problems. At his first assembly, Bumble looked with shock and admiration as a classmate urinated from the balcony. That was the real world, he concluded, but just as real—and not nearly so exciting—were the playground fights, where Bumble invariably came out second best. McFarland Junior High was a nightmare for Bill junior, who sat on the curb and cried every morning before boarding the school bus.

In the Northwest, his life did not seem to improve. He was younger than his sister and could not ride a horse nearly as well. He was smaller than his father and could not keep his brisk pace on the mountain trails. When the Justice went on one of his famous mountain climbs, his son would always fall behind. "Dad wanted to go up the mountain at ninety miles an hour," Bill junior remembered. "I wanted to go at thirty-five." The Justice did not seem to be sympathetic to his son. "I got encouragement from my dad," said Douglas Corpron, Jr., who climbed Mount Adams with the Douglases, "and I would have expected that Bill would have received some from his dad too. But Justice Douglas seemed to take the attitude: 'I'm an individual; you're an individual and we're each responsible for ourselves.' "

At home, the younger Douglas found his father unapproachable. Whenever he had a problem, he would seek the counsel and love of his mother. Why did he avoid his father? "Dad was scary," Bill junior remembered. "I felt from an early age I needed help in talking to that man. He would turn those blue eyes on me and make me squirm and feel self-conscious. His sternness and remoteness put me off. Mother would go to the bar and present my case to the old man. But she had the same problem with him. He'd stare at her and she would feel incomplete."

But Douglas was not just scary; he was also shy, and that may have explained part of his communications problem with his family. Though he was a great showman at parties, Douglas was basically an intensely private man. He did not make conversation easily and when he was trying to express a feeling, not a fact, he was conspicuously uncomfortable. The more sensitive the subject, the more inarticulate the Justice became. He attempted several times to tell his young son about the facts of life, for example, and finally in desperation took Bumble to a picturesque area in southern Oregon, where the two of them silently watched the mating of two brown pelicans. Another time, the father attempted to explain the dangers of sex to his frisky adolescent son. "There are good girls and bad girls," Douglas told Bill junior. "Yes?"

said Bumble expectantly. "That's all," said his father, and dropped the subject.

Millie, two years older than her brother, was generally acknowledged to be the "rebel" in the family. "You talk to my sister," said Bill junior, "and you'll know my father. They are exactly alike." Though she looked very much like her mother, Millie Douglas was the image of her father in spirit. Proud and tough-minded, she ran her own life and woe betide the person—including Justices of the U.S. Supreme Court—who stood in her way! The sparks between father and daughter began to fly early—at six o'clock in the morning, to be exact, when young Millie decided to practice the piano, only moments before her enraged father came storming down the stairs. "Once he took out a belt and said that he would hit me if I didn't do what he said," Millie recalled. "I said, 'You wouldn't dare.' And he didn't."

Unlike her brother, Millie never rebelled inconspicuously. At an early age, she realized that her father valued success, particularly academic achievement. So Millie, with considerable effort, managed to flunk out of private school in seventh grade. "He didn't like that very much," she said.*

Later, the stories of Millie's rebellion were as numerous and colorful to the family as her father's battles with law and the outdoors were to the public. As a teen-ager, Millie decided during a ride in the car that she wanted a part-time job. Absolutely not, said Justice Douglas. That was all she needed. Millie opened the car door at a stoplight, walked to a nearby drugstore and was hired as a weekend soda jerk. When she was old enough to date, her father made his opinion of her beaus well known. Once, Millie informed him that she was going to Alexandria, Virginia, to meet a sailor for a date. Out of the question, said the Justice. Millie met her boyfriend. Her father threatened punishment, but he never followed through. Millie never knew why he didn't punish her. But had he done so, it's fair to assume that she would not have bowed easily. "If I wanted to do something, I didn't see any reason why I shouldn't do it just because he said I shouldn't."

Millie seemed to hold a secret competition with her father. He

*Having proved her point, Millie brought home a report card with all A's the next year.

was the famous Justice who loved the outdoors, the pack trips, the horseback riding. So Millie learned to ride a horse well, better than her father, and as a teen-ager, she led parties of visitors on horseback through the back trails of the Wallowas. She enjoyed the rides and her own conspicuous talent as a rider and packer. She may also have enjoyed comparing her own prowess to her father's. "He was a terrible rider," she said. "He sat on the horse like a big sack of wheat. He had no respect for the horse. He rode like he drove a car, with his foot down on the accelerator until he got where he was going."

Even Justice Douglas's obvious pleasure and pride in his daughter's feats did not calm her. He bragged about her pack trips among friends and wrote about some of the more impressive exploits in his books. He wrote, for example, of one horseback trip in the Wallowa Mountains that began in sunshine but ended with rain and, finally, snow flurries. Millie, who had not expected the inclement weather, was riding without a jacket and was soon soaked and shivering. According to her father, he passed a whiskey bottle to her to warm her insides and her drooping spirits. It was a good story. The only trouble was that it never happened. "I was wet and miserable," Millie recalled, "but I just told him to get on with it. There was no passing of the whiskey bottle."

Her father simply could not resist a good story, about Millie or himself, on or off the mountain range, and if he embellished a little here and there, well, as he told his daughter after the first volume of his autobiography was published, there was such a thing as writer's license. It infuriated Millie. There were stories, true stories, that her father could have told. Like the time Millie was fifteen and riding with a young boy who was thrown and kicked in the head by his horse. Millie pushed her horse at a steady gallop until she reached a doctor, who returned with her to help her companion. Her father could not, it seemed, ever get it right, either telling stories that did not happen or not telling stories that did.

In Washington, Millie and Bumble would sit secretly on the stairs, out of sight of their parents, and eavesdrop on parties. Their father was always in the center of the crowd, telling his tall tales and jokes with relish and enjoying the rapt attention of his guests. Millie was repelled. "Dad was the showman, the genial host," she recalled sardonically, "encouraging some of his more vulgar friends to throw chicken bones over their shoulders. Then we would be paraded down to meet the company." When the two children were introduced, they smiled dutifully and cringed inside. "And this is your little son," Bill junior remembered the guests saying. "Are you going to grow up to be a famous judge like your father?" Bumble hated it just as he hated the photographers and reporters. "What bullshit, what artificiality," he thought. "Those people have glazed eyeballs; they don't really care."

The anger and resentment and rebellion were intense, but so was the love. Millie and Bumble adored their father and coveted their time with him. When he was not preoccupied with other matters, he could be kind and fun and loving. But those moments seemed exceedingly rare in their formative years, even when the Douglases were on vacation. Millie could remember only one sustained time when they had their father all to themselves. It was a summer during the war when the family took a long train ride west. Father received no telephone calls, dictated no memos, entertained no important officials. It was one delightful game of rummy from Washington, D.C., to Oregon.

But after the family arrived in Oregon, the mail sacks full of petitions to the Court soon followed. The postmaster at the tiny La Grande depot thrived on his seasonal burden, caused by the Justice's summer residency, but Millie and Bumble did not share his enthusiasm.

At the cabin, Douglas worked five or six hours a day on Court business. He did not like to be disturbed. When Millie or Bumble risked a peek into the cabin while their father was deep in legal papers, they were sorry. "He didn't get angry," Millie recalled. "He just gave you that cold stare—and that cut you off immediately."

The newspaper and magazine reporters invariably described Mildred Riddle Douglas, the Justice's wife, as a cheerful, pretty and very charming homemaker—a characterization used frequently by those who remembered Mildred in the early days of her marriage. As the years passed, and Douglas moved from New Haven to Washington, from Yale professor to Associate Justice of the U.S. Supreme Court, the description of Mildred, among her husband's friends, began to change. She was described as unambitious, unable to keep pace with her husband intellectually and, finally, as a sad, colorless little drudge.

To her children, both the public image and that of Justice Douglas's friends were very wide of the mark. For Millie and Bumble, Mildred Douglas was a wonderful human being and a perfect mother. They never put it in those terms, but the conclusion, after hearing them describe lovingly their mother's personality and affection, was inescapable. "In a large room, my mother felt very small," Bill junior recalled, "but in a small room, she radiated." And Millie, the hot-tempered rebel of the family: "Whatever my mother said, I listened to. If she said, 'Let's go to town, it will be fun,' I'd go and it *would* be fun. She put so much of herself into it. Dad just said to do it. There was no feeling."

Douglas's niece, Mrs. Florence Persons, recalled Mildred's engaging manner: "Children tend to like people who let them be themselves. Aunt Mildred was like that. She didn't thrust herself at you. You had the feeling she liked you. She was the kind of person children loved."

If Justice Douglas got up in the morning to do his work, as Bill junior has suggested, Mildred Douglas got out of bed to take care of her family. And in her own way, she performed her task with the zest and care and high intelligence that her husband applied to his. When her children were young, she would sit in front of the fireplace and read to them. It might have been something as frivolous as "Little Black Sambo" or "Raggedy Ann and Andy," or something more ambitious, like Roman mythology translated from the original Latin as she went along, but equally pleasurable. As her children grew up, Mildred remained gentle and kind and forever loving. It was to Mother they came when there was trouble. "She was the one who cured the nightmares and bathed the fevered brow," said Millie.

When they were in New Haven, Mildred had loved the small parties that she and her husband gave and she prepared carefully for them. By the time the guests arrived, the place settings had been neatly and attractively displayed, the food carefully prepared and in the oven, and all that was needed was the lively conversation. That had been provided, primarily, by her husband, while Mildred had sat nearby, smiling and enjoying the others enjoying themselves. When the parties had got larger and louder and more frequent as her husband rose in prominence and popularity, Mildred's enthusiasm had drained. And when the Douglases had attended important gatherings (after Douglas was on the Court, they often attended parties four or five times a week), Mildred's joy had turned to fright.

At one White House dinner, Mildred, to her utter consternation, had been seated next to President Roosevelt. As her husband later told the story, she had been so terrified that she could hardly raise her fork to her mouth. The President, always the charmer, had made a valiant effort to relax Mildred. It had not worked. For the entire evening, the best that Mrs. Douglas could offer was a quick monosyllabic "yes" or "no" to every question the President had asked.

Mildred loved her husband intensely throughout her life, even after their divorce in 1953. In the early years, there were enough moments of calm in Douglas's life to enable Mildred's tenderness and love to complement her husband's intense nature. But as the years passed, the quiet was replaced by the seemingly incessant demands on their time together. And the once loving conversations became unilateral ones, with the Justice barking orders to his wife. When she did not respond immediately and to his total satisfaction, Douglas would give her the icy stare that so frightened both Mildred and their children.

Douglas's impatience with his wife seemed to grow. The relationship took on more of the master-slave tones that so troubled some of his law clerks. Do this, do that. It seemed as if he wanted a wife to cook and iron his shirts and keep the household budget tidy, but the intimacy and sharing of a good marriage were, by the early 1940s, no longer there. Douglas insisted on absolute control of his own life and seemed to see his family as an extension of himself; so he demanded control of them as well.

The mornings were particularly bad. Douglas was always tense, but in the early mornings, when he was contemplating the demands of the day's schedule, he was as rigid as a steel trap. His wife could feel the tension and so could the children. He paced and ran his hand through his hair and drummed the table with his fingers. At the breakfast table, he said nothing. Instead he either read the newspaper or looked out the window, his lips pursed so tightly that the upper lip virtually disappeared.

Even on weekends, when he was supposed to relax, Douglas could never quite rid himself of the tension. He was in a hurry when the family was simply going to a shop or a movie theater. Douglas would pull the car to the curb and turn off the ignition. Mildred and the children would get out and wait for Douglas to lock all the car doors, open his door and walk around to the other side to meet them. It never happened that way. By the time the three of them were on the curb, Douglas had rolled up the windows and locked the doors and was already on his way. "He was always twenty paces ahead of us," said Bill junior. "Mother would plead with him to slow down, but he never did."

Whenever Douglas treated his wife or children as responsible, independent members of the family, they were thrilled. He asked Mildred, for example, to draw plans for a second cabin in Oregon, and Mildred went about the task with zestful excitement. When Douglas asked his son to show him how to tie a complicated knot, Bumble ran to his room and began immediately to practice for his performance in front of the old man. Both Mildred and Bill junior tried eagerly to prove to themselves and, they hoped, to Douglas that they were worthy of his companionship and love. The instances were rare, but always remembered.

Shortly after Douglas's Court appointment, when Mildred was in Oregon caring for her ailing mother, her feelings for her husband glistened in her letters to him: "People have heard that I'm here and are so anxious to meet me. Most of them had a chance to know me quite well ages ago but never took advantage of it. I'm so anxious to hear how you and the babes are getting along. I can hardly wait for a letter." And three days later, she wrote again, addressing her husband as "darling": "Gee, it was good to hear from you . . . do tell me all about the party at the White House. Hug Mil and Bub for me—I'm lonesome for you and them."

But within the week, Douglas had sent his wife a second letter, apparently criticizing her handling of the household bills. She replied that "if you would like to, you keep the checkbook from now on, then you will know how much it really costs to run the house with rent, servants, coal and tuition, etc."

Despite the widening gap between them, Mildred continued to care. In 1942, she and the children stayed in Washington while the Justice took a trip west. She wrote to him: ". . . the 27th can't come fast enough. We'll meet you in the car." She enclosed notes from Bumble and Millie as well. From Bumble "Hi-ya pop. Hurry up and come home. Write me another letter if you have time." And from sassy Millie: "Hi-ya pappy. Are you sure you didn't have to be carried out too, at that party of Roy's?" (Roy Schaeffer was one of Douglas's closest friends in Oregon.)

And in 1944, Mildred is again in the Oregon cabin, writing to her husband, reminding him of his children and her love for him. Speaking of Bumble, she wrote that "I couldn't resist those big shining eyes and that grin. I'm putty where he is concerned. . . . Millie was in the La Grande horse show last Wednesday—an old fashioned side saddle girl in the parade. She looked simply beautiful and stole the whole show, a proud beauty, her nose was high in the air . . . write me all you do and how the Court looks, if Owen J. [Roberts] speaks and Frankfurter has retired and tell Hugo hello for me. Much love."

By this time, the marriage was unraveling. Still, Mildred never criticized her husband in front of the children and did not allow them to complain either. But Mildred's loneliness had been apparent for several years and now there were rumors that Justice Douglas had an eye for beautiful women, not necessarily limited to the one to whom he was married. By 1944, guests at the Douglas home sensed the tension. "I could feel the unhappiness," recalled Mrs. Douglas Corpron, Sr. "He never touched her [Mildred] or showed affection or appreciated her. He bossed her around and he bossed the kids around, too, and they resented it."

But neither Mildred nor her husband seriously thought about divorce during his early days on the Court. For Mildred, the reason was simple. She still loved her husband and was totally devoted to him. She would never ask for a divorce and would accept it only after Douglas himself had forced the issue. For Douglas, the decision to seek a divorce came slowly. Divorce challenged every moral lesson his mother had taught him as a youngster. Marriage was sacred, he had been told, and his mother had supported her view with a constantly expressed love for her late husband. Julia Douglas had demanded high achievement from her elder son in his academic work; it should be no different in his personal life. The admission of failure did not come easily.

CHAPTER NINETEEN ―――――――――――――――――――

ONE SOUL TO SAVE

IN 1942, the war in Europe had not turned into the Allied rout of the enemy that Americans, given propaganda and history, had expected. News from the Pacific was even worse. After the vicious battles at Bataan and Corregidor had been reported, word was passed in the American press of an insane Japanese martial spirit. Government propaganda and the press's image stamped a Japanese stereotype in the American public's mind. According to U.S. public opinion polls, the Japanese were treacherous, sly, cruel and warlike.

Politicians, including President Roosevelt, did nothing to temper the public hysteria. FDR issued an order authorizing the Secretary of War and designated military commanders to prescribe "military areas," and at their discretion to exclude "potential enemies" from those areas. Congress followed with a resolution that made it a misdemeanor to disobey orders issued by the military authorities. The executive and legislative actions resulted in curfews and the ultimate evacuation of about seventy thousand native-born American citizens of Japanese descent and their incarceration in "relocation centers" in other parts of the U.S.

The sweep of the executive and legislative actions was breathtaking. The evacuations meant certain financial ruin to thousands and a loss of liberty and dignity to all affected by the orders. No attempt was made to distinguish between loyal and disloyal Japanese Americans, or between citizens and aliens. Nobody seemed to care. "The Japs live like rats," said the governor of Idaho, "breed like rats and act like rats. We don't want them." Progressive politicians, like California's Attorney General Earl Warren, were no less emotional. "If the Japs are released," said Warren, "no one will be able to tell a saboteur from any other Jap."

The restraints on Japanese Americans raised important constitutional questions about the scope of governmental power in time of war. In 1943, the Court offered its first opinion on the subject. The case involved Kiyoshi Hirabayashi, an American citizen born to Japanese parents, who was completing his final year at the University of Washington. Hirabayashi had defied military authorities and had been sentenced to two three-month prison terms for violating a curfew order and for failing to report to a "Civil Control Station" as a preliminary step to exclusion from the Seattle area. Afterward Hirabayashi went to court, claiming that his rights to due process under the Fifth Amendment had been violated.

The issue raised by Hirabayashi was argued at great length between Justice Douglas and his law clerk, Vern Countryman. The clerk said the punishment was a clear violation of Hirabayashi's constitutional rights. Douglas disagreed. The military order forcing Japanese Americans to evacuate their West Coast homes, Douglas said, was no trumped-up excuse for government tyranny; it was, Douglas firmly believed, a military necessity. Douglas told Countryman that a U.S. general he had talked to the previous summer was convinced Japanese submarines were off the West Coast.

"I said there was nothing to support the curfew classification but race," Countryman recalled. "I also said to him: You were in the army; you know not to believe a general. The Justice wouldn't budge."

In that critical wartime hour, the Court majority, including Douglas, decided that the job of separating the disloyal from the loyal Japanese Americans was particularly difficult and the military needn't try, since the interest of national security was paramount. The military had acted reasonably in concluding that residents having ethnic affiliations with the enemy, like Hirabayashi, might be more dangerous than others.

In a separate opinion, Douglas reminded readers of the Court decision that the disastrous bombing of Pearl Harbor made a Japanese invasion of the West Coast a real threat. As a result, the military commanders who wanted to clear the area of those of Japanese ancestry were acting within the boundaries of sound military judgment. It would, of course, have been better if the authorities could have screened the loyal from the disloyal Japanese Americans. But in wartime, wrote Douglas, "speed and dispatch may be of the essence."

"That was the worst opinion that Douglas ever wrote," said Vern Countryman. As if to prove that two wrongs make a right, Douglas joined Hugo Black's majority opinion a year later that sanctioned the exclusion of a Japanese American named Korematsu from San Leandro, California. Although the majority spoke in lofty terms of individual rights, it had no difficulty in dismissing Korematsu's in the paramount interest of the war effort. In one sentence, Justice Black rattled off the reasons: (1) the U.S. was at war with the Japanese Empire; (2) our military authorities feared the invasion of the West Coast and felt the security measures to be justified; (3) the military decided that the urgency of the situation demanded that all citizens of Japanese ancestry be segregated temporarily from the West Coast; and (4) Congress determined that the military should have that power.

The Court majority said that race prejudice was not an issue in the case. So it was left to Justice Frank Murphy to wonder, in dissent, why only Japanese Americans were singled out as a group, when there was no proof of group disloyalty. Could there be any explanation other than the prejudgment by the military—now condoned by the U.S. Supreme Court—that Japanese Americans were not to be trusted?

The Douglas votes in the *Hirabayashi* and *Korematsu* decisions were not so surprising as they might appear to those who knew his reputation only as that of a stalwart libertarian. For Douglas, like other justices who had established reputations as civil libertarians, including Hugo Black and, later, Chief Justice Earl Warren, felt that he owed primary allegiance to his country's survival.

Douglas's deeply felt patriotism was no passing fad. As a Whitman College undergraduate, Douglas had hungered for the taste of battle in World War I and when that honor was denied him, he was deeply disappointed. During World War II, Douglas often expressed to friends his frustration at being tied to the Court and he once told FDR of his desire to sign up for active duty. So when U.S. military authorities claimed that the West Coast evacuations were a military necessity, Douglas was, predictably, sympathetic.

But Douglas's votes in *Hirabayashi* and *Korematzu* were exceptions to his general libertarian code, even in wartime. What distinguished America from Germany and Japan, Douglas once told a wartime audience, was our people's willingness to honor the individual rights of all Americans. "Hitler would say: 'What a weak rod on which to lean in comparison with the forced unanimity of my people. How can one man dare to hold out against the State?' We know the answer. America has always known the answer. Recognition of the smallest minority is written in blood as well as ink in our Bill of Rights."

Even though issues of loyalty held a special poignancy for Douglas, he resisted, in case after case, the temptation to accept the government's rigid tests for allegiance. In 1943, he joined the majority opinion that reversed the *Gobitis* decision and struck down the compulsory flag salute in a public school as a violation of the First Amendment rights of Jehovah's Witnesses. He rejected a U.S. government argument that it had the statutory authority to deport a naturalized citizen who had joined the Communist Party before he had been granted U.S. citizenship. And writing for the Court majority, Douglas said that a Seventh-Day Adventist could not be denied citizenship simply because he refused to take up arms in defense of the country. "The effort of war is indivisible," wrote Douglas. "And those whose religious scruples prevent them from killing are no less patriots than those whose special traits or handicaps result in their duties far behind the fighting front."

Douglas also wrote the majority opinion in which the Court first curbed the oppressive regulations of Japanese Americans. The case involved Mitsuye Endo, who had been sent to a detention camp with other Japanese Americans but had later satisfied military authorities of her loyalty to the United States. Still, the War Relocation Authority would not allow Endo to leave the detention camp until she had convinced officials she had secured a job in a community that was not "unfavorable" to Japanese Americans.

By what right could the government continue to detain Endo after she had proved her loyalty? Douglas found the question unanswerable. His opinion for the Court was confined to a careful parsing of the language of the executive orders authorizing the detention, since, Douglas declared, the government could not have intended a greater restraint on the individual citizen than the orders "clearly and unmistakably" indicated. He found no such justification. Once he had satisfied himself that there was no explicit authorization for Endo's continued detention, Douglas addressed the larger issue raised by the Endo case: "A citizen who is concededly loyal presents no problem of espionage or sabotage. Loyalty is a matter of the heart and mind, not of race, creed or color."

Douglas had second thoughts about the Court's decisions in *Hirabayashi* and *Korematzu,* later admitting that they "were extreme and went to the verge of wartime power." But he was always proud of his *Endo* decision. In fact, he nominated it for a place in his book, *An Almanac of Liberty,* which was devoted to his libertarian beliefs.

By the end of the war, it sometimes seemed that the justices were as exhausted by their internal feuds as by their Court calendar. Justice Owen Roberts had become so embittered by the decisions of his activist colleagues, particularly Hugo Black, which he believed to be without judicial foundation, that he had refused to have lunch with the other justices. Finally Roberts resigned, but even the resignation did not quiet the friction. Black would not sign the justices' traditional farewell testimonial. When Frank Murphy, whom Roberts disliked intensely, sent Roberts a sentimental note of farewell, Roberts sarcastically referred to Murphy's letter as "the Saint's farewell note." After Justice Black had refused to withdraw from a case in which his former law partner had been an attorney, Justice Jackson wrote a short statement that was a thinly veiled attack on Black's ethics. Frankfurter and Douglas's antipathy for each other had not subsided. And a very weary Chief Justice Stone stood by helplessly.

After Stone died, on April 22, 1946, stories circulated around Washington that Jackson, who had taken a leave of absence from the Court to serve as the American prosecutor at the Nuremberg war crime trials, was being seriously considered as Stone's successor. Just as quickly, other stories circulated that Black and Douglas had sent word to President Truman that they would resign if Jackson was named Chief Justice. Black and Douglas denied the stories, but suspicions lingered, particularly in the minds of Jackson and his closest friend on the Court, Felix Frankfurter.

The report of Black's and Douglas's opposition to Jackson's nomination was accompanied by detailed published accounts of the feud between Black and Jackson. The accounts were topped off by a tirade, delivered by Jackson from Nuremberg, accusing Black of "bullying" in judicial conference and biased decision-making. If Black again failed to withdraw from a case in which Jackson perceived a conflict of interest, Jackson promised that he would make his earlier written attack on Black "look like a recommendation by comparison."

President Truman's awareness of the internal division on the Court was one reason that he went outside the Court to select Fred Vinson, his Secretary of the Treasury, as Chief Justice. It was the first of a spate of mediocre Court appointments by Truman. No one denied that Vinson had been a competent politician and effective government administrator. But his capacities for leadership were decidedly political, not intellectual, and that fact was readily apparent after Vinson had presided at his first judicial conference. "He [Vinson] is confident and easy going and sure and shallow," Felix Frankfurter observed. "He seems to have the confident air of a man who does not see the complexities of problems and blithely hits the obvious points."

Vinson claimed the title of Chief Justice, but did very little else to suggest that he was anything more than a figurehead leader of the Court. The true leadership was split between Felix Frankfurter, who led the restrained majority, and Hugo Black, who was the forceful spokesman for the activist minority which included Douglas, Murphy and Wiley Rutledge. Justices Jackson and Douglas gave strong intellectual support to the respective sides, but neither possessed Frankfurter's and Black's proselytizing instincts.

The Court division was recognized by Professor C. Herman Pritchett of the University of Chicago, who used statistical summaries to support his conclusions. He noted, for example, that in one judicial term Douglas agreed with Black 79 percent of the time, more than with any other colleague. Pritchett concluded that the Black and Douglas votes "show them to be generally more concerned for the protection of civil liberties and the rights of criminal defendants, more likely to support the government in its tax and regulatory activities, more desirous of limiting judicial review of administrative action and more likely to vote for labor than their colleagues."

Professor Arthur M. Schlesinger, Jr. also took a turn at analyzing the struggle on the Court, though he rejected Pritchett's austere statistics in favor of broader generalizations. The battle, according to Schlesinger, was between the proponents of judicial restraint (Frankfurter/Jackson) and those of "the Yale School" (Black/Douglas). The Frankfurter majority believed the Court threatened the democratic process by issuing the broad, policy-laden, libertarian decisions advocated by Black and Douglas. The Yale School, Schlesinger wrote, believed that policy-making was inevitable, not just for the legislator or executive, but for a judge as well, and "that any judge chooses his results and reasons backwards."

Black and Douglas, according to Schlesinger, consciously chose results that were consistent with their vision of the American democratic tradition. They voted for "liberal interests, not constitutional doctrines," Schlesinger suggested, "for the trade union against the employer, for the government against the large taxpayer, for the administrative agency against the business, for the injured workman, for the unprotected defendant, against the patent holder." For Schlesinger, the Black/Douglas approach was best summed up by Harvard Professor Thomas Reed Powell's comment that "the less favored in life will be the more favored in law."

In public, Douglas gave little credence to judicial labeling. "Those tags," said Douglas, "once you get into the middle of deciding cases, don't become very meaningful." And yet in private, Douglas engaged in just such labeling, telling his friend Fred Rodell that the personal frictions on the Court had been overplayed by the press, but the philosophical struggle had not. "The basic issues of liberalism vs. conservatism cannot be worked out by pleasing personalities," Douglas wrote Rodell. Any judicial appointment "is important only in terms of the balance of power."

Behind the labels for Black and Douglas, whether "Yale School" or "liberal," was the carefully conceived constitutional philosophy of Hugo Black. Basic to that philosophy was the belief that the protections of the First Amendment enjoyed a preferred place in the constitutional scheme.* Occasionally both Black and Douglas admitted that the time, location and manner of speech could be limited, but even then, they placed a special burden on the government to justify any restraint on First Amendment rights. It was a burden that the government rarely satisfied. When, for example, the Court majority accepted the argument by the city of Trenton, New Jersey, that an ordinance designed to regulate loudspeakers had not infringed on First Amendment rights, Black and Douglas dissented. They charged that the ordinance was not narrowly drawn, and under its general language, a Trenton official could censor those amplified messages he did not like. Frankfurter, who had voted to sustain the ordinance, found the dissenters' fears overblown and the talk of a "preferred position" for the First Amendment "a mischievous phrase."

It became increasingly obvious to Court observers that the Frankfurter majority would justify government restraints on speech that appeared reasonable, and just as obvious that Black and Douglas would reject that deferential position, constantly raising the specter of government censorship. A Court majority found nothing wrong with the arrest of a student street-corner orator in Syracuse, New York, who called President Truman a "bum," the American Legion a "Nazi gestapo" and urged blacks in his audience to fight for the rights that had been deprived them. The speaker made some members of the audience uncom-

*Actually, the theory of a "preferred position" for First Amendment rights did not originate with Black or Douglas, but with Harlan F. Stone.

fortable. There was milling about in the crowd, and some listeners spilled into the street. In addition, an irate member of the audience told one of the two policemen on the scene that he would attack the speaker if they didn't arrest him. Under these circumstances, the Court majority concluded, the arrest of the speaker was reasonable.

To Black and Douglas, the Syracuse police had arrested the wrong man. They should have jailed the irate listener, not the speaker, because the speaker was entitled to special protection under the First Amendment. "A speaker may not, of course, incite a riot," wrote Douglas in dissent. "But this record shows no such extremes. It shows an unsympathetic audience and the threat of one man to haul the speaker from the stage. It is against that kind of threat that speakers need police protection. If they do not receive it and instead the police throw their weight on the side of those who would break up the meetings, the police become the new censors of speech."

Besides holding tenaciously to his broad reading of First Amendment guarantees, Black, with Douglas's support, continued to promote his "incorporation" theory. As he had argued since his early days on the Court, Black insisted that the Fourteenth Amendment "incorporated" the Bill of Rights and made them applicable to the states. That interpretation of the Fourteenth Amendment would have resulted in a dramatic expansion of the protection of criminal suspects in state proceedings.

But the Court majority, led by Frankfurter, refused to adopt Black's theory. Instead the Court embraced a more flexible standard for the states, first fully articulated by Justice Benjamin Cardozo. For Cardozo and, later, Frankfurter, states violated the due process clause of the Fourteenth Amendment* only if they had failed to observe standards of fundamental fairness. That approach, Frankfurter believed, allowed the states the needed flexibility to experiment in a criminal justice system that, historically, had not been closely supervised by the Supreme Court. At

---

*The debate between Frankfurter and Black focused primarily on the interpretation of the due process clause of the Fourteenth Amendment, though Black claimed that his incorporation theory was based on the entire first section of the amendment.

the same time, by selective intervention, the Court prevented the states from grossly violating a defendant's rights in state criminal justice systems.

That left altogether too much discretion to the states, Black believed, a discretion that could not be squared with the explicit guarantees of the Constitution. "I fear to see the consequences of the Court's practice of substituting its own concepts of decency and fundamental justice for the language of the Bill of Rights," Black wrote (in dissent). "I would follow what I believe was the original purpose of the Fourteenth Amendment—to extend to all the people of the nation the complete protection of the Bill of Rights."

Even Douglas, a man of powerful intellect and expansive ego, did not deny Hugo Black's leadership of the libertarian wing of the Court. Nor did he covet Black's role. To Douglas, both Black and Frankfurter were revivalist preachers, always seeking new judicial converts. That was not Douglas's style or goal. "I haven't been much of a proselytizer on the Court," he later admitted. "I've had the theory that the only soul I had to save was my own."

But Douglas was never a man to live in anyone's shadow for very long, even one so imposing as Hugo Black's. In his earliest years on the Court, Douglas had seemed content to follow Black's lead, particularly in civil liberties cases. At the same time, he distinguished himself as a prolific worker, a master of detail in complex corporate cases and an occasional innovator who seemed more willing than his colleagues to break new constitutional ground.

It took a dozen years on the Court for a justice's judicial philosophy to mature, Douglas once said, and he seemed slightly ahead of schedule. By the middle and late 1940s, Douglas had built on his earlier administrative and judicial experience to forge a philosophy that was markedly different in both style and substance from Black's, though most of his conclusions continued to coincide with his colleague's. The Douglas opinions were characterized by direct, incisive forays that cut through technical verbiage to the core legal issues. His opinions were frequently written on behalf of the "little guy," whether he was challenging a corporate president or a police sergeant.

Like Brandeis, Douglas linked economic and personal freedom in one constitutional chain. He was wary of consolidated power, economic or political, believing that the public interest was best served when responsibility was spread into many hands. That was the best guarantee, he believed, that the fortunes of the people would not be dependent on the selfish interests of a few at the top of the corporate or political ladder. He abhorred economic monopoly and was just as wary of government officials who were not answerable to the people. He insisted on strict accountability to the public by corporations, government bureaucrats and policemen. When they did not meet his standards, Douglas did not hesitate to intervene.

Black was the theoretician of the activist school, reading history and the literal language of the Constitution to support his broad libertarian views. Douglas was the pragmatist, providing practical, contemporary insights to fill Black's doctrinal structure. But Douglas, unlike Black, did not feel bound by history or judicial precedent. The law survived, Douglas believed, because of its adaptability to new circumstances. What may have been a correct interpretation fifty years ago, then, might be obsolete today because the times and society's values may have changed. "It is, I think, a healthy practice (too infrequently followed) for a court to reexamine its own doctrine," Douglas wrote in 1949.

That functional philosophy of law pervaded Douglas opinions, even in cases far afield from civil liberties. In one of his most noteworthy (but little publicized) opinions, Douglas devised the modern system of public utility rate-making and, in the process, boldly overturned a judicial precedent that had been the law for almost half a century. The earlier Court had established the rule that a utility rate be "reasonable" and later Court decisions developed the "reasonable" standard, based on speculative, rather than actual, utility costs. That standard had frequently enabled utilities to reap excessive profits.

Douglas wasn't interested in speculative costs or abstract theory of what was "reasonable." "It is not theory but the impact of the rate order which counts," he wrote. "If the total effect of the rate order cannot be said to be unjust and unreasonable, judicial inquiry . . . is at an end. The fact that the method employed to reach that result may contain infirmities is not then important."

Result, not theory, was Douglas's judicial litmus test. By substituting his practical formula for the earlier theoretical one, Douglas enabled a utility to earn a return sufficient to attract capital, but not so much as to produce excessive profits at the public's expense.

Where First Amendment freedoms were at stake, Douglas was even more aggressive in cutting through obstructive legal language. He destroyed the Post Office Department's argument that the "smoking car" humor of *Esquire* failed to satisfy a statutory standard that a magazine be published for the "public good" (and, thus, qualify for second-class mailing privileges). Congress did not intend that the second-class mailing privilege be manipulated by the Anthony Comstocks in the Post Office Department, Douglas asserted. "What is good literature, what has educational value, what is refined public information, what is good art," wrote Douglas, "varies with individuals as it does from one generation to another. There doubtless would be a contrariety of views concerning Cervantes' *Don Quixote,* Shakespeare's *Venus and Adonis* or Zola's *Nana.* But a requirement that literature or art conform to some norm prescribed by an official smacks of an ideology foreign to our system."

Douglas carefully scrutinized police behavior, alert to both obvious and subtle forms of intimidation. Speaking for the Court, Douglas threw out a confession of a fifteen-year-old, obtained by police officers who had worked in relays from midnight until 5:00 A.M. "A 15-year-old lad, questioned through the dead of night by relays of police, is a ready victim of the inquisition," wrote Douglas. "Mature men possibly might stand the ordeal from midnight to 5 A.M. But we cannot believe that a lad of tender years is a match for the police in such a contest. He needs counsel and support if he is not to become victim first of fear, then of panic. He needs someone on whom to lean lest the overpowering presence of the law, as he knows it, crush him."

With each libertarian opinion, Douglas's standing among political liberals was enhanced. Among legal scholars, however, his reputation was not so sturdy. Douglas was guilty, some scholars suggested, of inattention to legal detail and indifference to precedent. It was hinted that he pandered to the general public, which did not understand or appreciate the intricacies of the law. Professor Paul Freund of the Harvard Law School made the point gently but firmly. "When Douglas first came to the Court, he wrote a little differently," said Freund. "He took more pains with his opinions. In areas such as railroad reorganization, he was quite masterful in getting command of the intricate facts. Later, it seemed to me he showed less interest in painstaking opinions. His opinions seemed written more for a general audience. It was as if he got bored with the lawyer's craft."

A number of Douglas opinions during the Vinson Court years lent credence to Freund's observations. Even when Douglas agreed with a dedicated proceduralist like Frankfurter in result, his opinions often showed an impatience with tightly reasoned argument. It seemed as if he considered elaborate opinions to be unnecessary exercises in technical pedantry. A Douglas opinion that confirmed the Court majority's long-held view that state legislatures were to be given wide leeway to regulate social and economic affairs illustrated the point.

To encourage its citizens to vote, the Missouri legislature had enacted a statute that allowed any employee to leave work for four consecutive hours while the polls were open on election days. Further, the statute prohibited an employer from deducting wages for the time the employee was gone during working hours. A man named Grotemeyer left work at 3:00 P.M. one election day (giving him four hours before the polls closed), which was one and a half hours earlier than he normally left on an average workday. Grotemeyer's employer deducted $2.40 from Grotemeyer's weekly paycheck—i.e., withholding wages for the hour and a half Grotemeyer was gone during working hours. The employer was later fined under the statute for penalizing Grotemeyer.

For Douglas, the constitutional issue was quickly resolved. First, the employer's liberty-of-contract claim (i.e., penalizing him for withholding wages interfered with his freedom to deal with his employees) had not been recognized by the Court since the sweatshop days of the early part of the century. Second, Missouri's statute was simply a form of minimum wage which the Court had accepted as legitimate state economic regulation for decades. Third, the state's police powers to regulate its citizens included the right to protect the suffrage, for according to Douglas, the right to vote was "basic and fundamental."

The entire opinion required only five printed pages. And yet it covered constitutional doctrine that had embroiled the Court in controversy for several decades. Until Douglas had so announced, it was not clear that a state's statute which provided time off to vote was a minimum wage law or that a state's police powers (usually limited to regulations of health, safety or morals) included protection of the right to suffrage or that the right to vote in state elections was recognized under the Constitution as "basic and fundamental." The Douglas opinion significantly expanded the frontiers of constitutional law and did so with very quick strokes of the pen.

Was Douglas's reasoning correct? The six* members of that Court who joined Douglas's opinion apparently thought so, and today it still stands as good constitutional law. To be sure, Douglas could have taken his readers through a more thorough reasoning process, developing the police powers doctrine of the state more intricately and announcing the basic and fundamental right to suffrage with more impressive judicial documentation. It was not an exhaustive treatise, but few of Douglas's later opinions were.

When Douglas paid close attention to formal legal rules, critics charged that he did so merely to achieve a desired result. That complaint was made in a case involving an unfrocked priest named Terminiello, who had delivered a speech in Chicago to the Christian Veterans of America. The speech was both stupid and vulgar. Terminiello referred to Eleanor Roosevelt as "one of the world's Communists," and to Jews as "scum." He also predicted that there would be violence in the auditorium where he was speaking; that was about the only accurate statement Terminiello made all evening. A protesting crowd outside got out of hand despite the efforts of police to keep their demonstration peaceful. Stones, ice picks and bottles were hurled through the doors and windows of the auditorium. Terminiello was arrested and found guilty by a jury of disorderly conduct.

Douglas, writing for a five-man Court majority, overturned

---

*A seventh member of the Court, Justice Frankfurter, agreed with Douglas's result, but not his reasoning.

Terminiello's conviction. The trial court judge's instruction to the jury was flawed—decisively flawed, according to Douglas. The judge had defined "breach of the peace" to the jury under the relevant state statute as conduct that "stirs the public to anger, invites dispute, brings about a condition of unrest, or creates a disturbance." But speech that angered or invited dispute, Douglas reasoned, was the expression that should be protected by the Constitution's free speech guarantee.

"A function of free speech under our system of government is to invite dispute," Douglas wrote. "It may indeed best serve its high purpose when it induces a condition of unrest, creates dissatisfaction with conditions as they are, or even stirs people to anger. Speech is often provocative and challenging. It may strike at prejudices and preconceptions and have profound unsettling effects as it presses for acceptance of an idea."

How could Felix Frankfurter disagree with that inspiring defense of free speech? Frankfurter, in dissent, suggested that Douglas had ignored elementary rules of judicial analysis and procedure. The Terminiello case, Frankfurter noted, had been argued through the Illinois courts on the assumption that the charge to the jury was not to be read out of context—as Douglas had done—but in the setting in which the speech had been made. On that basis, the state court had found that Terminiello's speech had incited violent disorder. Terminiello's attorney did not even raise in the state courts the issue of the judge's instruction, and, said Frankfurter, the U.S. Supreme Court had no authority to reverse a state court's judgment on a ground that was not argued before the state courts themselves.*

Douglas was applauded in the liberal press for his *Terminiello* opinion and Frankfurter chastised. Irving Dilliard of the *St. Louis Post-Dispatch* compared Douglas's position to the earlier advocates of free speech, Justices Holmes and Brandeis, and suggested that those two judicial saints would have been disappointed in Frankfurter. "The last thing they [Holmes and Brandeis] would have approved," wrote Dilliard, "would have

---

*Professor Vern Countryman recalled that Douglas once asked him to research the question of when an appellate court would reverse on the basis of an error not raised below. His conclusion: "Whenever it wants to."

been state action whittling away the Bill of Rights."

Frankfurter's close friend Professor Freund wrote Dilliard in response to his editorial, suggesting that Frankfurter was not opposed to intervening when a state had violated the First Amendment but that he had properly insisted on procedural integrity in the *Terminiello* case. Freund added that Holmes and Brandeis were also sticklers for procedural integrity and that one of Brandeis's most famous statements on freedom of expression had come after he had upheld, on procedural grounds, the conviction of a defendant who had attempted to exercise First Amendment rights. After Freund sent Frankfurter a copy of the Dilliard editorial and his own letter to the journalist, Frankfurter replied that Dilliard's commentary was not "an edifying exhibit on the state of American journalism." He added, "I say this because Dilliard is way above the average of the lot in single-mindedness and responsibility, within the limits of his understanding."

If, as Frankfurter suggested, it had been only the inability of the press and his colleagues in the majority to fully understand his views on constitutional procedure, it would seem only a matter of time until the Frankfurter position would have been accepted. But it is the Douglas opinion, not the Frankfurter dissent, that is the law today and that has become a staple for constitutional texts on the First Amendment. And that may be the most telling commentary on so many Douglas opinions.

Douglas was not writing for the *Harvard Law Review*, but perhaps it was important that he was not. For if he had played the scholarly game, delivering long, heavily documented treatises, dwelling on technical aspects of the law, he might not have reached the substantive issues that would be crucial to future generations of Americans. But he did reach those substantive issues—the fundamental right to vote in state elections, for example, and the high place of free speech in our society—and his opinions became increasingly important in the second half of the twentieth century.

"I Ain't A-runnin'"

Appointed for life, Justices of the U.S. Supreme Court, according to theory, leave political ambitions in the robing room. In fact, judicial office has never been so inhibiting. Associate Justice Charles Evans Hughes, for example, resigned from the Court to campaign as the Republican candidate for President in 1916, returning to the Court in 1930 when President Hoover appointed him Chief Justice.

Other justices have resisted the temptation of politics, despite a lively interest by others in their candidacy. Pressed in 1875 to seek the presidency, Chief Justice Morrison Waite refused. "The office [of Chief Justice] came to me covered with honor," Waite said, "and when I accepted it my chief duty was not to make it a stepping stone to something else, but to preserve its purity." Unless he unequivocally withdrew his name from political consideration, Waite added, the public would suspect that his judicial decisions were made with an eye to political advantage. The statement effectively ended talk of a Waite candidacy.

The names of both Hughes and Waite were invoked several times during the 1940s as an admonishment to Justice William O.

Douglas, who was mentioned prominently as a potential candidate on the national Democratic ticket in all three presidential elections of that decade. At first, Douglas decided to make no public statement of his intention to stay on the Court, believing that such a statement would unnecessarily draw attention to himself. But as his candidacy was discussed with increasing frequency, Douglas was advised to leave the Court, as Hughes had done, or to take Waite's course and declare publicly his irrevocable decision to stay. Douglas, however, ignoring both pieces of advice, remained on the Court but consistently refused to make a public statement of an irrevocable decision to stay there.

In a letter to Felix Frankfurter shortly before the Democratic convention in 1940, Douglas denied all political ambition:

> Dear Felix: There is considerable talk in Washington about putting me on the ticket. I discount it very much. I do not really think it will come to anything. But it is sufficiently active to be disturbing. It is disturbing because I want none of it. I want to stay where I am. This line to you is to ask you, should the matter come your way, to scotch it. You need not be told any reasons. You know hosts of them—from the ones Brandeis would give, on down. I am *most* serious about this—probably more serious than the possibilities justify. But I write you just in case!

But three years later, Frankfurter was certain that Douglas was running for the presidency.

"How many plugged nickels would you give for Bill Douglas's chance of becoming President?" Frankfurter whispered to Justice Frank Murphy during an oral argument before the Court.

"Well, I think all the other contenders for the nomination will kill themselves off and that will leave only Bill," Murphy replied.

"I didn't ask for his chances to become a candidate but his chances to become President," said Frankfurter.

"Well, no Democrat will be elected in '44, but Bill will be named, I believe . . . he will run in such a way as to make himself available the next time thereafter."

"I am surprised, Frank, that it doesn't shock you to have this Court made a jumping-off place for politics."

The story of Douglas's "political ambitions" stretched for

more than a decade and was considerably more complex than either Douglas or Frankfurter ever suggested.

For Felix Frankfurter, his Court appointment was timely, since Frankfurter, at fifty-six, had effectively been preparing at the Harvard Law School for the job for twenty-five years. Douglas had never been so settled in his career. The picture of perpetual motion, Douglas had been appointed Sterling Professor of Law at Yale at thirty-two, chairman of the SEC at thirty-eight and Associate Justice of the U.S. Supreme Court at forty. Even for the ambitious Douglas, the Court appointment had seemed premature. "I'm too young to go on the Court," he had told his SEC assistant, Gerhard Gesell, after his appointment had been announced.

That the Douglas appointment was untimely occurred to others as well. Here was a young man whose successful past seemed to promise an equally successful future. To confine Douglas's youthful energy to a sedentary job on the Court seemed to be an egregious waste of a public resource. It was not surprising, then, that only a few months after Douglas had put on his black robe, there were suggestions that he take it off. If Roosevelt did not run for a third term in 1940, some Washington pundits suggested that Douglas would be an excellent choice to take his place at the top of the Democratic ticket. And if Roosevelt did run for a third term, who would be a better running mate than Bill Douglas?

Douglas could provide a fine political balance for FDR, the argument ran, since Douglas was a Westerner in his manners and speech, even though he had spent his entire adult life in the East. He dropped his *t*'s in words like "kept" and "slept," wore a five-gallon hat and told tales of modern-day Bunyans like his Oregon hunting and fishing pal Roy Schaeffer. Douglas could carry a party into the wee morning hours with his own stories of cherry-picking with itinerant farm workers, riding the rails and hiking through the beautiful Wallowas. But Douglas also had a powerful mind and a sophisticated Eastern legal education to deal with the nation's most protracted problems. An unshakable New Dealer, he had shown professional mettle at the SEC in his successful negotiations with the Wall Street establishment and his early decisions on the Court.

Talk of a Douglas candidacy, whether for President or for Vice-President, made some of his admirers, such as *The New York Times*'s Arthur Krock, uncomfortable. Krock wrote: "The gossips have definitely put him [Douglas] in the 1940 picture. He will remain there until he takes himself out. And from now until the nomination is made—unless the President makes known his own receptivity*—every opinion written by Justice Douglas will be weighed on the scale of political ambition. This will damage him and hamper the Supreme Court."

Douglas did not take Krock's advice, and maintained a public silence whenever his candidacy was discussed. But even without a public comment from Douglas, his candidacy was a lively topic of conversation among New Dealers. After FDR announced his intention to run for a third term, voluble Tommy Corcoran was spreading the word that he had talked to Roosevelt about a running mate and the President's first choice was Bill Douglas. Jim Farley, Roosevelt's chief political strategist, corroborated, in private conversation, Corcoran's report that Douglas was at the top of the President's list for a running mate. Harry Hopkins said "the New Dealers were strong for Douglas" but that he didn't think Douglas "wanted the job particularly." He added, however, that he thought Douglas would take it "if the President asked him to."

In a letter to Roosevelt before the 1940 Democratic convention, Douglas did not say a single word about his desire (expressed a week earlier to Frankfurter) to stay on the Court. Instead Douglas talked politics. While in Texas, where he had addressed a state bar meeting, Douglas wrote the President that his foreign policy was popular in Texas, that FDR would carry the state in the 1940 election and that Roosevelt was "the only one who can beat Willkie."

Roosevelt did not seem to know of—or did not take seriously —Douglas's privately stated desire to stay on the Court. The President had told Harold Ickes, for example, that he "kept turning over in his mind all who might be available" for the vice-presidency. The list included Douglas. But FDR told Ickes that he finally eliminated Douglas after he had consulted various party leaders. "They told me that Bill Douglas would not do," Roose-

*At the time of Krock's column, Roosevelt had not declared his candidacy.

velt said, according to Ickes, "because he was not well enough known."

Had Douglas been so adamantly opposed to leaving the Court as he suggested privately to Frankfurter, he could easily have relayed the message to Roosevelt. The President knew that Douglas was perfectly capable of making his professional intentions known. When, for example, Roosevelt spoke to Douglas in 1942 about the possibility of his becoming director of the War Manpower Board while serving on the Court, Douglas told the President directly and explicitly that it was a bad idea. "Unless I resign from the Court and take an administrative post," Douglas wrote FDR, "I am inclined to the view that any real undertaking on my part to iron out difficulties between department heads and others who have authority and who in many instances have a real hostility would not prove to be helpful and might injure the Court."

After Roosevelt had selected Henry Wallace as his running mate in 1940 and had been elected for a third term, there was again talk of Douglas leaving the Court, with the presumed destination to be a place on the 1944 Democratic ticket. Again Douglas privately denied political ambition, telling his close friend Fred Rodell that "I am here [on the Court] for keeps if I have my way." But he still refused to state publicly what he had written privately.

As the 1944 election approached, that public silence not only stirred Felix Frankfurter to deliver lectures to Frank Murphy on the need for justices to lead a monastic existence,* but provoked him to think of every Douglas judicial vote in purely political terms. Thus Frankfurter found Douglas's *Hirabayashi* opinion, upholding the curfew restriction on Japanese Americans, "full of cheap oratory." Douglas's conclusion in *Schneiderman* v. *U.S.* that the federal government, with explicit statutory authority, could deport a former Communist, Frankfurter was certain, was pitched to "the anti-Communist sentiment." Justice Frankfurter was also

*The Frankfurter sermon would have been considerably more effective if the speaker had not been practicing exactly what he preached against. Felix Frankfurter never cut himself off from the political world around him after *he* entered the "monastery." In fact, he was so busy advising the President on everything from the selection of a new Chief Justice in 1941 (Stone, a Republican, Frankfurter told FDR, would stand for national unity) to the conduct of the war that Stone himself complained that Frankfurter was "getting a little out of scale."

convinced that Douglas (and Black) had switched their votes in the second compulsory flag salute case *(West Virginia Bd. of Education* v. *Barnette)* for political reasons. "Those great libertarians," said Frankfurter, referring derisively to Douglas and Black, agreed with his constitutional analysis "until they heard from the people."

The charges revealed more about Frankfurter's hostility toward Douglas than it did the facts. Douglas's opinion in the Japanese exclusion case was not "full of cheap oratory," but was devoted primarily to a discussion of the statutory language under which the military had acted. His analysis of the statute under which the government had attempted to deport an ex-Communist was so technical that only trained lawyers—pro- or anti-Communist—would have had the will or expertise to appreciate it. And Douglas's vote in favor of a tiny band of irascible religious fundamentalists in the second flag salute decision would hardly have promoted his candidacy for the presidential nomination of a major national party.

Still others, less suspicious than Frankfurter, were watching Douglas, particularly after Roosevelt announced that he would run for an unprecedented fourth presidential term. The only question that remained for the Democrats was whether FDR would again choose Henry Wallace as his running mate or look elsewhere, perhaps to Justice Douglas.

Shortly before the Democratic convention, Roosevelt dined at the White House with Democratic leaders, including George E. Allen, an influential businessman. After the dinner, the President and his guests retired to his study, where they reviewed candidates for the vice-presidency. Roosevelt was told that Wallace's name should be eliminated because his left-wing views would hurt the ticket. To the surprise of Allen, Roosevelt then injected the name of Justice Douglas.* "He spent some time extolling Douglas. He said in the first place, he had the following of the liberal left wing—the same kind of people Wallace had. He had practical experience from the backwoods of the Northwest. He

---

*FDR had mentioned Douglas as a possibility to others as well. He had told Wallace that Douglas was a "picturesque figure" who might add strength to the ticket on the West Coast.

looked and acted, on occasion, like a Boy Scout and would have, in Roosevelt's opinion, appeal at the polls. Besides, said Roosevelt wryly, Douglas played an interesting game of poker."

After the President had finished his promotion of Douglas, the leaders sat in silence. "No one wanted Douglas any more than they wanted Wallace," Allen recalled. The President sensed this, according to Allen. The group then discussed the possibility of Harry Truman. Roosevelt was concerned about Truman's age, sixty, and again brought up the name of Douglas, who, at forty-five, was so much younger. But the leaders were still not enthusiastic about a Roosevelt-Douglas ticket. According to Allen, Roosevelt then said to Robert Hannegan, the Democratic national chairman: "Bob, I think you and everyone else want Truman." Much relieved, the Democratic leaders wanted to leave before the President changed his mind. As Roosevelt escorted them to the door, Allen recalled, the President said, "I know that this makes you boys happy, and you are the ones I am counting on. I still think Douglas would have greater public appeal."

Although the party bosses had apparently persuaded Roosevelt that the best choice would be Truman, Roosevelt, with characteristic political acumen, kept all his options open. He wrote Senator Samuel D. Jackson, permanent chairman of the convention, that if he were a delegate, he would vote for Wallace. The letter fulfilled an earlier Roosevelt commitment to Wallace. But the President added: "I do not wish to appear in any way dictating to the convention. Obviously the convention must do the deciding. And it should—and I am sure it will—give great consideration to the pros and cons of its choice." To Wallace's dismay, Roosevelt had, in effect, assured that the convention delegates in Chicago would pick FDR's running mate.

With his name carried in most news accounts as a possible running mate with Roosevelt, Douglas acted both publicly and privately as he had in 1940. He refused publicly to declare that he was not available for political office. Privately, Douglas wrote a colleague, this time Chief Justice Stone, not Frankfurter, that he did not seek political office and, indeed, would not accept the vice-presidential nomination if it was offered. "I think political ambitions are incompatible with performance of our judicial functions," Douglas wrote.

At the same time, Douglas had given close friends like Tommy Corcoran, and sympathetic colleagues, like Frank Murphy, the distinct impression that he would welcome the opportunity to run with Roosevelt. That was also the view of Frankfurter, who wrote Chief Justice Stone before the Democratic convention. "There have been presidential hopefuls on the Court since 1789—too many of them," Frankfurter wrote Stone, "but never before, I believe, has any Justice sought a vice-presidential nomination!"

At the convention, a small coterie of Douglas supporters, led by Corcoran, began to corner delegates. The pitch: if Henry Wallace was on the ticket again, it would be a sure handicap and would possibly spell defeat for Roosevelt. Douglas had a liberal outlook, and none of Wallace's liabilities.

At the same time, however, the Truman forces, led by Democratic Chairman Hannegan, were working even more skillfully for their candidate. Hannegan's job was made slightly more difficult because of a note he had been given by the President, dated the opening day of the convention, in which the President endorsed Truman and Douglas as possible running mates. "You have written me about Harry Truman and Bill Douglas," FDR wrote. "I should, of course, be glad to run with either of them, and I believe that either one would bring real strength to the ticket."

A controversy later arose over the note, with some accounts, including Douglas's, suggesting that the President had originally placed Douglas's name ahead of Truman's and that Hannegan had had the order switched before making the note public at the convention. But Judge Samuel R. Rosenman, who inspected the documentary evidence, concluded that Hannegan had not altered the note. Harry Hopkins, a principal Roosevelt adviser, may have provided the most accurate summary of the events leading to Truman's selection:

> I am certain that the President had made up his mind on Truman long before I got back to the White House last year. I think he would have preferred Bill Douglas, because he knew him better and he always liked Bill's toughness. But nobody really influential was pushing for Douglas. I think he had gone off fishing out in Oregon or someplace. And Bob Hannegan was certainly pushing

for Harry Truman, and the President believed he could put him over at the convention. So the President told him to go ahead and even put it in writing when Bob asked him to.

With every important Democratic leader lined up against him* and no ground swell of public support, Douglas probably could not have captured the vice-presidential nomination in 1944 unless Roosevelt had given him his strong and unequivocal endorsement. But the President, preoccupied with the war and reluctant to cause friction among Democratic regulars, would not dictate his choice to the delegates. In addition, Douglas himself made no effort to press his candidacy.

After the convention had selected Harry Truman as FDR's running mate, Douglas sent Chief Justice Stone a second letter, reiterating his earlier message. "I felt pretty relieved when the Convention was over," Douglas wrote. "For awhile, I feared that pressure might be put on me to go on the ticket. It was not. Every one of my friends knew that I had no political ambitions and that I had but one desire of staying where I am."

At least one close Douglas friend, Abe Fortas, corroborated the Justice's story. "Douglas was subjected to a lot of blandishments and a lot of pressure from a lot of different people," said Fortas. "Nothing he did, so far as I know, showed him being influenced by political objectives. When the great opportunity came, he opted out. In 1944, he said he wouldn't take the vice-presidency. I can tell you that on my own knowledge. It wasn't put to him in terms: 'Here is the vice presidency, you can have it.' Persons who, to me, and, I'm sure, to him, were in a position to speak authoritatively for those who had power to have him nominated, asked if he would go along and he said no. He was in Oregon at this dramatic moment."

But another Douglas friend received a very different impression. He was economist Eliot Janeway, at that time a journalist with Time Inc., who remembered: "Douglas thought he had the vice-presidential nomination in 1944 and he wanted it. But he was

*Several of Douglas's admirers, including Fred Rodell, blamed Douglas's failure to get the nomination, in part, on labor leader Sidney Hillman, chairman of the CIO political action committee, who, it was said, objected to having the Justice on the ticket.

afraid to make an obvious move. It would have looked bad since he was still on the Court."

Had Douglas rejected the possibility of a place on the Democratic ticket, as he repeatedly suggested, he presumably would have told his good friend and most enthusiastic supporter, Tommy Corcoran, to give up the chase. He did not. Instead Corcoran kept lobbying for Douglas to the end, fully convinced that his man had—and wanted—a political future. Corcoran and Eliot Janeway (both observed by Justice Murphy making frequent visits to Douglas's chambers before the Democratic convention) never believed that Douglas took himself out of contention in 1944. It was, rather, "the Truman crowd," most notably Bob Hannegan, who, according to both Corcoran and Janeway, undermined the Douglas candidacy.

Felix Frankfurter was almost certainly wrong in believing that Douglas used the Court as a stepping stone to national elective office. That would credit Douglas with a calculated foresight that is supported neither by documentation nor by Douglas's firm grasp of political reality. But to go to the other extreme, as Douglas has suggested, and conclude political ambition never passed through his mind, is equally mistaken.

To be sure, Douglas never threw his hat in the political ring in 1944, but neither did he effectively take it out when it was thrown in by others. He went on record with those whom he cared about most—namely, members of the Court, like Chief Justice Stone, and close friends like Fred Rodell—that he had no political ambition. But he did not eliminate the possibility of political lightning striking, as he could have by announcing publicly his irrevocable decision to stay on the Court. To serve with Franklin D. Roosevelt could not have been a totally unattractive prospect. Indeed, both Roosevelt and Douglas himself believed that Douglas had extraordinary talent which could have been put to good use in the executive branch of government.

Shortly after Truman became President, Douglas, in fact, considered the possibility of moving from the judicial to the executive branch. With important vacancies still to be filled in the cabinet, Douglas admitted to Fred Rodell that an offer from Truman to be his Secretary of State or War might be tempting. The rumors Douglas had heard, however, made James Byrnes the front runner for State, though Douglas was also aware from "general talk" that Secretary of War "might come this way." He might consider either cabinet post if it was offered, wrote Douglas, depending on the timing of the offer and "the state of affairs when it happened." Neither offer was made to Douglas, but other opportunities to leave the judiciary would arise. And when they did, Douglas did not show the detachment of a man who had committed his professional life to the Court.

In 1946, Douglas was only forty-seven years old, but he had already served on the Court for seven years—and he was slightly bored. He still wrote more opinions than most of his colleagues. And he cared about the values that he defended in his opinions. Yet Douglas privately complained to friends that the Court's work was confining and did not fully satisfy his intellectual appetite or temperament.

Douglas had already begun to test his ideas outside the Supreme Court in magazine articles and public speeches whose subjects invariably transcended strictly legal issues. With the increased public exposure, Douglas created a new image: that of the statesman—or politician, depending on how favorably one viewed Douglas's extrajudicial activity. No one denied, however, that the Justice offered outspoken views on the direction in which America should be headed at home and abroad.

Douglas used the Bill of Rights as his springboard to a broader political vision. He wanted the Truman administration to combat communism, but not at the price of suppressing individual freedoms. His strategy in fighting communism, in fact, included a firm commitment to political liberties that totalitarian regimes denied. But Douglas went further.

"The real victory over Communism will be won in the rice fields rather than on the battlefields," Douglas declared. "If we want the hundreds of millions of people of the world in the democratic ranks, we must show them the way with practical programs of social reconstruction."

In his speeches, Douglas celebrated the virtues of the common man; he also strongly supported industrial democracy, in general, and collective bargaining and the vitality of labor unions in particular. He advocated a tough stance toward the Soviet Union, but also supported the United Nations and promoted the idea of international peace through cooperative social and economic programs. He was both a democrat and a Democrat, a left-of-center supporter of labor and a liberal reader of the Bill of Rights. But he was no pie-in-the-sky socialist, as many Democrats thought Henry Wallace to be. Douglas was, in sum, a tough-minded liberal who might appeal to that faction of the Democratic party whose allegiance President Truman seemed to be losing at an alarming rate in the postwar period.

It appeared to be a shrewd political move, therefore, for Truman to look to Douglas to fill the vacancy left by the resignation of Secretary of the Interior Harold Ickes. The departure of Ickes, one of the last holdovers from the New Deal, brought widespread lamentations from the liberal Democratic community. "One has the feeling," the *New York Post* commented, "that a poorer and poorer cast is dealing desperately with a bigger and bigger story."

Besides assuaging liberals in the Democratic party who did not like the Truman administration's increasingly conservative tone, a Douglas appointment made sense for other reasons. First, Douglas enjoyed a reputation as a good administrator and a committed conservationist, two attractive credentials for Interior. Moreover, Truman may have felt that he owed Douglas a favor, since he had foiled any hopes the justice might have had for the vice-presidential nomination in 1944. Finally, by bringing Douglas into the administration, Truman might well set him up to run with the President in 1948, when Truman would need to bring the discontented liberals in his party back in the fold.

Before contact between Douglas and the Truman administration was made, rumors of Douglas's appeal and availability circulated around Washington. The *Washington Star* reported that Tommy Corcoran was promoting the Douglas appointment at a dinner party at the home of Representative Lyndon Johnson of Texas. Besides Corcoran, the Johnson dinner guests included Speaker of the House Sam Rayburn, Abe Fortas and Douglas himself. Later, it was reported that Rayburn saw Bob Hannegan and the President on Douglas's behalf.

Corcoran, naturally, continued to promote the Douglas appointment, as did James Forrestal, Truman's Secretary of the Navy. Writing to the President, Forrestal tried to persuade the

President that Douglas, a loyal New Dealer and friend of Ickes, would not give Truman trouble. "If Bill went in," Forrestal told Truman, "he would be loyal to you." Truman later discussed the matter with his close adviser Clark Clifford, and told Clifford that he wanted Douglas at Interior. Forrestal was sent to the Court to make Douglas the offer. Douglas said he wanted to think about it. Later, both Clifford and Truman talked to Douglas about the appointment. The Justice said that he was interested in the appointment, but still refused to commit himself.

"Douglas was very interested in the Interior appointment," Clifford recalled. "There were appealing facets to the job." The cabinet post would have provided Douglas with a showcase for his considerable administrative talents as well as a natural opportunity for him to express his strong commitment to the protection of the environment. It would also have given him an opportunity to leave the Court and take up a more active political life. Finally, it could have set up Douglas very nicely for the 1948 election, either as Truman's running mate or as a presidential candidate in his own right. Did Douglas have political ambitions? "Of course, he did," said Clifford. "He had a lot of ideas that he wanted to try out."

On February 20, 1946, *The New York Times* reported that the Douglas appointment was imminent, delayed only by some lingering doubts of Justice Douglas. Still, the *Times* reported, "friends of Mr. Douglas were confident today that he would step down from the Court to enter a new field. Following his visit to the White House yesterday, Mr. Douglas is understood to have exchanged views with former Secretary Ickes and afterward to have decided to accept the President's offer."

But while still considering the offer, Douglas had also conferred with Chief Justice Stone, who expressed deep displeasure over the prospect of losing Douglas. As a general principle, Stone had told Douglas he did not approve of members of the Court leaving their positions to take up administrative or political duties. The Chief Justice had complained bitterly when Justice Owen Roberts had taken time away from his judicial duties to conduct a government inquiry into the bombing of Pearl Harbor. Later, Stone was disappointed when Justice Jackson had taken leave to become the American prosecutor at Nuremberg. And now Douglas was going to join those who had "left him in the lurch."

The Chief Justice also spoke to the President, reiterating his opposition to the Douglas appointment. He needed Douglas on the Court, Stone told Truman, because he was one of its most talented (and prolific) members. Luring Douglas away with a cabinet offer, Stone said, would do a profound disservice to the Court.

On February 22, Douglas wrote the President, declining the offer to join his cabinet as Secretary of the Interior. His resignation from the Court, Douglas wrote Truman, "in the middle of a term would create serious difficulties." Douglas added: "Against this feeling, there is my strong affection for you and a desire to help with this huge problem."

The Douglas refusal did not dampen the rumors of his political availability. In fact, talk of the Interior offer only intensified speculation about Douglas's political future. Whether Douglas ran with Truman in 1948 or on his own, his candidacy seemed compelling to his admirers. Among them was *Times* columnist Arthur Krock, who made the Douglas case for 1948: "He [Douglas] was once strongly encouraged by Mr. Roosevelt to think of himself as a successor in the White House and steward of the New Deal; he is young and ambitious, chafes under the confinement of judicial life and has a definite domestic and foreign program. His latest political appearance, though brief and abortive, has prompted many political managers and others to take another look at the record and personality of Justice Douglas."

Soon enough the political "managers" were taking Krock's advice. With the 1948 Democratic convention only a few months away, the word was out that the Democratic bosses had okayed Douglas as Truman's running mate. These were the same bosses —New York's Ed Flynn, Chicago's Ed Kelly and New Jersey's Frank Hague—who turned thumbs down on Douglas in 1944 when FDR suggested the Justice as *his* running mate. Douglas, the argument ran, would balance the ticket geographically and would give a needed New Deal flavor to appeal to Democrats in the East and Middle West. Douglas's strong civil rights and labor stands would not sit well with Southern conservatives, but the bosses had already made the judgment that Southern support was not critical.

Stories of the impending Douglas candidacy provoked a familiar fury in the chambers of Justice Frankfurter. Frankfurter told Justice Stanley Reed "that there was a good deal to Bob Jackson's clever remark this morning that the Court should adjourn until after the election." Later, he wrote Reed: "I think I know the history of the Supreme Court with sufficient intimacy to be confident in saying that never has it been so deeply drawn into the mire of politics as it has in the last few years." Frankfurter did not hide the target of his criticism: he attached a newspaper column of Joseph Alsop's which had discussed the Douglas candidacy for Vice-President in 1948.

Douglas continued to allow the speculation of his candidacy to swirl about him in the early months of 1948. But word was passed to the press that Douglas rated his position on the Court above the vice-presidency. In Douglas's mind, however, the presidency "would be something else again," *U.S. News* reported.

The liberal wing of the Democratic party picked up the theme. The Americans for Democratic Action wanted to substitute Douglas (or General Dwight D. Eisenhower) for Truman at the head of the Democratic ticket. According to the ADA, Douglas had turned in a perfect political report card. He was correct on civil liberties ("completely uncompromising"), industrial relations (a strong advocate of collective bargaining), the United Nations (he was for it) and communism ("The antidote to Communism," Douglas had said, "is effective democratic government"). Under Douglas's leadership, the ADA believed, "we could expect the cause of liberty and economic justice to be secure in America and to be championed throughout the world."

For the third time in as many Democratic presidential campaigns in the forties, Douglas mixed his signals. On the one hand, he authorized the publication of a letter to Irving Dilliard of the *St. Louis Post-Dispatch* in which the Justice wrote that "I have done everything I can to stop any friends of mine from promoting me for any political office. If any one of them is writing letters or otherwise trying to inspire college students or others to organize clubs for me, they are acting against my express desires and wishes." And later he issued folksy statements denying his candidacy. "I never was a-runnin'," he told reporters, "I ain't a-runnin' and I ain't goin' tuh."

But Douglas never fully convinced friends, like Tommy Corcoran, that he was serious. "Bill Douglas wanted to be President," Corcoran said firmly. Members of the press questioned Douglas's intentions as well. Shortly before the 1948 Democratic convention in Philadelphia, Robert Bendiner reported in *The Nation* that despite Douglas's avowed desires to stay on the Court, he really couldn't make up his mind yet whether to actively seek the Democratic presidential nomination. The indecision, Bendiner suggested, was not based on the principle that he could best serve the country on the Court, but rather on the practical political risk faced by any Democrat in 1948, including Douglas, of competing against the Republican candidate, Governor Thomas E. Dewey of New York. And if Douglas lost in 1948, his chances in 1952 would be diminished. Democratic politicians from Montana, Colorado, Minnesota and Washington had met with Douglas, Bendiner reported, and told the Justice that they could line up uncommitted delegates for him if he would only declare his availability. Douglas said neither "yes" nor "no," but rather simply looked out the window.

Douglas's fence-sitting presented a stark contrast to the other attractive noncandidate, General Eisenhower. Eisenhower did not want to run for office in 1948 and issued three separate statements saying that he did not want the Democratic presidential nomination and, finally, that if it were offered to him he would not accept it.

On the same day that Ike had issued his final, Sherman-like, statement that he would not accept the Democratic nomination for President, Douglas refused to comment on ADA President Leon Henderson's statement that his organization would shift all its support to Douglas. Four days later, Douglas told a reporter for the *Philadelphia Inquirer* that he did not plan to be a candidate. Would Douglas accept the nomination if he were drafted? "I have no comment at this time," Douglas replied.

"Tell those amateurs at the ADA," Harry Truman reportedly said to Washington attorney Paul Porter, "that any shithead behind this desk can get renominated." Douglas did not see the 1948 scenario as clearly as the President. Until the last minute—even after the Democratic convention in Philadelphia had opened

—Douglas thought he had a chance. "I was on the telephone from Philadelphia when Leon Henderson was telling Douglas there was no hope," Joseph Rauh, Jr., long-time ADA leader, recalled. "Douglas had been talking to supporters, giving them advice, encouraging them. Even when Henderson called, Douglas seemed reluctant to pull out."

"A professional politician probably would have known it was hopeless for Douglas in 1948," Rauh said. "Ike could have appealed to all factions but Douglas could only have gotten the nomination by knocking Truman off from the left. Unlike Ike, Douglas had to win by the normal political rules; you don't upset an incumbent President except on an issue. But Douglas was still on the Court so he couldn't seize on an issue."

Truman was easily renominated by the Democrats in Philadelphia on the first ballot. After he had secured the Democratic presidential nomination, Truman turned to the business of selecting a running mate. His first choice was Douglas. Eleanor Roosevelt telephoned Douglas to urge him to take Truman's offer. But Douglas again expressed his reluctance to resign from the Court to run with the President. Still, close friends of Douglas's reported that he had not ruled out the number two spot entirely. Douglas had yet "to be persuaded of the wisdom of becoming President Truman's running mate," *The New York Times* reported. "It thus became apparent that only an appeal from the President in the name of the party could swing Mr. Douglas around to an attitude of availability."

Truman made the personal plea by telephone, reaching Douglas in Oregon's Wallowa Mountains. Truman remembered the conversation: "I call him, tell him I'm doing what FDR did to me. He owes it to the country to accept."

After considering the President's offer for several days, Douglas turned it down. "I feel deeply that my greatest service to the nation at the present time is to remain on the Supreme Court," Douglas said in a prepared statement. "I have reached that conclusion with the greatest respect for the judgment of those who think otherwise. And so I say definitely and finally that I am not available for any public office." Two weeks later, Douglas wrote the President, explaining his decision. "Basic in my thinking," wrote Douglas, "was the thought that politics had never been my profession, and that I could serve my country best where I am. I weighed the pros and cons many times before I called you back. I do want you to know that I greatly appreciate the confidence you expressed in me. I will always cherish your friendship. I assure you it would have been a pleasure to stand shoulder to shoulder with you in the fray."

There were other, less inspiring, reasons for Douglas to decline Truman's offer. "Why be a number two man to a number two man?" asked Tommy Corcoran. "In 1948," recalled Clark Clifford, "Douglas, like just about everybody else, thought Truman was going to lose; there was no reason to go on the ticket."

Truman, too, sensed that Douglas's rejection was based on more than devotion to the Court. "He [Douglas] belongs to that crowd of Tommy Corcoran, Harold Ickes, Claude Pepper crackpots whose word is worth less than Jimmy Roosevelt's," Truman later wrote. "I hope he has a more honorable outlook. No professional liberal is intellectually honest. That's a real indictment— but true as the Ten Commandments. Professional liberals aren't familiar with the Ten Commandments or the Sermon on the Mount." In a memorandum shortly after Douglas had turned him down, Truman viewed the Douglas refusal in cold political terms: "I'm inclined to give some credence to Tommy Corcoran's crack to Burt Wheeler that Douglas had said he could not be a No. 2 man to a No. 2 man."

After 1948, there was speculation in the press, and suspicion in the White House, that Justice Douglas still coveted political office. A searing Douglas dissent in a 1949 antitrust decision was interpreted by the *Times*'s Arthur Krock as an address to a political constituency, not to the facts of the case. And in 1951, when Douglas announced that the U.S. should recognize Red China, President Truman viewed Douglas's public statement as political and bluntly told him so. "I am sorry that a Justice of the Supreme Court has been willing to champion the interest of a bunch of murderers by a public statement," Truman wrote Douglas. "You have missed the boat on three different occasions, if you wanted to get into politics." And then the President gave Douglas some advice: "Since you are on the highest court in the land, it seems to me that the best thing you can do is to give your best effort to the Court and let the President of the United States run the political end of foreign and domestic affairs."

Douglas had already taken half of Truman's advice. He had written a letter to Truman in September 1951, later made public, that declared in unequivocal terms that he would make the Court his lifetime career. He would never, thereafter, give serious consideration to high political office.

Why Douglas waited eleven years to make his intentions so clear is open to speculation. He may have accepted the political reality that it was virtually impossible to run for the presidency from the Court, as Charles Evans Hughes and Harry Truman seemed to understand better than Douglas. Moreover, his marriage to Mildred was breaking up at this time and Douglas may have concluded, as Tommy Corcoran advised him, that a divorce would present an insurmountable obstacle to high political office. Finally, Douglas may simply have come to terms with his national role, realizing that as an associate justice of the U.S. Supreme Court, he possessed a potent political power base.

"The Court became Douglas's power center," said Eliot Janeway, "and it had none of the problems posed by administrative responsibilities and patronage of political office." For the rest of his days on the Court, through the fifties, sixties and into the seventies, then, Douglas would ignore the second part of Truman's advice and he would speak out on every public issue that he considered vital to the national interest.

————————————————————

A MAN'S MAN

BILL DOUGLAS was, in his friend Fred Rodell's words, "a man's man." His clothes were scruffy and so were his language and his sense of humor. His hobbies were mountain climbing and horseback riding and backpacking, all activities that rewarded bodily prowess. Even his choice of companions, like Roy Schaeffer, the burly outdoorsman who ran a successful dude ranch in Oregon's Wallowa Mountains, corroborated Douglas's virile image.

Schaeffer was the quintessential Westerner, a man, said Millie Douglas, "after Dad's own heart. He was a good storyteller and he had great strength and stamina. Dad and Roy complemented each other."

Douglas met Schaeffer in the summer of 1939 while the Douglas family was vacationing in the Wallowa Mountains. Soon the two were horseback riding into the deepest recesses of the Oregon mountain range. Stunned by the beauty of the region, Douglas fantasized aloud about owning a small tract of land in the mountains, just enough to build a cabin for a family retreat. The problem, Douglas thought, was that the entire area was desig-

nated a national forest. A short time later, as Douglas and Schaeffer hunched forward in their saddles and looked at the Lostine
River from a spectacular vista high above, Schaeffer waved to a
clearing which Douglas later described as "one of the loveliest
spots God ever created."

"I'll give you this piece," Schaeffer said.

That piece, it turned out, was part of over one thousand acres
of an old mining claim that Schaeffer had purchased. Douglas
protested about the price but not the piece of land. He and
Schaeffer later came to terms on a purchase price, and two years
later, the Douglases, Roy Schaeffer and a carpenter were busily
constructing the first of three log cabins that would serve as the
haven for the Douglas family, cabinet members, journalists and
local cowboys for years to come.

Roy Schaeffer stories dominated countless Douglas conversations as well as substantial portions of two Douglas books. Born
on a winter day in 1888 in the Wallowa valley when the tempera-
ture was sixty degrees below zero, Schaeffer learned early—and
well—every skill he would need to survive in the wilderness. He
could build a lean-to in a driving snowstorm, or expertly dig a
hole under the massive drifts. He knew how to shoe a horse, shear
sheep, tan leather and shoot a .22 Remington with uncanny accuracy. He could also drag a 185-pound buck out of a canyon and
wield a mighty ax. "Roy Schaeffer is the man I would want with
me," Douglas wrote, "if I were catapulted into a dense woods
anywhere from Maine to Oregon."

There was a gentle side of Roy Schaeffer that Douglas admired
almost as much as his toughness. Douglas saw Schaeffer calm a
wild and trembling mare simply by talking to her in an assuring
low voice. He taught Douglas to kneel down silently in a mountain stream, touch the underbelly of a passing rainbow trout and
lift it effortlessly out of the water. Once, in the Wallowa wilderness with young Bill Douglas, Jr., he wrapped his huge arms
around the base of a tree, showing affection as a father would for
a member of his family.

Fred Rodell shared Roy Schaeffer's reverence for nature. But
unlike Schaeffer, Rodell offered a polished intellectual component to his friendship with Douglas. A slightly built Yale Law

School professor, Rodell became a close Douglas friend while he was a favorite Douglas student at Yale. The friendship was based, initially, on intellectual compatibility; Rodell flaunted a carefree brilliance in the classroom—quick, uninhibited, incisive—not unlike his mentor's. The two also shared a determined unpretentiousness. They dressed down, not up, and their conversations were full of rough words and sexual allusions. Asked what they usually talked about on their many fishing expeditions, Rodell replied, "Dirty limericks." And though Rodell had no formidable physique to match Roy Schaeffer's or Douglas's, his love of the outdoors was comparable and he celebrated it with Douglas on mountain trails and in trout-filled streams throughout the country.

Since Douglas's SEC days, Rodell had pledged his loyalty to Douglas in print and in private letter, assuring Douglas and the nation that Douglas was, in character and in ideas, the best public servant that America had to offer. Douglas returned that devotion with a rare, abiding trust. As Douglas's confidant, Rodell knew of his friend's intense distrust of Felix Frankfurter and his frustration with a Frankfurter-dominated Supreme Court majority.

Douglas and Rodell also shared a crude sense of humor; the two never seemed to tire of trading dirty jokes. "Do You Know Americans," which Douglas sent to Rodell, was an example:

> Two women sat on a bench in a London street. One said to the other, "Do you know Americans?" "Do I know Americans, why 'twas just tonight," the other replied, "that me old man says to me, 'Go down and get me a bucket of beer' and as I was returning who does I run into but an American. Before I could say 'Trafalgar Square'—he grabs me by the ass, shoves me under a tree, downs me, ins me, outs me, wipes his tallywacker on me petticoat, drinks me old man's beer, pisses in the bucket and stalks off whistling 'God Save the King.' And you asks me: 'Do I know Americans?' "

When he uncovered a particularly pleasing example of a favorite art form, the dirty limerick, Douglas passed it on to Rodell:

> There was a young fellow named Feeny,
> Who put high proof gin on his weeny,
> You may think him uncouth,

> For he added vermouth,
> And slipped his best girl a martini.

Another time, Douglas gloried in a limerick about Justice Robert Jackson, one of his least favorite colleagues on the Court. After stories of Jackson's difficulties at Nuremberg had been reported in Washington, Douglas sent Rodell a limerick he said he had heard:

> There was an upstart called Jackson,
> Who went to Germany for action,
> Not to bring men to justice,
> But to feather his *nest*ice,
> And finally fell flat on his *ass*ton.

The most memorable letters from Douglas to Rodell were touching expressions of love for Fred and his ailing wife, Katherine. In 1946, the news that Katherine was seriously ill with tuberculosis was followed by a letter that told of Douglas's sadness about "your Katherine." When Rodell's wife seemed to take a turn for the better, Douglas expressed relief and happiness and made plans to bring the Douglases and Rodells together: "I was delighted to hear your voice last night. I knew not only from what you said but from the lift in your voice that Katherine was over the ordeal of the operation. That was good news. I know the path to recovery will be slow. But I am sure she is in the clear. . . . We have plenty of room in our new place. The Rodell suite awaits you. . . . And give Katherine our love."

To help Katherine Rodell's recovery, Douglas suggested that Fred take a job in a warmer climate so that his wife could recuperate under more favorable conditions than the brittle New England winter offered. "Shouldn't all of us get on the ball to see what can be worked out in New Mexico?" Douglas asked. "We should be doing some planning on it right away." In a short time, Douglas had written the president of the University of New Mexico, recommending Rodell ("He is a grand promoter of ideas, a man of tremendous energy, resourcefulness, imagination and creative ability") for the deanship of the university's new law school. It was neither the first nor the last time that Douglas would promote Rodell for a professional position. It was, quite simply, what one true friend did for another.

Damon Trout was fun, the practical joke–loud party–pure silliness kind of fun that Douglas found irresistible. Trout and Douglas met, appropriately enough, at a loud party in 1940 in a Portland hotel. Although Douglas and Trout did not seem suitably matched—Trout had dropped out of school after the sixth grade, gone to sea and finally prospered in the marine electrical business —the two joked and partied and caroused together for more than three decades.

The affection was built around a mound of practical jokes. When Trout wrote Douglas that he was coming to Washington to visit, Douglas told Trout to come to the side entrance of the Court—where, unknown to Trout, Douglas had arranged for two guards to hide in the bushes. When Trout passed, the guards jumped out of the bushes brandishing their guns. "It scared the hell out of me," Trout recalled. Later, Trout fidgeted in the courtroom while his friend the Justice heard oral arguments. Finally a Court messenger handed Trout a note which read: "Let's get out of here and have a smile." That was the signal for Trout and Douglas to leave the formal activity in court and retreat to Douglas's chambers, where they spent the rest of the day drinking and telling stories.

From Outer Mongolia, Douglas sent Trout a postcard with the note: "I met a gal who says you're the father of her daughter." After Douglas built his Goose Prairie home, Trout nailed a sign to a tree trunk which read: "Absolutely nothing happened on this spot—September 6, 1859."

When Douglas and Trout were in New York City at the same time, Douglas took Trout with him, whether to a party at the Stork Club or to a critical discussion of Douglas's latest book. On the West Coast, Trout returned the favor, taking Douglas to his favorite bars and introducing him to pretty young women. One was a cocktail waitress named Catherine Heffernan, whom Douglas met through Trout at a Portland restaurant one night in 1965. She became Douglas's fourth wife less than a year later.

At the age of fifty, when most men have moved through the mid-life crisis and are contemplating the ravages of the aging process, Douglas seemed at the peak of his physical powers,

climbing, riding horseback, trekking with the step and determination of a man half his age. Then, suddenly, it all seemed over.

On October 2, 1949, the last day of the Court's recess, Douglas
had arranged to meet his old friend Elon Gilbert in the Cascades.
At Chinook Pass, Douglas mounted a huge cow horse, half registered thoroughbred, half American saddle, that Gilbert had
brought for him, and followed Gilbert's horse up the winding,
increasingly steep and rocky Cascade trail. After an hour, Douglas stopped to tighten the saddle girth of his mount while Gilbert
continued to ride over a crest and out of sight of his companion.
Douglas remounted, and as he later recalled:

> Suddenly the horse reared. Probably a hornet bit him. As he
> reared he wheeled and put his front feet on the side of the
> mountain. That put him practically straight up and down. I dis-
> mounted by sliding off his tail. Due to the pitch of the mountain
> the drop was about 8 feet. I lost my footing as I hit the ground
> and rolled. I rolled about 50 feet. I ended on a ledge—uninjured
> —not even a scratch. I raised my head to get up when I saw the
> horse. He was rolling too. I was in his path. He was only a few
> feet away. All I could do was duck. He rolled over me and I could
> hear all the bones break. Then he was gone and I was paralyzed
> with pain and unable to move. It took four hours to get me to the
> hospital and some morphine.

He should have died. His chest was crushed, twenty-three of his
twenty-four ribs were broken and his lung was punctured. "He
just lived because he wanted to live," said Elon Gilbert. "I suppose he would say it was all in a day's work."

The messages of concern streamed into Yakima's St. Elizabeth's Hospital from President Truman and FBI Director J. Edgar
Hoover and from obscure well-wishers like Harry E. Mock of
Marion, Indiana, who had broken three ribs himself and wanted
to commiserate with the Supreme Court Justice.

Sometimes Douglas responded to the outpouring of sentiment
with humor. To Harry Mock, Douglas wrote: "When you have
fourteen* broken ribs, a hiccup is a crisis, a cough a disaster and
a sneeze a calamity. And the most unfriendly act in the world
would be a pat on the back." But to his old friend and colleague
Jerome Frank, Douglas was serious and sentimental. "Your won-

*Fourteen turned out to be a preliminary, and optimistic, estimate.

derful letter came at the lowest point in my life—when it was touch and go," Douglas wrote. "What you said helped me hang on. . . . Thanks, Jerry, for the sentiments you expressed. I'll never forget."

Douglas had also received a note from a social acquaintance, Mercedes Davidson, the wife of a high-ranking Interior Department official, expressing her concern over the Justice's health. For Mercedes Davidson, it was "just a good 'get well' note," but to Douglas, it was a moving memento and the beginning, for him, of an amorous interest in Mrs. Davidson, who in time became the second Mrs. Douglas.

Douglas's marriage to Mildred was over in all but name by 1949 and it was apparent to anyone who observed the two of them in Douglas's room at St. Elizabeth's Hospital. Most of the time, Douglas simply ignored Mildred, even when she sat at his bedside. He was warm toward old friends Elon Gilbert and Dr. Douglas Corpron, but never toward Mildred. She spent much of her time in the hospital corridor. When Douglas did speak to her, it was usually to give an order. After Douglas had been told that the warm Arizona sun would be good for him, he instructed Mildred to drive a car to Arizona from Yakima, alone, because *he* wanted a car in Arizona.

"It wasn't fifty-fifty between Justice Douglas and his wife," recalled his nurse, Fern Ferris. "I thought she was a better woman than he was a man," she added. "That's just my opinion. Mrs. Douglas was warm and nice to be with."

Actually, it wasn't fifty-fifty between Douglas and any member of his family while he was hospitalized. He was cool to Millie, then a freshman at Whitman College, and to Bill junior too. But he was not cool with the hired help, and fired every nurse who was hired for him. That is, until Dr. Douglas Corpron hired Fern Ferris. "I just told him what he was supposed to do," Mrs. Ferris recalled. "I'd say, 'It's time for your bath.' He'd say, 'I don't want to take a bath.' I'd say, 'That's too bad.' "

After seven weeks in the Yakima hospital, Douglas was flown to a guest ranch in Tucson to continue his recovery. His spirits seemed to surge. Dr. Roy Hewitt "thinks I'll live and raise hell for many a year," Douglas wrote Chief Justice Vinson. "He thinks I am progressing better than a man has a right to expect. The total

number of ribs broken will exceed 17. In fact, they are sure of
only one thing—that one rib is not broken. So I'll bring back a
new championship, no doubt. I'm chafing in all this idleness.
Don't hesitate to shove things my way. I don't want to get too
rusty."

Douglas was parading his best spirits past the Chief Justice.
Actually, he was not feeling quite so good, he wrote Hugo Black,
nor was he so sanguine about his ability to take a share of the
Court's work. The shock of the accident and the long recupera-
tion, Douglas admitted to Black, had exhausted him.

"Justice Douglas is, indeed, a very fortunate man to have survived his serious injury with as little permanent injury as we
anticipate he will have," Dr. Hewitt wrote Chief Justice Vinson.
"His remarkable constitution has certainly been in his favor."

In a short time, reporters and photographers had flocked to
Arizona to record the recovery of the Court's most colorful justice. The Justice was photographed wearing a necktie displaying
a picture of Kendall, the horse who had thrown him and rolled
over him in the Cascades. The photograph appeared in *Time*
magazine with the caption: "Never a man to hold a grudge." And
between the covers of *Life*, Douglas was shown blowing up bal-
loons to strengthen "the judicial chest."

For Douglas, publicity at that time was not unwelcome. As he
recuperated, Douglas had been putting the final touches on a
manuscript that recounted his early life and love of nature. The
book, entitled *Of Men and Mountains*, would be published in the
spring of 1950 by Harper and Brothers. Before publication, John
Fischer, Douglas's editor at Harper's, suggested that the author
might hold a press conference to discuss his accident and mention that he was working on the book at the time of the mishap.
With luck, Fischer wrote Douglas, reporters would focus their
questions on the book rather than the accident. Douglas agreed
to hold the press conference.

Replying to Fischer's suggestions for editing changes and publicity, Douglas sounded like a typically ebullient author, hungry
for commercial success. Douglas's enthusiasm for his book was
particularly striking since, at precisely the same time, he had
dramatically recounted to Hugo Black his weak condition and
thoughts of resignation from the Court: "The bones are mending

O.K. But it takes a long time to get the full reserve of strength back. . . . I had been thinking that if I couldn't get back on the job in a month, I should resign. I do not want to cripple the work of the Court by my absence. But your letter is most reassuring and indicates that I will not cripple the Court if I stay away until March."

One day after writing Black, Douglas discussed publicity ideas for his book with his editor: "I might arrange to have a series of interviews here built around special episodes, e.g. (1) my first horseback ride since the accident (2) My use of the hills to restore my lung. . . . If the infantile paralysis phase is emphasized, the possibilities are endless. There is for example the Horace Heidt radio show—amateur hour—one of the best on the air. . . ."

Douglas followed through on his own publicity suggestions. He took that horseback ride, posing near a cactus for photographers. And he agreed to appear on the Horace Heidt show to discuss his book. After the book had been published, Douglas attended dinners in Yakima and La Grande in his honor and agreed to autograph his books in a Portland bookstore. He also attended an autograph party in Seattle, happily reporting to John Fischer that "they sold 77 copies that day."

Of Men and Mountains received excellent reviews—and with good reason. The book presented both the style and the substance of its author vividly. Douglas's climb from poverty and polio were recounted with the dramatic detail of the novelist. His adventures in the Cascades read like tales that filled most American boys' bookcases. The difference was that Douglas's stories were true, or at least close enough to the truth for reviewers to marvel and family members to only chuckle amusedly at the author's generous use of "writer's license." Reviewers even forgave Douglas's excesses, such as his slightly overdrawn descriptions of the Indian lore and botanical wonders of the Northwest. "There is an integrity of spirit," wrote Orville Prescott of *The New York Times,* a "contagious affection for others and an essential dignity in this mountain-climbing judge which command respectful admiration."

With the rave reviews and near-miraculous recovery from his accident, Douglas seemed to have the world pretty much as he wanted it. He now could return to the Court in good health and with a promising new career as a successful author. But outside the new glare of publicity, Douglas's personal life was torn asunder. He no longer loved his wife and he felt free to shop around for the emotional fulfillment he was not receiving at home.

The split between Bill and Mildred Douglas had been building for years, and accelerated in the postwar period. When Mildred alone, or with the two children, left Washington for the Oregon mountains, it was not a very well kept secret that the Justice, still in Washington, dallied with other women. From Oregon, Mildred would write to her husband, forlornly accounting for her days of washing, ironing, mending and cooking. And then the subject would usually turn to the Douglases' dwindling bank balance. Mildred would introduce the subject humorously: "It gets worser and worser, doesn't it! The lack of funds I mean. Since your telephone call, I have written about three more checks. . . . There are 33 millionaires in Walla Walla.* Do you mind if I elope with one of them?" But the financial pressures ultimately smothered Mildred's spunk: "I think the only thing to do is to cash those bonds of mine. . . ."

Douglas did not seem to appreciate his wife's problems or feelings. After she had received a particularly critical letter from him, she replied: "Your note of the 7th came this morning. If you meant it to be very cold and formal, it was. It put a cloud on my whole day. I hate to be reminded of my shortcomings I already know about. I do accomplish some things I think."

Mercedes Davidson seemed to be all that Mildred was not. She was stylish (not merely pretty, like Mildred) and scintillating in Washington society. Being the wife of an assistant secretary of the Department of the Interior, Mercedes had ample opportunity to show off her good looks and prickly-quick mind. Justice Douglas noticed.

Initially, Mercedes dismissed the attention the Justice showed as an innocent flirtation. But the calls from Justice Douglas at the office of Representative Helen Gahagan Douglas, where Mercedes was working, increased. "At first I couldn't figure it out," Mercedes remembered. But as Douglas's attentions toward her

*Mildred had visited Millie in Walla Walla, where she was attending Whitman.

intensified, it was obvious to Mercedes that the Justice had more serious plans for the two of them.

"He was a very difficult man to resist," Mercedes recalled. "He asked me to the Court for lunch [in 1950]. I thought it was innocent. It wasn't. . . . He didn't turn my head until the chase. A messenger would come to my house with two or three notes a day. There were little presents, a book, for example. He made up his mind and started charging. He figured out a way to corner you. He asked me to read the galleys for *Of Men and Mountains.* Then I did the research for him on *An Almanac of Liberty.* "

In time, the Justice had won his lady. They talked about common interests like horses (she was a better rider than he) and world affairs. "I learned so much from him," Mercedes recalled. "It was the best education I could have had. There was nothing about his philosophy of life I didn't agree with; we had total rapport."

If Douglas offered Mercedes an education, Mercedes offered the Justice a sympathetic ear. "I was his confidante," she said. "He talked about his childhood and how he hated the 'establishment.' He was an intellectual genius but insecure personally."

By 1952, the Justice wanted a divorce from Mildred so that he could marry Mercedes. It was not a decision that Douglas or Mercedes came to easily. For Douglas, it was the surprise ending to his fundamentalist Presbyterian fable. "Divorce was, in my Presbyterian heritage, a sin," Douglas wrote, "and I looked down on those who had gone that way." For Mercedes, it was the second roll of the marital dice and her friends told her she would lose again. She believed that her first husband had cheated on her long before she had accepted Douglas's advances and now, some of her friends told her, Douglas, who had a reputation as a woman chaser, would do the same.

For Tommy Corcoran, a Douglas divorce would be the end of his political dream: the American public, he felt, would never accept Douglas as President if he divorced Mildred. "I told Bill, 'in politics you don't get a divorce,' " Corcoran recalled. "Sure you have women. But you don't get a divorce. He would have been President if it hadn't been for this divorce business."

But the decision was only difficult for the Justice and Mercedes and their friends. It was intolerable for Mildred Douglas. At first her husband attempted to send emissaries, like Abe Fortas, to calm her. Other times, his sister, Martha, wrote long, reassuring letters. Finally in 1952 Mildred steadied herself and accepted the inevitable. She wrote Douglas:

> I hope it is possible for you to be patient with me, I have been packing, lifting and carrying until I've reached the end of my physical strength. What is the net result? The breaking up of a family—a fine family—one week—then thirty or fifteen minutes before a judge—it's all over—it never was—or one is supposed to believe it never was—I can't forget 28 years of devotion, loyalty and hard service that quickly and easily. I am physically and emotionally played out. . . . So will you please be patient? You are a famous and brilliant man. May God help you find it in your heart to forgive yourself, as our children and I do. With all good wishes, Mildred.

In 1953, Mildred Douglas was granted a divorce from her husband after twenty-nine years of marriage.

PART FIVE

THE MIDDLE YEARS

CHAPTER TWENTY-TWO

*R*USSIAN *R*OULETTE

On February 9, 1950, the junior U.S. senator from Wisconsin, Joseph McCarthy, delivered a speech to the Women's Republican Club in Wheeling, West Virginia, that would mark the beginning of an infamous era in American history. "In my opinion," McCarthy told his Wheeling audience, "the State Department is thoroughly infested with Communists." Then, applying one of his pet rules for public speaking—a speaker must be specific to make his points stick—McCarthy said, "I have here in my hand a list of 205, a list of names that were known to the Secretary of State as being members of the Communist Party and who nevertheless are still working and shaping the policy in the State Department."

Later, there would be a dispute over what McCarthy had actually said. His friends insisted that the senator had mentioned only fifty-seven cases. McCarthy himself could not remember exactly what he had said. It did not matter. McCarthy had touched a raw national nerve. Alger Hiss, a former State Department official, had been convicted of perjury in connection with charges that he had spied for the Communists. Americans had read about Communist Mao Tse-tung's victory in China and Russia's first atomic bomb explosion and the confession of Dr. Klaus Fuchs, a high-level atomic scientist, that he had passed atomic secrets to the Soviet Union while working in Great Britain and the United States. And now the Communists were in Washington, according to Senator McCarthy, in large numbers and in high positions, bent on destroying our democracy.

McCarthy repeated his charges in Salt Lake City and Reno and then wired the White House, demanding that President Truman do something. McCarthy's attacks captured headlines across the country and stirred the U.S. Senate to appoint a subcommittee to investigate the senator's statements. President Truman and his Secretary of State, Dean Acheson, issued angry statements of denial. At first the administration's denials and the skepticism of the Senate subcommittee's chairman, Democrat Millard Tydings of Maryland, seemed to pin down Senator McCarthy. But gradually support for the senator's crusade began to build, bolstered by wilder, and still unsubstantiated, charges by McCarthy that subversives were operating at high levels of the State Department.

Week by week, McCarthy became bolder and his opposition more timid. In the Senate, few Democrats risked a challenge to McCarthy's charges and the Republican leadership sat back to admire their young upstart. "Whether Senator McCarthy has legal evidence, whether he has overstated or understated his case, is of lesser importance," remarked Senator Robert Taft, the respected Republican leader. "The question is whether the Communist influence in the State Department still exists."

The political virus spread. Now Americans looked anxiously not only at their State Department but at every government institution, private organization and individual citizen. All new ideas were suspect and even old ones questioned. To prove patriotism, it seemed, every American had to love the flag, motherhood and apple pie, but even that last passion could be a problem. "If Communists like apple pie and I do, I see no reason why I should stop eating it," said one government worker, "but I would."

William O. Douglas was repelled by the orgy of suspicion. "The great danger of this period," Douglas wrote in *The New York*

Times Magazine, "is not inflation, nor the national debt, nor atomic warfare. The great, critical danger is that we will so limit or narrow the range of permissible discussion and permissible thought that we will become victims of the orthodox school." Douglas repeated the warning in other articles and speeches, but his views represented a distinct minority in the nation.

Few students of democratic governments expected the majoritarian institutions of government to resist a popular tide that suppressed the free expression of ideas. But the U.S. Supreme Court was different. Insulated from public pressure, attentive to the First Amendment's guarantee of free speech, the Court would hold its ground. That was the libertarian theory and it was tested dramatically at the height of the McCarthy era by Eugene Dennis and ten other leaders of the American Communist Party.

The Dennis trial had been one of the most raucous in U.S. courtroom history. The defendants and their attorneys, convinced that the prosecution for conspiracy to teach and advocate the overthrow of the government by force was a pure political act, responded in kind. They made the courtroom of U.S. District Judge Harold Medina *their* political arena. They harangued and harassed, producing both high drama and low comedy. When the defense objected to Judge Medina's scratching his head as calculated to prejudice the jury, Medina replied, "I want you gentlemen to understand that when I scratch my head, I am just plain scratching my head." The nine-month trial resulted in 15,937 pages of transcript, contempt citations for all eleven defense attorneys and criminal convictions for their clients.

The Supreme Court was spared the antics of the defense but not their troubling constitutional questions. The defendants had openly admitted teaching the works of Marx, Engels, Lenin and Stalin, and that, indeed, was the heart of the prosecution's case. But teaching alone, the defendants contended, was protected by the First Amendment's free speech clause. And if the Smith Act, under which the defendants had been convicted, made their teaching a crime, they argued, then the Smith Act was at odds with the Constitution.

Chief Justice Vinson's plurality opinion seized upon a watered-down version of Justice Holmes's "clear and present danger" test to uphold the convictions. Vinson identified the clear danger to the public order—communism—and then, in effect, committed all members of the Communist Party, including the eleven defendants, to its darkest subversive purpose. The Chief Justice was not deterred by the fact that no evidence at the defendants' trial had proved that they had translated their teaching into action or even incitement to action. "Obviously," wrote Vinson, "the words [clear and present danger] cannot mean that before the Government may act, it must wait until the putsch is about to be executed, the plans have been laid and the signal awaited."

Felix Frankfurter agreed with the result but contributed a concurring opinion with a weightier balancing of First Amendment interests against those of national security (which he ultimately favored). The critical paragraph in Frankfurter's opinion did not deal with the details of the Dennis case, however, but with the broader question of whether or not the Court should be sucked into the political maelstrom presented by the convictions of eleven American Communist leaders. Frankfurter did not think it should. "History teaches," warned Justice Frankfurter, "that the independence of the judiciary is jeopardized when courts become embroiled in the passions of the day and assume primary responsibility in choosing between competing political, economic and social pressures."

Only Justices Douglas and Black dissented. "Public opinion being what it is now, few will protest the conviction of these Communist petitioners," wrote Black. "There is hope, however, that in calmer times, when present pressures, passions and fears subside, this or some later Court will restore the First Amendment liberties to the high preferred place where they belong in a free society."

Douglas searched the record for evidence that the defendants had engaged in acts of terror or other seditious conduct which, he admitted, would not be protected by the First Amendment. But he found none, only the teaching of Marxist-Leninist doctrine. Teaching alone, said Douglas, was fully protected by the First Amendment.

Ironically, just such teaching of Communist doctrine, Douglas suggested, may have been responsible for its rejection in the United States:

Some nations less resilient than the United States, where illiteracy is high and where democratic traditions are only budding, might have to take drastic steps and jail these men for merely speaking their creed. But in America they are miserable merchants of unwanted ideas; their wares remain unsold. The fact that their ideas are abhorrent does not make them powerful. . . . The First Amendment reflects the philosophy of Jefferson "that it is time enough for the rightful purposes of civil government, for its officers to interfere when principles break into overt acts against peace and good public order."

During the McCarthy era, the loyalty oath became the nation's talisman. Federal employees were forced to sign oaths and so were state employees, teachers, prospective lawyers and labor union members. Private organizations were scrutinized by the U.S. Attorney General to determine if they were "totalitarian, fascist, communist or subversive." Legislative investigating committees, like the House Un-American Activities Committee, and ambitious prosecutors ran riot, bloating their reputations and destroying those who were their targets.

Douglas held no brief for Communists in the U.S. government or anywhere else; indeed, his anticommunism had been a matter of public record for years. But to Douglas, anticommunism never justified the deprivation of due process rights of American citizens, whether Communists or not.

Government loyalty hearings became a special target for Douglas, who attacked their unfairness and their devastating effects on their victims. The case of Dorothy Bailey provided Douglas with the opportunity to point out their evils. Bailey, a federal government employee, was charged with being a Communist and active in a Communist "front organization" on the Attorney General's subversive list. Her government review board stated that the case against her was based on reports, some of which came from "informants certified to us by the Federal Bureau of Investigation as experienced and entirely reliable." Bailey's counsel asked that she be given the opportunity to confront her accusers. The request was refused. Bailey's counsel requested that the names of the informants be disclosed. The request was refused. When her counsel asked if the informants had been active in a certain union, the chairman of the review board replied, "I haven't the slightest knowledge as to who they were or how active they have been in anything." Counsel then asked if Bailey's accusers had been under oath, and the chairman replied, "I don't think so." On the basis of the accusations of unseen, unnamed informers who were not under oath, Dorothy Bailey lost her job.

The Court split, four to four, thus, affirming a lower court ruling that upheld the loyalty board procedures in the Bailey case. The lower court had found that the loss of public employment did not require the strict guarantees of due process essential in a criminal trial, where a defendant's liberty was at stake. Douglas disagreed, asserting that the review board's procedures were both unconscionable and unconstitutional. "A disloyalty trial is the most crucial event in the life of a public servant," he wrote. "If condemned, he is branded for life as a person unworthy of trust or confidence. To make that condemnation without meticulous regard for the decencies of a fair trial is abhorrent to fundamental justice."

In that same opinion, Douglas attacked the Attorney General's list under which Bailey had been condemned, cutting to the core of the problem with a barrage of practical questions. What is a subversive organization? asked Douglas.

There are some who lump Socialists and Communists together. Does it mean an organization that thinks the lot of some peasants has been improved under Soviet auspices? Does it include an organization that is against the action of the United Nations in Korea? Does it embrace a group which on some issues of international policy aligns itself with the Soviet viewpoint? Does it mean a group which has unwittingly become the tool for Soviet propaganda? Does it mean one into whose membership some Communists have infiltrated? Or does it describe only an organization which under the guise of honorable activities serves as a front for Communist activities? . . . [The term "subversive"] will be given meaning according to the predilections of the prosecutor: "subversive" to some will be synonymous with "radical"; "subversive" to others will be synonymous with "communist." . . . These flexible standards, which vary with the mood or political philosophy of the prosecutor, are weapons which can be made as sharp or as blunt as the occasion requires. Since they are subject to grave abuse, they have no place in our system of law.

"Subversives" lists, Douglas believed, trampled not only procedural rights but First Amendment freedoms as well. He pursued the point after several New York schoolteachers challenged the state's Feinberg Law, which authorized the compilation of a list of subversive organizations. The New York law further stated that membership of any public school teacher in a listed organization was prima facie cause for dismissal.

The Vinson Court majority slid smoothly over the constitutional claim that the state law stifled freedom of speech and association. The Court said the teachers had a free choice: either work in the school system on its terms or "retain their beliefs and associations and go elsewhere."

That was an unconstitutional choice, Douglas declared in dissent.* No one needed the guarantee of free expression more than the teacher, Douglas wrote, and that guarantee was totally obliterated by the New York law. Douglas then described his Orwellian nightmare:

> The law inevitably turns the school system into a spying project. Regular loyalty reports on the teachers must be made out. The principals become detectives; the students, the parents, the community become informers. Ears are cocked for tell-tale signs of disloyalty. . . . Who heard overtones of revolution in the English teacher's discussion of *The Grapes of Wrath?* What was behind the praise of Soviet progress in metallurgy in the chemistry class? . . . What happens under this law is typical of what happens in a police state. Teachers are under constant surveillance; their pasts are combed for signs of disloyalty; their utterances are watched for clues to dangerous thoughts. A pall is cast over the classrooms. There can be no real academic freedom in that environment. Where suspicion fills the air and holds scholars in line for fear of their jobs, there can be no exercise of the free intellect. . . .

The Court majority was never attacked during the McCarthy era† and that could be taken as an endorsement for the philoso-

---

*Justice Frankfurter also wrote a dissent, consistent with his philosophy of judicial restraint, in which he argued that the Court should not have decided the case on the merits. Since no one had yet been fired under the Feinberg Law provisions, Frankfurter wrote, the Court should have avoided "constitutional adjudications on merely abstract or speculative issues."

†The same could not be said for Douglas and Black, whose dissenting opinions brought public attacks and sporadic calls for their impeachment. Douglas was also attacked by a

phy of judicial restraint expounded by Justice Frankfurter. But history will not treat so kindly the majority's "restraint" while civil liberties were crushed. For it is at just such a critical time that the Court's protection of individual liberties is most needed. Had a Vinson Court majority stood firm against the attack on civil liberties, the jobs and reputations of thousands, as well as the free expression of all, might have been preserved.

"Douglas and Black were the only Justices I would have wanted to clerk for at that moment," said Justice Hans Linde of the Oregon Supreme Court, who clerked for Douglas during the 1951 term. "I felt privileged to be on the side of a man of courage who was doing the right thing; the other clerks envied us." Even Frankfurter admirers, like his former clerk Philip Elman, said, "Douglas was sticking up for a lot of things that were right. During the Vinson Court years, Douglas and Black were on the right side."

During the McCarthy era, Douglas wrote many judicial opinions that shocked and angered a public intent on punishing real and imagined Communists. Even so, one controversial opinion stood above the rest. On Wednesday, June 17, 1953, Justice Douglas, acting alone and without consultation with the full Court, stayed the executions of Ethel and Julius Rosenberg, who had been convicted and sentenced to die for conspiring to pass atomic secrets to the Russians.

The conservative press was outraged. And so was Representative W. W. Wheeler, Democrat from Georgia, who introduced a resolution in the House to impeach Douglas.

Some of Douglas's colleagues were no less disturbed by his action, but their reasons were more complicated. Felix Frankfurter, having closed his own house for the summer, spent the night of June 17 at the home of his former clerk Joseph Rauh, Jr. "Sitting on our porch that evening," Rauh recalled, "he seemed angriest at Justice Douglas, whose actions at earlier stages of the case had not supported a full review of the case and who now at

---

colleague, Justice Jackson, who suggested in a memorandum that several Douglas opinions had resulted in "Communist victories."

the last minute pulled a 'grandstand' play." That view of Douglas's action was shared by Justice Robert Jackson, who later told columnist Marquis Childs about Douglas's earlier votes rejecting the Rosenbergs' appeals and suggested that his stay was an attempt to play to his liberal constituency with a popular solo performance. Although there is no record of how a third member of the Court, Justice Harold Burton, felt about Douglas's votes, his Court papers—as well as Frankfurter's and Jackson's—support the charge that Douglas had voted against hearing arguments presented by attorneys for the Rosenbergs on *five* separate occasions before dramatically issuing his stay of execution.

The story of Douglas's enigmatic behavior begins on June 7, 1952, the day the Justices of the Supreme Court first considered hearing the Rosenbergs' appeal.* The Rosenbergs' attorneys had appealed their convictions on four grounds: (1) The Rosenbergs had been charged with a conspiracy to commit espionage, not treason, but throughout their trial they had been branded as "traitors"; under the Constitution one could be convicted of treason only on the testimony of two witnesses for each overt act. Much of the evidence against the Rosenbergs, their attorneys argued, had been provided by a single witness or the uncorroborated evidence of an accomplice. (2) The death penalty violated the Eighth Amendment's prohibition against cruel and unusual punishment, since the Rosenbergs were, in effect, sentenced to death for treason without being accorded the constitutional safeguards for the crime. (3) The prosecution violated the federal criminal code by not providing the defense with a list of witnesses three days before trial. (4) U.S. District Judge Irving Kaufman had consistently shown hostility toward the Rosenbergs and deprived them of a fair trial.

The U.S. Court of Appeals for the Second Circuit had affirmed the Rosenbergs' conviction and sentence and had later denied the motion for a rehearing. But in rejecting the four grounds argued by the Rosenbergs' attorneys, the appellate court's three-judge panel indicated that it was split on the legal issues and that its rulings deserved consideration by the U.S. Supreme Court.

*The appeals also involved the legal arguments of Morton Sobell, who had been convicted and sentenced to thirty years in prison for his part in the conspiracy.

Only three members of the Supreme Court—Black, Frankfurter and Burton—voted to hear the Rosenbergs' appeal. Black voted to hear the case because he thought the Rosenbergs' first argument—that they had been sentenced to death, in effect, for treason without the required constitutional safeguards—presented a serious question for the Court. Frankfurter, who had a long-standing aversion to the death penalty, thought that every instance where a federal court had sentenced a defendant to death should be reviewed by the Court. Burton believed the Court should resolve questions about the treason clause and the validity of the death penalty.

At that time, Justice Douglas could have cast the decisive fourth vote for Court review of the Rosenberg case. He did not and, according to Felix Frankfurter's notes, voted against the Rosenbergs' petition with feeling. "His [Douglas's] 'denys' are usually curt and unaccompanied by argument," Frankfurter wrote. "His 'deny' this time was unaccompanied by argument. But it was uttered with startling vehemence." Only Frankfurter commented on the manner in which Douglas turned down the Rosenberg petition, but at least three other justices—Burton, Jackson and Douglas himself—noted his negative vote in their own records of the judicial conference.

On November 8, 1952, the Supreme Court turned down the Rosenbergs' petition for a rehearing by the same six to three vote. "Douglas again announced his 'deny' with unwonted vehemence," Frankfurter wrote. Again, Burton's, Jackson's and Douglas's records confirm Douglas's vote.

With their petition for rehearing rejected by the Supreme Court in November, the Rosenbergs' attorneys renewed their efforts in the U.S. District Court for the Southern District of New York in December 1952, introducing two new reasons why their clients' convictions should be overturned. First, they offered to present evidence that one prosecution witness had perjured himself on the witness stand. Second, they charged that prosecutor Irving Saypol had prejudiced their trial by out-of-court statements to the press during the trial which he failed to prove in court.

U.S. District Court Judge Sylvester Ryan refused even to let the Rosenberg attorneys argue the two issues and that decision was affirmed by the U.S. Court of Appeals for the Second Circuit. In affirming the lower-court decision, however, Circuit Court Judge Thomas Swan wrote that Saypol's conduct was "wholly reprehensible," but that the Rosenbergs had made the tactical error of not requesting a mistrial at the time. Besides, there was no evidence that any juror had read Saypol's announcement to the press. In February 1953, the appeals court granted the Rosenberg attorneys' petition to stay the execution until the U.S. Supreme Court could review the appellate court decision.

On April 11, the U.S. Supreme Court turned down the Rosenbergs for the third time. Only Justices Black and Frankfurter voted to hear their arguments. Justice Burton did not think the new arguments presented by the Rosenbergs' attorneys had merit. Again Justice Douglas voted to deny the petition—"in the same harsh tone," according to Frankfurter, in which he had denied their two previous requests.

That third refusal of the Supreme Court to hear the Rosenberg case deeply distressed Frankfurter. For Frankfurter, the integrity of the judicial process had always been the cornerstone of his philosophy and in the Rosenberg case, he was convinced, it had been severely compromised. The Saypol incident, branded "reprehensible" by the respected circuit court judge Thomas Swan, further convinced Frankfurter that the Court should have taken the case. So frustrated was Felix Frankfurter, in fact, that he decided to break one of his own rules: never to register a dissenting opinion to a Court's denial of certiorari. Later, however, Frankfurter reconsidered, fearing that his dissent might embroil the Court in controversy and be the basis for further disunity in the nation over the Rosenbergs' fate. Following discussion with Justice Black, Frankfurter and Black decided to limit their written comment to a single paragraph: "Mr. Justice Black and Mr. Justice Frankfurter, referring to the positions they took . . . last November, adhere to them."

But on May 22, 1953, Douglas wrote a memorandum to his colleagues that changed the entire situation and led to a chaotic judicial conference. "I have done further work on this case and given the problem more study," Douglas wrote. "I have reluctantly concluded that certiorari should be granted. Accordingly, I will ask that the order of denial carry the following notation:

'Mr. Justice Douglas, agreeing with the Court of Appeals that some of the conduct of the United States Attorney was "wholly reprehensible" but, believing in disagreement with the Court of Appeals that it probably prejudiced the defendants seriously, votes to grant certiorari.' "

On three previous occasions, Douglas had voted not even to hear issues in the Rosenberg case argued; now he had decided, without hearing oral argument, that the Rosenbergs had been seriously prejudiced.

Frankfurter was stunned by Douglas's reversal, but quickly realized that the new Douglas position renewed hope that the Court might yet hear arguments in the Rosenberg case. With Douglas joining Frankfurter and Black, only one more vote was needed to grant review. Frankfurter asked Chief Justice Vinson to reopen discussion on the Rosenberg case and then undertook a personal lobbying campaign to convince the two justices he felt most open-minded on the issue—Burton and Jackson—to vote to grant review. To Justice Burton, Frankfurter suggested that if the justices failed to grant certiorari, the Douglas dissent would be profoundly embarrassing to the Court; better, argued Frankfurter, that the whole Court act responsibly, since controversy over the Rosenberg case was now inevitable. Burton, however, resisted Frankfurter's arguments and still refused to vote for review. Frankfurter then went to Justice Jackson, telling him that he was unwilling to let the Douglas memorandum represent the Court's dissenting view. If the justices did not vote to review the Rosenberg case, Frankfurter told Jackson, he would have to write a dissent of his own.

Before the Court again considered the Rosenberg case, Justice Jackson's law clerk, William H. Rehnquist, the future Associate Justice of the U.S. Supreme Court, wrote a three-page memorandum to his boss telling why he did not think Jackson should vote to hear the case. "I would conclude that this proposal, or any proposal to change the court's views, would serve no purpose that has not been previously considered and rejected by the court," Rehnquist wrote. "In addition, it would be allowing one justice—WOD—to force the hand of the court and get the result which he now so belatedly wants." As to the suggestion that public opinion demanded the Court hear the case, Rehnquist wrote: ". . . the public opinion which has voiced itself in favor of the Rosenbergs is not even properly called 'left-wing' in the sense that the respectable liberal group in this country is behind it. It is a tiny minority of lunatic fringers and erratic scientist-sentimentalists."

Jackson had his own ideas on what he would do at conference. "Don't worry," Jackson told Frankfurter. "Douglas' memorandum isn't going down on Monday." He added, "Douglas' memorandum is the dirtiest, most shameful, most cynical performance that I think I have ever heard of in matters pertaining to law."

At the Monday conference, Jackson told his colleagues that he would vote to grant review because Douglas's threatened dissent had put the Court in a vulnerable position. Undoubtedly, said Jackson, there would be leaks to the press that at different times, four members of the Court—Black, Frankfurter, Burton and now Douglas—had voted to grant certiorari in the Rosenberg case. In addition, the dissent promised by Douglas would put the Court in the awkward position of having one of its members declare publicly that the Rosenbergs had not had a fair trial. By hearing arguments, Jackson contended, the Court would save itself embarrassment and put to rest any doubts about the fairness of the Rosenberg trial.

Jackson's vote made the fourth in favor of review—Black, Frankfurter, Douglas and Jackson—and so the justices began to discuss when the case should be heard. After the discussion had progressed for some time, Douglas, according to Frankfurter's record, spoke up: "He [Douglas] ought to say something, he started. What he had written was badly drawn, he guessed. He hadn't realized it would embarrass anyone. He would just withdraw his memorandum if that would help matters."

After Douglas had finished speaking, Justice Jackson addressed his colleagues. If Douglas withdrew his memorandum, said Jackson, the Court was in precisely the position it had been in before. With no Douglas memorandum, the Court could effectively avoid embarrassment—and reject the Rosenbergs' latest petition, as Jackson had wanted to do all along. With Jackson reverting to his earlier "no" vote, the Court again fell short, by one vote, of hearing the Rosenbergs' case. After the conference, Jackson, referring to Douglas, told Frankfurter triumphantly, "That S.O.B.'s bluff was called."

Later, Douglas told Hugo Black (who had been sick and had not attended the judicial conference) that he had withdrawn his memorandum because it was clear to him that the Court would only consider whether the Rosenbergs' petition for review should be granted, and not address the merits of the petition; he did not think it was worthwhile for the Court to grant such a limited hearing and then deny the petition. When Black later told Frankfurter Douglas's version of the conference, Frankfurter replied that Douglas had not told the truth. In fact, said Frankfurter, there had been four votes in favor of granting certiorari, ensuring that the Rosenberg case would have been heard on the merits if Douglas had not withdrawn his memorandum. Perhaps he had misunderstood Douglas, Black told Frankfurter.

On May 25, 1953, the Court issued a formal order denying the Rosenbergs' petition for review. Attached to the formal order was a notation that Justice Douglas "is of the opinion [it] . . . should be granted." No Douglas memorandum was filed.

Douglas's next vote in the Rosenberg case further complicated the puzzle. That happened at judicial conference on June 13, 1953, two days before the end of the Court's regular term and only five days before the Rosenbergs' scheduled execution. Attorneys had earlier tried to persuade Judge Irving Kaufman that many of the pretrial statements of the prosecution's chief witness, David Greenglass, and his wife, Ruth, contradicted later testimony and indicated that the couple had committed perjury. Kaufman rejected the arguments, calling the contentions "unsupported and incredible." The appellate court affirmed Kaufman's ruling and denied a further stay of execution. The Rosenbergs' attorneys applied to Justice Jackson for a stay of execution in order to give the defense additional time to prepare the briefs for an appeal of Judge Kaufman's ruling. Reluctant to act alone, Jackson referred the application to the full Court with the recommendation that the justices hear oral argument on the issue on June 15.

At the Court's judicial conference on Saturday, June 13, the justices were again deeply divided on resolution of the Rosenberg case and Justice Douglas again was at the center of the controversy. Four justices—Jackson, Black, Frankfurter and Burton—wanted to hear oral argument on the Rosenberg attorneys' motion to stay execution until they could prepare appellate briefs. But five members of the Court, including Justice Douglas, did not. Douglas told his colleagues that he would grant a stay of execution without oral argument, but that there was no end served by hearing oral argument on the motion. Having voted down Jackson's recommendation to hear oral argument, five to four, the justices then turned down the stay. This time Douglas switched sides—he wanted to grant the stay without oral argument and take the case on the merits. But Burton, who had been willing to hear oral argument, was unwilling to grant a stay without it. Again the vote was five to four, and again the Rosenbergs lost.

In adhering so stubbornly to his position, Douglas guaranteed that the Rosenbergs would not be heard in the Supreme Court on the new point of law raised by their attorneys. His vote was decisive.

On Monday, June 15, the Court formally rejected the Rosenbergs' motion for a stay of execution. That same day, the justices also turned down an application for habeas corpus based on the allegation that the Rosenbergs' prosecutor, Irving Saypol, had knowingly used perjured testimony of David and Ruth Greenglass. Black wanted to grant the application and Frankfurter argued for what he called an "open hearing" on the question. Justice Douglas, however, voted with the majority to deny the application and, according to Frankfurter, challenged Frankfurter's suggestion that there was a substantial legal basis for the Rosenbergs' attorneys' claims.

Three of Douglas's five votes to deny arguments in the Rosenberg case (on June 7 and November 8, 1952, and June 13, 1953), which in effect shut the door of the Court to the Rosenbergs, were a matter of public record, though not generally noticed by the press. But to his friends and admirers outside the Court, Justice Douglas was, on June 15, still the symbol of libertarianism. It was not surprising, then, that two attorneys who had not even been hired by the Rosenbergs approached Douglas to make a final plea on the Rosenbergs' behalf in the late afternoon of June 15.

For an hour and a half the attorneys made essentially the same arguments that had been made earlier in the day in the Rosenbergs' habeas corpus petition that the Court had turned down. Douglas told the attorneys that his difficulty with their petition was that they had failed to connect the government with the knowing use of alleged perjured testimony. Douglas added, however, that he would see the attorneys the next morning at 10:00 A.M. if they could present additional legal arguments to change his mind.

On Tuesday, June 16, Douglas heard the legal argument that would allow him to offer renewed hope to the Rosenbergs and assert his claim as the uncompromising libertarian. The argument: The Rosenbergs' indictment, trial and sentence had been secured under the wrong law, the Espionage Act of 1917. They should have been brought to trial under the Atomic Energy Act of 1946, since the conspiracy in which the Rosenbergs allegedly participated took place from 1944 to 1950. And under the Atomic Energy Act, a judge could impose the death penalty only on the recommendation of the jury and only with a showing that the offense had been committed with intent to injure the United States. Neither condition had been met in the Rosenberg case.

Douglas, who in Frankfurter's view had belatedly been "seized" by the Rosenberg case, had found the Atomic Energy Act point decisive. After hearing the attorneys' argument, Douglas sought the counsel of none other than Felix Frankfurter. Recalled Frankfurter: "The afternoon [of June 16], Douglas came to my office and set out for me the point concerning the Atomic Energy Act on which his decision eventually rested. It had been argued before him for the first time that morning by new counsel he had agreed to hear, and it troubled him. He thought it might have substance. He was after advice. I said I couldn't, of course, make a decision, but the point seemed to me one that should be looked into."

Frankfurter heard from Douglas several more times that Tuesday afternoon. Douglas also talked to Chief Justice Vinson, who rejected the new point. The Supreme Court had no power to revise the sentence imposed by a district judge, Vinson told Douglas; the Chief felt he had effectively disposed of the point in a published memorandum of November 17, 1952. Besides, Vinson said to Douglas, the attorney who had raised the argument had not been appointed by the Rosenbergs and had no standing to argue the point. Vinson nonetheless suggested that Douglas should raise the matter at judicial conference.

Later that night, Douglas drafted the judicial opinion that, twenty-four hours later, would reverberate throughout the nation and the world. He showed it to only one justice, Hugo Black, who thought it was an "enduring document." Douglas, however, had still not declared his intentions, and the next morning he telephoned Frankfurter once again to seek advice. Should he present the legal argument at judicial conference? Should he talk to Justices Jackson and Burton about it? Should he simply issue a stay of execution on his own?*

"Do what your conscience tells you," Frankfurter told Douglas, "not what the Chief Justice tells you."

The following day, Douglas stayed the Rosenbergs' execution. In his opinion Douglas said that he had not decided whether the death penalty had been improperly imposed. He had decided, however, that a new constitutional argument had been raised which presented a substantial legal question meriting full argument before the U.S. Supreme Court. "It is important," wrote Douglas, "that the country be protected against the nefarious plans of spies who would destroy us. It is also important that before we allow human lives to be snuffed out, we be sure— emphatically sure—that we act within the law. If we are not sure, there will be lingering doubts to plague the conscience after the event."

Immediately after releasing his judicial opinion, Justice Douglas left Washington and headed west by car, thinking that his stay would remain in effect until the full Court could hear arguments during the fall term. But in Uniontown, Pennsylvania, Douglas heard over the radio the announcement that Chief Justice Vinson had called a special session of the Court to hear the new arguments in the Rosenberg case raised by Douglas's stay.

Douglas later wrote Fred Rodell, expressing outrage at the Chief Justice's action. "No effort was made to reach me though my route and destination were known," he wrote Rodell. "The

*A single justice may issue a stay when the Court is in recess.

plan was to hold Court without me!! I just happened to hear about the Special Term by car radio!!!"

There was another version: Douglas, according to columnist Marquis Childs, had gone "on a motor trip with his then mistress, Mercedes Davidson. . . . Afterward [i.e., after he had granted the stay], nobody could find him—including the Pennsylvania state troopers. And, of course, poor old Fred Vinson, the Chief Justice, was wild, because he felt the troopers might find him under the most disturbing circumstances."*

Unknown to Douglas, two members of the Court had already laid plans to counteract his decision, even before he had formally issued his stay. The day before Douglas issued the stay, Justice Jackson arranged a meeting with Chief Justice Vinson and Attorney General Herbert Brownell to discuss their strategy if, as anticipated, Douglas stayed the Rosenbergs' execution. At the meeting, according to FBI documents, Jackson declared that Douglas had made a ridiculous mistake in hearing the new argument. If Douglas issued the stay, Vinson had promised to convene a special session of the Court on Thursday, June 18. Shortly after Douglas issued his stay, Attorney General Brownell petitioned the Court to vacate it on the grounds that the penalty clauses of the Atomic Energy Act did not pose a substantial legal question. Even before the Court convened at noon on June 18, then, two of its members—Vinson and Jackson—had made up their minds to reverse the stay.

According to Mercedes Douglas Eichholz, Douglas wept after he was personally informed by Chief Justice Vinson in the middle of the night of the Court's special session. "He felt betrayed," she recalled. "He was deeply hurt when Vinson pulled this conference on him. He was convinced he was right."

Later, Douglas told Fred Rodell the reasons that he thought Vinson had acted improperly: "The C.J. has no authority to convene the Court. That can be done only on a poll of the Court. . . . That was what Stone did for the *Quirin* case.† Here the whole

*Referring to Mercedes Davidson as Douglas's mistress was misleading. Douglas had lived separately from his wife for more than a year; the formal divorce proceedings took place a month after Vinson's announcement, and Douglas's marriage to Mercedes followed.

†In *Ex Parte Quirin*, Chief Justice Stone wrote an opinion for a unanimous Court during

Court was not polled . . . where is the power of the Court to set aside a stay? Congress granted it to a single Justice. Can five overrule Congress?" ·

Though he was angered by Douglas's "grandstand" play, Felix Frankfurter agreed with Douglas that the Chief Justice should not have convened the Court so hastily. In addition, Frankfurter was disconsolate "at the hopelessness in winning a majority for a full review of the case."

Douglas has suggested that Frankfurter's pessimism on the eve of the special Court session was justified. "When the Court was convened," Douglas wrote Rodell, "it was after the C.J. had talked with 6 [Justices] and got assurances of a vote of 5 to overrule me—in advance of argument—in advance of any exposure or explanation of the point!!"

During the nearly three hours of oral arguments on June 18, justices and attorneys were supposed to address themselves to two narrow questions: Did the full Court have the authority to vacate Douglas's stay? Did the apparent conflict between the penalty provisions of the Espionage Act and the Atomic Energy Act present a "substantial" question requiring further study and litigation? But neither all the attorneys nor all the justices stuck to their subject. "There never was a more crooked District Attorney in New York than the one who tried the Rosenbergs," blurted out John Finerty, associate counsel for the Rosenbergs. Justice Tom Clark suggested that Finerty confine himself to the relevant legal issues. No similar restraint was put on Justice Jackson, who sometimes seemed more concerned with the *consequences* of a ruling sustaining Douglas's stay than whether his stay raised a substantial legal issue. "The probabilities are that if the Atomic Energy Act covers this case," Jackson suggested to U.S. Solicitor General Robert L. Stern, "the whole case is out." In other words, if the Rosenbergs' sentences could be attacked under the Espionage Act, so could their indictments and convictions. Solicitor General Stern did nothing to calm Jackson's fears, admitting that he didn't think the government could succeed if it had to retry the Rosenbergs under the 1946 act.

World War II, holding that eight saboteurs could be denied access to the civil courts and be tried by a military commission.

The justices held two stormy conference sessions after oral argument, one on the afternoon of June 18 and the second the following morning. Black bitterly attacked the convening of the special session. It was wrong, he charged, to act so hastily and at the same time undercut the legitimate authority of one justice to issue a stay. Frankfurter followed up on Black's argument, questioning whether the Court had the authority to countermand Douglas's stay. Justice Burton supported the Douglas/Black/Frankfurter argument that it was improper for the Court to overrule Douglas. It would, said Burton, undermine the stay system. "Let it take due course," said Burton. "There is a substantial question. That's all we should pass on now."

"There were four who voted to keep my stay in force," Douglas later wrote. "Black, FF, WOD, Burton. If four felt it was justified, why the haste of five to get rid of it? After all it only takes four to grant cert. Why not respect for the views of four on a stay in a death case?"

It was a futile cause. Five members of the Court—Chief Justice Vinson and Associate Justices Jackson, Clark, Minton and Reed —voted to vacate the stay, taking Clark's position that it was "wrong to hold up [the case] any longer." When it was clear that a Court majority would not uphold the stay under any conditions, Justice Burton cast his vote with the majority, making the vote six to three.

On June 19, the justices entered the courtroom looking unusually grim. "Their expressions," reported *The New York Times,* "indicated that the conference at which the decision was hammered out might have been strenuous, perhaps bitter." In reading the Court's brief, unsigned opinion vacating Douglas's stay, Chief Justice Vinson suggested that there had been a great deal more furor than was merited by the legal questions that had been presented. He said, first, that the Court could overrule Douglas's stay because of its "responsibility to supervise the administration of criminal justice." Then he addressed the legal issue raised by Douglas. "We think the question is not substantial. We think further proceedings to litigate it are unwarranted. A conspiracy was charged and proved to violate the Espionage Act in wartime. The Atomic Energy Act did not repeal or limit the provisions of the Espionage Act. Accordingly, we vacate the stay entered by Mr. Justice Douglas on June 17, 1953."

It was that simple to Vinson. But in their dissenting opinions, Justices Black, Frankfurter and Douglas made a shambles of the majority's easy conclusions. Chief Justice Vinson had said the Court had the authority to vacate Douglas's stay, but Justice Black argued persuasively that that position was not justified by judicial precedent, federal statute or the language of the Constitution. In his concurring opinion, Justice Jackson had argued that the overt acts of the conspiracy had taken place before passage of the Atomic Energy Act and, therefore, to prosecute the Rosenbergs under the 1946 act would violate the constitutional provision against ex post facto laws. But some of the acts alleged in the Rosenberg conspiracy, countered Justice Frankfurter, in dissent, came after 1946 (and thus within the terms of the 1946 act).

"Where two penal statutes may apply, one carrying death, the other imprisonment—the Court has no choice but to impose the less harsh sentence," wrote Douglas in his dissent. "Before the present argument, I knew only that the question was serious and substantial. Now I am sure of the answer. I know deep in my heart that I am right on the law. Knowing that, my duty is clear."

After the Court's decision on June 19, President Eisenhower rejected a final appeal for clemency for the Rosenbergs because, he said, "the Rosenbergs may have condemned to death tens of millions of innocent people all over the world. The execution of two human beings is a grave matter. But even greater is the thought of the millions of dead whose death may be directly attributable to what these spies have done."

Out of respect for the Jewish Sabbath, the scheduled execution of Ethel and Julius Rosenberg on the evening of June 19 was moved up from the original 11:00 P.M. time. There were still rays of sunlight when Julius Rosenberg, thirty-five, clean-shaven and wearing a white T-shirt, was strapped into the brown-stained oak electric chair in Sing Sing prison's death chamber. He received the first shock of 2,000 volts at 8:04 P.M., then two more shocks. He was pronounced dead at 8:06 P.M. Ethel Rosenberg, thirty-seven, entered the death chamber a few minutes after her husband. She wore a dark-green print dress with white polka dots; her hair was close-cropped to permit contact of the electrode. She received three successive electrical shocks and was pronounced dead at 8:16 P.M.

Had Douglas voted to hear argument in the Rosenberg case at each of the five opportunities in which he cast negative votes, the Rosenbergs might still have died in the electric chair at Sing Sing. For a vote to grant certiorari by the Supreme Court is not an accurate barometer of the individual members' views on the merits of a case. Indeed, the justices are presumed to form their views on the merits of a case only after they have studied the appellate briefs and listened to oral arguments by attorneys and those of their colleagues in conference. After arguments on the merits in the Rosenberg case, Felix Frankfurter, for example, might well have concluded that the Rosenbergs had been treated fairly in the judicial process and that the death penalty was not forbidden by the Constitution.

It may be true, as Douglas contended, that the new legal argument presented on behalf of the Rosenbergs on June 16 was more substantial than the earlier ones, and that that point was decisive for him. What is troubling about the Douglas record, however, is that his earlier negative votes seemed so inconsistent with his whole judicial approach and philosophy. His reputation as a result-oriented libertarian justice was well documented. He had rarely based his judicial decisions on technical procedural grounds—when such grounds cut against the interests of individual defendants. And yet in the Rosenberg case, in vote after vote, Douglas seemed content to let the Rosenbergs go to their execution without even hearing a variety of legal arguments put to the Court by the Rosenberg attorneys. This was the same Justice Douglas who wrote in his opinion to stay the Rosenbergs' execution that "before we allow human lives to be snuffed out, we be sure—emphatically sure—that we act within the law."

In contrast to Douglas's behavior, Black, Douglas's long-time libertarian colleague, voted for review of the Rosenberg case at every opportunity, and was not so fastidious as Douglas seemed to be about it. On June 13, 1953, for example, Black agreed at judicial conference with Douglas that the Court should have heard arguments on the merits to stay the Rosenberg execution. But that did not stop Black, as it had Douglas, from voting to hear a technical procedural argument, if that was all that four justices were willing to grant at that time. Black would take the case one step at a time. Douglas would not, and it did not make sense.

Could political ambitions explain the Douglas behavior? Douglas did not want the Court to tackle the controversial Rosenberg case, the argument would run, because it would put him in an embarrassing position at a time when he might be considered for high political office. The theory fails on three counts. First, Douglas had never avoided difficult decisions in the past, even though they might have affected the public's view of him. Second, by 1952, when the first Rosenberg petitions reached the Supreme Court, Douglas had effectively eliminated himself from serious political consideration. Finally, all but one of the Douglas votes in the Rosenberg case came after the Eisenhower landslide victory in the presidential election of 1952.

But even without a "political" explanation, there was something profoundly unsettling about Douglas's behavior. Douglas, the outspoken champion of the underdog, insisted on dealing with the Rosenberg case on his terms alone, seemingly oblivious to the desperate pleas of the Rosenberg attorneys and several of his colleagues. In doing so, Douglas forced the Rosenbergs into a game of Russian roulette. The gun was pointed at the Rosenbergs and only Douglas knew which chambers contained the blanks. It was a deadly game, which Douglas seemed prepared to play for more than a year, as the Rosenbergs' lives teetered in the balance.

In his first volume of autobiography, Douglas did not mention his five negative votes in the Rosenberg case. He did, however, write with pride of his stay of the Rosenbergs' executions on June 17, 1953. That is the Douglas, the libertarian symbol, that he wanted the public to remember.

CHAPTER TWENTY-THREE ───────────────

STRANGE LANDS

IF "VIET CONG" had been substituted for "Viet Minh" and "American" for "French," the analysis would have provided an accurate blueprint for the U.S. disaster in Vietnam in the sixties: "The Viet Minh keeps the French pretty much in fixed positions. Then it goes around the flanks, suddenly appears far in the rear, or turns up in the midst of a French stronghold. Its troops come and go with apparent ease, disappearing as mysteriously as they arrive, melting away in the rice paddies like a phantom army. The Viet Minh is, indeed, so mobile that it seems to be everywhere in this country."

The analysis was contained in a book entitled *North from Malaya,* written by Justice William O. Douglas in 1952 and published the following year. In the summer of 1952, the Justice had taken to the bush to observe the fighting first hand. He found that the Viet Minh, vastly outnumbered in men and munitions by the French, rarely engaged the enemy in direct assault. Rather, the tactic was one of infiltration behind the French lines, where the guerrillas harassed and annoyed the French and, generally, kept them off balance. In order to be successful, the guerrillas had to possess

great reservoirs of expendable manpower and a cooperative community behind the French lines. Both conditions, Douglas observed, were met in 1952, as they would be in the 1960s when the
French were replaced by American troops.

Tracing the history and tragedy of colonial rule in Indochina,
Douglas lamented the fact that the U.S. had not encouraged the
dream of an independent Vietnam. The U.S. had supported the
French instead, and ensured years of guerrilla warfare. "Today,
the people are sick and tired of war," wrote Douglas. "Yet even
so, Ho Chi Minh has probably increased in popularity. The heavy
hand of the French is still on the land. The resistance movement
is stronger than ever; and Ho Chi Minh is the outstanding symbol
of it. There is little doubt that in a popularity contest Ho Chi
Minh would still lead the field."

Resistance to the Viet Minh had to come from the Vietnamese
themselves, not the French troops, Douglas argued. The French
could never win a military victory because they never could gain
the support of the Vietnamese, "who suspect every move of the
French, every promise, every ingratiating act." What could turn
the Vietnamese against the Viet Minh, Douglas argued, was a
"genuine democratic revolution." That meant sweeping reforms
which would uproot the landlords and the other vested interests
that had dominated the country's social, economic and political
fabric since the French had claimed control of the country in
1893. It also meant independence. "If the French refuse to make
that promise," Douglas wrote, "no political measure, no military
measure can arrest the processes of disintegration at work in the
country."

North from Malaya was the third book by Douglas in a series that
one reviewer termed travel books with "a social conscience."
Beginning in 1949, Douglas had embarked on what became annual summer pilgrimages to distant lands, from Afghanistan to
Nigeria, from the Kingdom of Swat to Kurdish villages in Iran.
"Traveling with Bill was like traveling with a magic carpet," said
his friend and frequent traveling companion, Elon Gilbert.

With typical Douglas energy, the Justice picked the brains and
won the hearts of the peasants in each region he visited. He
learned their customs and their miseries, dissected their governing hierarchies and property systems, agonized about the Com-

munist threat and pleaded for an enlightened foreign policy. In collecting his information, Douglas often avoided the VIP treatment. On his first visit to the Middle East and India, he met the Shah of Iran and Jawaharlal Nehru, but spent much more time (and space in his books) with ordinary villagers in what sometimes appeared to be a relentless determination to love everybody and everything he encountered.

As Douglas approached one Kurdish village, a local executioner welcomed his distinguished visitor by severing the head of a steer, dragging the animal across the road and proclaiming that the same should be done to all Douglas's enemies. The Justice found the ceremony "a robust, primitive, genuine welcome."

He was no less impressed by a gentler sign of hospitality after a fever and dysentery had forced him to turn back from a partridge hunt on Mount Kalar with members of the Baktiari tribe. As he struggled down the mountain, Douglas spotted a lone tent. He stumbled to the entrance and was greeted by a peasant. The man invited Douglas inside, rolled out a Persian carpet, told his guest to lie down and placed a blanket under his head. He brought Douglas a drink and then left him alone. Before he fell into a deep sleep, Douglas thought "how gracious and genuine a Persian's hospitality can be. When I walked into the tent, it became mine. I was left to myself . . . this was my new home."

Not everyone took a visit by Douglas so kindly. Russia's Iranian-beamed radio warned its listeners of a gang of American spies, led by "a certain Douglas," who were snooping around the Soviet-Iranian border. Their mission, according to the Russians, was to spy on border fortifications in pursuit of larger American imperialistic designs. When this "certain Douglas" scaled a peak in the region, the Soviet press headlined: "SUSPICIOUS FOREIGN 'ALPINISTS' IN IRAN." The Soviets even gave the spies ominous sobriquets; Justice Douglas became "Big Devil" and his son "Little Devil."

On his first two trips abroad, which included travel in Greece, Cyprus, Iran, Lebanon, Israel and India, Douglas jotted down notes on everything he had seen, smelled, heard and thought. The literary result of Douglas's efforts was the book *Strange Lands and Friendly People,* a title that Douglas agreed to only reluctantly. "It might describe the South Sea islands," Douglas wrote his

Harper editor, John Fischer. "It has a romantic touch—a travel-ogue flavor that I don't like and that is not the book." Despite Douglas's suggestions for another title ("Behind the East" or "Go Warmly to the East"), Fischer held fast to the original title. Douglas's fears that readers would not take the book seriously were not realized. *Strange Lands and Friendly People* was made a November 1951 selection of the Book-of-the-Month Club. "The eye-and-ear-witness reporting is magnificent," wrote Eric Seva-reid, then Chief Washington correspondent for CBS, in the *Saturday Review.*

Strange Lands contained its quota of travelogue descriptions of the lands and peoples that Douglas visited, but even here, there was a special touch. An associate justice of the U.S. Supreme Court, no less, was describing a Ghashghai shooting contest or applying his electric razor to a Lebanese peasant or buying a basket from an eight-year-old villager in the Himalayas. More important, there was the prodigiously adhesive mind at work, explaining in lucid detail the primitive methods of farming in the Middle East or the centuries-long rich history of the Persian tribes.

In fact, Douglas's insistence on a detailed narrative of the tribes of Persia had been the only serious point of disagreement with his editor. After Fischer suggested "fairly drastic" revisions of the section on the Persian tribes, Douglas succumbed to a serious case of author's vanity. He dashed off an outraged letter, pointing out the section's value to posterity. "That material is new, unique, original. It cannot be found in any language. That material will be invaluable for many years; it cannot be duplicated; no other person can write it; the region is closed. When the Iron Curtain falls around Persia, this material will be the only source material available showing the character, temper, etc. of the people be-hind it. These tribes in my lifetime will write Middle East history —and I think it will be glorious—that part of the book cannot be revised as you propose." In the end, both Douglas and Fischer softened their positions, with the author agreeing to cuts and the editor making changes that would ensure that the pace and sub-stance of the section were consistent with the rest of the book.

If there was a weakness to the book, it was Douglas's suggestion to the reader that the author could know an individual, a tribe, a country or a continent merely by focusing his extraordinary mind on the subject for a few weeks. His frenetic pace and facile pen skipped past subtle facts in a way that sometimes made the difference between enduring analysis and an entertaining journal. His analysis of India, for example, was occasionally strikingly naïve. He had asked a young village boy if the caste system still oppressed the country. "The boy turned to me," Douglas wrote, "wide-eyed at my inquiry, and said in full sincerity, 'there is no such person [as an Untouchable] in all of India anymore.' " With that illustrative conversation, Douglas concluded that Gandhi's teachings and India's law had begun to take hold in the back country. Douglas was also rather too charmed and impressed with Prime Minister Nehru and claimed, prematurely, that India was aggressively attacking its social and economic problems.

At times the author indulged in instant character analysis which provided smooth and entertaining reading but was of questionable accuracy. He quickly sized up a female Communist guerrilla in Greece as "a tigress who would spit in the face of her firing squad." And in Israel he met a "quiet, soft-spoken man" named Moshe Dayan, who fought dutifully for the Jewish homeland but longed to devote his life to his only two enthusiasms, his family and his farm.

Still, Douglas was no ordinary traveler and chronicler, and *Strange Lands* and his later books provided readers with important insights that other writers, spending years in the same regions, would not offer. Douglas saw the poverty but also the essential dignity of the peasants he met. He listened to their pleas for better medical care, schools and roads, and for land reform. He embraced their causes as his own.

And as he was to show later in Vietnam, Douglas exhibited a remarkable, almost prophetic, capacity to pinpoint the weaknesses of U.S. foreign policy. Douglas wanted the U.S. to sever ties with unrepresentative regimes and support the grass-roots needs of the people. He challenged a U.S. policy that measured friends by their allegiance to our foreign policy and spooned out rewards largely in the form of munitions. He urged that the U.S. place advisers in the villages, not in the national capitals with the government bureaucrats. He was convinced that U.S. policy could succeed only by means of enlightened assistance programs that brought the peasants better living conditions. The goal, Douglas believed, was to assure not a solid military alliance or a sympathetic vote in the United Nations—but a strong, independent Third World nation. That, to Douglas, was the most effective antidote to communism.

More than six months before *Strange Lands and Friendly People* was published, Douglas had already proposed a second travel book, this one on the mountains that stretched across northern India, Pakistan and Afganistan. His Harper editor, John Fischer, was not interested. He wrote Douglas that the Justice's new agent, Helen Strauss, had demanded too high a figure for an advance. Besides, Fischer told Douglas, he didn't think there was a substantial market for such a book.

"I think Fischer made a mistake," his boss, Cass Canfield, recalled. "Fischer told me that he thought Douglas was probably written out. I think Jack [Fischer] said, 'Oh, God, another book on mountains; we've already had two [*Of Men and Mountains* and *Strange Lands and Friendly People*]. Of course, he was completely wrong."

There was another version of why Douglas switched from Harper's to Doubleday for his second travel book, *Beyond the High Himalayas.* "My impression," said Ken McCormick, Douglas's editor at Doubleday, "was that we got him because he was propositioning any woman at Harper's who would look at him. It was embarrassing and I think Cass Canfield decided that this was no way for a justice of the U.S. Supreme Court to act. He was just screwing around and Canfield decided 'that guy has to go; I don't care if he's President of the United States.' " Though Canfield admitted that Douglas "knew how to handle an attractive lady" and "handled" at least one attractive woman employee at Harper's, he denied that Douglas's uncommon interest in Harper's female staff was the reason for his departure from the publishing house.

Douglas was not above talking about sexual adventures (not his own, of course) in his books. In the first chapter of *Beyond the High Himalayas,* he recounted the romantic escapades of his bus driver, Gillu, who had been assigned to drive the Justice from Manali, India, to the base of the Himalayas, where Douglas was scheduled to begin his mountain trek. The distance was only 125 miles, but with Gillu in the driver's seat, the trip took fourteen hours. The problem, Douglas discovered, was that Gillu, the father of ten children, was visiting girlfriends in every village along the way.

Douglas's accounts of his own experiences in the Himalayas did not offer his readers romance, but offered something equally compelling: high adventure. Shortly after Douglas and his party (which included an interpreter, a cook and porters to carry the supplies) began their climb, they were hit by late monsoon rains and winds. As Douglas trudged up the narrow trail, he noticed the corpses of dozens of animals killed by the storm. When the driving rain turned to sleet and hail and the winds reached hurricane velocity, the Justice wondered in characteristically dramatic prose —one part King Lear, one part Billy Graham—if his party might be the next victim:

> Right now it seemed that my own destruction was near. My feet were heavy with water and mud. I was so chilled I could hardly move. I did not think I could long endure. My breath was short. I felt icy hands at my throat, choking me. A cruel fate overhangs this Himalayan venture, I thought, a fate that has dogged it from the start. And then a prayer came to my lips as I bent into the wind and steeled myself for the battle of survival. In a few moments, I was gasping from the effort of walking. I stopped and looked up. A swirling cloud had taken a quick upward twist and given me new hope. For there was the dak bungalow a couple of hundred yards ahead of me. Could I make it? It seemed that unseen hands reached out and helped me over the last cruel stretch. . . .

He made it. And when Douglas was safely inside the dak bungalow, he greeted his porters with a smile and a warm pat on the back, as a general rallies his troops after the battle is over. "We had won together against the fury of the spirits," Douglas concluded. "A tremendous clap of thunder shook the bungalow. Death was abroad. But inside there was warmth, contentment and the companionship of men bent on high adventure."

Douglas's books about his travels never had a single focus. In one chapter Douglas would take the reader to the edge of a jagged Himalayan peak and in the next he might be lecturing on the inequities of the land tenancy system. He sprinkled his narrative with a light dose of humor, relishing the tale spread by his porters that he wore a "magical hat" (a tropical white glass helmet) that held back the rain, gently declining the invitation of a Lahuli woman who offered sexual favors and refusing to pay 800 rupees in damages for kicking a stubborn mule named Moti ("Moti and her mother and her grandmother wouldn't be worth 800 rupees," an irate Douglas told the mule's owner).

The storyteller's delight in poking fun—at himself or others, as the situation inspired—recurred throughout Douglas's books. In one of his later books, *West of the Indus,* for example, the author proudly told the reader that his second wife, Mercedes, had been in charge of repairing all mechanical malfunctions in a 1956 Chevrolet station wagon that the couple and a friend drove on a seven-thousand-mile trip from Karachi, West Pakistan, to Istanbul, Turkey, in the summer of 1957.

"Do you mean to say that you stood by while Mercedes changed tires?" a staid Washington hostess asked Justice Douglas upon their return.

"Yes, ma'am."

"Do you mean to say you sat in the shade while your wife crawled under the car to fix the muffler?"

"Taking pictures of her at work," Douglas replied.

"You mean to say you let a woman do all that work and you never lifted a finger?"

"I was busy taking pictures."

"Why, I never heard of such a thing—and Mercedes coming from the South, too."

"But you forget she's the mechanic. I, myself, can't tell one end of a screwdriver from another."

"Never heard of such a thing," the woman snorted. "I would think that it would have been much more proper if Mercedes had taken the pictures, while you fixed the car."

"But you see," Douglas replied, "pictures of a man fixing a car are a dime a dozen. Pictures of a woman fixing a car—especially pictures taken by her husband—tell a better story."

For every humorous anecdote, there was an even larger dose of Douglas's political philosophy. Contemplating the U.S. role in post–World War II Asia, Douglas recommended that America treat the Asian countries sensitively and with understanding, for, he suggested, whole civilizations carry the characteristics of either maleness or femaleness. "We are the aggressive male figures that shake the earth and remake it," Douglas wrote. "Asia is the female that silently creates, that builds slowly, patiently, that hangs on passionately to her past." Douglas was not concerned that his observations were vulnerable to charges of gross over-simplification and sexism. His purpose was to reach his reader with an arresting metaphor so that he could emphasize once again his overriding theme of the need for an enlightened foreign policy.

"We must play the masculine role with intelligence," he wrote. "We cannot win Asia by long, drawn-out, indecisive military engagements such as we have been conducting in Korea. We are pitting East and West in a bloody conflict. That is the way to make a tigress out of the female, an enemy more dangerous than any male can ever be. Asia needs more than a show of strength; Asia needs affection from those who represent the masculine component in the planetary scheme. If Asia knew our affection as well as our power, we could be wedded to her in great and noble deeds."

The imagery was strained and the assumptions sometimes questionable (was it the West's fault that it was locked in bloody struggle in Korea?), but the message was unmistakable. The United States should support independence movements in Asia with generous economic and social service assistance at the grass-roots level. In addition, we should accept Asian cultures and aspirations on their terms, not ours. That policy, in the long run, would be the best weapon against Soviet imperialism.

Douglas had no quarrel with the Russian people, only with their Communist rulers. And so, when he visited the Soviet Union in 1955, he exhibited the same good will and understanding that had characterized his earlier trips to the Middle East and Asia. Douglas's attitude was particularly striking when contrasted with that of his traveling companion, Robert F. Kennedy, fresh from Red-hunting as counsel to the Senate Investigations subcommittee.

The two traveled together at the request of Joe Kennedy, who in 1950 had asked Douglas to take his son Bobby with him on a planned trip to Russia. Douglas and Kennedy applied for visas but were repeatedly turned down. Finally, in 1955, with Stalin dead and Khrushchev planning a conference in Geneva with President Eisenhower, the Soviets relented.

Upon their arrival in Russia, Douglas and Kennedy were informed that an interpreter, who had been assigned to them months in advance, was not available. Douglas responded by returning to their hotel room and saying loudly, in the direction of what he assumed to be a concealed microphone, that he was going to call Khrushchev and complain about their rude treatment. Within an hour, an interpreter arrived and the remainder of their stay in the Soviet Union seemed to go much more smoothly. They ate a twenty-one-course meal at a collective farm near Baku, saw the tomb of Tamerlane in Samarkand and argued about academic freedom with an English-speaking professor at the University of Tashkent.

Curiously, Douglas was the soft-spoken member of the traveling team. "Douglas, the judge, was all suavity," Kennedy later recalled. "His technique was to appear interested and accommodating, drawing out the people with whom he talked until, having won their confidence, he could hit them with a factual issue and hope for a frank response." Young Bobby, on the other hand, was relentlessly hostile when attempting to gather information from the Russians.

Douglas and Kennedy differed in conclusions as well as tactics. While he doubted that the Soviet government's objectives had changed, Douglas thought that the Russian people wanted friendship and peace with the United States. Bobby was more skeptical. "We all want peace," he told one interviewer, "but are apt to be blinded by the bear's smile." And later he said: "My feeling is that before we make a great number of concessions we have to have something more concrete from the Russians, such as the dissolution of the Comintern and a workable disarmament plan."

Both Douglas and Kennedy termed the trip a success. Not only would Douglas get another book out of the experience *(Russian Journey),* but he felt he had given Joe Kennedy's closed-minded son a good political lesson as well. Before the trip, Bobby appeared to view the Russians as soulless fanatics; afterward, according to Douglas, he saw them as human beings and achievers, "people with problems." The experience, Douglas later contended, would help convince Kennedy to finally abandon his devotion to Senator Joseph McCarthy.

Douglas also made Kennedy a believer in his personal style of diplomacy. "He [Douglas] was a man who was able to tell them [the people of other countries], in ways they understood, of our views and beliefs. He could speak with wisdom of our laws and explain our system of government. He could talk to them also in every-day terms, of many other matters in which they were deeply interested—how much cotton was produced per acre in South Carolina or how much wheat in Nebraska. The many who have seen him in his travels, read his books, and heard his friendly words have been moved and inspired."

But Douglas was not content simply to inspire with his trips and books. He wanted his views on U.S. foreign policy adopted by the administration and he introduced his own style of diplomacy to accomplish that aim. In the early fifties, he wrote President Truman from abroad and conferred with him at home in an attempt to persuade him to relax the cold war tension.

Later, he undertook a one-man lobbying effort with important members of Congress to promote his ideas. After Douglas returned from Southeast Asia in the early fifties, for example, he hosted a luncheon for Ngo Dinh Diem (Douglas believed him to be the one Vietnamese leader who had preserved his integrity in the face of French corruption). Among the invited guests were Senators Mike Mansfield of Montana and John F. Kennedy of Massachusetts, whom Douglas wanted to impress with the nationalist, not Communist, nature of the underground movement in Vietnam. After the luncheon, Douglas was satisfied that his guests came away with "a new orientation to the problems of Vietnam."

Although Douglas's views were not accepted in the State Department, he articulated a foreign policy that had significant influence here and abroad, particularly in Third World countries. Through his books, Douglas reached millions around the world and exposed them to his foreign policy ideas. Though many of the ideas had first been announced in the forties, Douglas was able, in his books, to populate those ideas with the flesh and feelings of the peasants he met, and package them with humorous anecdotes and personal adventures. In this way, he made his liberal ideas palpable to more conservative citizens in the United States and abroad. As important, Douglas became a conspicuous symbol for liberal political thought at the height of the cold war, when such symbols, and such thought, particularly among America's leaders, were very rare indeed.

In promoting his ideas, Douglas used his position as an associate justice of the U.S. Supreme Court to full political advantage. He declared the principles of his foreign policy in speeches and books without the fear of political reprisal or restraint of office that inhibited high-echelon members of the State Department. Had he been Secretary of State, for example, Douglas could not have pursued his goals in the same aggressive, outspoken style. Douglas's innovative ideas, to be sure, did not form the centerpiece for a new U.S. foreign policy. But they were, and are, available to generations that may not feel so bound to the past.

POTBELLIED MEN

CHIEF JUSTICE Earl Warren once speculated on William O. Douglas's career had Douglas been born at an earlier time in American history. He might have come by sea with George Vancouver in 1792, the Chief Justice thought, or a decade later, joined the Lewis and Clark expedition which charted a trail across the continent. But still more likely, according to Warren, Douglas would have explored the West with Captain Frémont and Kit Carson. Warren had no doubt that regardless of whose heroic company Douglas would have chosen to keep, he would have done his pioneering while sitting on the Court and producing his usual high quota of judicial opinions.

In his own way, Douglas replicated the Chief Justice's admiring fantasy portrait in his twentieth-century life. The West had, unfortunately for Douglas, already been won and thoroughly explored, but that did not deter him from putting his own indefatigable energies to the task once again. In some ways he was able to do better than Lewis and Clark, Captain Frémont and Kit Carson. With the advantages of better maps and jet transportation, Douglas could cover more ground in a shorter time.

At the slightest call, Douglas would pack his camping gear and appear wherever he was promised outdoor adventure. Once, two Texas attorneys and outdoorsmen, Bob Burleson and Jim Bowmer, had planned a trip to Santa Helena Canyon in their state's Big Bend country and sent out invitations to several prominent outdoorsmen, including Douglas, whom they had never met. To their surprise, they received an immediate, enthusiastic response. "I'll be in Texas next month to make a speech," Douglas wrote. "Can we go then?" They could and did. After the adventure, Douglas was asked by a reporter if his companions were close friends of his. "They are now," replied Douglas.

Even when he was confined to the Washington, D.C., area by his Court duties, Douglas seemed able to spring free for a few hours when the spirit was irresistible.

"Want to go for a walk, Charlie?" Douglas would ask a frequent hiking companion, Charles Reich, who later wrote *The Greening of America.*

"Those were the magic words," Reich recalled. "In an hour we would be walking together along the C & O Canal towpath; the Justice's step quick, impatient, never pausing; both of us propelled by his energy."

Douglas exulted at the discovery of a good trout stream as much as at an energizing towpath. After he had fished a superb stream called Silver Creek, near Hailey, Idaho, Douglas wrote Fred Rodell: "That is the best dry fly stream I have seen. I can recommend it without reservations. It's a honey. Any day you wish me to meet you at Silver Creek, I'll be there."

"Bill was a damn good fly fisherman," recalled Gene Marsh, who, with his twin brother, Frank, was one of Douglas's favorite fishing companions. "He was a purist," said Marsh. "He only fished with fly, mostly dry fly, and he fished with light tackle and rod."

Another of Douglas's frequent fishing partners, Elon Gilbert, remembered the thrill he and Douglas experienced fishing in the Wallowa lakes. "You could see the fish in the bluish, transparent water as the fish made their run. As the fish turned, it flashed beautiful rainbow colors off its sides."

That was one of the experiences, Gilbert suggested, that brought Douglas back regularly, seemingly compulsively, to the

Northwest. "I always felt that Bill's residence in Washington was terminated each summer in the way a man might be held by an elastic band," said Gilbert. "Just as soon as he could, he came back. It was remarkable not that he came back, but that he stayed in the East. He was more one of us."

Douglas's love of fishing combined the joy of the sportsman with the curiosity of the insatiable student. He carried on an extended correspondence with Major Roderick L. Haig-Brown of British Columbia, an expert on Pacific salmon. And he was always ready to present a Brandeis brief in favor of dry fly over live bait fishing. "I would rather hook a one pound rainbow with a dry fly on a 3½ ounce rod," Douglas once wrote, "than a four pounder with bait or hardware." The preference, Douglas added, was based on the combination of the Justice's highly developed sense of competition with his reverence for nature's wonders. It takes a trout only one tenth of a second to detect the dry fly, Douglas observed, so they are tougher to catch. Dry bait, therefore, was doubly satisfying to Douglas, since it required greater skill of the angler and at the same time left the undeserving fishermen empty-handed and the streams full.

No one enjoyed the culminating moment of the successful angler more than Douglas. "Set rock at 45 degree angle," Douglas told friends who wanted his favorite trout recipe, "and heat upper side with fire; salt and pepper trout and roll in flour and place on heated face of rock; do not turn; rock will cook underside and campfire will cook topside; serve when trout is deep brown."

The outdoors provided Douglas with countless causes as well as innumerable pleasures. He organized or joined scores of "crusades," as he called them, to save a river or a lake or a patch of woods from private industry or government bureaucracy. His most celebrated hike occurred in 1954 after plans had been announced to convert 180 miles of the long-abandoned C & O Canal—a favorite area for hikers and avid naturalists which ran from Washington, D.C., to Cumberland, Maryland—into a parkway. "It is a refuge, a place of retreat, a long stretch of quiet and peace at the Capitol's back door," Douglas wrote to the *Washington Post,* protesting a *Post* editorial commending the parkway plan. Then he joined thirty-six other conservationists who demanded that the C & O be made a national historic park.

Government authorities ignored the demand, so Douglas and his fellow crusaders led a well-publicized protest march through the area.

As a result of the hike, plans for the freeway were put aside, and in 1971 (the government bureaucracy did not give up without a fight), the C & O was made a national park. Six years later, in a ceremony in the Capitol, the area was officially dedicated to Douglas.

Douglas did not limit his environmental or other causes to extrajudicial activities. He also used his judicial opinions to take his message to the people. In one opinion, supported by no other member of the Court, Douglas suggested that America's trees and rivers deserved the legal status given individual citizens, private corporations and even ships to bring a lawsuit. He urged a standing rule permitting environmental issues to be litigated

> in the name of the inanimate object about to be despoiled, defaced, or invaded by roads and bulldozers and where injury is the subject of public outrage. . . . before these priceless bits of Americana (such as a valley, an alpine meadow, a river or a lake) are forever lost or are so transformed as to be reduced to the eventual rubble of our urban environment, the voice of the existing beneficiaries of these environmental wonders should be heard. Perhaps, they will not win. Perhaps, the bulldozers of "progress" will plow under all the aesthetic wonders of this beautiful land. That is not the present question. The sole question is, who has standing to be heard?

Like John Muir, Douglas was not satisfied simply to love the wilderness and fight for its preservation, but insisted on recording what he saw and heard and felt. Thus, after an adventure in some remote wilderness, he would return to the Court (usually a day or even hours before the scheduled session), his notebooks filled with his memories and observations. During the Court term, sometimes while hearing oral argument, Douglas would develop his notes into book-length narratives.

In his nature books, Douglas could be lyrical or didactic, his personal adventures dramatic or humorous, as his mood, and the surroundings, inspired. Not surprisingly, in one of his first nature books Douglas returned to his early love, the Northwest. In *My*

Wilderness: The Pacific West, the reader was first transported to the Brooks Range of Alaska, where "all of the noises of civilization have been left behind; now the music of the wilderness can be heard." Later in the book, Douglas wrote of his pleasure in observing Mount Adams, which he had scaled in 1945. "If the sun sets clear, there is a moment before the mountain is swallowed up by darkness when it is brightly luminous, incandescent, a startling ball of cold light." And in nearby Goose Prairie, Douglas observed: "Nursery of splendid trees. Garden of brilliant flowers. Abode of birds without number. Greenhouse for succulent mushrooms. Gateway to wild and high country. . . ."

But the sights of the Northwest did not always inspire Douglas to poetic wonder. On a road in his beloved Cascades, Douglas counted twenty-seven automobiles ahead of him. It was a sign that *anyone* could reach his wilderness. And that did not please him. Nature's pleasures should be shared only by the hearty, the deserving, the true believers. But to Douglas's dismay, any TV-watching, beer-guzzling suburbanite could jump into his car and in a few hours behold the vistas that Douglas had sometimes trekked for days to discover. These mountains, his mountains, were captured as cheaply as a drive-in movie. It was, in his view, sacrilegious. "Potbellied men, smoking black cigars, who never could climb a hundred feet," lamented Douglas, "were now in the sacred precincts of a great mountain."

At night in the Cascades, Douglas did some mental calculations. Only two percent of the land area of the United States remained in a roadless, wilderness state, he figured. Now was the time for all good, hearty, vigilant wilderness enthusiasts to defend their turf. If action was not taken immediately, even the remaining two percent of wilderness would be desecrated by the automobile, trampled by the soft and flabby city slicker. "We need high Alpine meadows which can only be reached by foot," Douglas warned, and "peaks which can only be conquered by daring."

That same message was delivered in a sequel, *My Wilderness: East to Katahdin.* This time Douglas began in Arizona, paused in Colorado's Maroon Bells wilderness area, where he spotted America's smallest bird, the cassiope hummingbird, listened to a sharp wind play a symphony in the Australian pine of Florida's

Everglades and, finally, returned to the scene of earlier pleasure, the Katahdin Mountains in Maine.

"The pull of Katahdin," wrote Douglas, "like that of an old love, was always strong." He gloried in the sight of the goshawk and red-tailed hawk overhead, the red squirrel below, the lakes and the laurel, the wild strawberries and even the brown adder snake. But again his reverie was interrupted by the gloomy thoughts of a vanishing wilderness. The warning and even the language was reminiscent of the earlier book: "Civilization has destroyed the Maine wilderness. The roar of motorboats and of planes has shattered its sacred precincts. Man, though soft, flabby and unfit for adventure, now can go anywhere." Surveying the beauties of Maine's Katahdin and Baxter state parks, Douglas wrote that "God made the wilderness for man and all other creatures to use, to adore, but not to destroy."

Whether writing about distant lands or about natural wonders in the United States, Douglas refused to let his reader sit back and simply enjoy his guided tour. Douglas's books, all his books, taught his view of the world and the need to preserve the basic values he deemed crucial. In his books about his world tours, Douglas stressed democratic values and the need for social and economic development. In his nature books, Douglas lectured on environmental protection.

He did not pull punches. In *Farewell to Texas: A Vanishing Wilderness,* Douglas accused the utility companies, federal agencies, stockmen, lumber barons, vandals, oil companies and ranchers of despoiling Texas, and labeled them "the modern Ahabs." They were the villains of the tale, those "who see a tree and think in terms of board feet . . . see a cliff and think in terms of gravel . . . see a river and think in terms of dams." And like the ancient king of Samaria who coveted Naboth's vineyard and killed him to get what he wanted, the modern Ahabs had coveted all the state's unspoiled areas and had slowly squeezed all life out of the precious wilderness. To hear Douglas tell it, there was not a single state park or wilderness trail worthy of the name in the entire state of Texas. That was not true. But his readers could pardon the Justice his hyperbole because his heart was pure and his message urgent. "When we think of conservation, nature trails, back-packing, camping and outdoor recreation," Douglas concluded, "we must say farewell to Texas—unless the dedicated minority receives an overwhelming mandate from the people."

Outside Texas, Douglas was no more sanguine. Walden Pond, he observed, was no longer Thoreau's peaceful refuge but a garish collection of hot dog stands, bathing beaches and trailer camps. Lake Tahoe, Nevada, was no better. Originally "a shining jewel in the mountains," it had been ruined by sewage. And the Mississippi, "once a proud and majestic concourse . . . [now] collects sewage, garbage and industrial wastes all the way." To Douglas, highways became daggers pointed "at the heart of any wilderness that lies ahead" and their sponsors, like New York's Robert Moses, the environmentalist's executioner.

What was to be done? Never a small thinker, Douglas proposed a second Bill of Rights. This version would protect individual Americans who wanted to get out of their cars into hiking shoes and backpacks against the "powerful forces"—the government bureaucrats, strip-mining executives and lumber barons—who worked against them. For Douglas, protection of the environmentalists was given the same high place as protection of speech and religion, and for many of the same reasons. The nature-lovers in the country represented, according to Douglas, the essential value of individuality in an increasingly standardized society. "The wilderness is a refuge for automated man," wrote Douglas, and "offers an important alternative that brings into one's drab life an endless wonder and excitement of nature's flair for individuality rather than conformity."

In the wilderness protected by Douglas's second Bill of Rights, all motorized equipment would be barred, as would all mineral claimants. Existing sewage disposal systems would be replaced with distillation processes that would return pure water to the rivers. Douglas's Bill of Rights would automatically create the presumption in a court of law that any project destroying the basic character of a free-flowing river would be declared against the common good. He would direct the Bureau of Public Roads, by statute, to conserve all natural beauty in the country even if to preserve it would cost more than if the government bureaucrats allowed throughways to "gobble" up the land. To serve as watchdog for his Bill of Rights, Douglas would create an Office of Conservation, with the status of a cabinet-level department, to elevate, coordinate and plan all the conservation needs of the nation.

Douglas did not enjoy much greater tangible success in implementing his environmental ideas than he did in winning over the State Department to his foreign policy. No wilderness Bill of Rights has been adopted, and trees and rivers still lack standing in the U.S. Supreme Court. But Douglas has had an impact, and it has been far greater than his C & O Canal success. Since he began fighting for ecological causes, the American public has become more aware of and willing to fight for those same causes. The hostile forces are still there—the commercial companies and government bureaucrats who would destroy the land and pollute the water for their own interests. But now there are more people and even agencies in government (for example, the Environmental Protection Agency) willing to fight for rivers and lakes, valleys and ridges, mountains and paths.

Douglas, of course, could not claim sole responsibility for the movement. But he was there early and he was committed and visible. He offered the movement a hero.

NATIONAL TEACHER

Aｌｅｘａｎｄｅｒ Mｅｉｋｌｅｊｏｈｎ taught philosophy, not law, but a tiny book that he wrote on the meaning of the First Amendment quickly became recognized as a seminal work in constitutional theory shortly after its publication in 1948. In his book, *Free Speech and Its Relation to Self-Government,* Meiklejohn read the First Amendment's command that "Congress shall make no law abridging the freedom of speech" and concluded that the framers of the Constitution meant what they wrote. "No law" could only mean "no law."

For Meiklejohn, so long as speech focused on public policy, it was fully protected. The speech could advocate, in the strongest terms, socialism, communism, even anarchy; it did not matter. The critical public purpose to be served by the free expression of even the most revolutionary ideas was the American citizenry's right to decide, through a limitless flow of information, how it was to govern itself.

Because Meiklejohn insisted that the protection of public discussion was absolute, he naturally rejected Justice Oliver Wendell Holmes's "clear and present danger" test, which countenanced governmental restraint when the discussion posed a "clear and present danger" to public order. "The unabridged freedom of public discussion is the rock on which our government stands," wrote Meiklejohn. "With that foundation beneath us, we shall not flinch in the fact of any clear and present—or, even, terrific—danger."

Meiklejohn's absolute commitment to public discussion was pure and idealistic, too much so even for Justice Douglas, who, with his colleague Hugo Black, were commonly considered to be the Court's most dedicated libertarians. In the late forties and early fifties, Douglas's fiery First Amendment rhetoric tended to hide a persistent unwillingness to abandon Holmes's clear and present danger test. His most outspoken judicial opinions in that period denounced government restraint on speech, but always with the careful notation that the government had not presented evidence of a clear and present danger.

Douglas's brave dissent in 1951 condemning the convictions of Eugene Dennis and ten other American Communist leaders had pointedly stated that the government had not proved that the defendants had done more than teach Communist doctrine, hardly enough to meet Holmes's test. All the time that Douglas had quietly held to the Holmes test, he was promoting the principle of free speech under the First Amendment in the strongest possible terms. In *Dennis,* for example, he wrote: "Full and free discussion has indeed been the article of our faith. We have founded our political system on it."

A year after *Dennis,* Douglas wrote in a dissent: "The First Amendment is couched in absolute terms—freedom of speech shall not be abridged." His words in that 1952 opinion were provoked by a majority decision that had upheld the conviction under a state group libel law of a racist named Joseph Beauharnais. Beauharnais had been arrested after he had distributed pamphlets calling on the "one million self respecting white people in Chicago to unite" so that they would not be "mongrelized by the Negro." Douglas had not approved of Beauharnais's racist blather any more than had the Court majority, but he found no evidence that the distribution of Beauharnais's pamphlets presented a clear and present danger to public order. Again, the Holmes test.

But with each dissenting opinion, Douglas became increasingly convinced that the Holmes test was unworkable since, he believed, the Court majority was systematically diluting the test of all meaning. He perceived a Court majority subtly substituting a "reasonableness" standard for the tougher "clear and present danger" and, in the process, sanctioning virtually any restraint on public discussion that the government considered desirable. That suspicion was shared by Alexander Meiklejohn, who in 1953 wrote what Douglas later described as a "devastating" criticism of Court decisions "which have allowed freedom of speech to be abridged."

It may have been more than a coincidence that during the year in which Meiklejohn published his "devastating" criticism, Douglas's judicial opinions involving the scope of free expression assumed an absolutist coloration. "The command of the First Amendment," Douglas wrote in one dissent in 1953, "is that there shall be *no* law which abridges those civil rights. The matter is beyond the power of the legislature to regulate, control or condition." The "reasonableness" standard, Douglas noted, "has been slowly creeping into our constitutional law. It has no place there."

A year later Douglas puzzled over a claim that the First Amendment allowed the censorship of obscene movies under a narrowly drawn statute. "In order to sanction a system of censorship," wrote Douglas, "I would have to say 'no law' does not mean what it says, that 'no law' is qualified to mean 'some' laws. I cannot take that step." Finally, in 1957, Douglas presented his own constitutional test: The First Amendment guarantees of free expression are absolute, he said, and should be suppressed only when the expression "is so closely brigaded with illegal action as to be an inseparable part of it."

With the announcement of his own constitutional test, Douglas had not only caught up with Alexander Meiklejohn but had passed him in his commitment to a literal reading of the free expression clauses of the First Amendment. For Meiklejohn had limited his absolutist view to the discussion of public issues; he did not extend that same protection to private speech uttered for private purposes. Douglas made no such distinction. To him, the First Amendment command was as insistent, and complete, whether the expression the government wanted to suppress was found in Lawrence's *Lady Chatterley's Lover* or Lenin's *The State and Revolution.* In applying the same standard to so-called obscene literature as he did to other forms of expression, Douglas recognized that he (and Justice Black, who held similar views) was unlikely to persuade a majority of his colleagues of the wisdom of his views. "My views on obscenity are so far out of line with the majority view of the Court," Douglas wrote Professor Edmond Cahn of New York University Law School, who preached a libertarian philosophy similar to Black's and Douglas's, "that it seems almost hopeless to keep pounding away for them." But he did.

Despite his persistence, Douglas was unable to persuade a majority of his colleagues in the fifties that the First Amendment's command was absolute or, more generally, that the Court had a special libertarian mission. The dominant philosophy was that of judicial restraint; First Amendment freedoms, as other individual liberties, were weighed carefully against the reasonableness of the government's restraint. The guiding spirit of that philosophy was, of course, Felix Frankfurter.

Douglas feared that Frankfurter's dominant influence went far beyond the Court; indeed, he was convinced that it had even penetrated that academic bastion of libertarianism, the Yale Law School. The thought that Yale could be dominated by followers of Felix Frankfurter appalled Douglas, but the evidence seemed everywhere. Wesley Sturgis, a former Douglas colleague at Yale and a close friend, had been succeeded as dean by Harry Shulman, a Harvard-trained labor expert. An early Douglas clerk, Vern Countryman, had been denied tenure at Yale even though Douglas had given him strong support.* On the other hand, former Frankfurter clerks, like Alexander Bickel and Harry Wellington, had been welcomed to the Yale faculty and seemed to have had no trouble obtaining tenure. In teaching and writing about constitutional law, Yale's Bickel made no secret of his admiration for the Frankfurter philosophy of judicial restraint and his utter disdain for Douglas's opinions. The Frankfurter philoso-

---

*Countryman, ironically, later was granted tenure at Harvard.

phy, both Douglas and his inside source on the Yale faculty, Fred Rodell, believed, gradually began to dominate the school's thinking.

When Frankfurter himself had been asked to speak to a Yale Law School alumni meeting in Washington, D.C., in 1954, Douglas had noted the fact, unhappily, in a letter to Rodell. He also had expressed dismay when Yale's Dean Shulman delivered the 1955 Holmes Lectures at Harvard, a sure sign to Douglas that cross-fertilization had taken hold, with the Harvard philosophical strain increasingly dominant. Douglas's anger at the turn of events became so intense that he discouraged his own law clerks from accepting teaching appointments at Yale. His 1959 law clerk, Steve Duke, said that Douglas advised him not to go to Yale. "He said he didn't think I'd like the climate there. I think it had to do with the Countryman thing. Also Yale had added Bickel and Wellington. He thought the Frankfurter influence had taken over."*

In Douglas's view, the battle was not being lost just on the Court and in New Haven, but in the larger arena of public opinion. He distrusted all unfavorable reviews of his books, and frequently suggested that the unimpressed reviewer was a hatchet man for Frankfurter. When his book *We the Judges,* a comparative study of the Indian and American constitutions, received a critical review from Harvard political scientist Robert McCloskey, Douglas suspected the work of one of "FF's boys." And when Fred Rodell informed Douglas that an article he had submitted to the *New Republic,* criticizing Alexander Bickel's constitutional position, had been turned down, Douglas concluded that the rejection "shows what a hold the FF regime has on that sheet." When, later, *The New York Times* sent Anthony Lewis to cover the Supreme Court, Douglas was chagrined to learn that Lewis had spent a year at Harvard on a Nieman Fellowship, "learning the true faith."

Douglas was not, however, above his own subtle form of media manipulation. An opportunity arose after Professor Edmond Cahn wrote Douglas that he was concerned about the reviewer *The New York Times* would select for his new publication, *The*

---

*Duke rejected Douglas's advice and became a professor of law at Yale.

Predicament of Democratic Man. The book, Cahn wrote, was a completely outspoken defense of a libertarian philosophy which, he was certain, would displease certain of Douglas's colleagues (including, presumably, Felix Frankfurter). Cahn was afraid that the *Times* would send the book to an unsympathetic reviewer, who would do a hatchet job. To avoid that danger and assure the book a fair appraisal, Cahn suggested that Douglas let Francis Brown, the *Times* book review editor, know in advance that he would be willing to review the book.

Douglas wrote Brown the next day: "Dear Mr. Brown: Some of my friends were telling me about galleys on a forthcoming book by Professor Edmond Cahn of New York University. . . . What they told me about it excited my interest so much that I thought I would drop you a note indicating my interest in case you decide to review the book. I know nothing about the MS, but my friends were so interested that I judge it to be a very challenging and provocative document. . . ." Douglas sent a copy of his letter to Cahn with the notation that "This may have precisely the wrong effect—for the man is not very friendly."

Douglas needn't have worried. "I don't know anything about Edmond Cahn's book," Brown wrote Douglas, "but I would be very happy to have you review it if it is the kind of thing that interests you."

Cahn was elated, certain that the *Times* or some other prominent newspaper would seize the opportunity to have his book reviewed by Douglas.

With Douglas's mounting private fears that the Frankfurter philosophy was spreading, his public attacks on that philosophy intensified. He was no longer content to engage in the "more or less polite duel of ironies and sarcastic allusions," as Edmond Cahn put it, that had characterized his earlier criticism of the Frankfurter-dominated Court opinions. In 1958, Douglas published a book, *The Right of the People,* that signaled a direct, aggressive, unadorned attack on the philosophy of judicial restraint.

Too many members of the judiciary, Douglas wrote, had taken the view, advocated in a series of lectures by Judge Learned Hand, that the prohibitions of the First Amendment are "no more than admonitions of moderation." If Hand was correct, and the First Amendment conveyed "a mood, not a command," then the language of the First Amendment did not mean what it said. Hand's constitutional interpretation, Douglas charged, "has done more to undermine liberty in this country than any other single force. That notion [that the prohibitions of the First Amendment are "admonitions of moderation"] is, indeed, at the root of the forces of disintegration that have been eroding the democratic ideal in this country."

Although the specific attack was on Judge Hand, Douglas did not camouflage his disdain for all who represented Hand's philosophy. The Douglas criticism, inevitably, reached Felix Frankfurter as well. The "balancing" tests that Frankfurter had supported were openly condemned by Douglas as foreign to the First Amendment.

The philosophical struggle between the libertarians (Douglas/Black) and the proponents of judicial restraint (Frankfurter/Hand), as Douglas saw it, was a continuation of the fight waged among the Constitution's framers. Thomas Jefferson, the spiritual father of the Bill of Rights, had successfully pleaded the case for a First Amendment that would stand against government tyranny. On the other hand, Douglas noted, Alexander Hamilton had argued that there was no need for a Bill of Rights. Rather, Hamilton believed free expression should be dependent on public opinion and what he called "legislative discretion."

Frankfurter and Hand, Douglas suggested, followed the Hamilton interpretation of the First Amendment. By adopting a "reasonableness" standard and presuming virtually every legislative act to be "reasonable," Frankfurter and Hand had, in effect, resurrected Hamilton's maxim of "legislative discretion."

Douglas claimed, for himself, a sturdier Jeffersonian faith in the people and their rights under the First Amendment. "The philosophy of the First Amendment is that man must have full freedom to search the world and the universe for the answers to the puzzles of life," Douglas wrote. "Unless the horizons are unlimited, we risk being governed by a set of prejudices of a bygone day. If we are restricted in art, religion, economics, political theory, or any other great field of knowledge, we may become victims of conformity in an age where salvation can be won only by nonconformity."

Besides stating his absolutist interpretation of the First Amendment in *Free Speech and Its Relation to Self-Government,* Alexander Meiklejohn had written: "And to us who labor at that task of educating Americans, it becomes, year by year, more evident that the Supreme Court has a large part to play in our national teaching. That court is commissioned to interpret to us our purposes, our own meanings."

Although he had belatedly embraced Meiklejohn's absolutist view of the freedom of public discussion, Douglas was not so tardy in accepting the pedagogical role for the Court that the philosopher advocated. Since his early days on the Court, Douglas had accepted the Court's role of "national teacher." Even in the 1940s and early 1950s, Douglas's opinions, in part, had been admired (and criticized) for their conspicuous appeal to a lay audience. Douglas knew exactly what he was doing. During the McCarthy era, for example, Douglas's dissents, he later admitted, were calculated to touch "the conscience of our people."

But Douglas saw his mandate to be larger than even Meiklejohn had envisioned. Not satisfied merely to teach through his judicial opinions, Douglas communicated his broad philosophy of government to the American people in his books. One of these, *An Almanac of Liberty,* is illustrative.

Almanac was laid out like a calendar, with Douglas presenting a one-page history lesson for each day of the year. In his foreword, Douglas warned lawyers and historians away from the book, which, he admitted, might be too condensed to satisfy "their appetites for detail." Douglas had another audience in mind, the common man, who would be shown the broad outlines of a democratic faith—Douglas's democratic faith—without becoming bogged down in the technicalities of law or close historical analysis.

The Douglas *Almanac* was not confined to his interpretation of constitutional guarantees. His philosophy, Douglas wrote, was "more the small town than the city; more free enterprise than big business; more the man who risks his life than he who risks his dollar; more the farmer than the middleman; more the cooperative than the cartel. My *Almanac* ranks freedom to eat with freedom to speak, the right to property with the right to privacy, the right to work with freedom from racial discrimination. My *Almanac* is concerned with the Sermon on the Mount, the United Nations, workmen's compensation, social security as well as with habeas corpus and the Fifth Amendment."

Douglas did not, however, deny his "common man" a cogent discussion of civil liberties. Quoting Meiklejohn approvingly and taking the philosopher's First Amendment message to his readers, Douglas wrote that "Our philosophy is premised on the belief that national security will be better assured through political freedom, than through repression." He also advocated the constitutional view, only adopted by Douglas in 1952, that unauthorized governmental wiretapping violated the Fourth Amendment's guarantee against unreasonable searches and seizures. "Wiretapping may catch criminals who might otherwise escape," Douglas wrote, "but a degree of inefficiency is a price we necessarily pay for a civilized, decent society." The need for a decent, civilized society was again emphasized when Douglas spoke of the value of the Fifth Amendment's protection against self-incrimination: "The Fifth Amendment is an old friend, and a good friend," he wrote. "It is one of the great landmarks in man's struggle to be free of tyranny, to be decent and civilized. It is our way of escape from the use of torture. It protects man against any form of the Inquisition. It is part of our respect for the dignity of man. It reflects our ideas of the worth of rugged individualism."

When the law is wrong, Douglas wrote in a telling passage of *An Almanac,* it ought to be changed. Judges had often used precedent to preserve the status quo, at the expense of human rights. That was bad policy and worse constitutional law. "The Constitution is written in general terms," wrote Douglas. "The language gathers meaning from a judge's experience and philosophy. What other judges may have said it meant cannot be binding on the newcomer. For the Constitution was written for all ages."

In the 1960s, Douglas's commitment to First Amendment guarantees exceeded even Hugo Black's. Since their early days on the Court, both Black and Douglas had insisted on special protections for speech, press and assembly, but both had admitted those rights could be exercised only where people had a right to be for such purposes. Neither would allow an uninvited orator, for example, to deliver his message at a session of Congress or a murder trial. During the civil rights protests of the sixties, Black and Douglas frequently disagreed on where demonstrators had a right to exercise their First Amendment rights.

At the height of the civil rights movement, thirty-two Florida A & M University students sang hymns and danced in front of a county jail to protest the arrests and incarceration of their fellow students who had demonstrated against segregated public theaters. They, too, were arrested under a state trespass statute. In 1966, Justice Black wrote the majority opinion in *Adderley* v. *Florida* for the Court, upholding the arrests and convictions. Civil rights protesters had ample opportunity to demonstrate against segregation policies without marching on the county jail, said Black. They could, he admitted, demonstrate on the state capitol grounds, for those grounds are open to the public. "Jails, built for security purposes, are not," wrote Black. The Florida trespass statute, he added, "is aimed at conduct of one limited kind, that is, for one person or persons who trespass upon the property of another with a malicious and mischievous intent." Black concluded that the statute was properly invoked in the case.

It has been suggested that Justice Black's commitment to civil liberties waned in the middle sixties, when the civil rights protests became more raucous and his own health precarious. His opinion in *Adderley* gives some credence to that suggestion, since under another reading of the facts in the case, one could reasonably conclude that the students were not at the county jail "with malicious and mischievous intent," as Black contended, but to protest the arrests of their fellow students and civil rights demonstrators. Under that view, the protest, which did not compromise the security of the jail, was neither malicious nor mischievous. That was Douglas's position.

He wrote in dissent:

> The jailhouse, like an executive mansion, a legislative chamber, a courthouse, or the statehouse itself, is one of the seats of government whether it be the Tower of London, the Bastille, or a small county jail. And when it houses political prisoners or those who many think are unjustly held, it is an obvious center for protest. The right to petition for the redress of grievances has an

ancient history and is not limited to writing a letter or sending a telegram to a congressman; it is not confined to appearing before the local city council, or writing letters to the President or Governor or Mayor. . . . Conventional methods of petitioning may be, and often have been, shut off to large groups of our citizens. . . . Their [the protesters'] methods should not be condemned as tactics of obstruction and harassment as long as the assembly and petition are peaceable, as these were.

Protests against U.S. involvement in the Vietnam War presented even greater difficulties for Black, as Mary Beth Tinker and two other Des Moines secondary school students discovered. In 1965, the three students had worn black armbands to their schools to publicize their objections to the U.S. involvement in the Vietnam War and their support for an immediate truce. School authorities asked the students to remove their armbands, and when the students refused, they were sent home and suspended. The school authorities' action was challenged by the students as a violation of their First Amendment rights to free expression. A U.S. district court upheld the school authorities, and a federal appeals court affirmed the decision.

Justice Abe Fortas wrote the majority opinion for the U.S. Supreme Court, reversing the lower court decision. His opinion was supported by his former teacher Justice Douglas, but not by Justice Black. Fortas found nothing in the trial record to suggest that the students' armband display had interfered with discipline in the school or violated anyone else's rights. Instead Fortas concluded that the action of school authorities had been based on the "urgent wish to avoid the controversy which might result from the expression, even by the silent symbol of armbands, of opposition to this Nation's part in the conflagration in Vietnam." That was unacceptable. Students, wrote Fortas, "may not be confined to the expression of those sentiments that are officially approved. In the absence of a specific showing of constitutionally valid reasons to regulate their speech [he did not find it here], students are entitled to freedom of expression of their views. . . ."

What Justices Fortas, Douglas and other members of the Court majority took to be the students' exercise of constitutional rights, Justice Black interpreted as a prelude to anarchy. The armbands distracted the attention of other students from their studies, Black wrote in dissent, "to the highly emotional subject of the Vietnam War." Black predicted that as a result of the Court majority's holding, other students "will be ready, able and willing to defy their teachers on practically all orders. This is most unfortunate for the schools since groups of students all over the land are already running loose, conducting break-ins, sit-ins, lie-ins and smash-ins. . . ."

Douglas expressed his own thoughts about the protection of "symbolic" speech in another case when he addressed the issue of the government's right to make the burning of draft cards by young men protesting the Vietnam War unlawful. He wrote: "Action is often a method of expression and within the protection of the First Amendment. Suppose one tears up his own copy of the Constitution in eloquent protest to a decision of this Court. May he be indicted? Suppose one rips his own Bible to shreds to celebrate his departure from one 'faith' and his embrace of atheism. May he be indicted?" Douglas did not think so unless the expression was accompanied by action that interfered with a legitimate community purpose (for example, if the protest created traffic problems). He applied the same standard to draft card burning and declared that it, too, was protected by the First Amendment.

Hugo Black's reading of the Constitution made no attempt to accommodate new movements of the modern age. Though he never retreated from his commitment to the freedom of expression, Black found some of the protests of the sixties over segregation or Vietnam beyond the pale of his constitutional protection. Douglas had no such problem; indeed, the new events presented a challenge to him to see that the Court's interpretation of the First Amendment met the contemporary needs of the nation. *His* First Amendment provided a steady constitutional escort for civil rights demonstrators, even those singing in front of a small Florida county jail, and for Vietnam War protesters, whether students wearing armbands or young men burning their draft cards.

For Black, every guarantee of individual rights was contained in the Constitution. If he couldn't find the protection expressly stated in the Constitution, Black dismissed it. He refused, for example, to accept the theory that electronic eavesdropping by the government was a violation of the "unreasonable search and seizure" clause of the Fourth Amendment. Douglas did not find the language of the Constitution so confining. Writing of the various devices the government might use to overhear conversations, Douglas claimed that the "nature of the instrument that science or engineering develops is not important. The controlling, the decisive factor is the invasion of privacy against the command of the Fourth and Fifth Amendments."

Douglas's willingness to look beyond the explicit language of the Constitution to protect what he considered to be the essential rights of Americans was dramatically demonstrated when he wrote about the right to privacy. His belief in the right to be let alone, nowhere expressly guaranteed in the Constitution, became, in fact, the overriding theme of Douglas's libertarian philosophy and represented his most significant contribution to constitutional law.

The outline of Douglas's constitutional views on privacy was first presented in a lone dissent in 1952. The Court majority had held in the case that a transit company in the District of Columbia could broadcast radio programs, including music, news and commercial announcements, on its buses and streetcars. Douglas wrote that the captive listeners in the vehicles had been deprived of their constitutional right to privacy.

> This is a case of first impression. There are no precedents to construe, no principles previously expounded to apply. We write on a clean slate. The case comes down to the meaning of "liberty" as used in the Fifth Amendment. Liberty in the constitutional sense must mean more than freedom from unlawful governmental restraint; it must include privacy as well, if it is to be a repository of freedom. The right to be let alone is indeed the beginning of all freedom. Part of our claim to privacy is in the prohibition of the Fourth Amendment against unreasonable searches and seizures. It gives the guarantee that a man's home is his castle beyond invasion either by inquisitive or by officious people. A man loses that privacy of course when he goes upon the streets or enters public places. But even in his activities outside the home he has immunities from controls bearing on privacy. He may not be compelled against his will to attend a reli-

gious service; he may not be forced to make an affirmation or observe a ritual that violates his scruples; he may not be made to accept one religious, political, or philosophical creed as against another. Freedom of religion and freedom of speech guaranteed by the First Amendment give more than the privilege to worship, to write, to speak as one chooses; they give freedom not to do nor to act as the government chooses. The First Amendment in its respect for the conscience of the individual honors the sanctity of thought and belief. To think as one chooses, to believe what one wishes are important aspects of the constitutional right to be let alone.

In *The Right of the People,* Douglas expanded his privacy theory. Relying on moral and religious teachings as well as the Constitution, Douglas wrote of "natural rights" that "protect man, his individuality, and his conscience against direct and indirect interference by government." Some of those rights were found in the express language of the First, Fourth and Fifth Amendments, but others, Douglas claimed, were contained in the "penumbra" of the amendments, "implied from the very nature of man as a child of God."

By 1961, Douglas was prepared to defend his unique theory of privacy, first fully articulated in *The Right of the People,* in a judicial opinion. The occasion arose after a Court plurality had refused to decide the issue of the constitutionality of Connecticut's statute prohibiting the use of contraceptives and giving medical advice on their use. The case was brought by two married couples and a physician. The couples claimed that they had sought contraceptive advice from the physician, who had not given it for fear of prosecution. The Court plurality concluded that there was a "tacit agreement" among state law enforcement officials that the statute would not be enforced. Based on that conclusion, the Court had decided that it would not "be umpire to debates concerning harmless empty shadows."

Douglas declared in dissent that the Court should have taken the case and struck down the statute. "If [the state] can make this law, it can enforce it. And proof of its violation necessarily involves an inquiry into the relations between man and wife. That is an invasion of the privacy that is implicit in a free society. . . . This notion of privacy is not drawn from the blue. It emanates from the totality of the constitutional scheme under which we live."

In 1965, the same Connecticut law was challenged again, this time by a licensed physician and the executive director of the Planned Parenthood League of Connecticut, who had been arrested for violating the statute. At oral argument Justice Douglas did not ask a single question. He saved his energy for his judicial opinion for the Court, which would stand as one of the most important constitutional decisions of the twentieth century.

The constitutional right to privacy, Douglas declared in *Griswold* v. *Connecticut,* was supported by the First, Fourth, Fifth and Ninth Amendments.

> [S]pecific guarantees in the Bill of Rights have penumbras, formed by emanations from those guarantees that help give them life and substance. Various guarantees create zones of privacy. The right of association contained in the penumbra of the First Amendment is one. . . . The Third Amendment in its prohibition against quartering of soldiers "in any house" in time of peace without the consent of the owner is another. . . . The Fourth Amendment explicitly affirms the "right of the people to be secure in their persons, houses, papers and effects against unreasonable searches and seizures." The Fifth Amendment in its Self-Incrimination Clause enables the citizen to create a zone of privacy which government may not force him to surrender to his detriment. The Ninth Amendment provides: "The enumeration in the Constitution of certain rights, shall not be construed to deny or disparage others retained by the people."

Douglas was not satisfied merely to rely on the "penumbras" and "emanations" from the Bill of Rights. "We deal with a right of privacy older than the Bill of Rights," he concluded, "older than our political parties, older than our school system. Marriage is a coming together for better or for worse, hopefully enduring and intimate to the degree of being sacred. . . ."

The Douglas opinion outraged many legal scholars, who found his pinning of privacy labels to various constitutional amendments, without thoroughly documenting his conclusions, reckless to the point of being irresponsible. And his reference to a right "older than the Bill of Rights," seemed to be a throwback to a "natural law" period of constitutional decision-making which had been thoroughly discredited. Douglas's "accordion-like" opinion, wrote Professor Paul Kauper in the *University of Michigan Law Review*, suggested that Douglas and others on the Court could convert their subjective values into constitutional law.

A similar criticism was expressed by Douglas's dissenting colleagues, most notably Justice Hugo Black. "I like my privacy as well as the next one," Black wrote, "but I am nevertheless compelled to admit that government has a right to invade it unless prohibited by some specific constitutional provision."

The philosophical collision could not have been more pronounced. Black's philosophy was based on a literal reading of the Constitution. He searched in vain for a right to privacy. Douglas, possessing a more expansive libertarian creed, did not hesitate to look beyond the explicit language of the Constitution to protect what he considered to be the contemporary needs of the nation. To be sure, Douglas collected few accolades in the nation's leading law reviews for his *Griswold* opinion. The criticism was, in part, justified. Douglas did not provide a thorough analysis to support this new constitutional right to privacy. Indeed, his analysis in *Griswold* was not even as persuasive as his earlier writings on the subject had been. But the decision endures because Douglas's conclusion was correct. In declaring a right to privacy, Douglas had identified the most critical constitutional battleground for human dignity in the modern age.

CHAPTER TWENTY-SIX

Rich Man, Poor Man

O<small>NE WEEKDAY MORNING</small> in the early sixties, an associate justice of the U.S. Supreme Court stepped into the justices' private elevator, nodded to his colleague William O. Douglas, and then stood with noticeable discomfort as the elevator operator took the two justices to the floor of their chambers. After the elevator doors had shut, Douglas's younger colleague said to him, "I'm embarrassed. I've been on this Court for several years and I still don't know the name of that relief elevator operator."

"Don't worry about it," Douglas replied. "I've been here for more than twenty years and I don't know the name of anybody."

Douglas, of course, had exaggerated, but his comment was revealing. Known to the world through his books, speeches and opinions as a generous humanitarian, Douglas did not transfer that public good will to those whom he worked with on a daily basis. Many colleagues and staff thought of him as a lover of the masses who had very little use for individuals. To them, his compassion seemed to be intellectualized and most eloquently expressed in his publications.

Douglas's clerks were usually warned by his permanent staff

that they would be fired once or twice during the term. The firing, it was explained, was the Justice's way of showing displeasure. It would result in a particularly chilly office atmosphere for two or three days as well as extra work for members of the staff who had not been fired. But Douglas's mood would pass and, his clerks were told, they should report to work regularly as if the dismissal had never taken place.

Some clerks were put off by Douglas's addressing the messengers, who were black, by their last names. But when they realized that the clerks, who were white, were also addressed by their last names, no racist motive could be inferred. "At work he treated his messengers as messengers and he treated his clerks as messengers," said Steve Duke, Douglas's clerk for the 1959 term.

Duke learned not to take Douglas's impersonal manner personally. "You got the impression that Justice Douglas thought that clerking for him was the luckiest thing that could ever happen," said Duke, echoing the impression of earlier Douglas clerks. "So why should he be concerned about your personal feelings or your family?"

Douglas hired only one clerk a year in the fifties and early sixties, while the other justices took two. Still, he did not give them as much responsibility as the pair in some other justices' chambers. Work, yes, but not responsibility. Douglas expected his clerks to work the same twelve-hour-a-day, six-day-a-week schedule that he did, but those long hours were spent, primarily, checking citations or reading certiorari petitions. Clerks were usually asked their views on substantive constitutional questions *after* Douglas had written his draft opinion. And his basic reaction to criticism of an opinion was: "Well, that's a law school technicality."

"I felt intimidated by him," recalled Duke, "and so terribly inferior. He didn't do an awful lot to correct that impression." But despite the trial-by-fire atmosphere in the Douglas chambers, Duke left the experience with positive feelings toward Douglas and great admiration for his judicial work: "He (Douglas) didn't have time for bullshit. He did not think that discursive discussions with his clerks about pending cases were *helpful* to him or *necessary* for the nourishment of his clerks. They were, after all, very lucky to have the job. They had been duly forewarned of its terms and conditions. His work was far more important than their feelings. It is difficult to quarrel with such value judgments. Indeed, I think, impossible. If I were a justice, I think I would run my chambers substantially the way he did, if I had the gumption and the strength to do it. . . ."

Douglas was not significantly more accommodating in his relations with his colleagues on the Court than with his clerks. Many of the Court's members worked as though they were part of a judicial team of intellectual equals, each pulling his load toward the common good of the Court and the country. Not Douglas. First of all, he made it very clear that he did not consider all his colleagues his intellectual equals. That message was transmitted in small ways. Douglas insisted that he needed only one law clerk while his colleagues took two (and still complained of the heavy Court work load). At oral argument, while the other justices were listening intently to the attorneys, Douglas read a book or scribbled notes in his indecipherable scrawl for his next book or opinion. But then, suddenly, Douglas raised his head and directed a question to counsel. "You would think he wasn't paying attention but then he would ask that one question that would go to the jugular," said one colleague. "He never missed."

Douglas's colleagues were also aware that Douglas sometimes walked briskly from the bench to his chambers and dictated how he thought a case, just argued, would come out. That dictation took place before the justices met in conference to discuss it. Only a few minutes after the majority opinion was later circulated, Douglas circulated his dissent, written before he had even seen the majority's opinion. "It was extraordinary," said a colleague, "how he could anticipate both the conclusions and the reasoning of the majority."

At judicial conference, Douglas always seemed restless while his colleagues spoke. The only words that seemed to stir him in the 1950s and early 1960s were Felix Frankfurter's. "Felix had the habit in any case in which he had an interest to speak for exactly fifty minutes, the precise length of a Harvard Law School lecture," a colleague recalled. "Douglas would follow Frankfurter. 'When I came to conference,' Douglas would say, 'I thought the judgment should be affirmed [Frankfurter's position] but Felix has just talked me out of it.' It was his way of getting

Frankfurter's goat. More often, Douglas would say, 'I take the other view.' There was no advocacy at all."

Other colleagues remember Douglas presenting his judicial position at conference with great effectiveness. "The judicial conference has always been important to me," said one colleague. "I'm a team player. Bill Douglas wasn't. He didn't play the game. But with startling few words at conference and with startling lucidity, he would speak for one or two minutes and then he would shut up." Abe Fortas, who sat with Douglas on the Court from 1965 to 1969, corroborated this view. "Douglas would say very little at conference," Fortas said, "but what he said always went to the critical issue in the case." Justice Tom Clark described Douglas's contribution in conference slightly differently, but with similar admiration. "At conferences," Clark wrote, "Bill believed that rather than seeking harmony, one should seek disharmony. . . . Bill Douglas, the dissenter, was a catalyst at conference; indeed, his role was a crucial one."

The maverick streak in Douglas, reflected in his conduct at oral argument and in conference, persisted through the opinion-writing process. While others were busily drafting their opinions and submitting them to colleagues for comments (and, they hoped, approval), Douglas wrote exclusively for himself. "I always thought he enjoyed being a loner on the Court." said one colleague. "He was almost uncomfortable if anyone agreed with him. . . . He sometimes made it impossible for you to join him. He'd put two or three sentences in a dissent that were so outrageous, you just couldn't join him."

Both admirers and detractors among Douglas's colleagues agreed on one thing: if Douglas had made more of an effort to influence his colleagues through the decision-making process, he would have made their work product, and his, better. His opinions, even those with conspicuous flashes of insight, often appeared superficial or just plain sloppy. Nobody doubted that Douglas could have done a more thorough, scholarly job if he had chosen to. But he did not choose to and that indifference to detail was more infuriating than a showing of incompetence would have been.

Douglas's warning in *An Almanac of Liberty* to lawyers and scholars that he wasn't writing for them was equally apt for many of his later judicial opinions. After his first decade on the Court, Douglas appeared to have been interested more in communicating his broad philosophy to the readers of his judicial opinions than in satisfying a scholar's appetite for carefully documented legal arguments. He was not a lawyer's judge or a judge's judge or a scholar's judge. He was a people's judge, promoting his strong egalitarian philosophy regardless of whether or not his views were well supported by precedent.

Douglas had brooded for a lifetime about it. While he delivered newspapers in the early-morning hours and toted washing for his mother and mowed neighbors' lawns, other schoolboys seemed to enjoy a carefree existence. And their good fortune had nothing to do with merit or motivation, simply with money. Douglas felt poor and was certain that the others must have felt smugly rich. He expressed his bitterness occasionally, sitting at a campfire with a wealthy friend, Elon Gilbert, or during an intimate talk with his second wife, Mercedes, or in writing about the churchgoing hypocrites in Yakima's "establishment" who controlled the police and sanctioned their abuses of the underprivileged.

When Douglas had had his first taste of real power, as director of the SEC's study of protective and reorganization committees for bankruptcies and receiverships and, later, as a member and then chairman of the SEC, he had relished the opportunities to get even with the "establishment." The satisfactions were personal as well as professional in confrontations with the likes of John Foster Dulles, Wall Street lawyer Robert Swaine and the president of the New York Stock Exchange, Charles Gay.

On the Court, Douglas's sensitivity to the underdog was almost immediately apparent in his work. It was visible in his opinions castigating economic monopolies and in those giving the fullest civil liberties protections to vagrants, political dissidents and the lowliest criminal suspects. And it was evident in Douglas's broad interpretation of the Fourteenth Amendment's equal protection clause, which guaranteed first-class citizenship to racial minorities.

In the 1940s and early 1950s, Douglas had repeatedly supported Court decisions knocking down racially discriminatory barriers, from all-white political primaries in Texas, to restrictive covenants that kept blacks out of residential areas in Missouri, to a law that denied a black graduate student the same educational facilities available to whites in Oklahoma. In his book *We the Judges,* Douglas explained the importance of the equal protection clause: "Equal protection is the most important single principle that any nation can take as its ideal. Those who practice it give to each minority a sense of belonging. . . . Where there is a sense of belonging, there are ties of loyalty and devotion that no strains of politics can ever sever or destroy."

The challenge from South Carolina had come first. The issue was whether the state's enforced segregation of its public schools deprived blacks of the equal protection of the law guaranteed by the Fourteenth Amendment. At the Court's judicial conference in which the justices discussed the South Carolina case, Douglas and Black had made it clear to their colleagues that they were prepared to decide the issue. But the other members of the Court wanted a more complete lower-court record before considering the merits of the case.

Eventually the South Carolina case returned to the Court with the more complete record that the majority had wanted. The case was considered with other challenges to public school segregation from Kansas, Virginia and Delaware and was placed on the Court docket as *Brown* v. *Board of Education of Topeka* (the Kansas case).*

At the first oral argument, in 1952, Douglas made no attempt to hide his sympathies. The Douglas penchant for reaching the desirable result, and his frustration at listening to Frankfurter probe every subtlety presented by the constitutional challenge,† were evident when Frankfurter began to press one of the NAACP Legal Defense Fund attorneys, Robert L. Carter. At issue was the

---

*A companion case from the District of Columbia, *Bolling* v. *Sharpe,* was also considered.
†Frankfurter's persistent questioning of attorneys had always irritated Douglas, inspiring a story, perhaps apocryphal, that had made the rounds of Douglas admirers. One attorney who was to appear before the Court, so the story had been told, hired a lip-reader to learn what the individual justices' views were during oral argument, so he could pitch his best points to them accordingly. Throughout the argument, Douglas whispered to a colleague. Finally the attorney could not hold his curiosity any longer. "What's Douglas saying?" he asked. "He's saying," replied the lip-reader, "he wished that sorry little son of a bitch Frankfurter would shut up."

application of the doctrine announced in the 1896 case of *Plessy* v. *Ferguson,* which declared constitutional a law providing separate facilities for blacks in railroad cars. Fearing that the Court would reach for the *Plessy* precedent to justify separate school facilities, Carter had tried to put distance between his primary-school case and the nineteenth-century railroad case on the basis of the facts. Frankfurter had moved in.

"Are you saying that we can say that 'separate but equal' is not a doctrine that is relevant at the primary-school level?" asked Frankfurter. "Is that what you are saying?"

Carter struggled to respond. Fortunately for the attorney, Justice Douglas came to his aid.

"I think you are saying," interjected Douglas, "that segregation may be all right in street cars and railroad cars and restaurants, but that is all we have decided."

Carter grabbed the life preserver that Douglas had thrown out. "That is the only place that you have decided that it [segregation] is all right," he replied.

"And that education is different," said Douglas, leading Carter.

"Yes, sir," replied Carter.

"That is your argument, is it not?" asked Douglas. "Isn't that your argument in this case?"

"Yes," said Carter.

At the first judicial conference in *Brown* in December 1952, Douglas and Black rejected a cautious approach to the segregation issue. Black said that his reading of the Fourteenth Amendment commanded the Court to outlaw segregation. For Douglas, the issue was simply presented and decided. "A state can't classify by color for education," he told his colleagues. Douglas said, further, that a decision by the Court outlawing school segregation might raise social and political problems, but nonetheless, the Court should not delay its judgment.

Justice Frankfurter did not reveal his view on the ultimate issue, but proposed further argument on the history and scope of the Fourteenth Amendment. Frankfurter's purpose, he later suggested, was not just enlightenment on the dimensions of the Fourteenth Amendment. He was aware that at least two members of the Court, Chief Justice Vinson and Associate Justice Stanley Reed, were prepared to uphold the constitutionality of the separate but equal doctrine of *Plessy.* Frankfurter was unabashedly playing for time, attempting to coax a unanimous opinion out of his colleagues. And he was, as usual, irritated by Black and Douglas, particularly Douglas, whose behavior he considered "impetuous and unstatesmanlike."

Everything seemed to break Felix Frankfurter's way after that first judicial conference in 1952. He and his clerk, Alexander Bickel, drafted the questions about the history and effect of the Fourteenth Amendment that were given to the opposing attorneys for reargument. Before that argument, Chief Justice Vinson died and news of his death, reportedly, inspired Frankfurter to say, "This is the first indication I have ever had that there is a God." With the appointment of Chief Justice Earl Warren to replace Vinson, Frankfurter hoped, not only for a "no" vote on segregation, but for a new Chief Justice who could exercise the qualities of leadership to weld a unanimous vote on the issue. Warren did not disappoint him. Writing for a unanimous Court, the Chief Justice declared in the historic *Brown* decision that "separate educational facilities are inherently unequal."

It was a proud Frankfurter who wrote his friend Judge Learned Hand, retelling the story of the struggle to get a unanimous Court in *Brown.* But he could not resist getting in a dig at Douglas and Black, who had resisted his strategic maneuvering from the outset. "I will tell you that if the 'great libertarians' had had their way, we would have been in the soup."

For Frankfurter, the principled decision in *Brown* had been important, but so had the process itself. He had wanted the most complete lower-court record, meticulous research by the opposing attorneys, probing questions by the Court and careful deliberations by the justices in conference. And, for this momentous decision, Frankfurter had fought for a unanimous Court. With all those requirements met, Frankfurter could offer an implementation formula—that the public schools be desegregated with "all deliberate speed"—that would appear restrained. That formula was the best hope, Frankfurter believed, for the South's compliance.

Douglas had had little use for the intricate process that Frankfurter thought vital in *Brown* or other cases. He was, indeed, result oriented, as Frankfurter and other detractors often charged. He was also "impetuous" and "unstatesmanlike," in Frankfurter's terms; he did not worry about unanimity or the political impact of the Court's opinion. He was not a team player. But in Douglas's own terms, he was neither "impetuous" nor "unstatesmanlike." For he voted according to his conscience and his broad interpretation of the Fourteenth Amendment's equal protection clause.

Despite Douglas's frequent idiosyncratic ways, his views on civil rights and liberties almost perfectly matched those of three of his colleagues on the Court in the late fifties. Since their first days on the Court together, Hugo Black and Douglas had agreed on a generous interpretation of the civil rights and liberties protected by the Constitution. Chief Justice Earl Warren, at first a cautious member of Felix Frankfurter's restrained majority, at least in civil liberties cases, soon joined Black and Douglas. The final member of the "activist" minority bloc on the Court in the late fifties was William J. Brennan, who was appointed by President Eisenhower in 1956. Although a product of the Harvard Law School, Brennan resisted the intellectual attraction of Frankfurter's philosophy of judicial restraint. Brennan, like Black, Douglas and Warren, took a broad, aggressive view of civil liberties and rights.

But no matter how vehemently they held their opinions, the libertarian bloc usually fell one short of a majority. On the other side was Felix Frankfurter, regularly joined by Justices John Harlan, Potter Stewart, Tom Clark and Charles Whittaker. That side, in general, took a more cautious view in protecting civil rights and liberties than their more "activist" colleagues.

In 1962, however, Charles Whittaker announced that he would leave the Court, which raised the possibility that his replacement might turn the Court majority in a different direction. From his very first days on the Court in 1957, Whittaker had struggled, unsuccessfully, to keep intellectual pace with his colleagues. But he had a vote, just like the other eight members of the Court, and that vote had been recorded most frequently with Frankfurter's restrained majority. With the philosophical direction of the Court at stake, both Chief Justice Warren and Justice Douglas participated in the behind-the-scenes struggle to influence President

John F. Kennedy's selection to replace Whittaker.

The President's brother, Attorney General Robert F. Kennedy, had first recommended U.S. Circuit Court Judge William H. Hastie, a black and a Harvard graduate, to replace Whittaker. "I went up and saw [Chief Justice] Warren about Hastie," Robert Kennedy later recalled. "He was violently opposed to having Hastie on the Court. . . . He said, 'He's not a liberal and he'd be opposed to all measures that we're interested in, and he would be just completely unsatisfactory.'" Kennedy also spoke to Douglas, who told the Attorney General that Hastie would be "just one more vote for Frankfurter." The Hastie candidacy faltered.

Professor Paul Freund of Harvard, a close friend of Felix Frankfurter's and an eloquent advocate of his judicial philosophy, was also high on the list of top prospects submitted to the Kennedy administration. Douglas had anticipated the Freund candidacy as early as the summer of 1960. "The scuttlebutt is that the Harvard Law School was and is all out for Kennedy," Douglas wrote Hugo Black. "They apparently think they have a deal that Paul Freund will be named to the first Court vacancy!" After the Whittaker retirement had been announced, both Douglas and Chief Justice Warren were cool to the Freund appointment for the same reasons they opposed Hastie: Freund, they believed, would join the Frankfurter wing on the Court.

Ultimately, President Kennedy and his brother Bobby decided on Deputy Attorney General Byron R. White to fill the Whittaker vacancy. The President had served with White in the Pacific in World War II and had found his presidential campaign work in 1960 to be highly satisfactory. A Phi Beta Kappa graduate of the University of Colorado, an All-American football player, a Rhodes scholar and an honors graduate of the Yale Law School, White had impeccable paper credentials. Besides, he had proved himself to be a loyal and effective administration official in his steadfast insistence on protection of civil rights freedom riders through a hostile South. Explaining the choice of White, Attorney General Robert Kennedy said, "You [the Kennedy administration] wanted someone who, in the long run, you could believe would be doing what you thought was best. You wanted someone who agreed generally with your views of the country."

Shortly after White's appointment, Justice Frankfurter, who

had brilliantly argued the cause of judicial restraint on the Court for twenty-three years, fell seriously ill and was forced to retire. Before he left the Court, however, Frankfurter wrote one of his most impassioned defenses of his philosophy, in a case challenging the constitutionality of the malapportioned Tennessee legislature. Underrepresented urban dwellers in Tennessee, it was argued in *Baker* v. *Carr,* had been denied the equal protection of the laws.

Felix Frankfurter had written the Court plurality opinion in 1946 on a similar constitutional issue after the Illinois congressional districting scheme had been challenged. In his earlier opinion, Frankfurter had warned the Court against entering the "political thicket" presented by the issue of legislative malapportionment. Sixteen years later, Frankfurter had not changed his view. In *Baker* v. *Carr* he wrote: "There is not under our Constitution a judicial remedy for every political mischief, for every undesirable exercise of legislative power. The Framers carefully and with deliberate forethought refused so to enthrone the judiciary. In this situation, as in others of like nature, appeal for relief does not belong here. Appeal must be to an informed, civically militant electorate."

But there was a critical difference between Frankfurter's 1946 opinion and the one he wrote in *Baker* v. *Carr.* The later opinion was a dissent. The Warren Court majority, including Justice Douglas, said that the judiciary, braced by the equal protection clause of the Fourteenth Amendment, was charged with the responsibility of demanding legislative reform. That decision to enter the "political thicket" symbolized the egalitarian drive of the Warren Court and that drive would accelerate after Felix Frankfurter's retirement.

Although he generally supported civil rights claims that came before the Court, Justice Byron White disappointed many libertarians with his more conservative opinions in other areas, most notably that of criminal procedure. There were no such disappointments with the votes and opinions of the man chosen to replace Felix Frankfurter. He was Arthur J. Goldberg, an attorney long identified with organized labor, who was then serving as President Kennedy's aggressive, outspoken Secretary of Labor. With his appointment, Goldberg quickly joined the solid activist bloc of Warren, Black, Douglas and Brennan in both civil rights and civil liberties cases.

No justice on the Warren Court was more willing to dispense with legal formalities in pursuit of true equality under the law than Douglas. Since the Fourteenth Amendment applied only to state, not private, action, many members of the Court struggled to reach the appropriate constitutional judgment on the racially discriminatory actions of *private* restaurant owners in the South and in border states. In one case involving the arrest and convictions for disturbing the peace of sit-in demonstrators at a private, segregated restaurant in East Baton Rouge, Louisiana, the Court majority avoided the problem of finding state action in violation of the equal protection clause. Instead the majority overturned the convictions on due process grounds because they could find no evidence that the demonstrators had, literally, disturbed the peace, as required under the state statute.

Douglas found the majority's reasoning tortured. He wrote:

> If these cases had arisen in the Pacific Northwest—the area I know best—I could agree with the opinion of the Court. For while many communities north and south, east and west, at times have racial problems, those areas which have never known segregation would not be inflamed or aroused by the presence of a member of a minority race in a restaurant. But in Louisiana racial problems have agitated the people since the days of slavery. . . . This does not mean that the police were justified in making these arrests. For the police are supposed to be on the side of the Constitution, not on the side of discrimination. Yet if all constitutional questions are to be put aside and the problem treated merely in terms of disturbing the peace, I would have difficulty in reversing these judgments. I think, however, the constitutional questions must be reached and that they make reversal necessary. . . . It is my view that a State may not constitutionally enforce a policy of segregation in restaurant facilities. Some of the argument assumed that restaurants are "private" property in the sense that one's home is "private" property. They are, of course, "private" property for many purposes of the Constitution. Yet so are street railways, power plants, warehouses, and other types of enterprises which have long been held to be affected with a public interest. Where constitutional rights are involved, the proprie-

tary interests of individuals must give way. . . . One can close the doors of his home to anyone he desires. But one who operates an enterprise under a license from the government [here, the city of Baton Rouge had issued a permit to the restaurant owner] enjoys a privilege that derives from the people. . . . the necessity of a license shows that the public has rights in respect to those premises. The business is not a matter of mere private concern. Those who license enterprises for public use should not have under our Constitution the power to license it for the use of only one race. For there is the overriding constitutional requirement that all state power be exercised so as not to deny equal protection to any group. . . .

Douglas chided his colleagues again in a case involving black students who had been denied service at Hooper's Restaurant in Baltimore and were arrested and convicted of criminal trespass for refusing to leave the premises. The Maryland courts had upheld the convictions, but by the time the case reached the U.S. Supreme Court, the Maryland legislature had passed a public accommodations statute that undercut the basis for the sit-in protesters' convictions. Since the protesters' conduct no longer constituted a crime, the Warren Court majority decided to send the case back to the Maryland courts for reconsideration in light of the change in Maryland law.

Douglas did not join the majority. Instead he argued that the Court should have reversed the convictions and been done with the whole sorry mess. Congress had been considering a public accommodations section to the 1964 Civil Rights Act at the very moment the Court refused to face the issue squarely. It was, Douglas suggested, an issue that the whole nation was facing and the Court's ducking behind a legal technicality did neither the Court nor the nation high service. Reaching the issue that his colleagues refused, Douglas concluded: "Segregation of Negroes in the restaurants and lunch counters of parts of America is a relic of slavery. . . . When the state police, the state prosecutor, and the state courts unite to convict Negroes for renouncing that relic of slavery, the State violates the Fourteenth Amendment."

In those two sit-in cases, Douglas and Hugo Black did not agree, a phenomenon of recurrent frequency in the 1960s. As he accelerated his effort to translate his view of what was best for the

country into constitutional law, Douglas put more distance between himself and Black. He had shown his willingness to rely on
the "penumbras" of the Constitution in *Griswold*, an approach
totally rejected by Black. In attacking invidious discrimination,
Douglas showed himself to be no less a constitutional pioneer,
and made Hugo Black no less anxious about his pronounce-
ments.

Douglas had always been revolted by discrimination against
disadvantaged groups, and when that discrimination was linked
to an important societal interest, such as voting, he built a new
constitutional foundation to support his beliefs. He had opposed
a state poll tax because, he had decided in 1951, it made democracy's most basic right, voting, dependent on the amount of
money in one's pocket. No member of that 1951 Court joined
him.

In 1966, the makeup of the Court had changed radically and
now he found support for his view, which went far beyond the text
of the Constitution. Nowhere in that document did the framers
make it explicitly clear that the right to vote in state elections was
so fundamental that even a pauper could not be kept from the
polling booth. And yet Douglas, speaking for a Court majority,
made that the constitutional law. In rejecting Virginia's $1.50 poll
tax, Douglas put his case succinctly: "Wealth, like race, creed or
color, is not germane to one's ability to participate intelligently
in the electoral process. Lines drawn on the basis of wealth or
property, like those of race, are traditionally disfavored."

The Douglas opinion seemed so effortless that many who read
it might not have been aware that Douglas had made two dramatic breaks with the constitutional history of the equal protection clause. First, he had declared that voting in state elections
was a fundamental right which triggered the closest scrutiny by
the Court in considering the constitutionality of government restraints on that right. Second, he had suggested that a state's
classification on the basis of wealth, like race, would also provoke
the Court's closest study.

In sum, when voting was the interest and wealth the basis for
the classification, Douglas declared that the Court would demand
a compelling argument by the state for the legitimacy of its regulation. It was a standard that was improbable to meet in theory

and virtually impossible to realize in fact. And that was precisely as Douglas intended.

Hugo Black wrote an angry dissent. His reading of the equal protection clause of the Fourteenth Amendment required only that a state's regulation be reasonable. That requirement was easily satisfied by an argument that the poll tax (1) raised revenue and (2) assumed that those who had to pay for the voting privilege would exercise the franchise more responsibly than those who had been given it free. To insist on a "compelling" state interest to justify the poll tax, Black wrote, was inventing constitutional doctrine. He had objected to it when Douglas wrote about "penumbras" that established the right to privacy in *Griswold* and he now registered the same complaint about Douglas's interpretation of the equal protection clause. Reviewing his objections in *Griswold* to what he considered the Court's manipulation of the Constitution to meet present-day problems, Black stood by his position that it was inexcusable for Douglas and the Court majority "to write into the Constitution its notions of what it thinks is good governmental policy."

But to Douglas, good governmental policy and sound constitutional law were often synonymous, and that was particularly true when policy and law reinforced his strong egalitarian views. Naturally, Douglas wanted to spread the seeds of his philosophy. He took special satisfaction in a majority that built on his earlier-articulated view that the right to interstate travel was fundamental and made it an accepted constitutional doctrine. And he used the "fundamental right" analysis to insist that states provide counsel to indigent defendants for the first appeal of their conviction: "There is lacking that equality demanded of the Fourteenth Amendment where the rich man, who appeals as a right, enjoys the benefit of counsel's examination into the record, research of the law, and marshalling of arguments on his behalf, while the indigent, already burdened by a preliminary determination that his case is without merit, is forced to shift for himself."

None of the Douglas opinions expanding the reach of the equal protection clause were models of legal scholarship. Douglas did not offer exhaustive support from judicial precedent for his decisions, nor did he foresee every future implication. But that did not detract from the importance of the Douglas opinions. Professor Kenneth Karst of the UCLA Law School, discussing Douglas's contribution to constitutional law, has written: "Of course, for constitutional growth to be enduring, principled explanations must be made along the way. Someone must build the doctrinal bridges. But, especially today, someone is also needed who will lead an assault party over the chasm before there is a bridge and make the bridge possible." Douglas led the assault.

THREE WIVES

THE PARADOXES proliferated. Douglas loved mankind but, as many of his colleagues, clerks and secretaries realized, did not often have much use for its individual members. He was named Father of the Year in 1950, but his children, by that time, deeply resented his inattention to them and their mother. He wrote eloquently about the sanctity of marriage in his pioneering privacy opinion in 1965, the year in which his third marriage was breaking up and he had already cast an attentive eye on Catherine Heffernan, who would become the fourth Mrs. Douglas.

The man who could cut to the core of a complex legal problem on the Court or an oppressive land-tenancy system abroad could not put his personal life in order. Douglas tried to meet his emotional needs with the same bold thrusts that had worked so successfully in his public life. He moved with the familiar energy and determination, but the emotional insecurity persisted.

To the outside world and most of his friends, Douglas remained the tough-minded libertarian with the indomitable spirit. But his few intimates knew his emotional fragility. He craved adulation and respect, and when it was not given, he suffered.

Though he appeared charming and confident with women in public, he was profoundly insecure with female company. He could not accept criticism from women, no matter how lightly offered, without feeling humiliated. He once told Mercedes, his second wife, of another woman he had been seeing (before their courtship), who had criticized his dancing; since then, Douglas could not step on a ballroom floor without being self-conscious. And when the criticism was pointed, as when Agnes Meyer, the wife of the publisher of the *Washington Post,* had the temerity to call Douglas a "boor" to his face, the Justice, Mercedes recalled, was deeply offended.

Even little Felix Frankfurter could upset Douglas, though Douglas never gave his judicial antagonist the satisfaction of knowing it. After Douglas had married Mercedes, members of the Court gave the couple a wedding present. Frankfurter alone refused to join in the gesture. "It didn't bother me at all," Mercedes recalled, "but it bothered Bill."

Douglas's second marriage had started off happily enough in 1954, with the Justice taking great pride in Mercedes's wit, spirit and good looks. Mercedes continued to be Douglas's confidante, as she had been during their courtship, one who would listen for hours as he vented his feelings. On conference day, Douglas, who had communicated little thought and no feeling to his colleagues, would unwind at home. "I was there to catch his outpouring," she recalled. "He knew he could tell me anything about the Court and I wouldn't pass it to anyone and I never did." Douglas also talked about himself, frequently recounting the hard times of growing up in Yakima, his great love and admiration for his mother and his hatred of the "establishment."

But the discussion was not always so personal. Douglas would routinely take his new wife on an awesome intellectual tour of the political, economic and social problems of the world. "Living with a man like that was like living with a couple of Ph.D.'s," Mercedes recalled.

The couple's public image was upbeat. Mercedes was the spirited Southern belle who could make gracious conversation at Georgetown cocktail parties or change a flat tire in the boiling Middle Eastern sun. And Douglas was, well, Douglas, speaking with authority and charm and insight about the world's wonders and dilemmas. Together, they took the term "worldly" literally, traveling from continent to continent, summer after adventure-some summer.

But everything was done on his terms. He picked the countries to be visited, the books to be written (she would research them), the parties to attend, the friends to dine with. "I couldn't be a personality in my own right and live with him," said Mercedes. "He kept saying, 'We're going to do this, we're going to do that.' I should have gotten mad but I didn't."

Whenever he felt that his control of Mercedes was slipping, Douglas lost his temper. The arguments usually arose over his suspicions of her infidelity. She could not talk to male friends without making her husband uncomfortable. When they went to dinner parties, Douglas was forever on the lookout for any ro-mantic liaisons with other men. "He was fanatically jealous," she remembered. "If I even talked to another man too long, he would say, 'Why did you rub that man's leg? You were rubbing that man's leg all night.' We'd have these terrible arguments over imaginary things. I knew he was totally insecure, but he had total loyalty from me. He was never convinced."

Mercedes found Douglas increasingly difficult to deal with, even when the issue was no more controversial than his good health. After Douglas suffered a severe bursitis attack in the Northwest during the summer of 1956, his wife wrote Hugo Black for help. "What worries me the most is the depressions he gets in having to stay quiet," she wrote. "I thought a word from you might be cheering."

Five months later, Mercedes again confided in Black: "Bill still aches and groans and I am worried. The doctors all say that medically he is better, but the pain persists. How can we get him to accept the fact that he must slow up his routine of work and living? On the latter I have that pretty well under control but it is impossible for me to change his drive to work. Until Bill accepts himself the necessity and need to lessen his burdens, he is going to fight this thing. The tragedy, Hugo, is that he does not know he is doing this. To suggest it to him sends him into a defense and even more work. When you come back I'd like to see you and talk to you—and he must not know I wrote like this."

In time, both Mercedes and her husband were sending messages to Black, each without the other's knowledge. When the Douglases left Washington before the end of one Court term in the fifties for a trip abroad, Douglas wrote Black an apology for their early departure, blaming it entirely on Mercedes. "Mercedes thought we should stick to our plans and go," wrote Douglas. "She recognized that there would be some criticism but she did not think it very serious. I left word with the Chief to send for me in case of a deadlock or close decision. I can get back in two days. . . ."

Unknown to Douglas, his wife read his note to Black and fired off one of her own: "I happened to oversee a note Bill wrote you —and I noted he said—'Mercedes thought we should go ahead with our plans'—That disturbs me because I specifically tried to keep out of this decision he was wrangling with on Tuesday and Wednesday. He made the decision—and I suggested delaying through argument, etc. Anyway, no matter what I just wanted you to know I was not the influence that decided this. It's wrong and I know it—but Bill's headstrongness sometimes cannot be coped with—He is the only one who can. I only hope it won't cause him too much harm—and it doesn't end up 4 to 4 and he has to spend all he makes out of this 'venture' on a wild dash back to save the deadlock or his skin."

Mercedes's distrust of Douglas grew with their years together and her suspicions focused most frequently on his extramarital wanderings. Sometimes the romantic liaisons were imagined. Douglas's editor at Doubleday, Ken McCormick, remembered bar-hopping with Douglas in Washington, and his companion excusing himself at every tavern to call his wife to assure her of his best intentions. Other times, McCormick suggested, Mercedes's suspicions were perfectly justified.

"He started showing attentions to other women," Mercedes recalled, "and I wasn't a very good European wife. My mother said, 'If you'd just been a good European wife, it would have been all right.' There were various episodes but none of any consequence. I was dubious but I didn't think they were extended. He wouldn't be at a hotel where he said he was staying, so it became obvious. I should have realized this was going to happen before our marriage, since he always had the reputation of chasing women. But I thought I could make our marriage work."

And the marriage did survive the early jealousies and arguments. But in 1961, Douglas met Joan Martin, a petite twenty-year-old junior at tiny Allegheny College in Pennsylvania, and his marriage with Mercedes fell completely apart. Like the first meeting with Mercedes, Douglas's introduction to Joanie* Martin was an innocent chance encounter. She was working for a professor in the Allegheny College political science department who was to be Justice Douglas's host during a brief stay at the college. As the professor's student assistant, Joanie was given the privilege of accompanying her boss to the Youngstown airport to meet the Justice's plane.

"I have a very clear memory of the first time I saw him," Joanie recalled, "because as he came off the plane there was a gentleman in front of him, impeccably dressed in a dark suit with a briefcase, someone who looked as if he belonged in the legal world. Right behind him was this man wearing a beat-up hat and carrying a beat-up briefcase and sort of beating his coattails, with remnants of dust flying out. We extended our hands to the impeccably dressed gentleman but were tapped by the man behind him, who, with a twinkle in his eye, announced that he was Justice Douglas. It was that style that I knew from that day forward."

At dinner the first night, Joanie sat in awe as the Justice talked about his world travels to places she had only read about. He also talked about the law, spurring her interests in attending law school. "So here was a person who talked about law and foreign countries and all those things I had an interest in. I was very, very comfortable with him, because I had spent a lot of time as a child with my grandparents. So dinner was a very fascinating time for me to hear about places like Tibet and Afghanistan and Russia and Peru and all of the places he had been."

The next morning, after Douglas had finished breakfast with the president of the college, he came to Joanie's dormitory and invited her for a cup of coffee. They talked some more and then the Justice returned to Washington. In the months that followed, Douglas began sending her his books, and each time she would write a note to thank him. Her note would then be followed by

*The nickname she preferred.

another book. "This went on," Joanie said, "for about twenty books."

By the end of the school year, Joanie had read all the Justice's books and was fascinated. She decided to write her senior thesis on the Douglas philosophy; the "bottom line" for Douglas, Joanie told the faculty members reviewing her paper, "was his common sense capacity to know where the society should be headed."

In Joanie's senior year, the telephone calls and letters from Douglas increased, and at Christmas 1961, he sent her a handsome attaché bag. The Christmas present was "the first clue that there was some kind of emotional involvement," Joanie recalled. Still, she wasn't sure of his romantic intentions. "I flattered myself that it was like the relationship I had with my grandparents' friends. I enjoyed talking with them and they enjoyed listening and talking to me."

Douglas's broad knowledge of the law and the world was, naturally, mesmerizing to a young student. Joanie offered the Justice adulation, certainly, but that alone was not enough to sustain his interest. The two discovered much in common in their backgrounds. Both had been afflicted with polio as children, which enhanced their feelings as outsiders. Both had also witnessed tragedy in their families. Douglas's father had died when he was five; Joanie's father had been stricken by polio when she was a child and her mother had suffered a heart attack at the age of twenty-nine. As a result of her parents' illnesses, Joanie and her sister were sent to Detroit to live with their grandparents. Like Douglas, Joanie had worked regularly as a teen-ager. "I had to grow up fast to survive," she later recalled. "I was forced into a world of responsibility, grief and adults, long before most little girls have put their favorite little dolly to sleep for the last time."

In the spring of 1962, Douglas was scheduled to make a speech at the University of Buffalo Law School and invited Joanie, who lived in nearby Williamsboro, to hear him. She, in turn, invited the Justice to stay at her parents' house. At the airport, where Joanie and her mother met Douglas, "it was a very warm and happy reunion. It wasn't an intrigue. It wasn't a romance. It wasn't an affair. It was a very happy visit. At this point in his life, he was a very robust man. He had a sort of Spencer Tracy charm about him."

After her college graduation, Joanie decided to spend the next year in Washington, working for the Agency for International Development. Her main preoccupation that year was not U.S. foreign policy, however, but her now blossoming romance with Justice Douglas. They saw each other daily, dining out often. Washington buzzed with gossip, but it did not seem to bother Douglas. It made Joanie uncomfortable. "There was a buzz," she recalled. "I was so naïve I didn't realize how much of a buzz there was. I just wasn't happy. I wasn't too sure who I was or what I wanted for myself personally."

Talk of marriage came up increasingly in their conversation. "He'd say, 'You're going to be my wife' and I'd say, 'I don't know whether I'm going to be your wife' and he'd say, 'Oh, yes you are. I just know it in my bones.'" But despite Douglas's persuasive charm, he could not convince his young companion to be his wife.

At least, not in the spring of 1963. Instead Joanie left Washington and returned to her upper New York State home to think about her future. The Justice was soon off to Africa for one of his now familiar tours of the developing countries. But he did not forget Joanie. Several times that summer, the Justice telephoned from Africa. During one of those conversations, when Douglas once again proposed marriage, Joanie accepted.

"I think it was a call from Nigeria that did it," she recalled. "He was extremely dear to me. I decided to marry him because, I guess, I was miserable without him."

Mercedes was still Douglas's wife at the time he proposed to Joanie, but Douglas knew that their marriage was finished. The Justice had become increasingly withdrawn for two years, and in the summer of 1962, after Joanie came to Washington, Mercedes suspected another woman. Once during that summer, when Douglas was out of town, he wrote Mercedes to tell her that their marriage had deteriorated to such an extent that she should get a divorce. But Mercedes was not yet willing to give up on their marriage and she enlisted Douglas's friend Clark Clifford to sit down with them to help them effect a reconciliation. But Douglas would not accept it. In the fall, he moved out of their house, only to check in and out at will.

Within a few months of their separation, Mercedes discovered her husband's deep involvement with Joanie Martin, whom Mercedes described as a "twenty-year-old problem child." She concluded that Douglas was "mesmerized and under her spell" and that a divorce appeared inevitable. "After going through hell," she wrote Douglas's daughter, Millie, "I have finally reached the conclusion that I have to face this like one does death—I've collected myself and am working out of my grief—there's nothing else to do—as one must go on and I must find another life for myself—I can and will—but believe me—I find my love for him so strong, it is very hard."

Mercedes doubted that the Justice would marry "this child," but was full of bitterness toward Joanie and pity for her husband. "My theory is that he never ran around as a young man and hence his problem," she told Millie. "Also he needs adulation to the nth degree—she wrote her senior thesis on him—and I read it—the answer is in that. Also he has a tremendous self destructive instinct—whether that enters this I do not know."

In their last half-year as husband and wife, Douglas and Mercedes rarely saw each other. But when they did on Christmas Day 1962, Mercedes described her husband as looking "miserable." She wrote Millie: "I feel sorry for him—but I am impotent to help him. I know he's suffering great guilt feelings—but I believe his inability to face me—or his family is only part of the answer. . . . he is tragic in a way—geniuses are difficult and he is no exception—I only hope and pray his image will never be destroyed as it is important to many, many people the world over. He is a great man but an unhappy one. I hope he'll find peace—but we must all pray it will be with someone mature enough to help him."

A month after that sad letter, Mercedes wrote another to Millie, this time from St. Thomas, where she'd spent nine days in the sun. The change did wonders for her tan and helped revive her spunky, irreverent spirit.

He'll probably have several frustrating and unrewarding affairs before he reaches senility. He could hardly afford any more wives. Don't worry—I won't hand him the divorce on a silver platter—the reality of the situation as yet has not reached him— he wants to be sacrificial—and he'll really feel persecuted before

it's over. He knows I won't "bleed" him—but he asked for this
—so if he's broke after supporting your mom and me—it's his
own choice. . . . Tell Frank [Millie's husband] he forgets when a
Supreme Court Judge lays a babe, it isn't an ordinary man doing
so—it's the "robes"—and very little sex is needed! Now he can
chuckle—it's as if the gal got a chance to sleep with the Lord
himself!! . . . Well, as I said . . . if one is not philosophical—one
cannot survive—and I can do both. . . . I have no regrets over how
I've helped him and our life together. It took him two solid years
to get me even to consider marrying him—and a saga could have
been written about his pursuit. I refused to see him and go out
with him for one year before I finally went to his office for lunch
—it was like walking into a trap. . . .

Once over her hurt and anger, Mercedes did very nicely. The
divorce proceedings went smoothly and quietly on July 31, 1963,
with Mercedes telling the judge that on repeated occasions her
husband had told her he didn't love her and wanted to live apart.
"I called Bill afterward," she later wrote Millie, "to tell him I'd
been as discreet as I could for his sake and it had gone well—he
seemed relieved."

In that same letter, Mercedes told Millie that on August 6, one
week after her divorce from Douglas, she would marry Robert
Eichholz, a successful Washington attorney, whom she had
known since 1939. After the Douglases were separated, Eichholz
had renewed his acquaintance with Mercedes and, in time, had
made his serious intentions known. With her impending marriage
to Eichholz, Mercedes again felt affection toward Douglas. Neither she nor her new husband would do anything to hurt Douglas,
she told Millie, because they both believed in him and the importance of his work. She wished him the best, but predicted that his
life would be "hell" if he married Joanie Martin.

"Bill was always happy just before a marriage and one week
afterward," said Kay Kershaw, an old friend of Douglas's. The
first part of the statement seemed to be true in the summer of
1963. He wrote his daughter a characteristically brief, cheerful
note, assuring her that he was not crazy to marry twenty-three-
year-old Joanie Martin, as he was certain his daughter, then
thirty-four years old, had concluded. Joanie was a fine person, a

wholesome person, he said. In time, he was sure, Millie and Joanie would become good friends.

The transition period was smoother for Douglas than for his bride or her family. Crude, vile letters were written to the Martin family, suggesting in the most lurid terms that Joanie was a moral degenerate for marrying a man old enough to be her grandfather. Telephone callers delivered the same message. And there were threats to bomb the Martins' house, even to murder their daughter.

The couple was married in Joanie's parents' house, but it was not the quiet wedding both wanted. The third wedding for a Supreme Court Justice was news, national news, particularly when the jurist was William O. Douglas, and his bride was so young. The media converged on the Martin residence, and as if the inevitable circus atmosphere was not enough to fray the nerves of the participants, a television network truck drove through Mrs. Martin's cherished rose garden. Joanie's mother wept uncontrollably. After the ceremony, the Justice and his new wife had to lie on the floor of their departing car to evade the hordes of reporters and photographers.

The honeymoon, for Joanie, was quieter but no less traumatic than the wedding. The couple stayed at the Crescent Lodge near Forks, Washington, where Douglas worked on a book tentatively titled *The Last Frontier.* "I think Forks qualified," said Joanie. "It wasn't really a honeymoon except that I was going along with him," she said. They spent time in Forks, and visited Douglas's old friends Kay Kershaw and Isabelle Lynn at the Double K Ranch in Goose Prairie. Finally the couple went to a favorite lake of the Justice's in Oregon's Wallowa Mountains. Everywhere they went, the reception was cordial. But Joanie sensed that the politeness hid the curiosity about "this little friend who was trailing along after the Justice."

That summer, Joanie recalled, one person stood above all others in his understanding and compassion for the newlyweds. He was Chief Justice Earl Warren. The couple, with other members of the Court and their wives, had been invited to San Francisco for a celebration honoring the Chief Justice. Joanie approached the Chief Justice timidly, half anticipating that he would extend a perfunctory handshake and move on to the next guest. Instead

Warren put his arms around Joanie, in front of the national television cameras, and said, "Welcome to the family." Joanie was a Warren worshiper from that day forward.

The welcome in the nation's capital was not so warm. "People who had good manners exhibited them," said Joanie, "and those who didn't, who only had a superficial sense of good manners, well, I think my presence challenged that veneer. I began to dread cocktail parties because when people got a few drinks in them, they were less discreet. Also, the younger men thought they had a certain ability to make me happy in a way in which they assumed that an older man like the Justice could not compete. And they would make their proclivities known. They made passes at me. But they made themselves look boorish and foolish. So did older men, but not as old as my husband.

"Initially, it would hurt me very deeply to be treated in that fashion. My husband didn't know about it, though I know he suspected it might be a problem. But I always presumed that he thought that that conduct would speak for itself and that it wasn't necessary to address such boorish and obnoxious people. Basically, he was right, but when you are twenty-four years old and come from a cloistered background, you're always shocked, taken aback. You're hurt. You're not blasé. I suspect now I would simply open a man's shirt and pour my drink down it. But at the time, I would take refuge in the women's room and make sure my tears didn't show when I left. I was very vulnerable."

Feeling inadequate in the Washington social swirl, Joanie concentrated on making her marriage work at home. "I had been raised to be a wife," she said, "and it became a fetish with me. I would have the glasses chilled and his slippers out when the Justice came home and, I suspect, I grew increasingly boring."

But she was still a good listener and the Justice never seemed to tire of recalling the pain of his upbringing. "He never had a birthday party as a child," she said, "and I remember his telling me how much that hurt him." He spoke often of the scars of his childhood; there was also talk of the family's limited finances, of his father's death, of the lawyer bamboozling his mother out of her last savings, of his polio. He talked about his drive to overcome the effects of polio, and Joanie knew the pain. "I understood what he was saying, I understood how he hurt inside, because I had also been an outcast. We really enjoyed talking about some of those things because we really understood each other. We understood what those hurts were and why they were there."

Douglas also spoke glowingly of his mother's strong character and steely determination to see that her children succeeded. Douglas would tell Joanie of how, intuitively, he and his mother understood each other. "When we went by his little house in Yakima," Joanie recalled, "he would tell me how he and his mother sat facing each other, she mending clothes and he reading, the two of them enjoying the nonverbal communion and feeling at peace." Like Mercedes before her, Joanie was presented with a portrait of Julia Douglas that was awe-inspiring. "You could take all of his wives and stack us back to back and you wouldn't come up with the profound influence of his mother on him," Joanie said. "The greatest compliment he could pay you was to say you reminded him of his mother.

"I think he kept looking for the same relationship with his wives that he had with his mother. A mother's love doesn't ask for anything back. It's total support, all-giving, all-forgiving. But wives ask for things back. He wasn't able to make that distinction."

Life, then, for Joanie became almost a sacrificial act. Every activity was measured against her husband's interest, for it was his interest that was important. Predictably, Joanie experienced the same identity crisis that Mercedes had. Except she had neither the confidence nor the maturity of Mercedes, who at least attempted to challenge Douglas's total control of her life.

"I was perfectly happy to be a wife in one way, but in another, I didn't know where I was in the picture," said Joanie. "I was just walking around with this enormous name. I didn't have any personality anymore. His vote was so critical that I didn't dare shoot off my mouth or get involved. The options that were open to me were tea parties and fashion shows and cocktail parties. I was sort of a Washington kewpie doll. I was supposed to have my hair perfect and my clothes perfect and smile a lot and not say anything controversial. Not say anything at all. Just be dutiful and adoring. I just whacked. I couldn't figure out what I was supposed to do. I could only vacuum so many times and then the maid came. Even if I could sit down with older people, as I had in the past, and be comfortable with them, they weren't comfortable with me."

All the while, the Justice went about his appointed rounds, writing judicial opinions and books, traveling and trekking. And he seemed totally unaware of his wife's agony. "One of the things any woman close to Bill had to accept," Joanie said, "was that you more or less had to be an observer of him. He was the one who arranged whatever happened. Some of the things he arranged were wonderful, like our trip to Russia."

Other arrangements, like the long hikes Douglas planned, were not so wonderful. "I hated hiking, but I went," Joanie recalled. " 'If you're going to be a Douglas, Joanie,' he'd say, 'you're going to have to do these things.' I remember moments outdoors that I'm sure would match how people felt on the Bataan death march. I weighed eighty-eight pounds. I had sixty pounds on my back on one hike when I fell from a cliff into the ocean. I started menstruating two weeks early because my body was so shocked. I had to go three more days in the soaking rain. He forgot his air mattress so I had to give him mine. I slept on the sand. It was just incredible. But I wanted him to be proud of me, so I didn't say anything, but just kept hiking and hoping NBC wouldn't show up again with its film crew when my whole fanny was exposed from my clothes being ripped off my back."

Joanie couldn't hack it at home either. It wasn't that she wouldn't play by the Justice's rules; she wasn't always sure what the rules were. One Saturday morning, for example, a well-known photographer and his wife paid the Douglases an informal visit. Joanie described the scene: "Bill was up in his study. I offered them coffee. I was so excited to have real people in the house; people don't just drop in on you if you are a Supreme Court Justice. So I was excited to be able to do what was normal. So I talked and talked and served more coffee and was having the best time. About ten or fifteen minutes went by and Bill didn't come down. I knew he was hurt. So I went to the bottom of the stairs and called, 'Honey, we have guests.' He didn't answer. Another forty-five minutes went by. I couldn't figure it out so I went upstairs. He was blue with rage. He was so angry with me that he could hardly speak. He felt I had demeaned him by not coming to him immediately when the guests arrived. And he felt my calling him 'honey' in front of those people was also demeaning.

"I couldn't be a wifey at any time that we, as a couple, were exposed to the public. He felt it was inappropriate. But it was something I couldn't anticipate; other times, when he was hiking, he was sort of a 'grass roots' man. There were a lot of contradictions within him."

Joanie sensed the same insecurity in Douglas that Mercedes had and, like Mercedes, was increasingly incapable of dealing with it. "He had a need to be adored all of the time," said Joanie. "After forty years of public adoration and that mother, God help the wife who criticized the man. And if you were feeling less than adoring, well, it was a problem."

With the insecurity came the suspicions of infidelity that had plagued Mercedes. Once, in an airport, Joanie said, the Justice left her for seven hours without any money (he wouldn't allow her to carry money). She had offended him, she later learned, after she had let an airlines employee carry her bag. Douglas suspected that Joanie was making a pass at the man.

"I was always accused of making passes," she recalled. "It was so perplexing. First of all, I was monogamous, not only in the marriage, but he was the first person I had ever been involved with. So it wasn't as if I had had a series of affairs and then married him. But I was always having to prove something that wasn't provable. That I was faithful."

Joanie admitted that her insecurities were a match for her husband's. "I was terribly insecure as a young woman in Washington. Lots of women liked him. They were all at least three sizes bigger than I was in the important places. I couldn't figure out why he had married me when he had all of these things floating around. I just couldn't figure it out. Why me? When there were movie starlets and women who were sophisticated and knew their way around. Why? The more I was exposed to it, the more insecure I became. . . . I never had any illusion that I would be the last wife and that bothered me. I had a terrible sense of inadequacy at not being able to meet his needs. There was a point that the harder I tried to please him, the less there was of him. . . . He worked six, sometimes seven days a week, and I simply couldn't understand that. I knew people worked hard but I knew he couldn't be fired and I couldn't understand why he couldn't spend a little more time with me."

Douglas hid his disenchantment behind a frenetic schedule that took him, increasingly, out of town for extended periods. When he was at home, Joanie was left with the distinct impression that her presence made no difference. "Life with Justice Douglas was very, very lonely," said Joanie.

In the spring of 1964, less than a year after her wedding to Douglas, Joanie left. For the next two months she traveled incognito throughout Europe. When she returned, she noticed a renewed responsiveness from her husband, and her hopes for the marriage were briefly rekindled. But the difficulties persisted and Joanie saw less and less of her husband. When she suggested that she accompany him on one of his trips, his "no" was so emphatic that she "sort of felt he had another agenda."

"When Bill Douglas decides he wants another woman, that's it," said Joanie. "During our marriage, I knew it. How? I just knew. Women just know. I wasn't at all surprised by the sequence of events because it was the same pattern when I had been on the other side. Exactly the same. I think that the agony that Mercedes and I lived with was, one, that we really loved him and, two, we didn't know how to make him happy. I don't think we can blame ourselves, because I don't think he knows or knew how to be happy."

Cathy Heffernan worked as a cocktail waitress at the Three Star Restaurant in Portland, Oregon, to help pay her way through Marylhurst College. One August night in 1965, Douglas's old friend Damon Trout remembered, he dropped into the Three Star for a drink. Cathy, a fragile twenty-two-year-old with blond hair cut in a Mia Farrow pixie style, came to his table and Trout ordered a "smile." So Cathy smiled. After Trout explained that "smile" also meant the best Scotch in the house, she brought the drink and sat down with her customer to chat. Trout was charmed and thought his friend Bill Douglas would be too.

The next night, Douglas, having finished delivering a speech in Portland, told his friend Trout that he wanted a "smile." Trout drove the Justice to the Three Star, where Cathy Heffernan served the two men, and then sat down to chat and joke with them for a few minutes.* "I loved her the first time I saw her," Douglas said later. And after he and Trout left the Three Star, Douglas stunned his companion by telling him he wanted to marry the young woman he had just met.

"I was surprised," Trout recalled. "A Supreme Court Justice and this little girl?"

Douglas could not be deterred, even by the nuns at Cathy's school, who frowned upon a courtship of one of their students by the sixty-six-year-old Justice. So, according to Trout, Douglas wrote letters to Cathy, sent them to Trout, and Trout's wife then put them in a fresh envelope and forwarded them to Cathy.

In December 1965, Douglas was in Portland again and asked Trout to call Cathy for him. But Trout was busy and Douglas's impatience spurred him to make the call himself. He had been attracted to her hands, he told Cathy over the telephone, and he wanted to see her again. Cathy considered Douglas's line laughable ("actually, my hands aren't very attractive"), but accepted his invitation anyway. The two dined at the London Bar & Grill in Portland's Benson Hotel and talked well into the night. He talked of his background and his travels and she talked of hers.

Catherine Heffernan was the second child and only daughter of Curtis and Mary Heffernan. Her father was the chief night clerk at the Portland yard office for the Spokane, Portland and Seattle Railroad. Her mother processed prisoners' pictures at the Multnomah County jail in Portland. Cathy grew up in northeast Portland, in a modest, tidy wood-frame house. "There was no time, effort or money to raise me genteelly," said Cathy, who learned early to fend for herself. Strict Irish Catholics, the Heffernans sent Cathy to parochial schools. But though she remembered the nuns always telling her what to do and think, Cathy's independent spirit could not be denied.

When she was eighteen, Cathy was searching for adventure and decided she wanted to go to Europe. After she saw an ad in a magazine for a European youth hostel, she asked permission

---

*Cathy recalled her first meeting with Douglas slightly differently. She said that her boss at the Three Star Restaurant, Vic Harris, called her over to Douglas and Trout's table, introduced her to them and invited her to join them, which she did.

from her school to take a high school equivalency test so that she could leave parochial school early. Her request was denied. Undaunted, Cathy immediately began to make plans for a summer trip to Europe. It cost three hundred dollars for a European summer, she calculated, so she took a part-time job at a Portland restaurant to pay for it. The summer of her eighteenth year, Cathy bicycled and hitchhiked across Europe. By the time she returned to New York, she was out of money and had to ask a stranger for five dollars for groceries. She then wired her father for assistance to get back to Portland.

The story suggested a tale of another resident of the Northwest, forty-five years earlier, whose own independence and love of adventure had taken him to New York with his pockets almost empty. After his momentary insolvency in New York, William O. Douglas had enrolled at the Columbia Law School. After hers, Cathy Heffernan took a train (free, through her father's arrangements) back to Portland, where she continued her studies at Marylhurst, did volunteer work with mentally retarded children and still found the time to hold her job at the Three Star Restaurant.

At that first dinner together, Cathy Heffernan and Bill Douglas chattered away about world problems and about their lives. "We understood each other," Cathy recalled. "The most apparent thing since that first night together was that I understood him as a human being before I understood him as a public figure. I had great sympathy for him as a human being. The overwhelming impression from that first evening forward was that he was a man with broad insights who could communicate them without making me feel uncomfortable. I didn't know Bill as a complex figure. He talked with ease and tried to make the problems, for example, of the developing countries understandable to me."

Douglas asked Cathy to dinner the next night and then he asked to meet her parents.

By February 1966, Joanie Martin Douglas had begun divorce proceedings, moved out of the Douglas residence, taken a job at the United Nations and moved into an apartment in New York City. When Douglas came through New York on his way to Albany to deliver a speech, he stayed at Joanie's apartment. The arrangement seemed to suit both of them. He could pursue his career and his other interests. She could have a career and, simultaneously, be free of what had become, for her, an increasingly oppressive social life in Washington. Joanie had even thought that the loose relationship might hold the marriage together.

But by this time, Douglas had decided that he wanted to marry Cathy Heffernan. On June 24, 1966, Joanie and Bill Douglas were divorced. Less than three weeks later, the Justice and Cathy Heffernan left Portland by plane for Los Angeles to attend a dinner with some of the Justice's friends. After Cathy decided to stay an extra day, she and Douglas went shopping. At one small shop, a saleslady, Mrs. Lee Epstein, brought out a light-blue silk evening dress.

"Well, Mrs. Epstein," said the Justice, "why don't you bring out a wedding dress for her?" Douglas's immediate purpose was to purchase a dress for Cathy to wear at the wedding of President Johnson's daughter Luci, but the idea of buying a dress for Cathy's wedding did occur. As the Justice and Cathy left the store, Douglas told Mrs. Epstein with a twinkle, "If you can convince Cathy to marry me, I'll make you Secretary of the Navy."

"We hadn't really talked marriage plans specifically," Cathy recalled, "but it was always in the air. It seemed this was the only time to do it, since we could keep it a secret."

Cathy returned to Mrs. Epstein's shop and confided that she and the Justice had decided to get married. Mrs. Epstein offered her daughter's home in Encino for the wedding, an offer that Douglas and his bride-to-be accepted. The couple needed a marriage license in a hurry, and again Mrs. Epstein came to their assistance, sending one of the shop's delivery boys with them to the Santa Monica courthouse. They picked up the license and bought matching gold wedding bands.

Cathy then arranged to have her hair cut, but by the time she had returned to the hotel from the beauty parlor to dress for the 6:00 P.M. wedding, she had second thoughts. "I don't want to get married," she said to the Justice, sobbing. Douglas just laughed, and the more Cathy cried, the more he laughed. At that moment, reporters, who had heard that Justice Douglas had taken out a marriage license, knocked on the hotel room door. Cathy ran into the bathroom while the Justice talked to the reporters. Douglas came back and said, "It's no secret anymore. They know we're getting married. What are we going to do?"

Cathy stopped crying, combed her hair and walked bravely to the door, where she held her first press conference, telling the reporters that she would become the fourth Mrs. William O. Douglas.

The marriage to Cathy came along so fast, Douglas wrote his daughter, that he had no time to call, cable or write. The couple wanted a private wedding with no publicity, he said, but word was leaked. Cathy conducted her first press conference with aplomb, Douglas wrote. In a later letter, Douglas provided Millie with a brief sketch of his new wife: Cathy's weight (108 pounds), eye and hair color (blue and blond), religion (devout Catholic), work (teaching mildly disturbed children) and future plans (M.A. in sociology followed, probably, by community work). He was certain that Millie would love Cathy.

On their honeymoon in Goose Prairie, Douglas was more demonstratively affectionate with Cathy than he had been with anyone in years. Visitors observed the Justice walking with his arm around his new bride, calling her "sweetie," beaming while Cathy told of their travel plans. The age difference seemed to melt away as both Cathy, twenty-three, and Bill Douglas, sixty-seven, acted like young newlyweds. At a bookstore, Douglas picked up a copy of *Of Men and Mountains* and showed Cathy a picture of himself as a teen-ager. "Look at me in that picture, sweetie," he said. "I could really climb in those days." Cathy giggled and said, "I wasn't even thought of in those days," and then skipped off with Tinker Bell ease, leaving the Justice grinning.

Defying the best predictions of family and friends on both sides, the frolicking good humor and affection of the honeymoon continued. When they traveled abroad, Douglas would indulge in one of his antic teases and Cathy would gleefully join in. On a trip to China, Douglas told the vice-mayor of Shanghai that Cathy was a famous wrestler. The vice-mayor looked over the slight Mrs. Douglas and replied that she seemed ill equipped for the sport. Douglas told the vice-mayor that Cathy had developed a new training technique that built strength but not muscles. Cathy held her laughter in and the couple spent the remainder of the tour graciously refusing invitations for a demonstration from the famous American wrestler.

At home, Douglas was equally adept at playing pranks on his wife, and the two would laugh about them afterward. When the couple visited former President Eisenhower at Walter Reed Hospital, the Justice whispered to the Presbyterian minister in attendance that Cathy was in desperate need of religious counsel. And then Douglas tiptoed out of the room, leaving Cathy to politely decline the minister's help.

Cathy shared her husband's adventuresome spirit as well as his silliness. She told the story of one particularly memorable three-day pack trip in the Cascades: "We planned to spend the night at Horseshoe Basin. Clouds formed soon after we got there. We couldn't be seen by the pack train. They had our food and clothes. We had half a Hershey bar between us. Bill said, 'We'd better get wood because they've passed us by.' It snowed and rained all night. The Hershey bar didn't get any bigger. We sat around the fire and Bill told stories all night long. When dawn broke, there were a couple of inches of snow on the ground. Bill was still telling stories when the pack train finally found us at noon the next day."

Cathy was unpretentious and determined to stay that way. She would not attempt to do what she didn't like or be someone other than herself. And the Justice accepted her on her terms. "I'd rather run a river in the wilderness than bake a cake," said Cathy, so they both agreed that she should spend more time outdoors than in the kitchen. Indeed, the Justice actually shared the cooking and cleaning for the first time in his forty-two years of marriage. On special occasions, such as Thanksgiving, Cathy accepted the culinary challenge but had no illusions about the results. On her first attempt at the traditional feast, she cheerfully passed the booze from guest to guest in hopes that any after-effects would be attributed to the bottle, not her turkey.

Behind the pixie cut and ready smile, she was a very tough-minded young woman. "She's the only one of Dad's wives," said Douglas's daughter, Millie, "who categorically refused to wait on him." And early in their marriage, Cathy gave notice that she not only would not wait on her husband, she would not be intimidated either. Once, in a fit of anger, Douglas threatened to take away all Cathy's credit cards. "Here," she said defiantly, "take them." He retreated.

The same independent spirit that braced her for her husband's forays helped her to survive and, ultimately, thrive in an unconventional marriage. Cathy set the tone early, telling a reporter who asked if the stares that followed her in public bothered her: "These people who can't understand my marriage often have a life experience which is like a blackboard that's completely filled," she said. "And some people's blackboards are very small."

Where Joanie tried immediately after her marriage to Douglas to establish a close relationship with Douglas's daughter (who by this time was teaching school in England and living with her second husband), Cathy kept her distance until she and Millie had got to know each other. And she took Douglas's friends and Washington society as she found them, not trying to impress them or overwhelm them with her sophistication or sincerity.

And what, she was asked, did she expect of a marriage to a man forty-four years her senior? "We intend to make our life together the fullest, most complete one possible—whether it's one year, ten years or twenty."

Cathy's effect on her husband was magical. He knocked himself out taking her around Washington, thinking up things he thought she would like to do. They went to the ballet (though Cathy caught him napping), concerts and black-tie dinners. At every occasion, the Justice treated her with greatest consideration and affection.

Douglas's good cheer spread to the office. He seemed more relaxed. "He even jokes around the office!" observed Nan Burgess, who had been Douglas's secetary since 1957. "He goes home fairly early unless terribly busy and doesn't work Saturdays unless he has a deadline for a manuscript or Court work. I wouldn't have believed it if I didn't see it myself. He *laughs!!*"

The concerts and foreign travels and Douglas's newly acquired cheerfulness at the office came to an abrupt halt on June 5, 1968. It was a Monday and Douglas was sitting at the bench, listening to oral arguments. Suddenly, he collapsed in his chair. He was immediately carried to his chambers, where he revived, began pacing and then collapsed again. He had suffered a heart attack. At Walter Reed Hospital, doctors examined Douglas and con-

cluded that his heart could no longer produce the required sixty-
two beats a minute. A two-inch transistorized machine called a
pacemaker was therefore installed in Douglas's body to maintain
his heartbeat at a normal rate.

"I was with him right after the operation [installation of the
pacemaker] and he looked well and chattered like a monkey," Bill
Douglas, Jr., wrote his sister. Bill junior, who had interrupted an
acting tour (he was then performing at Dartmouth College) to be
with his father, added these admiring words about Cathy: "Cathy
has been beautiful, at the hospital all day and into the night, really
loving him and making him happy or as happy as he could be."

After Douglas had fully recovered from his heart attack, Cathy
continued to contribute to her husband's happiness, and that
contribution was visible for all around them to see. In return she
received his love, which, from this complicated man, was not
something to be taken for granted. She also was offered a new
life, far from Marylhurst College and Portland's Three Star Restaurant. The whirlwind tours of Africa and Asia came so often
that Cathy sometimes wished the couple would pause from what
seemed to her to be the routine of 25,000 miles every two
months. But even a fatigued Cathy Douglas was having fun and
filling her inquisitive mind with new ideas.

Besides the trips, Douglas offered his young wife unique educational and career opportunities. First he had made certain that
Cathy enrolled at American University to fulfill the credit requirements for her degree in sociology. But predictably, as she listened
to her husband's experiences and ideas, her mind had turned
toward another discipline, the law. On her first day at the American University Law School, Cathy realized that every one of her
fellow students knew who she was and, she suspected, was waiting
for her to make a mistake. But Cathy adjusted and so did her new
colleagues. She graduated from the law school in 1972 and received a master's in law from Georgetown University in 1974.

After law school, Cathy joined the prestigious Washington law
firm of Leva, Hawes, Symington, Martin and Oppenheimer. She
quickly proved that she had more than her name to contribute.
"She's a star at meeting people," said Marx Leva, the senior
partner at the firm. "She can sit in a meeting and pick up an issue

more quickly than the others." He added, "I think she can charm a bird out of a tree." After only five years of full-time practice, Cathy was serving as general counsel to the Women's National Bank, sitting on the board of directors of National Public Radio and co-chairing the Americans for Alaska organization, which lobbies for legislation to preserve vast lands in Alaska as wilderness. She also accepted numerous invitations to speak or attend ceremonies in honor of her husband.

In Douglas's last years, when his health became increasingly precarious, there was occasional talk in Washington that Cathy was spending too much time building her career and too little time taking care of her husband. But members of Douglas's immediate family did not see it that way. "He made Cathy into what he wanted all of us to be," said Millie. "He had her finish college and go to law school. Now she's making a career. She is his product. He has made her into a successful lawyer. In this sense, she has repaid him for all he gave her."

PART SIX

THE LAST YEARS

IMPEACHMENT

IN THE BEGINNING, it was a petty, political attack, which did not deserve, or elicit, a serious response. On July 18, 1966, less than one week after Douglas had married his fourth wife, Representative George W. Andrews of Alabama called for the House Judiciary Committee to investigate the Justice's moral character. "If they find that he is a man of bad character," said Andrews, "he could be impeached." And even if he couldn't be impeached, said Andrews, the investigation would allow Douglas's character to be "x-rayed to the American people." Andrews's colleague, Representative Thomas G. Abernathy of Mississippi, added, "In all candor, he [Douglas] would do himself and his country a favor if he would quietly resign from the High Court and devote full time to that in which he appears to be most learned and proficient—linking the highways of matrimony."

Andrews's resolution provided some congressmen with a few moments of puerile snickering, but little else. Supported primarily by representatives from Southern states who did not like Justice Douglas's civil rights opinions, the resolution failed.

The second attack was neither petty nor political. On October

16, 1966, Ronald J. Ostrow, a respected reporter for the *Los Angeles Times,* wrote an article that laid out uncontested facts:

For six years, Douglas had served as president of the Albert Parvin Foundation, a tax-exempt organization that financed fellowships and other educational programs to promote international peace and understanding. Since 1962, Douglas had received a yearly salary of $12,000 for his services. The Parvin Foundation derived much of its income from a first mortgage on Las Vegas's Flamingo Hotel and gambling casino. The foundation also owned stock in the Parvin-Dohrmann Corporation, which supplied furniture to many of the hotels on the Las Vegas Strip. Albert Parvin, chief benefactor of the foundation, had a financial interest in three Las Vegas gambling casinos.

When asked by Ostrow about his $12,000 salary from the Parvin Foundation, Douglas said the money was assigned to him "largely as an expense account" for trips in connection with foundation work. His expenses, said Douglas, came "pretty close" to matching his annual salary. The fact that the annual salary amounted to almost one third of his $39,000 salary as a justice did not, said Douglas, raise any ethical questions in his mind.

In his article, Ostrow pointed out that Albert Parvin had entered into business deals with known gambling operators, including Edward Levinson. Levinson had been involved in various enterprises with Bobby Baker, the former secretary to the Senate, but had invoked the Fifth Amendment privilege against possible self-incrimination and had raised other objections in refusing to answer questions of the Senate Rules Committee investigating the dealings of Baker.

Ostrow did not suggest that Douglas had any connection with Edward Levinson or any other gambling operator with whom Parvin had done business. What he did suggest was that Douglas's connection with Albert Parvin's foundation and his salary of $12,000 a year, derived, in part, from Las Vegas gambling income, did not present a justice of the U.S. Supreme Court or the Court itself in the most favorable light.

Canon Four of the American Bar Association's Canon of Judicial Ethics stated that "a judge's official conduct should be free from impropriety and the appearance of impropriety." In practice, the ABA had never been rigorous in the enforcement of the canon. Moreover, federal laws governing the conduct of judges were not particularly strict. At the time of Ostrow's article in the *Times,* federal judges were not required to disclose their financial holdings or outside income. And it was left to the individual judge to decide whether personal involvement or interest demanded that he disqualify himself from a case.

Douglas told the *Times'*s Ostrow that a judge's power to disqualify himself was a safeguard against conflicts of interest that might arise from his outside activities. He noted that no company in which the Parvin Foundation had an interest had been before the Supreme Court.

On the Senate floor the day after Ostrow's article was published, Senator John J. Williams (Republican, Delaware) said the Parvin Foundation's payments to Douglas raised a serious question about the "propriety" as well as the "legality" of the Justice's foundation salary. Williams pointed out that the $39,000 a year that justices of the U.S. Supreme Court received for life was presumed to insulate members of the Court from the necessity of earning outside income. If the Supreme Court did not take prompt action, Williams warned that he would ask for a full-scale investigation by the Senate Judiciary Committee on justices' outside income. Later in the day, Senator Williams wrote Chief Justice Warren about Douglas's involvement with the Parvin Foundation. "There is a grave question as to the propriety of his [Douglas's] accepting such payments," Williams wrote, "and I would appreciate your reviewing these charges and advising me whether or not the Supreme Court condones such practices and if not, what steps will be taken to protect the integrity of the Court."

Chief Justice Warren responded to Senator Williams in a letter which stated that Douglas's involvement with the Parvin Foundation was "a matter personal to Mr. Justice Douglas." The Chief Justice also enclosed a letter from Douglas to Warren, in which Douglas defended his involvement with the foundation against "some recent vicious press articles." First, Douglas assured the Chief Justice that the Parvin Foundation had no connection with the operation of any commercial enterprise. Second, he noted that many justices, past and present, had maintained connections

outside the Court, as trustees of colleges, law professors, authors
and owners of securities, and that it had always been the responsibility of the individual justice to disqualify himself when a conflict
of interest was perceived. Douglas stated that nothing coming
before the Court had involved the Parvin Foundation in any way.

The remainder of Douglas's letter described the foundation's
philanthropic activities, beginning with its sponsorship of fellowships at Princeton and UCLA for students from underdeveloped
countries. Douglas also mentioned an adult literacy program in
the Dominican Republic and the foundation's sponsorship of
occasional meetings between experts from the United States and
Latin America held at the Center for the Study of Democratic
Institutions at Santa Barbara. The focus of all foundation programs, said Douglas, was to educate current and future leaders
of Latin America about the strengths of a democratic society so
that they, in turn, could effectively combat the forces of communism.

Following Ronald Ostrow's story, the chief of the Washington
bureau of the *Los Angeles Times,* Robert J. Donovan, wrote letters
to the other justices, asking for opinions on whether there should
be a rule governing their outside activities. Further, Donovan
inquired about each justice's personal policy on accepting outside income and participating in nonjudicial activities. The responses could not have been encouraging to Donovan. Justice
Harlan wrote Donovan that it was his policy not to discuss the
affairs of the Court or its individual members with the press.
Justice Black wrote Donovan that he thought any rule binding
justices would encroach on their constitutional independence.
Black wrote that he personally had drawn very little outside income while serving on the Court and that he did "not consider
it to be a part of my responsibility or duty to sit in judgment upon
the outside activities of my brethren on this Court."

With the hands-off response of other members of the Court,
including the Chief Justice, and Douglas's strong defense of his
involvement with the Parvin Foundation,* the furor gradually

*Privately, Douglas dismissed the attack as instigated by the FBI, which, he said, did
not want him to take part in a case before the Court involving Fred B. Black, Jr. Black,
a former associate of Bobby Baker, had challenged his conviction of income tax invasion
on the ground that the FBI had illegally tapped his telephone.

subsided. By the end of November, Douglas's connection with the Parvin Foundation was no longer news. Although Douglas had told Chief Justice Warren that the increased activities of the Parvin Foundation would make it difficult for him to continue as its president, he nonetheless continued (and accepted an increase in his annual salary to $12,765).

Both before and after the controversy arose over his connection with the Parvin Foundation, Douglas maintained a close personal relationship with Albert Parvin. To Parvin, the Justice was a great man whose ideas needed to be translated into tangible activities that he hoped the Parvin Foundation could provide. In fact, Douglas's book *America Challenged,* in which the Justice had outlined the dangers that communism posed to Latin America, had given Parvin the idea for his foundation in the first place. Parvin, then, offered Douglas adulation and money to engage in the traveling and the good-will ventures that he had thrived on for more than a decade.

For his part, Douglas openly claimed Parvin as a close friend and invited him to rub shoulders with some of the most powerful men in the world. For example, at a 1964 dinner at Washington's F Street Club, honoring Douglas's twenty-five years on the Court, Albert Parvin had sat at Table One, together with, among others, Douglas himself, President Lyndon B. Johnson and Chief Justice Earl Warren. In his remarks that evening, Douglas said that "if compassion, conscience, fair-dealing, courage, humility are on occasion mine, I got them from the Lyndon Johnsons, Earl Warrens, Hugo Blacks, . . . Albert Parvins, and all the rest of you with whose friendship I have been blessed."

In May 1969, both Douglas's relationship with Albert Parvin and his position as the paid president of Parvin's foundation again came under public attack. It occurred shortly after *Life* magazine had published the details of a financial relationship that another associate justice of the U.S. Supreme Court, Abe Fortas, had arranged with another charitable foundation, this one created by financier Louis Wolfson. *Life* reported that Fortas had accepted a fee of $20,000 from Wolfson's foundation at a time when Wolfson was under investigation by the Securities and Exchange Commission for selling fraudulent securities. Reports then circulated that President Richard Nixon's Attorney General, John Mitchell, had met secretly with Chief Justice Warren to tell him that the Justice Department had far more serious information on Fortas's extrajudicial activities than had been made public. A legal contract, Mitchell had learned, required Wolfson's foundation to pay $20,000 a year for as long as Fortas or his wife lived. For Fortas sympathizers, the Mitchell action smacked of an ugly squeeze play by the Nixon administration to force Fortas off the bench. They did not like it, but they could do nothing about it.

Douglas was in Brazil at the time *Life* broke the Fortas story. When he returned to Washington, he went directly from the airport to the Fortas home in Georgetown. Fortas later described Douglas's loyalty during the crisis: "Of course, he was there. As Lyndon Johnson used to say, 'He was a good man to lay behind the log with.' "*

Douglas and Fortas stayed up all night discussing Fortas's dilemma. Could Fortas survive the attack in the press now that it had been enthusiastically joined by the Nixon administration? Fortas was despondent. Douglas gently consoled his long-time friend, but he never wavered in his advice. Stick it out, he told Fortas. Do not bow to political pressure. Do not let the media and Richard Nixon run you out of office.

But each day that Fortas clung to his position on the Court brought more pressure from politicians and the press for his resignation. Finally, on May 15, 1969, Fortas resigned, the first justice in Supreme Court history to do so under the pressure of public criticism. A major consideration in his decision, Fortas has suggested, was the fear that had he not resigned, his critics would have driven from the Court not only Fortas himself, but also Justice William O. Douglas.

For conservative politicians, including the man who sat in the White House, there were tantalizing similarities between the Fortas arrangement with the Wolfson Foundation and the Douglas arrangement with the Parvin Foundation. Both Fortas and Douglas had accepted substantial income from foundations financed by businessmen whose dealings had come under scrutiny of law

---

*The old Texas expression that Johnson used referred to someone to be trusted behind a log during an Indian attack.

enforcement officials. Wolfson had been convicted of selling fraudulent securities. Albert Parvin had been named, though not tried, as a co-conspirator in a stock fraud case involving Louis Wolfson. Ironically, the Parvin Foundation had hired Fortas's wife, a prominent Washington attorney, as its tax adviser.

But the distinctions between the Fortas situation and that of Douglas were even more striking. Although Albert Parvin had known Wolfson and done business with many gamblers of unsavory reputation, he, unlike Wolfson, had never been the object of legal proceedings by the government. "I am sick that what I have done in the course of honest business," Parvin said, "has reflected on a man as great as Justice Douglas. . . . Yes, I knew Wolfson and I know lots of gamblers and I have points in almost every Las Vegas hotel—but I don't break the law and I never would and nothing should reflect on a man like Justice Douglas."

It was never clear what Fortas was being paid to do for the Wolfson Foundation except respond to a vague directive to work in the field of juvenile delinquency. As president of the Parvin Foundation, on the other hand, Douglas actually ran the organization and took an active role in the implementation of its very tangible and highly praised programs in the United States and Latin America.

But those distinctions did not persuade Douglas's critics, and the numbers were growing. Even those who admired Douglas began to question the propriety of his relationship with the Parvin Foundation. The *Washington Post*'s Alan Barth, for example, had long applauded Douglas's libertarianism, but he questioned the wisdom of Douglas's accepting outside income from the foundation. Noting that the justices' salaries had recently been raised to $60,000 a year, Barth wrote: "Congress fixed this sum for the salary of Supreme Court justices with the thought that it would satisfy men to whom honor, public service and the pursuit of a high calling mean more than money. . . . Is it not time, then, for the Justices of the Supreme Court to lay down for themselves a new canon of conduct—a hard and uniform and unequivocal canon recognizing the extraordinary caliber and character of their office?" Barth suggested two "commandments" for the justices. One dealt with the problem of justices' latent political ambitions and would have prohibited them from ever accepting another government appointment or elective office. Barth's second commandment confronted directly the problem presented by Justice Douglas's involvement with the Parvin Foundation: "Thou shalt receive no remuneration from any other employer than the United States."

In the House of Representatives, H. R. Gross (Republican, Iowa), who had prepared articles of impeachment against Fortas, now suggested that the House Judiciary Committee look at Douglas's relationship with the Parvin Foundation. In the Senate, Senator John Williams again asked that Douglas's activities be reviewed, this time by the American Bar Association's Ethics Committee. At the same time, House Minority Leader Gerald R. Ford, impressed by the quantity of mail to Congress critical of Douglas, had quietly decided to conduct his own investigation of Douglas's activities. Later, in the summer and fall of 1969, Ford and his staff, with help from Clark Mollenhoff, an assistant to President Nixon, and Assistant Attorney General Will Wilson, who offered Ford confidential FBI files, would begin to accumulate a mound of information on Douglas.

Just as members of Congress were once again beginning to train their eyes on Douglas's connection with the Parvin Foundation, the foundation announced that it had sold $2 million of its stock in the Parvin-Dohrmann Corporation. *The New York Times,* in reporting the transaction, noted that Justice Douglas had received more than $85,000 from the Parvin Foundation over a seven-year period, and that Douglas's foundation salary in 1967 alone had been equal to one fourth the amount of all grants given by the Parvin Foundation in that year. At the same time, another newspaper story revealed that Douglas had been paid $4,000 to conduct two seminars at the Center for the Study of Democratic Institutions, a California study center which was financed, in part, by grants from the Parvin Foundation.

Later in that same week, Douglas resigned as president of the Parvin Foundation. According to the statement released by the foundation, Douglas had been expected to resign for more than a month (which would have predated the Fortas resignation). Douglas had written the foundation's board of trustees a memorandum, according to a foundation spokesman, which indicated that the augmented activities of the foundation made it increasingly difficult for him to continue. "I probably cannot carry it [the burden of foundation responsibilities] while I remain on the Court," Douglas was quoted as writing in his memorandum. "While the foundation pays me a salary," Douglas wrote, "there is not enough left after income tax to pay the cost of the new and promising activities of the foundation."

Douglas's cutting of financial ties with Parvin blunted the most damning criticism of him, but not for long. Two days after the announcement of Douglas's resignation, a *New York Times* reporter discovered a letter from Douglas to Albert Parvin in which the Justice accused the Internal Revenue Service, and the Nixon administration indirectly, of attempting to drive him off the Court. In the letter, Douglas discussed an ongoing IRS investigation of the operations of the Parvin Foundation. IRS agents had been working since 1967 to see if Albert Parvin had been using the foundation to serve his financial interests and as a cover to avoid payment of taxes. Despite the three-year investigation, no charges were ever brought against Parvin. When asked about the prolonged study, a spokesman for the IRS denied that the inquiry was motivated by personal or political considerations.

"A manufactured case," Justice Douglas assured Albert Parvin in his letter. "The strategy is to get me off the Court. I do not propose to bend to any such pressure." Had the letter stopped there, it would have been newsworthy only as another example of the outspoken opinions of Mr. Justice Douglas. But Douglas did not stop there. Instead he suggested ways that the foundation finances could be set apart from Parvin's control. Douglas admitted that his suggestions wouldn't help Parvin with his present difficulties with the IRS, but he thought they might shield him from future IRS investigations.

It was just a piece of friendly advice from Douglas to Parvin. The only problem was that federal law forbade federal judges from engaging in the practice of law. Could Douglas's tax advice to Albert Parvin be interpreted as a violation of that code? Through the Court's press officer, Douglas said that he "knew very little" about the foundation's problems and had never served as Parvin's legal adviser. For the moment, the denial deflected criticism, but Douglas's critics filed the item in their growing dossier on the Justice.

Meanwhile Douglas's colleagues became increasingly uncomfortable with the constant surveillance of one of their brethren by the press and members of Congress. Privately, retiring Chief Justice Warren considered both Douglas's and Fortas's outside incomes improper and felt that both had let the Court down. Publicly, Warren announced that four members of the Court—Justices William Brennan, Potter Stewart, Byron White and Thurgood Marshall—had voluntarily agreed to give up outside compensation for non-Court activities, in keeping with a mandatory rule that had recently been imposed on lower federal court judges by the Judicial Conference of the United States. Warren had been unsuccessful, it was noted, in achieving unanimity in his desire to get all the justices to commit themselves voluntarily to the Judicial Conference rule. Missing from the list of those willing to accept the rule were Justices Hugo Black, John Harlan and William O. Douglas.

Although Douglas maintained a calm exterior, he was concerned about the controversy. "It seems as if the campaign against me is increasing in volume and that impeachment proceedings are likely," he wrote his old friend Fred Rodell on June 19, 1969.

Clement Haynsworth, Jr., was the dour, aloof chief judge of the U.S. Court of Appeals for the Fourth Circuit whom President Nixon had nominated to succeed Abe Fortas on the U.S. Supreme Court. Haynsworth was also a Southerner and a judicial conservative, two credentials that were attractive to the President and anathema to many political liberals. Still smarting from the forced Fortas resignation, liberals picked over the Haynsworth résumé with the care of microbiologists. "Haynsworth would have been confirmed in a minute ten years ago," said Nixon aide John Sears. "But his appointment came at a time when Christ himself would have drawn at least one 'no' vote on principle alone."

It did not take liberals long to find grounds to oppose the Haynsworth nomination. While a judge, Haynsworth had cast the deciding vote in a case involving Darlington Mills, a North Carolina textile concern that was doing $50,000 worth of business with Vend-a-Matic vending machine company. Haynsworth was vice-president and director of Vend-a-Matic at the time of the suit.

"There was literally no choice whatsoever for Judge Hayns-worth," said John Frank, the nation's leading authority on dis-qualification of judges, "except to participate in that case and do his job as well as he could." Haynsworth's opponents rolled out other minor charges of conflicts of interest. But on the ethics issue, the worst to be said for Clement Haynsworth, Jr. (and *The New York Times* said it) was that "none of his alleged misdeeds has turned out to be more than an imperceptive man's neglect in which there was neither profit nor, it would seem, expectation of profit."

While the Senate debated Clement Haynsworth's ethics, House Minority Leader Gerald Ford told the press that he, too, was concerned about the ethics of Supreme Court Justices, most par-ticularly those of Justice William O. Douglas. Actually, Ford did not volunteer the details of his ongoing investigation of Douglas, but when he was asked by a *Washington Post* reporter to confirm or deny the investigation, Ford confirmed it. "If the Senate votes against a nominee for lack of sensitivity," said Ford, alluding to the Haynsworth controversy, "it should apply the same standards to sitting justices."

He did not mean to hold Douglas hostage for Haynsworth's confirmation, Ford assured the press. Few believed him. "The transparency of Mr. Ford's moves does him no credit either as a statesman or tactician," *The New York Times* editorialized. "We think that he will find that anti-Haynsworth Senators will hardly be induced to switch by a poorly veiled threat." The editors at the *Times* were correct. On November 21, 1969, in a tense ten-minute roll call, thirty-eight Democrats and seventeen Republicans com-bined to vote down Clement Haynsworth, Jr., the first Court nominee to suffer that fate in thirty-nine years.

Congressional supporters of Haynsworth were bitter about his defeat and several, including Ford, looked vengefully to Douglas. A loosely organized impeach-Douglas effort was organized in the House, with the single goal of filing articles of impeachment against Douglas during the 1970 congressional term. Gerald Ford, H. R. Gross of Iowa and Clark MacGregor of Minnesota, all Republicans, were supporters of the cause, though Ford, the most prominent among them, denied to the press that he would assume a leadership role in the effort.

Despite the threats, the likelihood of Douglas's forced removal from the bench still seemed remote. First of all, Douglas had history on his side. Though the U.S. Senate had failed to confirm twenty-four men nominated to the Court by U.S. Presidents, now including Haynsworth, it had never voted conviction to impeach a sitting member of the Court. Moreover, the Democrats controlled Congress and would not likely purge one of their own from the Court. That view had been corroborated earlier when talk in Congress of Douglas's impeachment had fizzled. Douglas himself had seemed to help his own cause by resigning as president of the Parvin Foundation. Finally, his judicial colleagues had shown no enthusiasm to pursue the matter, nor had the Ethics Committee of the American Bar Association, which refused to take any action.

But two events in the early months of 1970, one created by Douglas, the other completely out of his control, once again provoked a serious impeach-Douglas movement in Congress. The first was the publication of Douglas's book *Points of Rebellion*, a diatribe against governmental and corporate power. In this thin (ninety-seven pages) volume, Douglas pummeled the "establishment" with aggressive dare words that seemed pitched to the disenchanted younger generation. Douglas sent shivers of admiration through his youthful followers and simply shivers through his critics when he wrote: "We must realize that today's establishment is the new George III. Whether it will continue to adhere to his tactics, we do not know. If it does, the redress, honored in tradition, is also revolution." *Evergreen* magazine, which spliced bold ideas with bald scenes of copulation, found Douglas's rhetoric in *Points* sufficiently titillating to publish excerpts.

Unfortunately, Douglas had very little of substance to say in *Points* that he had not already said better in earlier publications. Worse, much of what he said this time around was patent nonsense. He had written magnificently of the dangers of conformity during the height of the McCarthy era. Now times had changed, but Douglas's observations had not. And so he wrote of the stultifying atmosphere in the country, in which, he said, free expression was being suppressed on college campuses and in the public forum. But despite those in government (most conspicuously, Richard M. Nixon) who wanted to suppress radical ideas that made them uncomfortable, Americans enjoyed more and freer channels of speech than ever before. And a large measure of the credit could go to Douglas and other members of the Warren Court majority, who had insisted that debate on public issues be "uninhibited, robust and wide-open."

American Scholar magazine quickly dismissed *Points of Rebellion* as "hackneyed." But conservative critics, like *National Review* columnist Ernst van den Haag, savaged the book. Parodying the Warren Court's definition of obscenity, van den Haag suggested that *Points* was utterly without redeeming social value, although it did not violate current community standards, such as they were. The book was news, wrote van den Haag, just as a bishop's coming out for burlesque would be news: "being a bishop is not, nor is favoring burlesque, but being a bishop favoring burlesque is."

Douglas's book was published at a time when a large segment of American voters was genuinely concerned about order in the country. A Supreme Court Justice's talk of revolution, predictably quoted out of context by Douglas's enemies, was profoundly unsettling. To make matters worse, Douglas seemed to flaunt his "anti-establishment" credentials by allowing excerpts to be sold to *Evergreen,* where nude bodies cavorted only a few pages away from Douglas's prose. It was bad enough to pander to the younger generation. But to make substantial sums of money from the effort, made many of those in Congress whom Douglas had charged were responsible for the nation's "political bankruptcy" very angry.

Douglas's political antagonists were further provoked in April when the Senate, by a vote of 51 to 45, rejected President Nixon's second nominee to the U.S. Supreme Court in five months. He was G. Harrold Carswell, an unremarkable lower federal court judge from Florida who could boast neither exceptional legal training nor conspicuous competence on the bench. He was, however, a white Southerner and that point was made clear, too clear, when Carswell's earlier commitment to segregation was revealed by the press.

G. Harrold Carswell was in a very different category from Clement Haynsworth. An honest and competent, if not innovative, judge, Haynsworth had failed to be confirmed primarily for political reasons. Carswell showed neither the skills nor the judicial temperament that would have distinguished him as a lower federal court judge, much less as a justice of the U.S. Supreme Court. Still, conservatives in the Nixon administration and Congress insisted on lumping the two failed Court nominees together, victims, they suggested, of a liberal vendetta. Inevitably, they counterattacked.

Shortly after the Carswell defeat, the Vice-President of the United States, Spiro T. Agnew, announced that Haynsworth and Carswell had "been denied seats on the bench for statements that are much less reprehensible than those, in my opinion, by Justice Douglas." On Capitol Hill, Congressman Ford reported that a "bi-partisan" group in the House of Representatives would press an investigation into Justice Douglas's fitness for office. According to Ford and others, Ford was a moderating influence on some of his colleagues, who were angrier and more emotional about the issue. "Jerry was in the position of being stampeded or of staying in front of the pack," said one Capitol Hill source.

Later, on the floor of the House, Ford specified the charges against Douglas:

1. Douglas had sold an article on folk singing to *Fact* magazine for $350 at a time when the magazine's publisher, Ralph Ginzburg, was a defendant in a libel suit pending in the federal courts. The suit eventually reached the Supreme Court, where a majority sustained a lower-court judgment against Ginzburg. Douglas dissented. Had Douglas sold his soul and vote to Ginzburg for $350? Apparently Ford thought so, terming Douglas's participation in the case a "gross impropriety."

2. Douglas had served as a "well-paid moonlighter" for the Parvin Foundation since 1962. Ford was not content, however, to remind his colleagues in the House of the Douglas-Parvin connection, a charge that had first been reported in 1966 and debated both before and after Douglas resigned from the foundation in May 1969. Instead Ford embellished the charge by dropping the names of an assortment of gamblers and mobsters, from Bugsy Siegel to Meyer Lansky to "Ice Pick Willie" Alderman. Some of them had never done business with Albert Parvin; none had ever been directly connected with Douglas.

3. Douglas had worked for the "leftish" Center for the Study of Democratic Institutions in Santa Barbara, California. The center's transgressions, in Ford's view, had included sponsoring a 1965 meeting of New Leftists and a 1967 meeting of student militants. There was no evidence that Douglas had participated in either event. Ford failed to mention that the center had also sponsored symposiums in which such non-leftists as the new Chief Justice of the United States, Warren E. Burger, had participated.

4. Douglas's *Points of Rebellion* was an "inflammatory volume" which subscribed in spirit to "the militant hippie-yippie movement." Ford was further appalled by the company Douglas's literary efforts kept, but bravely refrained from describing the explicit sex scenes in the issue of *Evergreen* that carried excerpts from *Points*.

Ford's attack was a blustery blend of fact and innuendo that would have been ludicrous if it had not been so serious. Nothing in Ford's potpourri of charges could fairly fit into the category of impeachable offenses in the Constitution.* But that did not deter Ford. "An impeachable offense," Ford said, "is whatever a majority of the House of Representatives considers it to be at a given moment in history."

Fortunately for Douglas, while Ford was making his speech on the floor of the House, Representative Andrew Jacobs, Jr. (Democrat, Indiana) marched to the well of the House and dropped into the hopper a resolution to impeach Douglas. By his action, Jacobs, a liberal Democrat, transferred the Douglas investigation from a select committee (favored by Ford) to the Judiciary Committee, which was chaired by liberal Democrat Emanuel Celler of New York. Later, Ford and other Douglas critics in the House charged that the investigation of Douglas by a judiciary subcommittee, also chaired by Celler, was a "whitewash." "The committee's investigation was a travesty," Ford later wrote. "Members didn't hold public hearings, examine witnesses under oath or make public the pertinent documents they obtained." Celler's subcommittee also managed to keep the investigation going be-

---

*Under Article II, Section 4, of the Constitution, a justice can be impeached for "Treason, Bribery, or other high Crimes and Misdemeanors."

yond the November elections, and thereby took pressure off many congressmen, whose constituents were outraged by Douglas's conduct, to vote impeachment.

The first tangible result of the political attack on Douglas was a tenfold jump in sales of *Points of Rebellion*. "It was like being banned in Boston," said a spokesman for Douglas's publisher, Random House.

Meanwhile Douglas went jauntily on his way, appearing to welcome his newest claim to notoriety. At a symposium on *Points of Rebellion* held at the Brooklyn Law School, Douglas listened indifferently as Sidney Hook, the noted conservative philosophy professor from New York University, attacked *Points* as "sheer caricature of the situation in this country." Hook added, "Exaggeration, thy name is Justice Douglas."

When it was his turn to speak, Douglas gestured with his thumb toward Hook and said, "I recommend that he not even open my next book," which, Douglas promised, would be "very, very upsetting." Later, he looked wistfully out the window and noted that it was a much better day for a hike than a symposium full of earnest declarations of opposition to violence.

No threat of impeachment, not even a resolution, signed by 110 members of the House of Representatives, that called for the investigation into the charges leveled against him, could shake Douglas's complacency. But a few of Douglas's close friends, like Clark Clifford, Ben Cohen and David Ginsburg, did not share Douglas's attitude. They had carefully analyzed Ford's speech on the floor of the House and the resolution calling for an investigation, and had concluded that the impeachment proceeding was nothing less than an effort by the Nixon administration to stifle dissent and build a campaign issue for the fall election. Despite Ford's strong denial, they believed that the Nixon administration was deeply involved in the effort and that for both Douglas's and the nation's sake, the Justice had to fight back.

"We called a meeting in Washington," Simon Rifkind, a close Douglas friend and law school classmate, recalled. "Bill did not take the matter as seriously as we did. He had been on the bench a long time and was fearless of what he could be accused of. He was indifferent to the opinion of the man on the street. If Mr.

Ford wanted to fulminate, it was okay by Douglas. He treated the whole controversy with contempt.

"But we finally convinced him that the matter was serious and that he needed counsel. If possible, we thought his attorney should be a young man, in his forties or fifties, preferably a Republican and a WASP. That's how I got elected." (Rifkind was sixty-eight years old, a Democrat and a Jew. He was also a former federal judge, was a senior partner in the powerful New York law firm of Paul, Weiss, Rifkind, Wharton & Garrison, and was generally acknowledged to be one of the toughest and shrewdest attorneys in the country.)

Douglas told Rifkind to do what he thought was appropriate. Rifkind put Douglas "under wraps," vetoing any Douglas speeches or articles that might be controversial. More important, Rifkind organized a team of lawyers who, in Rifkind's words, "prepared for Ford's impeachment attack like we would a murder trial." With Douglas's full cooperation, they studied every piece of paper in Douglas's office that did not relate to Court business. They also read and analyzed every speech and newspaper article critical of Douglas and tracked down every rumor that attacked their client. And they met every wild attack with a cool, detached legal response. If, for example, the anti-Douglas forces charged that Douglas had been in Santo Domingo for political purposes, Rifkind and company would produce documentary evidence that Douglas had been in Buffalo on the particular day mentioned. Responding to Ford's specific charges, Rifkind wrote:

1. On the Ginzburg case: "The Justice never has had any dealings with Ralph Ginzburg."

2. On Douglas's connection with the Parvin Foundation and Albert Parvin's associations with alleged international gamblers: "The foundation has no connection with the international gambling fraternity. . . . Justice Douglas does not know the alleged underworld persons named in the attacks upon him. . . . In serving as a director of the Parvin Foundation, and receiving modest compensation for such services, Douglas follows a long precedent—as, for example, did Chief Justice Warren Burger and Justice Harry Blackmun with respect to the Mayo Foundation and the Kahler Corporation."

3. On the Douglas association with the Center for the Study of Democratic Institutions: "Mr. Douglas has participated in the activities of one of the free world's great academic institutions . . . so have Chief Justice Earl Warren, Chief Justice Warren Burger . . . and scores of other distinguished Americans."

4. On *Points of Rebellion* and the excerpts in *Evergreen:* "The attack on the Justice's book . . . is not only profoundly subversive of the First Amendment, but is based upon an inexcusable distortion of what the Justice actually wrote. . . . The book . . . is a patriotic call for our democratic processes to meet challenges of the day so as to pull the rug from under a small minority advocating violent rebellion. . . . The Justice did not authorize its [*Evergreen*'s] editors to reprint a portion of his book. Pursuant to its standard contractual rights, Random House made that decision."

Rifkind was equally adept at diffusing Ford's constitutional argument. Although the Constitution provides for impeachment for conviction of treason, bribery "or other high Crimes and Misdemeanors," Ford had argued that the impeachment clause should be read with the phrase in Article III that stated that judges of the Supreme Court and inferior courts "shall hold their Offices during Good Behavior." He was bolstered by a legal study by two Detroit lawyers which concluded that "it is the conscience of Congress" that determines whether conduct of judges is impeachable. "If a judge's misbehavior is so grave as to cast substantial doubt upon his integrity," the study concluded, "he must be removed from office, regardless of all other considerations."

Rifkind insisted that members of the subcommittee of the House Judiciary Committee investigating Douglas concentrate exclusively on the impeachment clause. "A careful examination of the Constitution itself," wrote Rifkind, "clearly demonstrates that Federal judges may be impeached only upon charges of 'Treason, Bribery, or other high Crimes and Misdemeanors.' There is nothing in the Constitution . . . to suggest that Federal judges may be impeached for anything short of criminal conduct." Later, in response to Ford's position, Rifkind wrote: "Mr. Ford's definition of an impeachable offense means that judges serve at the pleasure of Congress. This is so utterly destructive of the principles of an independent judiciary and the separation of powers that I could not believe that convincing historical support could be found for so radical a proposition. Now that I have read the Kelly [one of the Detroit lawyers] memorandum I am more than ever convinced that Mr. Ford's view is historically and legally as untenable as it is mischievous."

On December 3, 1970, the three Democratic members of the subcommittee investigating Justice Douglas concluded, as Ford had anticipated, that there were no grounds for impeachment. The two Republican members of the committee refused to join the majority. One of the Republicans, Representative Edward Hutchinson of Michigan, admitted that he would not have demanded Douglas's impeachment, but criticized the committee for not facing the issue of whether Justice Douglas's activities "seem so improper to merit congressional censure or other official criticism of the House."

The massive (924 pages) subcommittee report effectively ended all serious talk of Douglas's impeachment. It met Ford's exaggerated charges, as Rifkind had, with carefully documented responses. But the report, while blunting impeachment talk, raised serious questions about the propriety of Douglas's conduct. Among the report's findings:

1. From 1960 to 1969, Douglas made more money from his off-the-bench activities than from his judicial duties. His judicial salary totaled $389,749.26. For the same period he received $377,260.19 in fees for writing and lecturing. The Parvin Foundation paid him at least $96,680. (Not included in the subcommittee report were figures on Douglas's outside income for 1970; in the first six months of the year alone, he earned $20,568.10 from lectures, articles and books.)

2. Douglas had tried to borrow money from Albert Parvin to buy lots adjoining the Douglas house in Goose Prairie, Washington. Parvin told Douglas he would be happy to make the loan, but that it might be embarrassing to Douglas. The loan was not made.

3. As president of the tax-exempt Parvin Foundation, Douglas had once approved a loan of its funds at a loss for the personal use of the foundation's benefactor, Albert Parvin.

4. Douglas and his wife accepted expensive gifts, including a portable bar and a set of sterling flatware, from Albert Parvin.

Douglas also bought $3,350.23 worth of furniture, apparently at cost, through the Parvin-Dohrmann Corporation.

The impeachment of Justice Douglas would have dealt a devastating blow to our constitutional system. The Constitution's framers had not intended to give Congress the power through the impeachment clause to remove judges for partisan political reasons. George Mason, one of the framers, had suggested, for example, that the term "maladministration" be included among impeachable offenses. But James Madison had objected that so "vague a term will be equivalent to a tenure during the pleasure of the Senate."

If political conservatives who did not like Douglas's opinions could harass him and ultimately drive him from the Court on charges that the Constitution's framers clearly did not intend to be impeachable offenses, then the judiciary could no longer be considered independent. It would be subservient to the political will of the legislature.

Short of impeachment, however, some of the charges against Douglas did raise serious questions about his judgment. His financial obligations and his peripatetic life style undoubtedly placed severe strains on his salary as a U.S. Supreme Court Justice. He supplemented that income by lecturing for large fees and writing books. Some of his books were very good and others, like *Points of Rebellion,* seemed to have been churned out for the quick buck. Douglas engaged in other matters, like heading the Parvin Foundation, that could have presented conflicts of interest. There was nothing, to be sure, that was dishonest or patently unethical in what the Justice did. But if Douglas could globe-trot at Parvin's expense, other justices could do the same or worse. And as Parvin's generosity toward Douglas suggested, the line between proper and improper financial arrangements by justices with private businessmen was very thin indeed. Douglas had not crossed the line, but he had inched dangerously close to it. Next time, pressed by financial problems, he, or others following his example, might be compromised.

And what did the impeach-Douglas movement suggest about the target of the inquiry? First, that Douglas had antagonized many in the country with his liberal rulings and young wives.

Second, that Douglas and his friends seemed equal to any political challenge to push him off the Court. And third, that his judgment was fallible, though he was increasingly reluctant to admit it. In his latter years on the Court, Douglas began to assume that whatever he did was correct, simply because *he* had done it.

KING RICHARD

For fourteen months, B-52s pounded the Cambodian countryside with tons of bombs ordered personally by the President of the United States, Richard Nixon. The President did not tell the American public about the bombing, nor did he inform members of Congress. The President did not even trust responsible Pentagon officials with his secret; they were given false military reports. In 1970, the year after the bombing had begun, the President sent U.S. ground troops into Cambodia to sweep sanctuaries that the military believed were being used by the Communists to attack American units in South Vietnam. The American troops pulled out of Cambodia when their mission had been accomplished. But the bombing was later resumed, obliterating whole Cambodian villages and many thousands of Cambodian peasants.

The President never doubted that he had the constitutional authority to send our bombers and troops into Cambodia. In fact, he did not even bother to assign State Department lawyers the task of justifying his action until four days after he had dispatched the troops. When he did ask for a comprehensive legal brief for his constitutional authority to do what he had already done, he gave the assignment to his Assistant Attorney General, William H. Rehnquist.

The critical issue, not easily resolved by a reading of the Constitution or the opinions of the U.S. Supreme Court, was whether the President could initiate hostilities against a foreign power without a declaration of war by Congress. The Constitution gives Congress the exclusive power to declare war, but makes the President the commander in chief of the armed forces. Many past Presidents, from Jefferson to Lyndon Johnson, had initiated hostilities without a declaration of war and their actions were justified, Rehnquist argued, by the President's constitutional authority as the commander in chief. No Supreme Court decision, Rehnquist noted, had contradicted that view.

The primary problem with Rehnquist's interpretation was that no past President had presumed to do what Richard Nixon had done in Cambodia. During the nineteenth century, American armed forces had been used by Presidents on their own authority for such purposes as suppressing piracy and protecting American lives and property in backward areas where government had broken down. But the Cambodian invasion was a far cry from the suppression of piracy, and to suggest that the invasion and prolonged bombing was an effort to protect American lives and property in an emergency was stretching the constitutional point beyond recognition.

In the twentieth century, Presidents from Teddy Roosevelt to Lyndon Johnson had committed substantial troops to foreign soil. But even in the most questionable case of a President assuming constitutional authority, the involvement of massive manpower and weaponry by Lyndon Johnson in Vietnam, a strong argument could be made that the President acted with the implied consent of Congress. For though Congress had never declared war on North Vietnam, it had given various indications that it approved of Lyndon Johnson's actions, from the express endorsement of the President's policies in the Joint Congressional ("Tonkin Gulf") Resolution of 1964 to the continuous congressional appropriation of millions of dollars for the U.S. military effort.

Congress had never sanctioned Richard Nixon's Cambodian

adventure. In fact, Congress had pointedly approved military appropriations only so long as the funds were not used to finance an extension of the war in Southeast Asia. And if the continuous bombing of Cambodia was not an extension of the war, what was it?

The question occurred to Representative Elizabeth Holtzman of New York and to several military officers, who, in April 1973, joined her in bringing suit against the Nixon administration to stop the bombing in Cambodia. They made their constitutional argument before U.S. District Judge Orrin Judd in the Southern District of New York, the same judge who had earlier ruled that Lyndon Johnson's actions in Vietnam had been given Congress's imprimatur and, therefore, were constitutional. This time, however, Orrin Judd ruled against the President. He said that Richard Nixon had not been supported by congressional action, as Lyndon Johnson had. He said that Richard Nixon had acted and was continuing to act without constitutional authority. He said, finally, that the bombing in Cambodia must stop.

Could a single U.S. district court judge in New York City stop the bombing in Cambodia? Administration officials did not wait for the answer, but immediately appealed Orrin Judd's decision to a higher court. The U.S. Court of Appeals for the Second Circuit, exercising characteristic judicial caution, stayed Judd's order and set argument on the merits of the issue for August 15. By this time, the Justices of the U.S. Supreme Court had scattered to their summer retreats. Undeterred, Representative Holtzman carried her argument to Justice Thurgood Marshall, who was authorized to hear such appeals in the Second Circuit when the Supreme Court was not in session.

The task of Thurgood Marshall was made more complicated because Congress, with the President's grudging consent and after the initiation of the Holtzman suit, had set an absolute deadline of August 15 for the cessation of the bombing of Cambodia. It was already August 1. Any decision by Marshall or, later, the full Supreme Court would be rendered academic in just two weeks. Should the judiciary go on record, nonetheless, with a decision on the constitutionality of the President's actions? Holtzman did not hesitate to give her answer. "Lives are being risked every day and every day we're spending $5 million on this war," she said. "The incredible thing would be to have it on my conscience or the conscience of any American to have somebody killed in a war that was unconstitutional."

The argument of Elizabeth Holtzman contained considerable moral authority. Holtzman also seemed to have constitutional authority on her side, as Justice Marshall, in his twelve-page opinion, admitted. "A fair reading of Congress' actions concerning the war," wrote Marshall, "is that the legislature has authorized only 'partial hostilities'—that it has never given its approval to the war except to the extent that it was necessary to extricate American troops and prisoners from Vietnam. Moreover, this Court could easily conclude that after the Paris Peace accords, the Cambodian bombing is no longer justifiable as an extension of the war which Congress did authorize and that the bombing is not required by the type of pressing emergency which necessitates immediate Presidential response."

Ultimately, however, Justice Marshall did not rely on the text of the Constitution or on moral authority for his conclusion. Instead he leaned on a venerable judicial tradition, formalized as the "political question" doctrine. The essence of that doctrine is that some issues are of such political import, and so defy the rational standards under which courts are obligated to work, that they are better left to the political branches of government to resolve. To Marshall, the issue he was asked to decide seemed to fit into the "political question" category. In refusing to reinstate Judge Judd's order to stop the bombing in Cambodia, Marshall noted that the judiciary was probably the least qualified branch of government to weigh foreign policy and that problem was compounded when he, a single jurist, was asked to make such a momentous decision. The bombing continued.

Although it is always open to a litigant to make a constitutional argument to a second Supreme Court justice after the first has ruled unfavorably, the option is rarely taken. An argument takes time and money, and it is generally assumed that one member of the Court will not take it upon himself to reverse a second member. Reading down the list of members of the Court, beginning with the newest appointee, William H. Rehnquist, it seemed that Representative Holtzman had only one realistic choice in seeking a reversal. It was, of course, Justice Douglas, a man with a long history as the Court's maverick liberal, who had expressed, on many occasions, his serious doubts about the constitutionality of U.S. military involvement in Southeast Asia.*

Justice Douglas met the attorneys in the Holtzman suit in a Yakima courtroom, about a forty-minute ride from his mountain retreat in Goose Prairie. The argument lasted for an hour, with the attorney for Representative Holtzman arguing that the President was acting unconstitutionally and the attorney for the government urging Douglas to exercise judicial restraint in the face of a protracted political problem. At the end of the hour, Douglas said that he was returning to Goose Prairie to ponder his decision. He also said that the attorneys would not have to wait long for his opinion. He did not, he added, intend to wait until his decision would become moot at the August 15 bombing deadline.

Less than twenty-four hours later, at 9:30 A.M. on August 4, Justice Douglas reinstated the lower-court order to stop the bombing in Cambodia. In his opinion, Douglas first paid his respects to his colleague Thurgood Marshall, whose own opinion was entitled to "the greatest deference." But once the judicial amenities were completed, Douglas reversed his colleague, offering a provocative reading of constitutional law with a larger statement on the politics and morality of the bombing in Cambodia.

The legality of the Cambodian bombing presented an issue, to Douglas, that was no different from that of an ordinary capital case. He explained: "The classic capital case is whether Mr. Lew, Mr. Low or Mr. Lucas should die. The present case involves whether Mr. X (an unknown person or persons) should die. No one knows who they are. They may be Cambodian farmers whose only 'sin' is a desire for socialized medicine to alleviate the suffering of their families and neighbors. Or Mr. X may be the American pilot or navigator who drops a ton of bombs on a Cambodian village. The upshot is that we know that someone is about to die."

Just as he had been willing to stay the execution of Ethel and Julius Rosenberg two decades earlier, Douglas was ready to do the same for the unknown Cambodian peasants he was sure

*Douglas had written eight opinions dissenting from the Court's denial of certiorari where the issue of the constitutionality of U.S. military involvement in Vietnam was raised. In those opinions, Douglas had also expressed his doubts on the merits of the issue.

would die without his decision. The analogy between an ordinary capital case, such as the Rosenbergs', and the Cambodian challenge was not quite apt. In the Rosenberg case Douglas was preserving the status quo so that the Rosenbergs' attorneys might argue a new point of law. With his opinion ordering a bombing halt in Cambodia, Douglas was not preserving the status quo but disrupting it, by effectively ruling that the President's action was unconstitutional.

Only Congress could declare war and Congress had not done so, Douglas wrote. And even if an undeclared war such as the one in Vietnam could be justified, "the Cambodian bombing is quite a different affair." Douglas strongly suggested (though he did not state it formally) that President Nixon's action was illegal and the judiciary was obligated to say so.

Despite Justice Douglas's order, the bombing in Cambodia did not stop. Officials at the Pentagon explained that they had refused to comply with Douglas's decision while the administration attempted to gain a reversal by the full Supreme Court. It took the administration a very short time to succeed. At 3:30 P.M. on August 4, only six hours after the Douglas decision was announced, eight members of the Supreme Court reversed Douglas. That had been accomplished by Thurgood Marshall, who, responding to Douglas's decision, had polled the other members of the Court by telephone. They had been unanimous in condemning Douglas's action.

Douglas did not respond graciously to his colleagues' rebuke. "The reported action of the Court was without precedent," he said. "From what I can learn, other members of the Court had not even read my decision." His colleagues' action, Douglas later asserted, was "a subversion of the regime under which I thought we lived."

The members of the Supreme Court returned to their summer vacations, having safely deposited the issue of the legality of the Cambodian bombing with the Court of Appeals for the Second Circuit, which had earlier agreed to hear arguments on the merits (and now moved the date of the argument up a week). Six days after Douglas had issued his opinion, the three-judge appellate court, by a two to one vote, ruled that the bombing was a political question beyond the competence of the judiciary to decide. The bombing continued until August 15, the day that Congress had mandated that it must stop.

Douglas's opinion was condemned by many sophisticated Court observers, even those who had abhorred the Cambodian bombing and had questioned Richard Nixon's right to initiate it. But condemning the Cambodian bombing was one thing; rushing to a dramatic judicial solution, as Justice Douglas had done, was quite another. The rationale for the bifurcated view was familiar, supported by many of the voluminous opinions of Justice Felix Frankfurter. Courts are not equipped to solve political issues, the argument went, particularly when they involve the imprecise calculations of foreign policy. In addition, the spectacle of one justice of the Supreme Court overruling the careful deliberations of another, as Douglas had done, did not encourage public respect for the judiciary.

Despite the persuasive intellectual tug of that position, there was something hauntingly compelling about Representative Holtzman's urgent plea and Justice Douglas's response. If the judiciary did not stop the bombing in an unconstitutional war, even for a week or two, lives would be lost and cautious judges would, in part, be to blame.

Two days after Douglas had ruled that the Cambodian bombing must stop, and the full Court overruled him, American planes bombed the Cambodian town of Neak Luong *by mistake,* killing 137 Cambodian soldiers and civilians. A day later, a U.S. plane again bombed the wrong target, killing eight Cambodians and injuring sixteen others. Later, a Cambodian military spokesman reported that there had been at least five U.S. bombing errors over Cambodia in the final weeks before the bombing cessation. No casualty figures were given.

Douglas's action in the Cambodian bombing litigation dramatized, perhaps more than any other single opinion in his last years on the Court, why he had built such a large following in the liberal political community and why, at the same time, he so exasperated the more conservative majority, including many of his colleagues on the U.S. Supreme Court. In his public opinions and private actions, Douglas epitomized the hero in American history, the single man who could make a difference, who defied the conventional wisdom of institutions and men with considerably more power than he possessed. From the U.S. Supreme Court, historically one of the sturdiest bastions of conservative political thought and style, Douglas pelted the political establishment with ideas that they did not want to hear from anyone, and most certainly not from a Supreme Court justice.

Douglas's isolation from the President as well as from the majority on the Court had been building for years, even before Richard Nixon was elected to the presidency in 1968. The split between Douglas and Lyndon Johnson over the President's Vietnam policies had, by the middle sixties, become deep and irreparable. The severance of the relationship was particularly shattering because the two had formed a close personal friendship when Johnson was a raw New Deal congressman from Texas. Douglas's first wife, Mildred, had tutored the Johnson children in Latin and Johnson had entertained Douglas in his home. Johnson promoted Douglas for Truman's cabinet after the war, and almost a decade and a half later, Douglas reportedly offered to leave the Court to campaign for Johnson for President. The respect that the two held for each other was generously expressed at the dinner in Douglas's honor in 1964. "Above all," said President Johnson, "Bill Douglas is the symbol of the Responsible Man— the one soul that makes the difference—the individual who cannot be denied—or defeated." And Douglas, in turn, said Lyndon Johnson taught him compassion, conscience, fair-dealing, courage and humility.

After that 1964 dinner, however, Douglas rode back to the White House with Johnson and lashed out at the President's Vietnam policy. "Douglas gave the President hell about his Vietnam war policy," recalled Sidney Davis, a Douglas friend who was present. "Douglas told the President that our position was not just and the President told him, 'This doesn't have anything to do with justice—this is war.' They argued for hours about it."

Later, Douglas put his protests into the official record, writing dissent after dissent, pleading with his judicial colleagues to respond to the constitutional question: could the President continue to escalate the war in Vietnam without a declaration of war from Congress? The Warren Court majority never agreed to hear arguments on the merits of the issue, presumably for the same reasons that the Burger Court avoided that issue and later the Holtzman suit challenging the bombing in Cambodia. The issues were fraught with political consequences for the Court and the country and did not, to a large Court majority, recommend themselves to judicial resolution.

In protesting the Warren Court majority's timorousness on the Vietnam War issue, Douglas came very close to delivering an opinion on the merits. In numerous opinions when the issue was pressed upon the Court, he suggested that the President's action in Vietnam was unconstitutional. Despite Douglas's protests, every member of the libertarian Warren Court majority, except William O. Douglas, persisted in ducking the Vietnam War issue.

Douglas escalated his private war with his judicial colleagues when the issue arose of the right of two draftees, one a devout Catholic and the other a humanist, to qualify for conscientious objector status during the Vietnam War. Both men said they were morally opposed to the Vietnam War because they believed it was unjust. The C.O. status was properly denied, wrote Justice Marshall for an eight-man Court majority, because the two draftees were not opposed to serving in all wars. To Douglas, dissenting alone, it did not matter whether the young men objected to all wars on moral grounds or simply the Vietnam War; the First Amendment protected their beliefs.

Douglas's isolation from his colleagues became the subject of a joke by his admirers. During a recess at the trial of Dr. Benjamin Spock in Boston in 1968, the story goes, it was reported that the Supreme Court had upheld the federal statute that made it a crime to burn draft cards. "What was the vote?" asked a dejected civil liberties attorney. "Seven* to Douglas," was the reply.

During the impeachment attempt in 1970 and for the rest of his days on the Court, Douglas was convinced that Richard Nixon had been the driving force behind Gerald Ford's investigation. Whether Nixon actually engineered the impeachment drive or simply offered moral support and the help of his staff, the President undoubtedly wanted Douglas off the Court. The reasons were scattered throughout Douglas's judicial opinions.

---

*Justice Marshall took no part in the decision.

For years, Douglas had opposed the unchecked power of the executive branch. In 1952, he had expressed that opposition in the most celebrated confrontation between the Court and the President in the post–World War II era. Joining five of his colleagues, Douglas had condemned President Truman's seizure of the nation's steel mills when a strike was threatened during the Korean War. In his concurring opinion, Douglas noted that the power assumed by the President properly resided in the Congress. "We pay a price for our system of checks and balances, for the distribution of power among the three branches of government," Douglas wrote. "It is a price that today may seem exorbitant to many. Today a kindly President uses the seizure power to effect a wage increase and to keep the steel furnaces in production. Yet tomorrow another President might use the same power to prevent a wage increase, to curb trade-unionists, to regiment labor as oppressively as industry thinks it has been regimented by this seizure."

No modern American President—not Harry Truman, certainly not Dwight Eisenhower, not even Lyndon B. Johnson—rivaled Richard Nixon's appetite for unchecked presidential power. As Arthur Schlesinger, Jr., has written, the imperial presidency grew to terrifying proportions during the terms of Richard Nixon. Nixon coveted both the trimmings of monarchy (what other President would have ordered operetta uniforms for White House guards?) and the arbitrary powers of monarchy itself. Neither Truman nor Johnson had carried out their most ambitious plans without consulting, before or immediately afterward, with Congress and the American people. But Richard Nixon ruled alone and in secrecy.

Douglas opposed Richard Nixon's imperial presidency in foreign policy, as his opinion in the Cambodian bombing suit demonstrated. He also delivered lectures on Nixon's domestic transgressions long before the revelations of Watergate had condemned the President to a sordid chapter in American history. Unlike his attack on the Cambodian bombing, Douglas's judicial opinions excoriating the Nixon administration's domestic policies trod familiar ground: the Bill of Rights.

In 1971, Richard Nixon censored the press in the name of national security. The challenge quickly became known as the

Pentagon Papers Case, because it involved the publication of the secret multivolume history of U.S. involvement in the Vietnam War that had been commissioned by the Secretary of Defense. First *The New York Times* had published a narrative and some of the documents from the study, which it had received from a former Defense Department employee, Daniel Ellsberg. When the Nixon administration succeeded in court in temporarily enjoining the *Times*'s publication, the controversy moved to the *Washington Post,* which had also obtained a copy of the study from Ellsberg. The *Post*'s publication was also stopped.

Because the case involved censorship, the most drastic invasion of the First Amendment freedom of the press, the U.S. Supreme Court agreed, within days of the lower-court decisions, to hear arguments. Appearing before the justices, U.S. Solicitor General Erwin Griswold dispelled any notion that he hoped to win the votes of the Court's most outspoken libertarians, Justices Black and Douglas. "You say that no law [abridging free press] means no law and that should be obvious," Griswold told Justice Black. "I can only say, Mr. Justice, that to me it is equally obvious that 'no law' does not mean 'no law' and I would seek to persuade the Court that is true." The government's main argument was that the publication of the Pentagon Papers could jeopardize ongoing diplomatic negotiations and consequently cost thousands of lives if the war were prolonged. That justified, in Griswold's view, the censorship because the national security interests of the United States outweighed the First Amendment claims.

Douglas remained silent during the Solicitor General's presentation, but became very active during the argument of the *Times*'s attorney, Yale Professor Alexander Bickel. In a hostile exchange, Douglas gave Bickel, the former Frankfurter clerk, a tongue-lashing for not claiming for his client an absolute right to publish. What the *Times* did claim, argued Bickel, was that the government show a much closer, direct link between the publication of the Pentagon Papers and the harm to the national security than the government had proved.

Six members of the Court rejected the Solicitor General's argument and their decision allowed the *Times* and the *Post* once again to go to press with their stories on the Pentagon Papers. The pivotal opinion was written by Justice Potter Stewart, who admitted that the Nixon administration had a constitutional right to protect the nation's security. The flaw in the government's position, said Stewart, had been that no evidence of "direct, immediate and irreparable" harm to the national security had been presented.

The language of the Stewart opinion was altogether too temperate for Justice Douglas, who wrote in his concurring opinion that the First Amendment

> leaves, in my view, no room for governmental restraint on the press. . . . The dominant purpose of the First Amendment was to prohibit the widespread practice of governmental suppression of embarrassing information. It is common knowledge that the First Amendment was adopted against the widespread use of the common law of seditious libel to punish the dissemination of material that is embarrassing to the powers-that-be. The present case will, I think, go down in history as the most dramatic illustration of that principle. A debate of large proportions goes on in the Nation over our posture in Vietnam. That debate antedated the disclosure of the contents of the present documents. The latter are highly relevant to the debate in progress.

Both of Richard Nixon's appointees who sat on the Court at the time dissented from the majority's view in the Pentagon Papers decision. Chief Justice Warren Burger, a "law and order" jurist who was best known for his criticism of libertarian Warren Court opinions in the criminal procedure field, found the newspapers' haste to publish irresponsible. "To me, it is hardly believable that a newspaper long regarded as a great institution in American life would fail to perform one of the basic and simple duties of every citizen with respect to the discovery or possession of stolen property or secret government documents. That duty, I had thought —perhaps naïvely—was to report forthwith, to responsible public officers. This duty rests on taxi drivers, justices and *The New York Times.*" The President's second appointee, Harry Blackmun, was so outraged by the newspapers' conduct that he was prepared to blame them for any harm to the nation that might come from publication of the Pentagon Papers. Neither Burger nor Blackmun devoted much space in their opinions to the value of the free press guarantee of the First Amendment.

By the time that President Nixon had completed his judicial appointments and made good on his promise to appoint "strict constructionists" to the Court, Douglas represented, more than ever, the extreme libertarian position on the Court's greatly diminished liberal wing. Justice Hugo Black, senior member of the famous libertarian partnership of Black and Douglas, was gone, succeeded by Lewis Powell, Jr. Like Black, Powell was a courtly Southerner and an excellent lawyer. But that was where the similarities ended. A former president of the American Bar Association and a partner in Virginia's most prestigious law firm, Powell had been a centrist in politics and promised to steer a similar course on the Court. Nixon's fourth appointee was the Assistant Attorney General who had argued the constitutionality of the President's Cambodian action, William H. Rehnquist. Throughout his legal career, Rehnquist had impressed everyone with two conspicuous attributes: his brilliance and his bedrock conservative philosophy.

Only a few months after his appointment had been confirmed, Rehnquist became embroiled in a controversy involving a constitutional challenge to the U.S. Army's widespread surveillance of civil rights and antiwar activists. The purpose of the army's surveillance, ostensibly, was to prepare for assistance in the event of civil disorder. A group of antiwar activists began a lawsuit to stop the army's operation, claiming that the surveillance violated their First Amendment rights to speech, press and association and their right to privacy.

As Assistant Attorney General, Rehnquist had been asked by the Senate subcommittee on constitutional rights if he thought that the government had the right to snoop on American citizens. Without hesitation, Rehnquist replied that he believed the government did have that power. At that same hearing, Rehnquist was asked specifically about the legal position taken by the antiwar activists who had challenged the army surveillance operation. The Assistant Attorney General said that he disagreed with the activists' contention that citizens could sue to stop army surveillance.

What made this 1971 exchange between Assistant Attorney General Rehnquist and the Senate subcommittee significant was the fact that less than a year later, as a justice of the U.S. Supreme

Court, Rehnquist cast the decisive fifth vote in support of his earlier view. Joined by the three other Nixon appointees to the Court and Justice White, Rehnquist ruled that the antiwar activists had not been harmed by the army's surveillance, and therefore did not have standing to initiate a lawsuit. Later, Rehnquist, criticized for having participated in a case in which he had already expressed his views, responded that "proof that a Justice's mind at the time he joined the Court was a complete tabula rasa [clean slate] in the field of constitutional adjudication would be evidence of a lack of qualification, not lack of bias."

Almost overlooked in the controversy over Rehnquist's participation in the case was one of the most stirring pleas for a return to the protection of civil liberties that Justice Douglas ever wrote. But before he reached the civil liberties issue, Douglas disposed of a procedural point on which, for many years, he had vehemently disagreed with his colleagues, even his libertarian colleagues on the Warren Court. The debate had focused on the "standing" requirement that had to be met before a litigant could argue his case in a court of law. The U.S. Supreme Court had always been wary of discontented citizens who wanted to complain in court about some government action. Traditionally, the Court had insisted that to have his day in court, a litigant must show a personal injury greater than that of an ordinary citizen or taxpayer. The Warren Court had eased that standard, but had never fully abandoned it. Douglas, on the other hand, had consistently argued that the "standing" doctrine was often just another way to frustrate the legitimate constitutional claims of American citizens. He would open the courts to all citizens with substantial constitutional grievances, and that included the antiwar activists who were protesting the army's surveillance operation. Having disposed of the "standing" issue, Douglas wrote:

> This case involves a cancer in our body politic. It is a measure of the disease which afflicts us. Army surveillance, like Army regimentation, is at war with the principles of the First Amendment. Those who already walk submissively will say there is no cause for alarm. But submissiveness is not our heritage. The Constitution was designed to keep the government off the backs of the people. The Bill of Rights was added to keep the precincts of belief and expression, of the press, of political and social activi-

ties free from surveillance. The Bill of Rights was designed to keep agents of government and official eavesdroppers away from assemblies of people. The aim was to allow men to be free and independent and to assert their rights against government. There can be no influence more paralyzing of that objective than Army surveillance. When an intelligence officer looks over every nonconformist's shoulder in the library, or walks invisibly by his side in a picket line, or infiltrates his club, the America once extolled as the voice of liberty heard around the world no longer is cast in the image which Jefferson and Madison designed, but more in the Russian image.

After Hugo Black was gone, Douglas felt an acute sense of loneliness on the Court. That isolation provoked a heightened state of anxiety which pervaded Douglas's thoughts, actions and writings in the last years of Richard Nixon's presidency.

Douglas's concern about the Nixon administration was apparent, for example, in a dissent to an obscure decision in which the Court denied the release on bail of a woman defendant who had maintained that her attorneys had been subjected to electronic surveillance by the government. The Nixon administration is a "regime where the 'dirty business' of wiretapping runs rampant," Douglas wrote. And then he threw in the one-sentence blockbuster that made the front page of *The New York Times*. "I am indeed morally certain that the conference room of the Court has been bugged," Douglas charged. He did not elaborate, but when the charge was denied by the FBI, Douglas did not retract it, either.

Douglas continued to remind the administration that he did not trust their motives or their word when he was again confronted, as he had been in the Pentagon Papers case, with broad claims of government secrecy in the interest of national security. The challenge developed after a newspaper article in 1971 indicated that President Nixon had received conflicting recommendations on the advisability of an underground nuclear test at Amchitka Island, Alaska. Representative Patsy Mink of Hawaii and thirty-two of her colleagues in the House requested release of the recommendations, and when that request was denied, brought an action under the Freedom of Information Act.

Among the legal positions that the Nixon administration had

argued, in defending its right to keep the details of its deliberations secret, was that it had classified six of the documents sought
by the members of Congress as "Secret" or "Top Secret." The
Supreme Court majority ruled that the administration's stamp of
"Secret" and "Top Secret" was conclusive on the issue and that
courts had no further role in the matter. "The majority makes the
stamp [of "Secret" and "Top Secret"] sacrosanct," wrote Douglas in dissent, "thereby immunizing stamped documents from
judicial scrutiny, whether or not factual information contained in
the document is in fact colorably related to interests of the national defense or foreign policy. Yet anyone who has ever been
in the Executive Branch knows how convenient the Top Secret or
Secret stamp is, how easy it is to use, and how it covers perhaps
for decades the footprints of a nervous bureaucrat or a wary
executive."

The reign of Richard Nixon was coming to an end in 1974. The
President had fought tenaciously, resentfully, from his first efforts
to plug the leaks of the "plumbers" to his desperate firing of
Special Prosecutor Archibald Cox. But he could not keep, for
very long, his secrets or his office. The press and the American
public became more insistent in their demands for an explanation
of the abuses of power by his administration. And all three
branches of government tightened the pressure. Senator Sam
Ervin's committee investigating Watergate became more asser-
tive in its claims on the President. Special Prosecutor Cox was
gone, but a new special prosecutor, Leon Jaworski, was at work.
And a previously undistinguished U.S. district court judge named
John Sirica listened attentively to Prosecutor Jaworski's arguments in the trial of several defendants involved in the Watergate
debacle, who were charged with, among other things, conspiracy
to obstruct justice. Richard Nixon was named as an unindicted
co-conspirator in the case.

During the trial, Jaworski requested tapes of conversations that
took place in the White House of Richard Nixon. The President's
lawyer, James St. Clair, argued that those taped conversations
were the privileged property of the President and off limits to
Prosecutor Jaworski and Judge Sirica. The tapes were, St. Clair
contended, the President's alone to hear since they involved mat-

ters of highly sensitive government policy. But Jaworski retorted that such a position put the President above the law and that that could not be possible under our constitutional system. Judge Sirica agreed with Jaworski and demanded that the President hand over the tapes.

From the very first day that Prosecutor Jaworski had requested the White House tapes, President Nixon had been adamant in his refusal to relinquish all of them. When Judge Sirica ruled that he must submit the tapes to the study of the court, the President appealed. While the matter was pending in the U.S. Court of Appeals for the District of Columbia, the U.S. Supreme Court agreed to hear arguments on the issue. At that time, the President suggested that he might remain defiant to the very end, that even if the Supreme Court of the United States ruled against him, he might ignore the decision. A constitutional collision appeared imminent.

Two hundred people waited overnight in front of the U.S. Supreme Court building before the doors opened at 9:00 A.M. on July 6, 1974. One hundred thirty-six of them were rewarded with seats that morning to hear the three-hour-and-two-minute argument in the case of the *United States* v. *President Richard Nixon*. Those spectators merged with lawyers, journalists and guests of the justices, four hundred in all, who listened to the constitutional arguments of Special Prosecutor Leon Jaworski and the President's attorney, James St. Clair. The casual air of St. Clair and the soft Texas twang of Jaworski were disconcerting to a few, who expected history to be made by more impressive actors. "I thought it would be different," said one spectator. "I thought they would, well, talk Latin or something. It was so . . . ordinary."

But there was nothing ordinary about the arguments, and the attorneys, the justices and Richard Nixon knew it. The stakes were not only Richard Nixon's presidency but the very constitutional fabric under which the country had been governed for the previous 185 years. Richard Nixon suggested that no cause, not even a criminal prosecution that challenged, indirectly, his right to govern, should force him to obey a court of law. If he was correct, then the President was immune from the check of a coequal branch of government. He could ignore the judiciary as he had ignored the Congress and the American people with his bombing of Cambodia. He could rule.

The final decision of the U.S. Supreme Court was unanimous.* The only opinion belonged, officially, to President Nixon's first Court appointee, Chief Justice Burger, although other justices drafted major portions of it. The Court said that it was and always had been the duty of the Supreme Court to say, finally, what the law was. In this case, the Court ruled, the President's argument must fail because against his general claim of privilege were the more pressing, specific needs of the criminal justice system. No one, not even the President of the United States, could set himself above that system.

Justice Douglas did not write a word. He did not have to. A unanimous Supreme Court, a Court that included three appointees of Richard Nixon, had said that the President had exceeded his constitutional authority. Douglas said, privately, that the decision in *U.S.* v. *Nixon* was one of the most important decisions in which he had participated in all his years on the Court.

Less than a month later, under mounting pressure for his impeachment, President Richard Nixon resigned.

*The vote was 8–0; Justice Rehnquist took no part in the decision.

CHAPTER THIRTY ────────────────────

FINISHING TOUCHES

In HIS LAST YEARS on the Court, Douglas was treated by his judicial colleagues like an eccentric great-uncle. They admired him but at the same time were grateful that there was only one in the family. "I often wondered what it would be like to have nine members like Bill Douglas," mused one member of the Court, who then answered with a metaphor: "If we had nine opera singers who all wanted leading roles, we'd have a lot of problems."

The Burger Court, even more than its predecessors, was for "team players." The leadership of the Court resided in a coalition of judicial centrists. Potter Stewart and Lewis Powell, both moderates in temperament and philosophy, were crucial members of the coalition. So was Bill Brennan, who, for all his doctrinaire liberalism, had always shown a shrewd political talent for lining up votes. Byron White kept his own counsel but would listen to reason.

Douglas was no help. No member doubted Douglas's genius, but that only infuriated his colleagues. At a time when the Court needed intellectual strength, Douglas seemed indifferent to the challenge. When the spirit moved him, Douglas, all agreed, could write a startlingly brilliant opinion. The trouble was not with the occasional flash of genius, but with the more common superficial treatment of a complex subject. "Some of his stuff was awfully shallow," said one colleague, more in sadness than in anger. "In his last years, Bill seemed bored, jaded," said another.

Douglas suffered in comparison to Hugo Black, who, one colleague recalled, "up to the day he left, acted like a young fellow right out of law school in his involvement and advocacy." On the other hand, Douglas seemed more interested in promoting his liberal philosophy, oblivious to the particular facts of the cases before the Court. "Bill didn't seem to be involved in the decision-making process," said a colleague.

Douglas's attitude was reflected in the way he presided at the justices' Friday conference on the rare occasion when the Chief Justice was away. As senior justice in the Chief's absence, Douglas conducted the meeting and stated the facts of each case before the justices deliberated. When he did preside, Douglas routinely finished the Court's business several hours earlier than usual. After the conference adjourned, Douglas would return to his office, satisfied that he had cut through all the nonessential business which seemed to bog down the Chief. It was a triumph of Douglas's incisive analysis, his staff surmised. But his judicial colleagues held a different opinion. "Bill didn't discuss anything," one said. "He would just say, 'This is a case involving such and such a statute. The issue is such and such. I vote to affirm.' No wonder we were out of there so early."

Douglas often put his new colleagues, appointed by Richard Nixon, on edge, throwing tantrums one minute and making gracious gestures the next. When Harry Blackmun was new to the Court and showing the strains of the job, Douglas did not help matters by responding to one memorandum from Blackmun's office with a blistering critique that bordered on the sadistic. But another time Douglas offered extravagant praise for Blackmun's concern for the environment and suggested that the two shared this common bond.

Douglas once jolted the genteel Lewis Powell after Powell quietly announced that he would be spending the Christmas vacation in his hometown of Richmond. "I'm going to be in my office working," growled Douglas, "and I think you should too." But when columnist Jack Anderson raised ethical questions about Powell's business connections, Douglas comforted his new colleague, saying, "If that's the worst the press says about you while you're on this Court, you'll have done very well."

Perhaps in retaliation for the discomfort Douglas sometimes caused them, his colleagues told anecdotes that pointed up Douglas's weaknesses. They knew the stories of Douglas's brutal treatment of his clerks and did not mind repeating them. And one remembered first seeing Douglas at a bar association meeting, holding hands with his third wife, Joanie, and remarking to his own wife what an affectionate couple they were. Six months later, Douglas and Joanie were separated. During the impeachment attack, it was recalled, Douglas made a rare appearance at the American Bar Association's annual meeting and wooed the organization's staid, conservative members as if he were a political candidate running for office. It was also noted that Douglas, the voice of the common man, monopolized the Court limousine. When a colleague finally was able to persuade Douglas to share the automobile, he discovered that the tension evaporated only after he asked Douglas about his past. "It was good for five or six mornings running," he recalled.

But ultimately, it was not Douglas's egocentricity or perceived hypocrisy that galled his colleagues nearly as much as what they considered his professional irresponsibility. It was not just that he was no team player; he seemed unaware that there was any team to play on. Nothing pointed this out so clearly, or aggravated Douglas's colleagues as much, as his habit of leaving Washington for his vacation home in Goose Prairie several weeks before the end of the term. Every member of the Court, from Brennan to Burger, resented it. "One of our brethren leaves town early," Burger once told the press, "and tries to conduct his business back and forth four thousand miles away or however far it is out there." One member of the Court recalled: "Sometimes he [Douglas] didn't even tell us he was leaving. Then he'd telephone from Goose Prairie to ask me to cast his vote on this, that and the other thing." Douglas's view was that he could conduct any outstanding business by correspondence and telephone. "If every

Justice had done that," said a colleague, "the Court couldn't have functioned."

Maintaining good relations with his colleagues was not a high priority for Douglas. In his last years, he was much more interested in putting the finishing touches on his libertarian judicial portrait. He attempted to do with the law what an artist might accomplish with brush, oils and canvas: bring harmony from natural chaos. Just as no team could duplicate the work of a Cézanne, no cooperative effort at the Court could, or should, Douglas believed, portray the essential truths of the law. Douglas worked quickly, seemingly without great effort, but his broad strokes and vivid hues (there were few grays) distinguished his legal compositions from those of any man who had ever sat on the U.S. Supreme Court.*

To the end, Douglas exhibited a Brandeisian spirit and toughness in his attack on illegal monopolies. He brooked no compromise, as Chief Justice Burger discovered only a few months after taking office. One year earlier, the Warren Court majority, including Douglas, had ordered the El Paso Natural Gas Company, the world's largest gas pipeline company, to divest itself of monopolistic holdings in the West. The new Chief Justice thought the Court had made a grievous error with its decision, and when the gas company petitioned the Court for a rehearing in the case, he saw his opportunity to correct the transgression.

Although there was a long-standing tradition on the Court that new justices would not vote on rehearing petitions, Burger thought the unwritten rule made no sense and decided to challenge it. If the Chief were able to vote, he believed that he had the votes for a rehearing and, eventually, for a reversal in the case. Douglas, however, had no intention of allowing a new Chief

*Douglas's critics pointed to his sloppy technique and the absence of subtle gradations of color. Douglas created unnatural harmonies, they charged, which covered the essential blemishes and grays of the law. His work deserved favorable reviews only if the absence of careful technique—and reality—were excused by the artist's inspired result. In painting, that might be possible; in law, Douglas's critics suggested, it was not. For a devastating attack on Douglas's tax opinions, see "The Behavior of Justice Douglas in Federal Tax Cases," by Bernard Wolfman, Jonathan L. F. Silver and Marjorie N. Silver, in Vol. 122 of the *University of Pennsylvania Law Review*, p. 235.

Justice to twist the rules and undercut a major antimonopoly decision that boldly reflected his own philosophy.

After Burger floated a memorandum to his colleagues, suggesting a change in the rule on rehearings which would have allowed him to vote in the El Paso Natural Gas case, Douglas sat down at his desk to compose a response. In ten pages, Douglas retold the history of the case, and accused the new Chief of manipulating the Court's rules and of an unconscionable attempt to reverse a one-year-old precedent. It was no way for any member of the Court, and certainly not a new appointee claiming to be a "strict constructionist," to behave. Douglas would not stand for it. If his colleagues accepted the new Chief's suggestion to change the rule and then granted a rehearing in the case, Douglas warned that he would publish his memorandum as a dissent to the official announcement of the Court's decision to rehear the case.

Stewart and Black spoke to Burger and warned him that Douglas would carry out his threat. For the sake of harmony on the Court, they told the new Chief, he must withdraw his suggestion. Shortly after that informal meeting, the Court announced that the rehearing petition was denied.

Douglas's views on the preferred position of the First Amendment never wavered. He did not even bother to view the raunchy movies shown at the Court when his colleagues attempted to decide which skin flicks were obscene. There was nothing prudish about Douglas; he just thought every movie was protected by the First Amendment. No exceptions. In a 1973 dissenting opinion, Douglas explained his view:

> Art and literature reflect tastes; and tastes, like musical appreciation, are hardly reducible to precise definitions. That is one reason I have always felt that "obscenity" was not an exception to the First Amendment. For matters of taste, like matters of belief, turn on the idiosyncrasies of individuals. They are too personal to define and too emotional and vague to apply. . . . I am sure I would find offensive most of the books and movies charged with being obscene. But in a life that has not been short, I have yet to be trapped into seeing or reading something that would offend me. I never read or see materials coming to the Court under

charges of "obscenity," because I have thought the First Amendment made it unconstitutional for me to act as a censor. . . .

He did not share his colleagues' difficulties in locating that fine line between the free exercise of religion, protected by the First Amendment, and the establishment of religion prohibited by the same amendment. From his earliest days on the Court, Douglas had read the free exercise clause broadly, as shielding all forms of beliefs, whether of Jehovah's Witnesses or of young men during the sixties and seventies who refused to serve in what they concluded was an immoral war in Southeast Asia. As to the establishment clause, Douglas had declared in 1952 that "we are a religious people whose institutions presuppose a Supreme Being." That did not stop him later, however, from constructing the highest wall separating church and state of any member of the modern Court. He voted "no" to public school prayers and "no" to government loans of textbooks to parochial schools. And in a case challenging a tax exemption for property used solely for religious purposes, Douglas, alone, voted to strike down the exemption. In his dissent, Douglas wrote: "The present involvement of government in religion may seem de minimis. But it is, I fear, a long step down the Establishment path."

Douglas was forever vigilant in pointing out the retreat of the Court, under Chief Justice Burger, in the field of civil rights. Even before Richard Nixon had supplied his full complement of Supreme Court Justices, it was clear to Douglas that the new majority forming would not stand firm against racism. When the mayor of Jackson, Mississippi, closed all the city's public swimming pools rather than comply with a court order to desegregate, the new Chief Justice voted with the majority which refused to lock Jackson into what Burger suggested was a financially doomed desegregation venture. Nixon's second appointee, Harry Blackmun, voted with the Chief, candidly admitting that a desegregated public swimming pool was a "nice-to-have-but-not essential" variety of public service.

Douglas dissented, concluding "that though a State may discontinue any of its municipal services—such as schools, parks, pools, athletic fields, and the like—it may not do so for the purpose of perpetuating or installing *apartheid* or because it finds life in a multi-racial community difficult or unpleasant. If that is its reason, then abolition of a designated public service becomes a device for perpetuating a segregated way of life. That a State may not do."

Douglas stalked racism in the public schools and parks and far beyond. When Moose Lodge No. 107 in Harrisburg, Pennsylvania, refused to serve Leroy Irvis, a member of the state legislature who was black, Irvis brought suit. No member of the Court denied that the club had discriminated against Irvis because of his color, but a majority decided that that was no business of the Court. The Fourteenth Amendment's equal protection clause was not relevant, the Court held, since this was not "state action" but involved the preferences of private citizens in the confines of a private club. To hold otherwise, wrote Justice Rehnquist, "would utterly emasculate the distinction between private as distinguished from state conduct."

Douglas disagreed, claiming in dissent that there was the required state action. He noted that the state of Pennsylvania had issued its quota of liquor licenses, including one to the all-white Moose lodge. Since the liquor license quota was filled, Douglas concluded that "the State of Pennsylvania is putting the weight of its liquor license, concededly a valued and important adjunct to a private club, behind racial discrimination."

Douglas's sympathy for the "little guy" pervaded his opinions in every field. Throughout his years on the Court, Douglas consistently voted for broad coverage of employees under federal statutes that provided compensation for injured workmen. He was equally determined to defend the rights of nonworkmen, indigents who challenged the subtle intimidation of vagrancy laws. Those laws were nothing more than a polite way for police to harass drifters, Douglas believed, and he fought for years to eliminate them. In 1972, Douglas wrote an opinion for the Court that invalidated a municipal ordinance which defined the crime of vagrancy to include "persons wandering or strolling about from place to place without any lawful purpose or object." Douglas stated that walking, strolling and wandering "are historically part of the amenities of life as we have known them."

During the Warren Court era, Douglas supported every majority opinion that extended the rights of criminal suspects, from

Gideon v. *Wainwright,* the decision holding that indigent defendants in state felony trials were entitled to counsel, to the controversial *Miranda* v. *Arizona,* in which the Court imposed a duty on police to warn defendants of their constitutional rights before they could be interrogated. Indeed, Douglas had anticipated some of the rulings in his earlier opinions. In one 1958 dissenting opinion, for example, Douglas declared that criminal suspects were entitled to counsel during police interrogation, a view that was later written into law. When the Burger Court broadened the constitutional rights of defendants, as it did in extending the right to counsel to state proceedings involving petty offenses, Douglas, appropriately, wrote the majority opinion. But when he detected a backtracking on the part of the Burger Court majority, Douglas invariably dissented.

The emerging Burger Court majority's insensitivity to the constitutional claims of the poor was exemplified when a bare five-man majority rejected the claim of Barbara James (who was receiving aid-to-dependent-children payments) that the state welfare department had violated her Fourth Amendment rights. A caseworker had come to James's apartment to inspect the premises to see if James continued to meet conditions for eligibility for welfare assistance. James refused to let the welfare worker in the door without a warrant. After all requests to inspect her apartment were rejected by James, her welfare payments were cut off. In court, James's attorney argued that the welfare department was forcing James to open her home against her will, and that constituted an illegal search, prohibited by the Fourth Amendment. Wrong, wrote Justice Blackmun for the majority. James was confusing a right with a privilege. A forced entry by police raised the question of a constitutional right. This was different. This was nothing more than a charity call. Mrs. James had no *right* to demand anything where charity (a welfare payment) was involved.

"If the welfare recipient was not Barbara James but a prominent, affluent cotton or wheat farmer receiving benefit payments for not growing crops, would not the approach be different?" asked Douglas in dissent. "Welfare in aid of dependent children, like social security and unemployment benefits, has an aura of suspicion. There doubtless are frauds in every sector of public welfare whether the recipient be a Barbara James or someone who is prominent or influential. But constitutional rights—here the privacy of the home—are obviously not dependent on the poverty or on the affluence of the beneficiary. It is the precincts of the home that the Fourth Amendment protects; and their privacy is as important to the lowly as to the mighty."

No constitutional right was more proudly protected by Douglas than that of privacy, a right that he had announced in *Griswold* v. *Connecticut.* When he saw the opportunity to expand the right, and sensed strong opposition from colleagues to the expansion, Douglas abandoned his traditional role as the Court's loner. Instead he joined the battle.

That happened after the Court heard cases from Texas and Georgia challenging those states' anti-abortion laws. The Texas statute made abortion a crime except when performed to save the life of the mother. The standards in the Georgia statute were broader, permitting abortion to preserve the life or health of the mother, to abort a fetus likely to be born with serious defects or one conceived as a result of rape. For Douglas, the issue in both cases of a woman's right to an abortion fit comfortably within his view of the constitutional right to privacy. Justices Brennan and Marshall supported Douglas's position. Although Justices Stewart and Blackmun were reluctant to expand the constitutional right so dramatically, both suggested in conference that the decision to abort in the early stages of pregnancy should be protected from state interference. They, too, leaned toward a ruling that would strike down the state anti-abortion laws, though on narrower grounds than Douglas, Brennan and Marshall.

In their comments on the cases at conference, Chief Justice Burger and Justice White made it clear that they were in favor of upholding the state statutes. That made the count five to two,* to strike the statutes.

The Chief Justice assigns majority opinions when he votes with the majority. Here, however, he was in the minority. As senior justice in the majority, Douglas assumed he would assign the majority opinion. But Burger issued the formal assignment from

---

*Though their appointments had been confirmed, Justices Powell and Rehnquist had not heard oral arguments in the abortion cases and did not participate in the voting.

his office, assigning the abortion decision to Harry Blackmun. Douglas dashed off an angry memo, accusing Burger of impropriety. The Chief responded by saying that the individual justices' positions in the abortion cases were so complicated that it was not clear who was in the majority. By assigning the opinion to Blackmun, he was simply asking one justice to focus the sensitive issues in the cases, which, he assumed, would be reargued. Blackmun supported the Chief's position, and attempted to assure Douglas that Burger's assignment was proper.

Douglas did not like it, fearing that at best, Blackmun would write a very narrow opinion striking the statutes but not expanding the right to privacy to the extent Douglas would have liked. At worst, Blackmun could change his mind entirely, with the help of some subtle pressure and persuasion by the Chief. For the moment, Douglas decided not to press the issue. He would withhold judgment until he saw a draft of Blackmun's opinion. Although Blackmun had been given the abortion assignment in December, the winter passed without a draft circulated from Blackmun's office. Word leaked out that Blackmun, a notoriously slow worker, was experiencing difficulties in putting his thoughts into written form.

When a draft was finally circulated in early May, none of Blackmun's colleagues was satisfied. Blackmun had not explicitly recognized that pregnant women had a right to privacy, but had simply asserted that the Texas anti-abortion law was vague and therefore unconstitutional. In the Georgia case, Blackmun based his decision on the need to protect a doctor's professional judgment, not on a woman's right to privacy. Stewart found both the style and the reasoning inadequate. Douglas saw major problems too, but he was more interested in the results (Blackmun had, after all, found the statutes unconstitutional) than in Harry Blackmun's style or reasoning. He wanted to hold Blackmun's vote. Douglas told Blackmun that his draft was one of the finest presentations of an issue he had ever read.

During the first week in June, Douglas erupted again, after Blackmun informed Douglas and other members of the Court that he would withdraw his abortion opinions. The lateness of the term, the sensitivity of the issue, the need for additional research, Blackmun wrote, all suggested to him that the cases ought to be put over for reargument next term. He requested that all copies of his earlier draft memorandum be returned.

Douglas suspected that the Chief was behind Blackmun's postponement idea. Reargument would give the Chief Justice additional time to work on Blackmun. And by the next term, the two new "strict constructionist" Nixon appointees, Powell and Rehnquist, excellent prospects to sustain the state statutes, could participate. If all the pieces fell into place for Burger, he could produce a five-man majority (Burger, White, Blackmun, Powell and Rehnquist) to sustain the anti-abortion statutes.

In a memorandum addressed to his colleagues, Douglas wrote that he, not Burger, should have assigned the majority opinion.

> When . . . the minority seeks to control the assignment, there is a destructive force at work in the Court. When a Chief Justice tries to bend the Court to his will by manipulating assignments, the integrity of the institution is imperiled. . . . The plea that the cases be reargued is merely strategy by a minority* somehow to suppress the majority view with the hope that the exigencies of time will change the result. . . . But that kind of strategy dilutes the integrity of the Court and makes the decisions here depend on the manipulative skills of a Chief Justice. . . .

Douglas reworked the memorandum, circulated it to his colleagues and flew west for his vacation, leaving behind the threat to make the memo public as a dissent if the abortion cases were put over for reargument. Rumors circulated in the press that the Chief was playing fast and loose with the abortion decision and that Douglas would soon have something public to say about it. Brennan pleaded with Douglas by telephone to reconsider for the sake of the institution. It would not look good, Brennan argued, for the justices to air their internal grievances in public. Douglas was unmoved; his threat remained. Only after Harry Blackmun personally pledged to Douglas that he would not change his pro-abortion position, only refine it, did Douglas agree not to publish his memorandum. The abortion cases were held over for the 1972 term.

*Under the Court's traditional rule, only justices who had sat on a case could vote for reargument. The votes of Powell and Rehnquist, therefore, did not count, Douglas argued.

Blackmun kept his word. After spending most of the summer in the stacks of the Mayo Clinic medical library in Rochester, Minnesota, Blackmun returned to Washington more convinced than ever that the early decision to abort was a private matter, to be decided by the expectant mother and her physician. His conviction was translated later in the term into sweeping Court majority opinions in which Blackmun declared that Texas's and Georgia's anti-abortion statutes were unconstitutional.

In his opinion on the Texas statute, Blackmun wrote that the decision to have an abortion was entirely protected from state interference in the first trimester of a woman's pregnancy. The state could regulate in the second trimester only in the interests of the health of the mother. Only in the third trimester, when the fetus reached viability, Blackmun continued, could the state protect the interests of the unborn child with an anti-abortion law.* It was an astoundingly broad affirmation of the constitutional right to privacy, first announced by Justice Douglas eight years earlier.

Douglas wrote a concurring opinion, elaborating on what he considered to be the constitutionally protected "Blessings of Liberty":

First is the autonomous control over the development and expression of one's intellect, interests, tastes, and personality. . . .

Second is freedom of choice in the basic decisions on one's life respecting marriage, divorce, procreation, contraception, and the education and upbringing of children. . . .

Third is the freedom to care for one's health and person, freedom from bodily restraint or compulsion, freedom to walk, stroll or loaf. . . .

Not surprisingly, no member of the Court joined Douglas's broad concurrence. He did not stick to the basic issue of the constitutional right of a woman to have an abortion. He did not have to. Harry Blackmun had taken care of that. But Douglas's contributions that day went far beyond his opinion. He had shrewdly applied pressure to Blackmun when it earlier had ap-

---

*In his opinion in the Georgia case, Blackmun rejected substantial portions of the statute, considered to be a reform measure, on more technical constitutional grounds.

peared that Blackmun might stray from the majority. Moreover, he had contributed his earlier opinion in *Griswold* v. *Connecticut,* establishing the constitutional right to privacy, on which the Court's anti-abortion decisions were critically based.

In the first volume of his autobiography, published in 1974, Douglas attempted to prove that his life, like his view of the law, could be reduced to undiluted purposes and results. The book, *Go East, Young Man,* provided a series of impressionistic glimpses of an indestructible achiever who became the second-youngest man ever to be appointed to the U.S. Supreme Court. The problems in his early life were there—the polio, the poverty, the frenetic work/study schedule at college and law school, the exhausting sixteen-hour days as a young New York corporate lawyer, his experiment with psychoanalysis while at Yale, his struggle at the SEC with the powerful financiers of Wall Street. But the experiences were dramatically portrayed as object lessons for his readers.

Family and long-time friends shrugged at the literary feat, bemusedly debating whether the book should be marketed as fiction or nonfiction. In each episode, Douglas triumphed, usually alone. Hard work and high moral purpose always brought their just results. Poverty could be overcome, just as the venal strategies of Wall Street's establishment could be exposed and corrected. Douglas did it all. It was not a modest book. Nor was it entirely candid.

The author devoted less than a page to his wife of twenty-nine years, Mildred, and only a short and significantly unrevealing chapter on his two children. He wrote of their talents but not of their feelings, or his. He did not mention his persistent fears and weaknesses (those not overcome by his seemingly indomitable spirit)—some of which he exhibited during the struggle to bring the autobiography itself to publication.

Douglas had first attempted autobiography with his book, *Of Men and Mountains,* which was greeted, on publication in 1950, by enthusiastic reviews and exceptional commercial sales. It, too, had dealt with Douglas's early years, but it was not intended to be definitive. Only a few years after publication of *Of Men and Mountains,* Douglas began to collect his thoughts for a larger, more ambitious book which would serve as the autobiography of William O. Douglas. For more than a decade, he kept his project to himself.

One spring day in 1969, Douglas picked up the telephone to dial the number of Dagmar Hamilton, a government instructor at the University of Texas in Austin. He asked her to come to Washington immediately and plan to stay for a week. He would not tell her the purpose of the trip. Hamilton trusted Douglas's judgment and quickly packed her suitcase.

Hamilton had first met Douglas in Washington in 1955 with her husband, Robert, who was then a law clerk to Associate Justice Tom Clark, and more significantly, was the son of Douglas's old Yale friend, Professor Walton Hamilton. After Dagmar had graduated from the American University Law School in 1962, Douglas asked her to do research for the book he was then writing. That project led to another and another, seven books in all. With each manuscript, Douglas gave her more responsibility. By the time she had worked on *The Three Hundred Year War: A Chronicle of Ecological Disaster,* Dagmar Hamilton was writing whole pages of the text. She didn't mind the anonymity. "They were his ideas," she said. "If he'd had the time to do the research, he would have said the same thing."

When she arrived at Washington's National Airport in the spring of 1969, Dagmar Hamilton took a taxi directly to the U.S. Supreme Court, called at the marshal's office and was led to Justice Douglas's chambers. Douglas greeted her warmly but said nothing about his reasons for asking her to come. He suggested that they take a walk outside the Court building.

Hamilton sensed that something was wrong. Douglas seemed tense, overwrought. As they walked, he told her why.

He was convinced, Douglas told Hamilton, that Richard Nixon had begun a methodical dismantling of civil liberties in the country. He feared for the country. He also feared for himself. He was certain, he said, that his office was bugged and that attempts had been made to steal his papers. He believed that his life was in danger.

"In the past," Hamilton recalled, "he had always understated his concerns. He was never maudlin. Suddenly, he was very emotional. He was so emotional, I was shaking all over."

When they returned to Douglas's chambers, Douglas unlocked the bottom drawer to his desk. It was stuffed with the shards of his life in manuscript form, which he had been working on for the last fifteen years. Douglas knew that it was wildly disorganized and badly in need of editing. He wanted Hamilton to take the manuscript, in its raw form, and mold it into a publishable autobiography. It was a matter of the utmost urgency, Douglas said, and it must be kept strictly confidential. Of all the people he knew, Douglas said, he trusted Hamilton to do the job. If she accepted the assignment, he wanted her to promise that she would place the completed manuscript in a warehouse where it would be safe from his enemies.

Hamilton spent the next week in room 210 of the Supreme Court building, sifting through Douglas's manuscript. It was difficult to follow at times, and in need of drastic editing. But it was William O. Douglas's story told in his words, and, therefore, fascinating. She told him that she would be happy to work on it. She did not, however, share what she considered Douglas's paranoia, and rejected the notion that it would be necessary to store the manuscript in a warehouse. Hamilton then returned to Austin, where she wrote Douglas a short letter saying that she thought the manuscript was a valuable historic document. Then, sensitive to Douglas's fear that his life was in jeopardy, Hamilton wrote that she hoped he would have many more chapters to his autobiography before it became final.

Douglas did not discuss the autobiography with Hamilton again for more than three years. In the fall of 1972, he told her that he was interested in talking to Random House about the manuscript. He wanted her to help with the book and suggested that she fly to New York to talk to Random House's president, James Silberman, and senior editor, Charlotte Mayerson.

"They must have thought I was some pickup," Hamilton recalled. "Who was I? I had never written anything under my own name. I was, then, only teaching part-time at the University of Texas.* I don't think Justice Douglas ever really told Random House what my role was or had been with past books. I think he

---

*Later, Hamilton became a full-time tenured professor at the University of Texas's Lyndon B. Johnson School of Public Affairs.

was uneasy about my dealing with Random House directly and simply didn't say anything to them about me."

There were some disagreements at the meeting. Relaying Douglas's wishes, Hamilton insisted that the autobiography not come out as a single volume. His Court years would come later, she said. But weren't the Court years the most interesting and salable period of Douglas's life? Hamilton was asked. Not necessarily, she replied. Douglas's early experiences in the Cascades, as *Of Men and Mountains* had shown, were highly readable. And in the first volume, Hamilton suggested, Douglas could also recount his experiences at the SEC and with FDR. Random House agreed to publish volume one of Douglas's autobiography, which would end with his appointment to the Court. Douglas signed the book contract.

In the spring of 1973, Hamilton began the editing process, taking the reams of copy sent by Douglas from Washington and converting it into a coherent manuscript. After she had completed about two-thirds of the editing, Hamilton was asked by Random House to send the remaining edited copy directly to New York. "I thought it was a mistake," Hamilton recalled. "I thought the Justice would find it threatening for me to work directly with Random House. With past books, I had always sent my editing suggestions to him first. He would simply incorporate the changes in his own copy of the manuscript. It saved face for him and sounded as if he'd thought of the changes himself."

It *was* a mistake. Without having complete control of the edited manuscript, Douglas felt that the book was slipping away from him. He became mistrustful of Hamilton and, later, despondent. He wrote Hamilton in August that the book was no longer his and suggested that he might burn it.

Hamilton realized that Douglas blamed her. In a letter, she attempted to explain her good intentions and repair their friendship. He did not reply. Hamilton sought Cathy Douglas's counsel. When Hamilton was in Washington (working for the House Judiciary Committee that was studying the possible impeachment of Richard Nixon), Cathy suggested that Hamilton invite the Douglases to dinner. She did. Douglas refused to come. On his birthday, Hamilton bought him a stone vase, picked a flower for it, and brought the present to his chambers. She was told that the Justice was out of the office; she knew he was not. Later, the vase was returned to her by Court messenger. No note was attached.

If Douglas's autobiography becomes a best seller, Bob Hamilton told his wife, he'll forgive you. The book was published in the spring of 1974. Dagmar Hamilton's name was not mentioned in the book and she was not sent a complimentary copy. But after the book appeared on the best seller charts, Douglas agreed to meet Hamilton for lunch.

"I saw the flotilla coming," Hamilton remembered. "There was his secretary, two law clerks, Datcher [his messenger] and the Justice. He felt embarrassed about meeting me one to one. After they sat down, Douglas asked if people wanted a drink. Nobody did. I ordered a glass of white wine and said, 'Things must be bad at the Court if nobody's drinking; I can tell you that some of us at the impeachment inquiry sure do.' Everybody laughed. The Justice then ordered a glass of white wine, the same one that I had ordered. For lunch, I ordered Maryland crab cakes. So did he. He never said a word about the book. But everything was okay again."

Anticipating a New Year's Eve 1974 in Nassau, Douglas approached the holiday break in rare good spirits. Before departure, Douglas ducked into his office, shocked his law clerks by offering them an unexpected vacation, wished his secretaries a happy new year, then told his driver to head for National Airport. After he and Cathy arrived at their Nassau hotel, Douglas unpacked while Cathy went downstairs. When she returned, Cathy found Douglas collapsed on the floor, groggy and having difficulty moving his left arm and leg. He was rushed to a local hospital, where he awaited the arrival of his personal physician, Dr. Thomas Connally (who was flown to Nassau at the direction of President Ford). Dr. Connally immediately recommended that the Justice be flown to Washington, where he could receive better care. Douglas had suffered a severe stroke.

When he arrived at Walter Reed Army Hospital, Douglas was placed in the intensive care unit. His old friend Abe Fortas visited him there and told reporters that Douglas might be back at the Court in three or four weeks. It was wishful thinking. In fact, those who observed Douglas in January 1975 knew that his chances of a full recovery, in three weeks or three years, were minimal. He did not have total control of his body, his mental concentration was seriously restricted, and he had difficulty speaking. To make matters worse, Douglas was not cooperative with the staff at Walter Reed. He refused, for example, to undergo a psychoneurological examination, standard for stroke victims. If the hospital made him take the exam, Douglas warned, he would issue a public statement charging that he was being forced to see a psychiatrist against his will.

Douglas's condition presented a quandary for the other members of the Court. No one knew when, or if, Douglas might return to his full duties. But they could not presume to decide for his doctors or for Douglas himself. It was Douglas's decision and he had already indicated that he fully intended to return to the Court. His clerks and secretaries had been shuttling between the Court and Walter Reed since Douglas's first week in the hospital. The eight justices knew, nonetheless, that Douglas's future on the Court was not clear. They agreed in January to delay arguments in five cases in which Douglas was likely to be the decisive fifth vote, rescheduling them for later in the term.

Chief Justice Burger was aware of Douglas's precarious condition and of the gap between that condition and Douglas's own optimistic assessment. Douglas wanted the Court's press officer to issue a statement referring to his stroke as his "fall"; Burger instructed the press officer to issue the statement of the "fall" under Douglas's name, not the Court's, and then ordered that no more information about Douglas's condition be given out. In the meantime, Burger quietly arranged for the Court carpenter to construct a ramp to allow Douglas's wheelchair to be pushed up to the elevated bench upon his return.

On Monday, March 24, Douglas returned to the bench for the first time since he had suffered the stroke. His appearance was shocking. The once robust body was thin and lifeless. His ruddy complexion was now pale and his eyes, bulging unnaturally, stared vacantly ahead. The Chief, aware of the delicacy of the situation, leaned over and asked Douglas if he would like to leave a few minutes before the lunch recess was declared. No, Douglas replied. When the recess was announced a few minutes later, the embarrassing moment that Burger had anticipated could not be avoided. The other eight justices stood and walked out, leaving Douglas, helpless and alone in his chair. Two Court policemen then appeared on either side of Douglas and slowly wheeled him down the ramp and out of the sight of the shaken spectators.

The following day Douglas held a brief press conference in his chambers which he hoped would assuage any fears that he was no longer capable of doing his job. As the fifteen reporters from the media were led into his office, they saw Douglas at his desk, scrawling a note on a pad with his right hand, his left arm lying motionless in his lap. A minute later, David Beckwith, then *Time*'s legal correspondent, remembered, Douglas tried unsuccessfully to rip two sheets from the pad. He could not hold the pad and tear the paper with his right hand. Douglas then put the pad in his lap, attempting to use his left arm to pin it down. Despite obvious effort, Douglas could not move his left arm. While the reporters watched uncomfortably, Douglas's secretary rushed over and tore off the sheets.

The Court press officer quietly asked if Douglas was ready to begin. The Justice looked bewildered, his mouth gaping open uncontrollably. After a pause, the press officer asked: "Do you have a statement, Mr. Justice, or would you like to entertain questions?" Douglas replied, "Yes." For the next five minutes, the reporters reluctantly participated in the awkward spectacle of a disabled justice trying to convince them that he was healthy. Speaking haltingly and slurring his words, Douglas invited all of them to join him on a fifteen-mile hike at the end of April. He assured them that he would sit in on all oral arguments for the remainder of the Court term. He did admit that he no longer had the energy he once had, but he had no intention of resigning. He was firm about the last point. He would not resign.

Rather than putting to rest the issue of his resignation, Douglas had only provoked further speculation. In his present weak condition, could Douglas do the work that taxed the capacities of eight healthy justices? Or would Douglas be forced to resign, allowing President Ford, the man who had tried to impeach him, to appoint his successor?

Douglas's mental condition deteriorated. He repeatedly addressed people at the Court by their wrong names, often uttered non sequiturs in conversation or simply stopped speaking altogether, retreating into glassy-eyed silence. On one occasion, Douglas adamantly refused to be wheeled into his own office, claiming it was the chambers of the Chief Justice.

As Douglas's condition worsened, the other members of the Court agreed informally to a strategy that would effectively nullify his vote. If the Court was split four–four and it was likely that Douglas would cast the decisive fifth vote for a majority, the case would be held over for reargument the next term. The justices also agreed not to grant certiorari unless there were four votes, excluding Douglas's, for review. One member of the Court explained: "Bill's votes were inconsistent with his prior positions. For example, he would vote to deny cert in cases where the issues were similar to earlier cases in which he had consistently voted to grant cert. So the purpose of the agreement was to protect Bill as well as the integrity of the Court."

Although he still possessed the extraordinary will power that had served him so well all his life, Douglas made no progress. Physical therapy did not help. Neither did medication. In April, the decision was made to move Douglas to New York's Rusk Institute of Rehabilitative Medicine, which enjoyed a worldwide reputation for its success in rehabilitating stroke victims.

At the Rusk Institute, the sight of Douglas, in constant pain and struggling to accomplish the most basic physical tasks, was disheartening to his staff. "I would be on the verge of tears," his secretary, Sandra Phillips Flax, remembered. "And he would reassure me. 'It could be worse,' he would say. 'At least I can read and write.' But his body would not do what he wanted. Just to break a hard roll at a meal was a major breakthrough. He never gave up. He even believed he would walk again."

The member of the Court who, above all others, had aggravated Douglas in his last years turned out to be the most solicitous. Unlike most of the other members, Chief Justice Warren Burger regularly inquired about Douglas's health and periodically sent him apricot preserves and vintage wine. "The Chief Justice was a saint," said Sandra Phillips Flax.

On July 24, 1975, after he had visited Douglas at the Rusk Institute, the Chief Justice said, through a hospital spokesman, that he was extremely pleased with Douglas's progress. It was not a candid statement. In fact, Douglas was making virtually no progress and Burger, Douglas's close friends and his family knew it.

In August, Douglas and his wife flew to Goose Prairie. A month later, Douglas made the mistake of deciding to hear oral argument in Yakima, a forty-minute drive from Goose Prairie, on an emergency request to prevent disclosure of grand jury records. Like the March press conference, the appearance in Yakima was intended to reassure the public that Douglas was still capable of fulfilling his judicial duties. And like the press conference, the Yakima appearance proved just the opposite. Douglas's physical helplessness was immediately apparent and his mental lapses were more frequent than ever. He seemed dazed, unable to concentrate on the attorneys' arguments. When the attorneys had finished, they waited for Douglas's signal to end the proceeding. But Douglas said nothing, absolutely nothing, for 9½ minutes while those in the courtroom shifted in their seats uncomfortably. Finally, Douglas broke the silence, thanking the attorneys for "a very helpful and a very spirited argument."

Shortly after that shattering experience, Douglas's friend, Charles Reich, received a letter from Isabelle Lynn who, with Kay Kershaw, operated the Double K Ranch in Goose Prairie. Both Lynn and Kershaw, old and devoted friends of the Justice's, felt that Douglas was in no condition to return to the Court. The problem, Lynn wrote Reich, was that no one could convince Douglas to retire. Could Reich, who was in San Francisco, come to Goose Prairie and argue the case for Douglas's retirement before the Justice? Reich said that he would, but only if he was asked to come to Goose Prairie by the Douglases. After telephone calls from both Cathy and Bill Douglas extending the invitation, Reich headed for Goose Prairie.

When he arrived, Reich found Douglas in obvious pain and not in complete control of his body or mind. At times, Douglas would fall asleep during a conversation or speak of events of the 1950s as if they had occurred only days earlier. "He was in much, much worse shape than he or the public realized," Reich recalled.

For three days, Reich pleaded with Douglas, telling him that his return to the Court would severely jeopardize his already weakened physical condition. If Douglas insisted on resuming his Court duties, Reich argued, he would also damage his extraordinary judicial reputation that had been built over more than three decades.

Someone had to defend the underprivileged, Douglas replied. "Even if I'm only half alive," Douglas told Reich, "I can still cast a liberal vote."

"Bill," said Reich softly, "you must resign. You've been a great justice for thirty-six years. But you can't be one anymore."

Still, Douglas was not prepared to retire. "I'm going back to Washington and try it," he told Reich. "I hope you'll understand, Charlie. I have to decide for myself."

Tension built at the Court as the new term began and Douglas insisted on assuming his seat. At judicial conference, Douglas frequently dropped off into an uneasy sleep even as his colleagues were talking. Invariably, pain forced him to be wheeled out of the room before the conference was completed. On the bench, Douglas experienced the same difficulties, dozing often during oral argument and then making untimely exits when the pain in his body became unbearable. His colleagues were, in turns, gracious and angry. The Chief was particularly sensitive to Douglas's fragile condition. Others, like Byron White, did not attempt to hide their annoyance that Douglas's stubbornness in clinging to his seat was jeopardizing the work of the Court.

By the end of October, doctors at Walter Reed were convinced that Douglas would never walk again. Moreover, they told him that he would remain paralyzed and in constant pain for the rest of his life. Douglas wanted a second opinion. But in New York, doctors at the Rusk Institute confirmed the bleak prognosis. They did hold out hope, however, that if he received sufficient rest, his condition *might* improve. Douglas returned to Washington in time for the Court's Friday conference but, again, he could not endure the pain and was forced to leave.

By the following Monday, Douglas had made the decision that he had obstinately avoided for almost a year. He would resign from the Court. With the help of his old friends Abe Fortas and Clark Clifford, he prepared a letter of resignation to send to President Ford. On November 12, 1975, just before noon, Douglas informed the Chief Justice of his decision. At lunch in the justices' private dining room that day (where they were celebrating Harry Blackmun's birthday), Douglas sat silently in his wheel-chair while the Chief made the announcement. "Bill wants me to tell you," the Chief said, "he's written a letter to the President."

There were tears but also relief among the justices. At last they could get on with their business with the expectation that in a short time they would have a ninth, fully functioning member of the Court. Their feelings of perfect good will toward Douglas were short-lived.

Even after his replacement, John Paul Stevens, a fifty-five-year-old judge on the U.S. Court of Appeals for the Seventh Circuit, had been confirmed by the Senate, Douglas insisted that he was still a member, the *tenth* member, of the U.S. Supreme Court. In Douglas's view, his resignation was a necessary formality, but it did not signify his retirement. Each time a member of the Court or staff suggested that Douglas's judicial career was over, he would put his acerbic pen to work to set them straight.

In a memorandum, the Chief Justice had delicately suggested that Douglas might move his office to the more "commodious" quarters once occupied by former Chief Justice Earl Warren. But Douglas knew that those offices were smaller than his and not equipped to accommodate the staff of a working justice. Douglas's reply to the Chief dripped with sarcasm, as he assured Burger that his present quarters were fine. In his memorandum, expressing his satisfaction with his present office, Douglas used the word "commodious" five times. Douglas's law clerk, Robert Deitz, recalled his boss's triumph. "It was marvelous to see how Douglas outmaneuvered the Chief Justice."

Douglas came to his office regularly, commanded a full staff (after Burger tried unsuccessfully to persuade him to cut it) and requested copies of briefs in important cases pending before the Court. And then Douglas did what the justices had most dreaded. He announced that he intended to write an opinion that he expected to be printed with those of the other members of the Court.

The case involved a challenge to the Federal Election Campaign Act of 1974, which had attempted to restrict the influence of large financial contributions to political campaigns. The statute provided for the financing of presidential campaigns through tax revenue, required detailed reporting of political contributions and expenditures, limited individual campaign contributions and imposed strict limits on campaign spending by political candidates. The case presented complicated statutory and constitutional issues which, ultimately, took the justices 237 pages to explain.

Although Douglas had officially retired, he contended that he was still a voting member of the Court on all cases in which cert had been granted or jurisdiction noted while he was still a sitting justice. That meant, in his view, that he could participate in the campaign financing decision. He wrote an opinion in the case and had it printed, assuming that it would be circulated with the opinions of other members of the Court. When it wasn't, Douglas was immediately alert to the significance of the snub.

In a memorandum from "Mr. Justice Douglas," Douglas charged that the justices' attempt to exclude him from their deliberations "tends to denigrate Associate Justices who "retire.' " Their ploy, he wrote, was pure "political maneuvering," which had no place at the Court. For the remainder of his thirteen-page memorandum, Douglas raised questions about the constitutionality of the spending and contribution limits of the statute. "A new party formed to oust the hold that the corporate and financial interests have," wrote Douglas, "is presently by the terms of this act unqualified to get a dime."

The familiar populist philosophy was there, but the memorandum lacked the power of earlier Douglas opinions. "Bill is like an old firehouse dog," Burger told a clerk, "too old to run along with the trucks, but his ears prick up just the same."

Everyone at the Court recognized the inevitable but Douglas himself. When he heard that the Court planned to announce the opinion in the campaign financing case, Douglas ordered his clerk to take his opinion to the Court press office for distribution.

"I won't do it," the clerk replied.

"You are a traitor," said Douglas, and vowed to take the opinion to the press office himself.

The clerk wrote a note to Justice White saying that "the tenth member of the Court wants to release his opinion." Court officials were then told to ignore Douglas's requests for assistance. Douglas got the message. He was no longer a member of the tribunal on which he had served so brilliantly for 36 years. The justice, whose tenure exceeded all who preceded him in the Court's 186-year history, had, finally, retired.

Douglas was seventy-seven years old when he assumed the status of a retired member of the Court. His physical condition got progressively worse and his periods of concentration shortened. Bill Douglas, Jr., sadly predicted in 1977 that his father would not live to celebrate another Christmas. But as usual, Douglas defied predictions as well as the laws of nature. He continued to work on the second volume of his autobiography, polishing it, trying to decide whether to purge the manuscript of passages uncomplimentary toward his fellow justices. After ignoring an interview request for this book for two years, he sent word only a few days after the long-awaited interview that he would like to read my manuscript before publication (a request that was refused). The Justice was not well but he was decidedly alive and, as his request suggested, he could still be remarkably alert and shrewd.

"Even at 20 percent," said Douglas's clerk Dennis Hutchinson, who in 1977 was helping him complete the second volume of his autobiography, "the Justice can be a terror. He's not the tartar he once was but when he's unhappy, I know it. Not long ago, he called me in. 'How can anybody with a fifth grade education write this sentence?' he asked, and then he threw the draft at me." While Hutchinson was speaking to me, Douglas's secretary interrupted to say that the Justice wanted him to call. "He says he's been waiting for two days to speak to you and either nobody gives you the message or you refuse to call. He wants you to call him at once. . . ."

Members of the Court, both those who agreed with Douglas and those who did not, felt his absence. "We miss him," said one who was close neither personally nor professionally to Douglas. Why? Those who attended Douglas's memorial service at the National Presbyterian Church that cold January day in 1980 could provide the answer. Douglas's vanity, pettiness, irascibility, even his bouts of meanness, would pass from memory. But his greatness would endure. William O. Douglas became a heroic symbol of the human spirit, offering an unwavering belief that the power and dignity of the individual could make the nation and the world a better place.

ACKNOWLEDGMENTS_____

This book could not have been completed without the help of a number of people: Wendy Weil, my agent; Amy Bonoff and Simon Michael Bessie, my editors at Harper & Row; E. Donald Shapiro, dean of the New York Law School, who encouraged me throughout the project; Dean Cycon, John Delmar, Barbara Friedman, Jay Itkowitz and Ronald Senese, who helped with the legal research; Natalie Simon, who interviewed Mrs. Lyndon B. Johnson, read and took notes on numerous periodicals and books and studied documents at the Truman Library in Independence, Missouri, and the Lyndon B. Johnson Library in Austin, Texas; Roger Newman, who provided insights and materials; Cathleen H. Douglas, who made many useful suggestions on sources; Nita Culwell Coker, who typed the entire manuscript expertly and with unfailing good cheer; Professor Vern Countryman of the Harvard Law School, who read and offered extremely valuable suggestions on portions of the manuscript dealing with Douglas's early work in the bankruptcy field as well as his later judicial opinions; Professor William L.Cary of the Columbia Law School and U.S. District Judge Gerhard Gesell, who read and provided useful comments about sections on Douglas's work at the SEC;

Professor Steven Duke of the Yale Law School and Dean Albert Rosenthal of the Columbia Law School, who read and made important comments on chapters about Douglas's Court years; Steven Adler, John Delmar and Marcia Simon, who read the entire manuscript and offered many helpful suggestions for its improvement; Sara, Lauren, David and Marcia Simon, who were forced to pretend, too often, that this book did not disrupt their lives.

Source Notes ———————————

The source notes are, for the most part, self-explanatory. I have used acronyms to identify frequently used sources after the initial entry. Douglas's autobiography, *Go East, Young Man,* becomes GEYM. Felix Frankfurter's Papers at the Library of Congress are cited as FFPLC. U.S. Supreme Court decisions and law review articles follow legal methods of citation: *West Virginia Bd. of Education* v. *Barnette,* 319 U.S. 624 (1943), means that the Supreme Court decided the case in 1943 and that the opinions begin at page 624 of volume 319 of the *United States Reports,* the official volumes of the Court's decisions. A law review article cited as 47 *Harv. L. Rev.* 565 (1934), means that the article was published in 1934 and can be found at page 565 of volume 47 of the *Harvard Law Review.*

Whenever possible, I have identified by name persons interviewed. Because of the sensitive nature of a number of the interviews, however, some persons requested anonymity. Those requesting anonymity include several members of the U.S. Supreme Court as well as some of Douglas's former law clerks.

Introduction

Page

2   "to take the government . . .": *Schneider* v. *Smith,* 390 U.S. 17, 25 (1968).
3   "Because of Bill Douglas . . .": William O. Douglas Memorial Service, National Presbyterian Church, Washington, D.C. 1-23-80.

Interview

4   Author's interview (AI) with William O. Douglas (WOD), Washington, D.C., 5-12-78.
9   Frankfurter's hosility, Joseph Lash, *The Diaries of Felix Frankfurter* (New York, 1975).
11   *West Virginia Bd. of Education* v. *Barnette,* 319 U.S. 624 (1943).

Page

13   Frankfurter's view, Felix Frankfurter, *Rosenberg Memorandum,* Felix Frankfurter Papers, Harvard Law School. (FFPHLS), Cambridge, MA.

Chapter One: Treasure

17   *Fergus Falls Weekly Journal* stories, 10-13-98, 10-15-98, 10-20-98; Otter Tail County Historical Society (OTCHS), Fergus Falls, MI.
18   History of Maine, *Fergus Falls Weekly Journal,* 7-12-29, OTCHS.
18   "a gift of God . . ." History of Maine Presbyterian Church, OTCHS.
18   Background of the Rev. Douglas, William O. Douglas, *Go East, Young Man* (GEYM), (New York, 1974), pp. 5, 6.
18   "When the hat . . .", Ibid., p. 6.
19   Background of Julia Fisk Douglas, GEYM, pp. 1, 2; AI with Martha Douglas Bost, Chicago, IL., 8-31-76.
19   "My life at times . . .", GEYM, p. 4.
19   "Mother resembled . . .", AI with Bost.
20   "sawdust pitched . . .", GEYM, p. 8.
20   "was watching . . .", AI with Bost.
20   "Father would . . .", Ibid.
20   WOD called "Treasure", Ibid.
20   " 'Treasure' walked . . .", Ibid.
21   "She soaked . . .", *Of Men and Mountains* (OMM), (New York, 1950), p. 31.
22   "I was about three . . .", GEYM, p. 8.
22   Julia Douglas's feelings, AI with Bost.
22   Memories of Estrella, GEYM, p. 9.; AI with Bost.
22   Memories of Cleveland, GEYM, pp. 11, 12; AI with Bost; Jack Alexander, "Washington's Angry Scotsman", *Saturday Evening Post,* 10-17-42.
23   "He knew me . . .", GEYM, p. 12.
24   "He was present . . .", OMM, pp. 22, 28, 29.
24   "I want to bring . . .", GEYM, p. 13.
25   "Like St. Francis . . .", Ibid.
25   "Mother always felt . . .", AI with Bost.

Chapter Two: Born for Success

26   History of Yakima, *Yakima Herald-Republic* supplement, Spring 1975.
26   "At times . . .", Gary L. Jackson, *Remembering Yakima,* (Yakima, 1975) p. 18.
27   "the devil incarnate", GEYM p. 17.
27   "I think we all felt . . .", AI with Bost.
28   Julia Douglas's standards, Ibid.
29   Julia Douglas's story, GEYM, p. 18.
29   Conversations with Rodell, AI with Fred Rodell, Bethany, CT, 7-8-76.
29   WOD's practical jokes, GEYM, p. 22; AI with Bost.
29   Douglases at the circus, Ibid.
30   Julia Douglas's Republicanism, GEYM, p. 7.
30   "I was hardly fourteen . . .", Ibid.
30   WOD as "stool pigeon", Ibid., pp. 60, 61.
30   WOD's feelings, AI with Elon Gilbert, Cowiche, WA., 8-17-76.
31   "South Front Street . . .", GEYM, pp. 61, 62.

Page

31   WOD apparently told no one, AI with Bost, Gilbert.
31   "Bill didn't resent . . .", AI with Gilbert.
31   "Douglas's view . . .", AI with W.H. "Ted" Robertson, Yakima, WA., 8-16-76.
31   "While there were . . .", GEYM, p. 60.
32   WOD's politics, Ibid., pp. 64–68.
32   WOD's silence with family and friends, AI with Bost, Gilbert.
32   WOD's priorities, AI with Bost.
33   Julia Douglas's views on education, Ibid.
33   WOD and Arthur behind the woodshed, Ibid.
33   "And knowing . . .", Ibid.
33   "We went . . .", GEYM, p. 21.
33   "He'd come into class . . .", AI with Grace Anderson, Yakima, WA., 8-16-76.
34   WOD's nervousness, AI with Bost.
34   Debate topic, *North Yakima Wigwam,* 1916, A.C. Davis High School, Yakima, WA.
34   WOD's preparation, AI with Bost.
34   WOD going blank, GEYM, p. 57.
34   N. Yakima basketball record, *North Yakima Wigwam,* 1916.
35   "Both Martha and Orville . . .", AI with Bost.
35   "Our papers . . .", Brad Emery letter to author, 10-26-76.
35   WOD's high school honors, *North Yakima Wigwam,* 1916.
35   "Born for success . . .", Ibid.
35   "As a cork . . .", Ibid.

Chapter Three: Escape

37   American leaders, Doris Faber, *The Mothers of American Presidents* (New York, 1968).
37   Julia Douglas's preferences, AI with Bost.
38   "Mama said . . .", Ibid.
38   Arthur's background, Ibid.
38   WOD and Arthur's rivalry; AI with Mercedes Douglas Eichholz, Washington, D.C.,
     4-18-77.
38   Martha and Julia Douglas's relief, AI with Bost.
39   "[Mother] set about . . .", OMM, p. 32.
39   WOD in foothills, Ibid., pp. 34, 35.
40   Martha's preparations, AI with Bost.
40   "if the mosquitoes . . .", GEYM, p. 19.
40   Julia Douglas's phobias, Ibid.
40   "Martha, do you . . .", AI with Bost.
40   "Try sleeping out . . .", *North Yakima Wigwam,* 1916.
41   Arthur and WOD camping, OMM, pp. 79–84.
41   "The shinbones . . .", Ibid., p. 82.
42   WOD horseback adventure, Ibid., pp. 51–62.
42   WOD and Gilbert, AI with Gilbert.
43   Meal with sheepherder, Emery letter to the author.
43   WOD and nature, see generally, OMM; GEYM, pp. 37–43.
44   WOD and Gilbert in the Cascades, AI with Gilbert.
44   "Dad told us . . .", AI with Millie Douglas Read, Lapover, OR, 8-27-76.
44   "I realized . . .", GEYM, p. 110.
44   "When one stands . . .", OMM, p. 90.

Page

45 "I felt at peace . . .", OMM, p. 49.
45 "Finally, I took . . .", GEYM, p. 110.
45 WOD's puritanism, AI with William O. Douglas, Jr., Portland, OR, 8-25-76.
46 WOD problems with women, AI with Eichholz.

Chapter Four: Rare Opportunity

47 Whitman background, Whitman College catalogue, 1917, Whitman College Library (WCL), Walla Walla, WA.
48 WOD's schedule, GEYM, pp. 97, 98.
48 WOD's work at Falkenberg's, AI with Jerry Cundiff, Walla Walla, WA, 8-20-76.
48 Color blind episode, Ibid.
49 "In time . . .", GEYM, p. 100.
49 Criticism of WOD at Beta, AI with Dr. William Wilson, Portland, OR, 8-26-76.
50 "Bill was against . . .", AI with Dr. Chester Maxey, Walla Walla, WA, 8-20-76.
50 WOD's family anxiety, AI with Read.
50 "Well, you've had . . .", AI with Wilson.
50 ". . . was a good Christian man . . .", GEYM, p. 103.
51 WOD article, "Souls Tempered with Fire", *The Codex,* June 1919, WCL.
51 WOD's achievement, AI with Cundiff.
52 Background on Professor Brown, GEYM, pp. 105, 106; commencement address of Dr. Chester Maxey, Whitman College, 5-29-55; "An Endowed Chair in Physics in Memory of Benjamin W. Brown", *The Whitman Alumnus,* May 1958, WCL.
52 "How wonderful . . .", GEYM, p. 106.
52 "Davis was . . .", Ibid.
52 Background on Dr. Davis, GEYM, Ibid.; *The Whitman Alumnus,* February 1947; profile of Davis, *Walla Walla Union Bulletin,* 3-13-47.
53 "warfare against mankind", Eric Goldman, *Rendezvous with Destiny* (New York, 1952), p. 192.
53 "Whitman Sees . . .", *Whitman Pioneer,* 5-11-17, WCL.
53 "the Huns will . . .", GEYM, p. 91.
53 WOD at recruiting office, Ibid., pp. 91, 92.
54 "hate the Germans . . .", Ibid., p. 93.
54 WOD as toastmaster, *Whitman Pioneer,* 2-4-19, WCL.
54 WOD activities, GEYM, pp. 97–116; *Whitman Pioneer,* 5-11-17, 2-4-19, 3-20-19, WCL; AI with Wilson, Cundiff.
54 WOD's debating activities, *Whitman Pioneer,* 5-11-17, 3-20-19, WCL.
55 "Orville Douglass showed . . .", *Whitman Pioneer,* 3-20-19, WCL.
55 "He just knocked . . .", AI with Wilson.
55 WOD tribute to faculty, Whitman faculty minutes, 4-19-20, WCL.
55 "Whitman to me . . .", WOD commencement address, 6-13-38, Whitman College, WCL.
56 "You can attend . . .", AI with Read.

Chapter Five: Frustration

57 WOD's finances, GEYM, p. 117.
57 WOD's discussions with Bond, AI with Cundiff.
58 Davis's influence, GEYM, p. 106.
58 Whitman graduates chose teaching, Whitman catalogue, 1917, WCL.

Page

58 Julia Douglas's choice, GEYM, p. 123.
58 WOD's frustration, Ibid., p. 119.
58 WOD's Rhodes interview, Ibid., pp. 119, 120.
59 WOD's conclusion, Ibid, p. 119.
59 WOD and Bailey, Ibid., pp. 122, 123.
60 "Resolved: That the principle . . .", Lolomi, Yakima H.S. yearbook, 1921, A.C. Davis H.S.
60 WOD's spare time, AI with Al Egley, Yakima, WA, 8-16-76.
60 Background on Mildred, AI with WOD Jr., Washington, D.C. 2-22-77.
61 WOD's interest in law, GEYM, pp. 123, 124.
62 WOD planning trip, Ibid., p. 127.
62 WOD leaving family, AI with Bost.
62 "When I get . . .", Ibid.
63 WOD's version of trip, GEYM, pp. 127–133.
63 Earlier version in which WOD pays for coach ticket, WOD profiles, *St. Louis Post-Dispatch,* 4-2-39, *Saturday Evening Post,* 10-17-42.
63 "the stranger—especially . . .", GEYM, p. 134.
64 WOD's meeting with Wilson, Ibid.; AI with Wilson.
64 WOD's first day at Columbia, GEYM, pp. 134–136.
65 Shanks's version, *Columbia Alumni News,* 4-14-39, Columbia Law School, New York, N.Y.

Chapter Six: Knuckles and Bones

66 Columbia undergraduates, *Columbia Spectator,* 11-22-22, 11-29-22, Columbia University Library (CUL), New York, NY.
66 Discussions at Columbia Law School, *Columbia Spectator,* 9-27-22, 10-28-22, 1-17-23, CUL.
66 Rifkind's schedule, AI with Simon Rifkind, New York City, 4-13-77.
66 Dewey's singing, GEYM, p. 139.
66 Robeson's football, Dorothy Butler Gilliam, *Paul Robeson, All American,* (Washington, D.C., 1976), p. 25.
67 "all knuckles and bones", AI with Rifkind.
67 "It cannot . . .", Julius Goebel, Jr., director, *A History of the School of Law, Columbia University* (New York, 1955), p. 226.
67 Stone's philosophy of legal education, Ibid., pp. 226–230.
67 Stone as teacher, Ibid., pp. 218, 219; GEYM, p. 146.
68 "Finally, one . . .", Ibid.
68 "He was unquestionably . . .", AI with Rifkind.
68 Moore as teacher, J. Goebel, op. cit., pp. 249–252. GEYM, pp. 145, 146; WOD, "Underhill Moore", 59 *Yale L.J.* 187 (1950).
69 WOD and Moore, GEYM, pp. 145, 146; WOD, "Underhill Moore", op. cit.
70 "It was our way . . .", AI with Harold Seligson, New York City, 1-6-77.
70 "The Doctrine of Imputed . . .", 24 *Colum. L. Rev.* 401 (1924).
70 "The Power of a State Bank . . .", 24 *Colum. L. Rev.* 633 (1924).
70 Public policy discussion, 24 *Colum. L. Rev.* 79 (1924).
71 "To obtain . . .", GEYM, p. 140.
72 Earlier version, WOD profile, *St. Louis Post-Dispatch,* 4-2-39.
72 WOD wedding and honeymoon, WOD profile, *The Oregonian,* 6-30-46.
72 "We blew . . .", WOD profile, *St. Louis Post-Dispatch,* 4-2-39.

Page

73   "I never felt . . .", letter from Mildred to WOD, 2-19-48, Millie Douglas Read letters (MDRL).
73   WOD avoided the market, GEYM, pp. 284, 285.
73   WOD's lack of funds, AI with Gilbert.
74   "Remember . . .", AI with Bost.
74   WOD and Moore, GEYM, p. 145.
75   "The world . . .", Ibid., p. 149.

Chapter Seven: Ducks in a Row

79   Fortas's suggestion, AI with Abe Fortas, Washington, D.C., 7-23-76.
80   WOD interviews, GEYM, pp. 149, 150.
80   Background on Cravath firm, Robert T. Swaine, *The Cravath Firm and Its Predecessors, 1819–1949*, Vol. II (New York, 1948).
80   Dulles's version of WOD interview, Leonard Mosley, *Dulles,* (New York, 1978), p. 76.
81   "For a poor . . .", R. Swaine, op. cit., p. 2.
81   "Douglas was not . . .", AI with John J. McCloy, New York City, 8-11-77.
81   Rifkind's decision, AI with Rifkind.
82   "alert, vigorous . . .", AI with Bruce Bromley, New York City, 1-25-77.
82   WOD's schedule, GEYM, pp. 150, 151.
82   WOD's salary, Cravath records, New York City.
82   "At the outset . . .", R. Swaine, op. cit., p. 4.
83   WOD and Swatland, GEYM, pp. 151, 152.
84   "Bill Douglas and I . . .", AI with McCloy.
84   Background on St. Paul collapse and reorganization, R. Swaine, op. cit., pp. 418–431; Max Lowenthal, *The Investor Pays* (New York, 1933); *Literary Digest* 3-28-25; *Literary Digest,* 12-11-26; *The New Republic,* 2-4-31.
85   "adverse criticism," R. Swaine, op. cit., p. 430.
85   Swaine's reference to Lowenthal, Ibid., p. 418.
85   "intervention in receivership . . . ," M. Lowenthal, op. cit., p. 143.
85   Key document, Ibid., pp. 189–192.
86   "One of my duties . . .", GEYM, p. 152.
86   "I don't think . . .", AI with McCloy.
87   He was not . . . , AI with Wilson.
87   WOD's return to Yakima, GEYM, pp. 156–158.
88   "I don't know . . .", AI with McCloy.
89   Court decision, *U.S., et al.* v. *Chicago, Milwaukee, St. Paul and Pacific Railroad Co.*, 282 U.S. 311 (1931).
89   "I don't remember . . .", AI with McCloy.
89   Frankfurter's defense of Sacco and Vanzetti, Felix Frankfurter, "The Trial of Sacco and Vanzetti", *The Atlantic Monthly,* March 1927.
90   "had written letters . . .", GEYM, p. 167.
90   WOD's article on railroad reorganizations, WOD, "Protective Committees in Railroad Reorganizations", 47 *Harv. L. Rev.* 565 (1934).
90   Lowenthal article, M. Lowenthal, "The Railroad Reorganization Act," 47 *Harv. L. Rev.* 18 (1933).

Page

Chapter Eight: The Battle of 1928

92   WOD's anxiety, GEYM, p. 150.

93   "a demure, quiet . . .", AI with Wilson.

93   Background on Columbia feud, J. Goebel, op. cit, pp. 272–305.

94   "That legal education . . .", Ibid., p. 273.

94   "go hammer . . .", Ibid., p. 299.

95   "It seemed to me . . .", AI with Judge Harold Medina, New York City, 1-25-77.

96   "I was indoctrinated . . .", Professor Richard Powell letter to author, 9-12-77.

96   "I was for . . .", AI with Medina.

96   WOD's views, GEYM, pp. 159–162.

96   "I had nothing . . .", Ibid., p. 161.

97   "The atmosphere . . .", J. Goebel, op. cit., p. 302.

97   "There was . . .", Ibid., p. 304.

98   "He [Butler] was . . .", GEYM, p. 161.

98   "Although the statutory . . .", J. Goebel, op. cit., p. 304.

98   Columbia resignations, Columbia Law School faculty minutes, 10-11-28, Columbia Law School, New York City.

98   Moore's silence, J. Goebel, op. cit., p. 305.

98   Columbia under Smith, Ibid., pp. 309–346.

99   WOD's version of resignation, GEYM, p. 161.

99   Faculty records of resignations, Columbia Law School faculty minutes, 6-1-28, Columbia Law School.

99   Announcement of resignation, Columbia Law School faculty minutes, 10-11-28, Columbia Law School.

Chapter Nine: The Nation's Outstanding Law Professor

100   Background on Hutchins, author's telephone interview with Robert M. Hutchins, 3-1-77; Hutchins profile in *The New York Times* (NYT), 5-16-77, p. 1.

101   "Naturally, the courses . . .", Ibid.

101   WOD's meeting with Hutchins, GEYM, p. 163.

102   "to proceed . . .", Yale Law School faculty minutes, 5-10-28, Yale Law School, New Haven, CT.

102   Yale in 1928, AI with Professor Thomas Emerson, New Haven, 7-9-76; AI with Rodell; AI with Judge Justine Wise Polier, New York City, 10-25-77.

102   Yale Law School atmosphere, AI with Emerson, Rodell, Polier; GEYM, pp. 164, 165.

102   Hutchins's approach, AI with Hutchins; Hutchins profile, NYT, 5-16-77; Dean's Report, 1928–1929, Yale Law School, Yale University Library (YUL), New Haven, CT.

103   "At Yale . . .", AI with Hutchins.

103   Hutchins's impression of WOD, Ibid.

103   "spoon-fed, coddled . . .", GEYM, p. 164.

103   "Douglas came . . .", AI with Emerson.

104   "In retrospect . . .", GEYM, p. 164.

104   "Douglas was . . .", AI with Emerson.

104   "His large classes . . .", AI with Rodell.

104   "He jumped . . .", AI with Emerson.

Page

105   "He made . . .", AI with Professor Myres McDougal, New York City, 10-27-76.

105   "The precision . . .", AI with Fortas.

105   "He was always . . .", AI with Rodell.

106   "For a young man . . .", AI with McDougal.

106   WOD article, "Vicarious Liability and the Administration of Risk", 38 *Yale L.J.* 584, 720 (1929).

107   "Gentlemen . . .", Dean's Report, 1928–29, Yale Law School, YUL.

109   Hutchins's resignation, Hutchins profile, NYT, 5-16-77.

109   "Bill Douglas . . .", GEYM, p. 164;

109   Hutchins's offer, *Time,* 1-27-36, p. 50, WOD profile, *PM,* 12-15-45, AI with Hutchins.

110   WOD's version, GEYM, p. 164.

110   "Last winter . . .", Dean's Report, 1930–31, Yale Law School, YUL.

110   WOD appearing to play off two institutions, AI with McDougal, Wilson.

110   "Professor William O. Douglas . . .", Dean's Report, 1931–32, Yale Law School, YUL.

110   "I never understood . . .", AI with Hutchins.

111   "Wall Street . . .", E. Goldman, op. cit., p. 248.

111   "It is still . . .", Dean's Report, 1929–30, Yale Law School, YUL.

111   WOD's Monday schedule, GEYM, p. 174.

112   WOD and Thomas findings and conclusions, Clark, WOD and Thomas, "The Business Failures Project—A Problem in Methodology", 39 *Yale L.J.* 1013 (1930); WOD and Thomas, "The Business Failures Project—II", 40 *Yale L.J.* 1034 (1931).

112   WOD's opinion on constitutional right of privacy, *Griswold* v. *Conn.,* 381 U.S. 479 (1965).

113   "It was expensive . . .", WOD and Thomas, "The Business Failures Project—II," op. cit., p. 1043.

Chapter Ten: Outward Calm, Inner Turmoil

114   Mildred's happiest days, AI with Rodell.

115   Mildred and her children, AI with Millie Douglas Read, WOD Jr.

115   "He was . . .", AI with WOD Jr.

116   Game of Murder, AI with McDougal.

116   WOD at banquet, AI with Rodell.

116   Poker parties, Ibid.

116   Background on Arnold, GEYM, pp. 167–169, 171, 172; AI with Emerson, Fortas, Rodell.

117   Mysterious note, remarks of Thurman Arnold at 20th anniversary of WOD's Court appointment, 4-17-59, Charles Clark Papers, Yale Law School Library.

117   "Please mention . . .", Ibid., GEYM, pp. 168, 169.

118   WOD and Arnold drinking, Ibid., pp. 167, 168.

118   "Passengers will . . .", Ibid., pp. 171, 172.

118   "Don't put . . .", AI with Judge Gerhard Gesell, Washington, D.C. 7-22-76.

118   "We counted . . .", remarks of Thurman Arnold, op. cit.

119   "Thurman and I . . .", GEYM, p. 172.

119   WOD's nervous tension, AI with Wilson.

120   "It is the imponderable . . .", GEYM, p. 178.

120   WOD's fears, Ibid., pp. 177–202.

121   "I went down . . .", OMM, pp. 105, 106.
122   WOD at Yale pool, Ibid., p. 188.
122   "The only thing . . .", Ibid., p. 183.
122   "Dad's idea . . .", AI with WOD Jr.
123   WOD's feelings about mother, AI with Cathleen Douglas, Washington, D.C. 4-18-77; WOD's demands on wives, AI with Millie Douglas Read, Mercedes Douglas Eichholz; AI with Joan Douglas Nicholson, Washington, D.C., 3-20-79.
123   "He is a great . . .", AI with Eichholz.

Chapter Eleven: The Road to Washington

124   "Did you hear . . .", E. Goldman, op. cit., p. 248.
125   "Only a short time . . .", Dean's Report, 1931–32, Yale Law School, YUL.
125   "Experience has shown . . .", WOD and C. Shanks, *Cases and Materials on the Law of Management of Business Units* (Chicago, 1931), preface.
126   WOD and Corbin exchange, Yale Law School, New Haven, CT, faculty minutes, 11-17-32, 12-8-32, Yale Law School.
126   "Douglas was a . . .", AI with Rodell.
126   "I think he was . . .", AI with McDougal.
126   "If you put . . .", William Leuchtenberg, *Franklin D. Roosevelt and the New Deal, 1932–40* (New York, 1963), p. 13.
126   "Hoover can calculate . . .", Ibid.
127   "balanced antithesis," Ibid., p. 10.
127   "It is common sense . . .", Ibid.
127   "A plague of . . .", Ibid., p. 64.
127   Background on Frankfurter, J. Lash, op. cit.; Harlan Phillips, *Felix Frankfurter Reminisces* (New York, 1960); Joseph Rauh, Jr., "Felix Frankfurter: Civil Libertarian," *Harv. Civil Rights L. Rev.*, Vol. II, No. 3 (Summer 1976).
128   "the most influential . . .", W. Leuchtenberg, op. cit., p. 64.
128   WOD's congratulatory letter, WOD to JF, 3-31-33, Jerome Frank Papers (JFP) YUL.
129   "Pecora has the manner . . .", W. Leuchtenberg; op. cit., p. 59
129   "to the ancient rule . . .", Ibid., p. 90.
129   "I haven't seen . . .", WOD to JF., 4-19-33, JFP.
130   "I can think . . .", JF to WOD, 4-24-33, Ibid.
130   WOD letter to *Times*, NYT, 4-9-33, p. 5.
131   First article, WOD and G. Bates, "Some Effects of the Securities Act upon Investment Banking", 1 *U. Chi. L. Rev.* 283 (1933).
131   Second article, WOD and G. Bates, "The Federal Securities Act of 1933", 43 *Yale L.J.* 171 (1933).
132   "I would have . . .", WOD to JF, 12-4-33, JFP.
133   *Yale Review* article, WOD, "Protecting the Investor", 23 *Yale Review* 521 (1934).
133   "If you would . . .", WOD to JF, 4-28-34, JFP.
134   "My dear Felix . . .", WOD to FF, 4-6-34, Felix Frankfurter Papers, Library of Congress, Washington, D.C. (FFPLC).
135   "The Connecticut crowd . . .", WOD to JF, 6-12-34, JFP.
135   Landis's call to WOD, GEYM, p. 258.

Page

Chapter Twelve: Lighting the Matches

139   "Your budget is . . ." GEYM, p. 259.
139   "It was a family . . .", WOD oral history transcript, John F. Kennedy Library, Waltham, MA.
140   Background on Kennedy, "Mr. Kennedy—The Chairman", *Fortune,* September, 1937; David E. Koskoff, *Joseph P. Kennedy: A Life and Times* (Englewood Cliffs, N.J., 1974).
140   "Each evening . . .", GEYM, p. 264.
141   "This was . . .", JF to WOD, 10-8-34, JFP.
141   "I sent . . .", WOD to JF, 10-10-34, Ibid.
141   "Dear Bill . . .", JF to WOD, 10-11-34, Ibid.
141   "finesse & high-powered . . .", WOD to JF, 10-16-34, Ibid.
141   "I am venturing . . .", WS to JF, 10-31-34, Ibid.
142   "Dear Bill . . .", JF to WOD, 11-3-34, Ibid.
142   "You are a swell . . .", WOD to JF, 11-5-34, Ibid.
142   "the best legal mind . . .", WOD to FDR, 12-7-37, official files, SEC, (SEC), Washington, D.C.
142   WOD's investigation, Report on Protective and Reorganization Committees, Parts I–VIII, Washington, D.C., 1937, SEC.
144   "Douglas was surgical . . .", AI with Fortas.
144   "He is not only . . .", WOD address to Duke Bar Association, Durham, N.C. 4-22-34, SEC.
144   "The earmark . . .", AI with David Ginsburg, Washington, D.C., 3-24-78.
144   "You stood me . . .", GEYM, p. 260.
144   "preconceived conclusions," R. Swaine, op. cit., p. 500.
145   WOD's view, AI with WOD.
145   WOD—Dulles confrontation, GEYM, p. 262.
145   WOD—Dulles exchange, Report on Protective and Reorganization Committees, Part I, pp. 830–831, SEC.
146   "Dulles posed . . .", GEYM, p. 262.
146   WOD—Untermyer confrontation, Ibid., pp. 262, 263.
147   "Their arrangement . . .", Ibid., p. 263.
147   WOD Jr's memories, AI with WOD Jr.
147   "He treated us . . .", AI with Millie Douglas Read.
147   "Douglas told me . . .", AI with McDougal.
147   "Douglas was always . . .", AI with Gesell.
148   WOD criticism of corporate trustee, NYT, 6-19-36, p. 1.
148   WOD criticism of bond houses, NYT, 6-4-36, p. 35.
150   "And now . . .", FF to WOD, 6-28-37, FFPLC.

Chapter Thirteen: Crusader and Irritant

151   Kennedy's SEC accomplishments, "Mr. Kennedy—The Chairman", op. cit.; "SEC", *Fortune,* June 1940.
151   "a going concern", JPK to FDR, 9-6-35, Franklin D. Roosevelt Papers (FDRP), Hyde Park, N.Y.
152   "this fool rumor . . .", WW to JML, 10-2-35, SEC.
152   Maloney telegram, FM to FDR, 12-7-35, FDRP.

Page

153 "Ben and I . . .", AI with Thomas G. Corcoran, Washington, D.C., 12-20-76.
153 "John didn't want . . .", James M. Landis oral history transcript, Columbia Oral History Collection (COHC), CUL.
153 "You're my man", GEYM, p. 264.
153 WOD meets FDR, WOD to FDR, 7-7-36, FDRP.
153 WOD credits FF, WOD to FF, 1-22-36, FFPLC.
153 "Sent to the . . .", *Time,* 1-27-36, p. 50.
153 "is not looked . . .", *Newsweek,* 1-24-36, p. 46.
153 "Washington thinks . . .", *Fortune,* March 1936, p. 198.
154 *Times*'s report, NYT, 1-17-36, p. 27.
154 WOD speech to investment bankers, NYT, 3-8-36, III, p. 1.
154 WOD's criticism of speculation, NYT, 7-12-36, III, p. 1.
155 "Floor traders . . .", NYT, 7-19-36, III, p. 1.
155 Rumors circulated, Ibid.
155 "When you honored . . .", WOD to FDR, 7-7-36, FDRP.
156 "In view . . .", WOD to SE, 7-8-36, Ibid.
156 "Call him . . .", FDR to MHM, 7-9-36, Ibid.
156 WOD's Chicago speech, WOD, (introduction and notes by James Allen), *Democracy and Finance,* (Port Washington, N.Y. 1940), p. 1.
157 "economic royalists . . .", W. Leuchtenberg, op. cit., p. 184.
157 Landis at SEC, "The Legend of Landis", *Fortune,* August 1934.
158 "At most . . .", Landis oral history transcript, COHC.
158 WOD's criticism of customers' men, WOD, *Democracy and Finance,* p. 107.
159 WOD Bond Club speech, NYT, 3-25-37, p. 37.
159 "spontaneous . . .", Ibid, p. 46.
159 "Do you suppose . . .", NYT, 10-24-37, VIII, p. 9.
160 Wall Street's preferences, NYT, 1-14-37, p. 35.
160 Harriman's advice, Daniel Roper to FDR, 9-18-37, FDRP.
160 "Since Mr. Douglas . . .", NYT, 8-10-37, p. 35.
160 "The Yakima school . . .", *Time,* 10-11-37, p. 61.

Chapter Fourteen: No Monkey Business

162 Background on confrontation between SEC and officers of New York Stock Exchange, Joseph Alsop and Robert Kintner, "The Battle of the Market Place," *Saturday Evening Post* (SEP), 6-11-38 and 6-25-38.
163 Gay's background, Ibid.; Literary Digest 1-29-38, p. 12. Whitney's background, J. Alsop and R. Kintner, op. cit., 6-11-38.
164 Exchange politics, Ibid.
165 WOD's thoughts, J. Alsop and R. Kintner, op. cit., 6-25-38.
165 WOD's version of appointment, GEYM, p. 281.
165 "a militant idealist . . .", *New York Herald Tribune,* 9-23-37, p. 26.
165 "What kind . . .", NYT, 9-23-37, p. 45.
166 *Herald Tribune* editorial, NYHT, 9-23-37, p. 23.
166 "we were taught . . .", *Time,* 10-11-37, p. 61.
167 Background on WOD's SEC policies, Fred Rodell, "Douglas over the Stock Exchange", *Fortune,* February 1938.
168 Behind the scenes battle, J. Alsop and R. Kintner, op. cit., 6-25-38.
170 WOD—Jackson exchange, Ralph F. De Bedts, *The New Deal's SEC,* (New York, 1964), pp. 162, 163.

Page

171   Feud went public, F. Rodell, op. cit.
171   "Bullshit", AI with Rodell.
171   "I have always . . .", NYT, 11-24-37, p. 39.
172   Wall Street cried "foul", Ibid.
172   Gay's statement, NYT, 11-30-37, p. 12.
173   WOD—Conway exchange, J. Alsop and R. Kintner, op. cit., SEP, 6-25-38.
173   Whitney's problems and downfall, Ibid.

Chapter Fifteen: In Brandeis's Footsteps

176   Discussion between FDR and his economic advisers, W. Leuchtenberg, op. cit., pp. 243–274.
177   "are taking . . .", NYT, 4-3-38, IV, p. 3.
177   "who have expressed . . .", NYT, 4-10-38, p. 2.
178   Crap game, WOD to JC, 12-8-37, SEC.
178   WOD at SEC, AI with Fortas, Gesell, Ginsburg, Emerson.
178   Hide and seek, AI with Gesell.
179   WOD as true believer, AI with Emerson.
179   "When most men . . .", WOD, *Democracy and Finance*, introduction by James Allen.
179   "I don't think . . .", AI with Gesell.
179   "The issuance . . .", WOD to FDR, 4-12-39, FDRP.
180   "we do not . . .", NYT, 11-9-37, p. 33.
181   "Government . . .", WOD, *Democracy and Finance*, introduction by James Allen.
181   "if we can . . .", NYT, 5-14-38, p. 2.
181   "It looks . . .", WOD to JPK, 4-2-38, SEC.
181   "We were doing . . .", AI with Fortas.
182   "Is the front . . .", GEYM, p. 298.
182   "We finished . . .", Ibid., p. 299.
182   Background on *New Yorker* investigation, SEC memorandum, 3-7-39, SEC.
182   "Does he habitually . . .", deposition of Ruth Lackman by W.J. Cogan and Philip Wagner, 2-21-39, SEC.
183   "My receptionist . . .", HR to DHS, 2-28-39, SEC.
183   "I was proud . . .", GEYM, p. 269.
183   "He gave loyalty . . .", AI with Fortas.
184   WOD on SEC appointments, WOD to FDR, 12-7-37, SEC.
184   "Once Douglas . . .", AI with Gesell.
185   Summary of SEC findings, J. Frank memorandum to files, 3-11-38, SEC; *In the Matter of Richard Whitney*, SEC.
185   "a honey", WOD to JPK, 10-29-38, SEC.
186   "The Wall Street Wail . . .", J. Frank to WOD, 9-30-38, Ibid.
187   WOD's complaint, WOD to WMM, 11-1-38, Ibid.
187   "it would have been . . .", memorandum of conference between SEC and Exchange officials, 12-17-38, Ibid.
187   "In the hearings . . .", RMH to WMM, 12-18-38, Ibid.
187   "IT IS NOT . . .", WOD to RMH, 12-17-38, Ibid.
187   "your decision . . .", JF to RMH, 12-19-38, Ibid.
188   "unfinished business," WOD statement, 12-22-38, Ibid.
188   "to take off . . .", WOD to FDR, 4-12-39, FDRP.
189   "too hot . . .", WOD to FDR, Ibid.

Page

189 "A bang up job," NYT, 12-30-38, p. 1.
189 Krock's toast, GEYM, p. 459.
190 "I had never . . .", Ibid., p. 465.
190 "The important . . .", Ibid., p. 455.
190 WOD at TNEC hearings, WOD testimony, 2-6-39, SEC.
191 "degrade moral values . . .", NYT, 2-10-39, p. 36.
191 Brandeis's endorsement of WOD, GEYM, p. 459.
191 Ickes conversation with FDR, Harold Ickes, *The Secret Diary of Harold L. Ickes, 1936–1939* (New York, 1954), pp. 588, 589.
191 Frank campaign, GEYM, p. 462.
191 WOD on FDR Court-packing plan, Ibid., p. 324.
192 WOD letters to Murphy, Rayburn and Farley, 2-14-39, SEC.
192 WOD letter to Brandeis, WOD to LDB, 2-20-39, Ibid.
192 "was delighted . . .", WOD to WL, 2-18-39, Ibid.
192 "In all candor . . .", WOD to JFD, 2-23-39, Ibid.
192 "stimulating . . .", WOD to JFD, 1-18-39, Ibid.
192 WOD's solicitations, Cameron Sherwood letter to the author, 11-30-77.
193 Support for WOD, AI with Maxey.
193 Borah's support, GEYM, p. 462.
193 WOD's attack, NYT, 3-16-39, p. 35.
193 Krock's analysis, NYT, 3-26-39, IV, p. 3.
194 "I have . . .", GEYM, p. 463.
194 Frazier's opposition, 84 *Congressional Record* 3706–13, 3773–88.

Chapter Sixteen: The Short Reign of Felix Frankfurter

197 Power of judicial review, *Marbury* v. *Madison*, 1 Cranch 137 (1803).
197 "Accustomed to trample . . .", Fred Rodell, *Nine Men: A Political History of the Supreme Court of the United States from 1790 to 1955* (New York, 1955), p. 134. *Dred Scott* v. *Sandford*, 19 How. 393 (1857).
198 "a self-inflicted wound", Charles E. Hughes, *The Supreme Court of the United States* (New York, 1928), p. 50.
198 Court tore great chunks, *Schechter Poultry Corp.* v. *U.S.*, 295 U.S. 495 (1935); *Carter* v. *Carter Coal Co.*, 298 U.S. 238 (1936); *U.S.* v. *Butler*, 297 U.S. 1 (1936); *Morehead* v. *Tipaldo*, 298 U.S. 587 (1936).
198 Court changes, *West Coast Hotel* v. *Parrish*, 300 U.S. 379 (1937); *National Labor Relations Board* v. *Jones & Laughlin Steel Corp.*, 301 U.S. 1 (1937); *Steward Machine Co.* v. *Davis*, 301 U.S. 548 (1937).
199 Court's mission, Robert McCloskey, *The American Supreme Court* (Chicago, 1960).
200 "the most useful . . .", J. Lash, op. cit., p. 39.
200 "brutality and injustice . . .", J. Rauh, op. cit., p. 498.
201 "Trotsky and . . .", Ibid.
201 "From the time . . .", Ibid., p. 501.
201 "What is urgently . . .", J. Lash, op. cit., p. 64.
202 "We were all . . .", H. Ickes, op. cit., p. 559.
202 "Do you know . . .", J. Lash, op. cit., p. 67.
202 "Judges cannot . . .", Ibid.
203 "zeal for self expression," Ibid., p. 76.
203 "He's too discursive . . .", Ibid.

Page

204 "I am bound . . .", FF to WOD, 12-2-41, FFPLC.

204 "disclose what . . .", FF to WOD, 12-20-40, Ibid.

204 Irritation of WOD, Black and Murphy, AI with Fortas; AI with Joseph Rauh, Jr., Washington, D.C., 3-23-78.

204 Background on *Gobitis* case, Alan Barth, *Prophets with Honor* (New York, 1974), pp. 108–130; John Garraty, ed., *Quarrels That Have Shaped the Constitution* (New York, 1964), pp. 222–242.

205 "Our beloved . . .", *Gobitis* v. *Minersville School Dist.*, 21 F. Supp. 581, 585 (1937).

206 "I come up . . .", J. W. Howard, *Mr. Justice Murphy* (Princeton, 1968), p. 287.

206 "I can express . . .", J. Lash, op. cit., pp. 68, 69.

207 "because of his . . .", Ibid., p. 69.

207 *Gobitis* decision, *Minersville School District* v. *Gobitis*, 310 U.S. 586 (1940).

208 "We think . . .", J. Garraty, ed., op. cit., p. 234.

208 "When a liberal . . .", Ibid., p. 235.

208 "there seemed . . .", Ibid.

209 Attacks on Jehovah's Witnesses, Ibid.

209 Companion cases, *Bridges* v. *California*, 314 U.S. 252 (1941).

210 Holmes's "clear and present danger" test, *Schenck* v. *U.S.*, 249 U.S. 47 (1919).

211 Background on Betts case, A. Barth, op. cit., pp. 80–107.

213 *Betts* decision, *Betts* v. *Brady*, 316 U.S. 455 (1942).

214 *Jones* v. *Opelika*, 316 U.S. 584 (1942).

Chapter Seventeen: An Uncluttered Mind

216 "the Axis", J. Lash, op. cit., p. 76.

216 "We are not . . .", J. W. Howard, op. cit., pp. 268–270.

216 "Us girls . . .", Ibid., p. 268.

217 "Felix thought . . .", AI with Philip Elman, Washington, D.C., 3-23-78.

217 "Every time . . .", J. Lash, op. cit., p. 174.

217 "two completely . . .", *Newsweek*, 11-24-75, p. 45.

217 "the most systematic . . .", J. Lash, op. cit., p. 175.

217 WOD's suspicions, AI with WOD; WOD to F. Rodell, 6-18-(undated), Rodell Papers (FRP), Haverford College Library, Haverford, PA.

217 Frankfurter's lobbying, J. Lash, op. cit., pp. 345–350.

218 Cabal of FF admirers, WOD to F. Rodell, 1-14-54, 2-9-55, 11-29-56, FRP.

218 "Douglas was . . .", AI with Fortas.

219 "that the line . . .", J. Lash, op. cit., p. 250.

219 Price-fixing decision, *U.S.* v. *Socony-Vacuum Oil Co.*, 310 U.S. 150 (1940).

219 Brandeis was pleased, Alpheus T. Mason, *Brandeis—A Free Man's Life*, (New York, 1946), p. 635.

220 WOD touched, WOD to FDR, 7-12-41, FDRP.

220 "gives some advantage . . .", FDR to WOD, 9-19-39, FDRP.

220 "Pitching and catching . . .", WOD to FDR, 9-19-39, Ibid.

221 "he [Douglas] was lots . . .", H. Ickes, op. cit., p. 601.

221 "Bill Douglas is . . .", H. Ickes, *The Secret Diary of Harold L. Ickes, 1939–1941* (New York, 1954), p. 53.

221 FF and WOD on government eavesdropping, *Goldman* v. *U.S.*, 316 U.S. 129 (1942).

222 Challenge to "Okie" law, *Edwards* v. *California*, 314 U.S. 160 (1941).

222 Challenge to Oklahoma law, *Skinner* v. *Oklahoma*, 316 U.S. 535 (1942).

Page

222   Court recognizes fundamental right to interstate travel, *Shapiro* v. *Thompson,* 394 U.S. 618 (1969).

223   Jehovah's Witnesses case, *Murdock* v. *Pennsylvania,* 319 U.S. 105 (1943).

224   FF's relationship with clerks, AI with Rauh, Elman.

224   WOD's relationship with clerks, AI with clerks (some of whom requested anonymity).

225   "Justice Douglas . . .", AI with confidential source (CS).

225   "which one . . .", Ibid.

225   "I thought . . .", AI with Professor Vern Countryman, Cambridge, MA, 5-18-78.

226   "He didn't create . . .", AI with CS.

226   "But that footnote . . .", AI with Countryman.

226   "He wasn't . . .", AI with CS.

226   "I doubt . . .", AI with Ginsburg.

227   "we were back . . .", AI with CS.

Chapter Eighteen: Illusion and Reality

228   WOD family profiles, *House and Garden,* August 1942; *Ladies Home Journal,* March 1943.

230   WOD Jr.'s memories, AI with WOD Jr.

232   "I got encouragement . . .", AI with Dr. Douglas Corpron, Jr., Yakima, WA., 8-18-76.

233   "You talk . . .", AI with WOD Jr.

233   Millie's memories, AI with Millie Douglas Read.

236   "Children tend . . .", AI with Florence Douglas Persons, Scarsdale, NY, 4-12-78.

237   Mildred at White House, AI with WOD Jr.

237   Tension between Mildred and WOD, AI with Read, WOD Jr.

238   "People have heard . . .", MD to WOD, 6-5-39, Millie Douglas Read letters (MDRL).

238   "darling: . . .", MD to WOD, 6-8-39, Ibid.

238   "if you would . . .", MD to WOD, 6-15-39, Ibid.

239   ". . . the 27th . . .", MD to WOD, 9-21-42, Ibid.

239   "I couldn't . . .", MD to WOD, 9-30-44, Ibid.

239   "I could feel . . .", AI with Mrs. Douglas Corpron Sr., Yakima, WA., 8-18-76.

239   WOD's view of marriage, GEYM, p. 144.

Chapter Nineteen: One Soul to Save

241   Treatment of Japanese-Americans, John M. Blum, *V Was for Victory: Politics and American Culture During World War Two* (New York, 1976).

241   U.S. public opinion polls, Ibid., p. 46.

242   "The Japs live . . .", Ibid., pp. 160, 161.

242   "If the Japs . . .", Earl Warren profile by Anthony Lewis, Leon Friedman and Fred Israel, editors, *The Justices of the U.S. Supreme Court, 1789–1969* (New York 1969), Vol. IV, p. 2728.

242   "I said . . .", AI with Countryman.

243   *Hirabayashi* decision, *Hirabayashi* v. *U.S.,* 320 U.S. 81 (1943).

243   "That was . . .", AI with Countryman.

243   *Korematzu* decision, *Korematzu* v. *U.S.,* 323 U.S. 214 (1944).

244   WOD's patriotism, GEYM, pp. 93–95.

Page

244   WOD's desire to enlist, WOD to FDR, 7-10-42, FDRP.

244   "Hitler would say . . .", WOD speech to American Jewish Congress, 3-1-43, FFPHLS.

244   *Gobitis* reversal, *West Va. Bd. of Education* v. *Barnette,* 319 U.S. 624 (1943).

244   Deportation decision, *Schneiderman* v. *U.S.,* 320 U.S. 118 (1943).

244   Seventh Day Adventist decision, *Girouard* v. *U.S.,* 328 U.S. 61 (1946).

244   *Endo* decision, *Ex Parte Endo,* 323 U.S. 283 (1944).

245   Douglas opinion in *Defunis* v. *Odegaard,* 416 U.S. 312 (1974).

245   Roberts's bitterness, J.W. Howard, op. cit., p. 392.

245   "the Saint's farewell. . . ." Ibid., p. 395.

245   Black-Jackson feud, Gerald T. Dunn, *Justice Black and the Judicial Revolution* (New York, 1977), pp. 224–249.

245   FF and WOD, AI with Elman, Fortas, Rauh, Rodell.

246   "he [Vinson] is confident . . .", J. Lash, op. cit., p. 274.

247   Pritchett statistics, NYT, 2-22-46, p. 24; WOD profile, *PM,* 12-15-46; C. Herman Pritchett, *Civil Liberties and the Vinson Court* (Chicago 1954).

247   "show them . . .", WOD profile, *PM,* op. cit.

247   Schlesinger analysis, "The Supreme Court: 1947", *Fortune,* January 1947.

247   "Those tags . . .", WOD profile, *PM,* op. cit.

248   "The basic issues . . .", WOD to FR, 6-7-46, FRP.

248   Black's philosophy, Hugo Black, "The Bill of Rights," 35 *N.Y.U. L. Rev.* 865 (1960); Hugo Black and Edmond Cahn, "Justice Black and the First Amendment's Absolutes", 37 *N.Y.U. L. Rev.* 549 (1962).

248   Loudspeaker decision, *Kovacs* v. *Cooper,* 336 U.S. 77 (1949).

248   "preferred position," Stone opinion (footnote 4), *U.S.* v. *Carolene Products Co.,* 304 U.S. 144 (1938).

248   Syracuse orator decision, *Feiner* v. *New York,* 340 U.S. 315 (1951).

249   Black-FF "incorporation" debate, *Adamson* v. *California,* 332 U.S. 46 (1947).

249   Cardozo standard, *Palko* v. *Conn.,* 302 U.S. 319 (1937).

250   "I fear . . .", *Adamson* v. *California,* Ibid., p. 89.

250   "I haven't been . . .", NYT, 11-11-73, p. E-14.

251   "It is . . .", WOD, "Stare Decisis", 49 *Colum. L. Rev.* 735, 746 (1949).

251   Rate-making decision, *Federal Power Commission* v. *Hope Natural Gas Co.,* 320 U.S. 591 (1944).

252   *Esquire* decision, *Hannegan* v. *Esquire Inc.,* 327 U.S. 146 (1946).

252   Interrogation decision, *Haley* v. *Ohio,* 332 U.S. 596 (1948).

253   "When Douglas . . .", AI with Professor Paul Freund, Cambridge, MA, 5-20-78.

253   Missouri voting decision, *Day Brite Lighting Inc.* v. *Missouri,* 342 U.S. 421 (1952).

254   Terminiello decision, *Terminiello* v. *Chicago,* 337 U.S. 1 (1949).

255   Dilliard editorial, *St. Louis Post-Dispatch,* 5-22-49.

255   Countryman's research, Countryman letter to author, 3-31-80.

256   Freund's response, PF to ID, 5-31-49, FFPHLS.

256   "an edifying exhibit . . .", FF to PF, 6-8-49, Ibid.

Chapter Twenty: "I Ain't A-runnin' "

257   "The office . . .", Morrison Waite profile by Louis Filler, L. Friedman and F. Israel, op. cit., Vol. II, p. 1249.

258   WOD's early silence, NYT, 7-7-40, IV. p. 3.

258   "Dear Felix . . .", WOD to FF, 7-2-40, FFPHLS.

Page

258   Frankfurter-Murphy exchange, J. Lash, op. cit., pp. 154, 155.
259   "I'm too young . . .", AI with Gesell.
260   "The gossips . . .", NYT, 10-26-39, p. 22.
260   Corcoran spreading the word, Harold Ickes, *The Secret Diary of Harold L. Ickes, 1939–1941*, (New York 1954), p. 229.
260   Farley corroborated, Henry Wallace oral history transcript, COHC.
260   "the New Dealers . . .", Ibid.
260   WOD letter, WOD to FDR, 7-9-40, FDRP.
260   "kept turning over . . .", H. Ickes, op. cit., p. 286.
261   "Unless I resign . . .", WOD to FDR, 7-10-42, FDRP.
261   "I am here . . .", WOD to FR, 6-30-41, FRP.
261   "full of . . .", J. Lash, op. cit., p. 251.
261   "the anti-Communist . . .", Ibid., pp. 215–217.
261   "getting a little . . .", J. Lash, op. cit., pp. 74, 75.
262   "Those great libertarians . . .", Felix Frankfurter oral history transcript, COHC.
262   Frankfurter's references, *Hirabayashi* v. *U.S.*, op. cit.; *Schneiderman* v. *U.S.*, op. cit.; *W. Va. Bd. of Education* v. *Barnette*, op. cit.
262   White House meeting, George E. Allen oral history transcript, Truman Library (TL), Independence, MO.
262   "picturesque figure", H. Wallace oral history transcript, COHC.
263   "I do not . . .", FDR to SJ, quoted in Henry Wallace oral history transcript, COHC.
263   "I think political . . .", WOD to HFS, 7-12-44, Harlan F. Stone Papers (HFSP), Library of Congress, Washington, D.C.
264   Corcoran impression, AI with Corcoran.
264   Murphy impression, recounted to Henry Wallace, H. Wallace oral history transcript, COHC.
264   "There have been . . .", FF to HFS, 8-22-44, HFSP.
264   "You have written . . .", WOD profile by John Frank, L. Friedman and F. Israel, editors, op. cit., Vol. IV, p. 2465.
264   WOD's account, AI with WOD.
264   Rosenman conclusion, WOD profile by John Frank, L. Friedman and F. Israel, editors, op. cit.
264   "I am certain . . .", Ibid.
265   "I felt . . .", WOD to HFS, 8-21-44, HFSP.
265   "Douglas was subjected . . .", AI with Fortas.
265   "Douglas thought . . .", AI with Eliot Janeway, New York City, 5-28-79.
265   Hillman's objection, Fred Rodell, "Bill Douglas—American," *American Mercury*, December, 1945.
266   Murphy's observations, recounted to Henry Wallace, H. Wallace oral history transcript, COHC.
266   Corcoran impression, AI with Corcoran.
266   Janeway impression, AI with Janeway.
267   "general talk", WOD to FR, 5-15-45, FRP.
267   WOD complaints, AI with Corcoran, Janeway.
267   "The real victory . . .", WOD, *Being an American* (New York, 1948) p. 205.
268   "One has . . .", Robert Donovan, *Conflict and Crisis: The Presidency of Harry S. Truman, 1945–1948* (New York, 1977) p. 183.
268   *Washington Star* Story, 2-21-46.
269   "If Bill went . . .", R. Donovan, op. cit., p. 183.
269   "Douglas was . . .", AI with Clark Clifford, Washington, D.C., 12-7-78.

Page

269 "friends of . . .", NYT, 2-20-46, p. 17.
269 Stone's view, NYT, 2-24-46, IV, p. 3.
270 "in the middle . . .", WOD to HST, 2-23-46, TL.
270 "He was once . . .", NYT, 2-24-46, IV, p. 3.
271 "that there was . . .", J. Lash, op. cit., p. 338.
271 "I think . . .", Ibid., p. 339.
271 "would be . . .", *U.S. News,* 1-30-48, p. 37.
271 ADA on WOD, ADA campaign pamphlet, 4-10-48.
271 "I have done . . .", WOD to ID, NYT, 6-6-48, p. 1.
271 "I never was . . .", NYT, 7-11-48, p. 5.
272 "Bill Douglas . . .", AI with Corcoran.
272 WOD's indecision, Robert Bendiner, "Politics and People," *Nation,* 6-12-48.
272 Eisenhower's statement, *New York Post,* 6-16-48.
272 WOD's silence, NYT, 7-6-48, p. 21.
272 "I have no . . .", NYT, 7-10-48, p. 1.
272 "Tell those . . .", AI with Rauh.
273 "I was on . . .", Ibid.
273 "A professional . . .", Ibid.
273 "to be persuaded . . .", NYT, 7-11-48, p. 1.
273 "I call him . . .", R. Donovan, op. cit., p. 405.
273 "I feel deeply . . .", NYT, 7-13-48, p. 4.
273 "Basic in my . . .", WOD to HST, 7-31-48, TL.
274 "Why be . . .", AI with Corcoran.
274 "In 1948, . . ." AI with Clifford.
274 "He belongs . . .", R. Donovan, op. cit.
274 Krock's comment, NYT, 6-17-49, p. 22.
274 "I am sorry . . .", HST to WOD, 9-27-51, TL.
275 WOD's letter, NYT, 1-14-52, p. 1.
275 Corcoran's advice, AI with Corcoran.
275 "The Court became . . .", AI with Janeway.

Chapter Twenty-one: A Man's Man

276 "a man's man", AI with Rodell.
276 "after Dad's . . .", AI with Read.
276 WOD and Schaeffer meeting, GEYM, p. 236.
277 "I'll give you . . .", Ibid.
277 Schaeffer stories, GEYM; OMM.
277 "Roy Schaeffer is . . .", OMM, p. 232.
278 "Dirty limericks", AI with Rodell.
278 "Do You Know Americans", WOD to FR, 5-29-46, FRP.
278 "There was . . .", WOD to FR, 7-9-46, Ibid.
279 "your Katherine", WOD to FR, 10-26-46, Ibid.
279 "I was delighted . . .", WOD to FR, 11-21-46, Ibid.
279 "Shouldn't all . . .", WOD to FR, 10-26-46, Ibid.
279 "He is a . . .", WOD to J.D. Robb, 2-3-47, Ibid.
280 WOD and Trout meeting, AI with Damon Trout, Portland, OR., 8-25-76.
280 "It scared . . .", Ibid.
280 "Let's get . . .", Ibid.
280 "I met . . .", Ibid.

Page

281 "Suddenly the . . .", Fred Rodell, "As Justice Bill Douglas Completes His First Thirty Years on the Court", 16 *U.C.L.A. L. Rev.* 704, 712, 713 (1969).

281 "He just lived . . .", AI with Gilbert.

281 "When you . . .", NYT, 10-11-49, p. 17.

281 "Your wonderful . . .", WOD to JF, 10-24-49, JFP.

282 "just a good . . .", AI with Mercedes Douglas Eichholz.

282 WOD's attitude toward Mildred, AI with Mrs. Douglas Corpron, Sr.; AI with Mrs. Fern Ferris, Yakima, WA., 8-18-76.

282 "It wasn't . . .", AI with Ferris.

282 "I just . . .", Ibid.

282 "thinks I'll . . .", WOD to FV, 11-20-49, Hugo Black Papers (HBP), Library of Congress, Washington, D.C.

283 WOD's exhaustion, WOD to HB, 12-23-49, HBP.

283 "Never a man . . .", *Time,* 11-28-49, p. 30.

283 "the judicial chest," *Life,* 12-5-49, p. 55.

283 Fischer's suggestions, JF to WOD, 12-12-49, Harper & Row Papers, Rare Book and Manuscript Library (RBML), Columbia University, New York City.

283 WOD's reply, WOD to JF, 12-14-49, Ibid.

283 "The bones . . .", WOD to HB, 12-23-49, HBP.

284 "I might . . .", WOD to JF, 12-24-49, RBML.

284 WOD pose, NYT, 1-24-50, p. 22.

284 that "they . . .", WOD to JF, 10-6-50, RBML.

284 "writer's license", AI with Millie Douglas Read.

284 "There is an . . .", NYT, 4-10-50, p. 17.

285 WOD dallied, AI with Eichholz, Janeway.

285 "It gets . . .", MD to WOD, 2-18-48, MDRL.

285 "I think . . .", MD to WOD, 2-19-48, Ibid.

285 "Your note . . .", MD to WOD, 2-12-(undated), Ibid.

285 WOD and Mercedes, AI with Eichholz.

286 "Divorce was . . .", GEYM, p. 144.

286 Mercedes's beliefs, AI with Eichholz.

286 "I told Bill . . .", AI with Corcoran.

287 "I hope . . .", MD to WOD, 3-8-52, MDRL.

Chapter Twenty-two: Russian Roulette

291 "In my opinion . . .", Eric Goldman, *The Crucial Decade, America 1945–1955* (New York, 1956), p. 142.

291 "I have here . . .", Ibid.

292 "Whether Senator . . .", Ibid., p. 215.

292 "If Communists . . .", M. Jahoda and S. Cook, "Security Measures and Freedom of Thought", 61 *Yale L. J.* 295, 307 (1952).

292 "The great danger . . .", WOD, "The Black Silence of Fear," NYT, 1-13-52, VI, p. 7.

293 Background on Dennis case, A. Barth, op. cit., pp. 170–174.

293 "I want . . .", Ibid., p. 173.

293 *Dennis* decision, *Dennis* v. *U.S.,* 341 U.S. 494 (1951).

295 WOD's views on due process, *Vital Speeches,* 7-1-53, p. 554.

295 *Bailey* decision, *Bailey* v. *Richardson,* 341 U.S. 918 (1951).

296 WOD's views in *Bailey* expressed in his opinion in *Anti-Fascist Refugee Committee* v. *McGrath,* 341 U.S. 123 (1951).

Page

297   Challenge to Feinberg Law, *Adler* v. *Bd. of Education,* 342 U.S. 485 (1952).
297   "Communist victories", memo of Justice Jackson in *Joint Anti-Fascist Refugee Committee* v. *McGrath,* FFPHLS.
298   "Douglas and Black . . .", author's telephone interview with Hans Linde, 10-22-73.
298   "Douglas was . . .", AI with Elman.
298   "Sitting on . . .", J. Rauh, Jr., op. cit., p. 515.
299   Jackson's view, Marquis Childs oral history transcript, COHC.
299   Background on the Court in the Rosenberg case, Michael E. Parrish, "Cold War Justice: The Supreme Court and the Rosenbergs", 82 *American Historical Review* 805 (October 1977).
300   "His [Douglas's] 'denys' . . .", F. Frankfurter, Rosenberg Memorandum, FFPHLS.
300   Burton records, Harold H. Burton Papers (HHBP), Library of Congress, Washington, D.C.
300   Jackson records, Robert Jackson Papers (RJP), University of Chicago Law School, Chicago, Ill.
300   WOD records, WOD clerk, Monty Podva, letter to author, 9-14-79.
300   Certiorari denied, *Rosenberg et al.* v. *U.S.,* 344 U.S. 838, 850 (1952).
300   "Douglas again . . .", Rosenberg Memorandum, FFPHLS.
301   Certiorari denied, *Rosenberg et al.* v. *U.S.,* 344 U.S. 889 (1952).
301   "wholly reprehensible", *U.S.* v. *Rosenberg et al.,* 109 F. Supp. 108, 116 (1953).
301   "in the same . . .", Rosenberg Memorandum, FFPHLS.
301   Frankfurter's views, Ibid.
301   "Mr. Justice Black. . . .", Ibid.
301   "I have done . . .", Ibid.
302   Frankfurter's strategy, Ibid.
302   "I would conclude . . .", Rehnquist memorandum, In Re *Rosenberg,* RJP.
303   "Don't worry . . .", Rosenberg Memorandum, FFPHLS.
303   "He [Douglas] ought . . .", Ibid.
304   "That S.O.B.'s . . .", Ibid.
304   Perhaps he . . ., Ibid.
304   "is of the . . .", *Rosenberg et al.* v. *U.S.,* 345 U.S. 965, 966 (1953).
304   "unsupported and . . .", NYT, 6-4-53, p. 13.
304   Court's Saturday conference, Rosenberg Memorandum, FFPHLS.
305   Court's actions, *Rosenberg et al.* v. *U.S.* 345 U.S. 989 (1953).
305   WOD's denial, F. Frankfurter, Rosenberg Memorandum-Addendum, 6-19-53, FFPHLS.
306   WOD and Rosenberg attorneys, Ibid.
306   WOD "seized", Ibid.
306   WOD talked to Vinson, Ibid.
307   "enduring document", Ibid.
307   "Do what . . .", Ibid.
307   WOD opinion, *Rosenberg* v. *U.S.,* 346 U.S. 313 (1953).
307   WOD heard the announcement, NYT, 6-18-53, p. 16.
307   "No effort . . .", WOD to FR, 6-25-53, FRP.
308   "on a motor . . .", M. Childs, oral history transcript, COHC.
308   Brownell meeting, M. Parrish, op. cit., p. 835.
308   "He felt . . .", AI with Eichholz.
308   "The C.J. has . . .", WOD to FR, 6-25-53, FRP.

Page

308   *Ex Parte Quirin* et al., 317 U.S. 1 (1942).
309   "at the hopelessness . . .", J. Rauh, Jr., op. cit., pp. 514, 515.
309   "When the Court . . .", WOD to FR, 6-25-53, FRP.
309   "There never . . .", NYT, 6-19-53, p. 8.
309   "The probabilities . . .", NYT, 6-19-53, p. 8.
310   Justices' stormy conferences, Burton, Conference Notes on WOD stay, HHBP.
310   "Let it take . . .", Ibid.
310   "There were four . . .", WOD to FR, 6-25-53, FRP.
310   "wrong to . . .", Burton, Conference Notes on WOD stay, HHBP.
310   "Their expressions . . .", NYT, 6-20-53, p. 7.
310   Court opinion, *Rosenberg* v. *U.S.*, 346 U.S. 273 (1953).
311   "the Rosenbergs . . .", NYT, 6-20-53, p. 1.
311   Rosenbergs at Sing Sing, Ibid., p. 6.
313   WOD on Rosenbergs' stay, GEYM, pp. 23, 469.

Chapter Twenty-three: Strange Lands

314   WOD on Vietnam, WOD, *North from Malaya*, (New York, 1953).
314   "The Viet Minh . . .", Ibid., p. 153.
315   "Today . . .", Ibid., p. 173.
315   "who suspect . . .", Ibid., p. 206.
315   "a social conscience," *Saturday Review*, 11-10-51, p. 17.
315   "Traveling with . . .", WOD profile, *Yakima Herald Republic*, 9-16-54.
316   "a robust . . .", WOD, *Strange Lands and Friendly People* (New York, 1951), p. 72.
316   "how gracious . . .", Ibid., p. 132.
316   "a certain Douglas", *Life*, 8-15-49, p. 59.
316   "Big Devil", NYT, 10-3-49, p. 32.
316   "It might . . .", WOD to JF, 5-2-51, RBML.
317   "The eye-and-ear . . .", *Saturday Review*, 11-10-51, p. 17.
317   "fairly drastic", JF to WOD, 2-13-51, RBML.
317   "That material . . .", WOD to JF, 2-18-51, Ibid.
318   "The boy turned . . .", WOD, *Strange Lands and Friendly People*, p. 309.
318   "a tigress . . .", Ibid., p. 15.
318   "quiet, soft-spoken . . .", Ibid., p. 264.
319   WOD's advance, JF to WOD, 4-11-51, RBML.
319   "I think . . .", AI with Cass Canfield, New York City, 6-11-79.
319   "My impression . . .", AI with Ken McCormick, New York City, 5-22-79.
319   "knew how . . .", AI with Canfield.
319   Gillu's adventures, WOD, *Beyond the High Himalayas*, (New York, 1952), p. 27.
320   "Right now . . .", Ibid., p. 40.
320   "We had won . . .", Ibid.
321   "magical hat", Ibid., p. 78.
321   "Moti and her mother . . .", Ibid., p. 115.
321   "Do you mean . . .", WOD, *West of the Indus*, (Garden City, NY, 1958), pp. 3, 4.
322   "We are . . .", WOD, *Beyond the High Himalayas*, pp. 232, 233.
323   WOD and RFK in Russia, WOD, *Russian Journey*, (Garden City, N.Y., 1956).
323   "Douglas, the judge . . .", Arthur M. Schlesinger, Jr., *Robert Kennedy and His Times*, (Boston, 1978), p. 123.
323   "We all want . . .", Ibid., p. 129.

Page

323   "My feeling . . .", Ibid., p. 127.
324   "people with problems", Ibid., p. 129.
324   "He was a man . . .", R.F. Kennedy tribute to WOD at U.S. Supreme Court, 4-20-64.
324   WOD letters to HST, 10-19-50, 9-25-51, TL.
324   WOD luncheon, WOD oral history transcript, Kennedy Library, Waltham, MA.
324   "a new orientation . . .", Ibid.

Chapter Twenty-four: Potbellied Men

326   Warren's speculation, Chief Justice Earl Warren, "Mr. Justice Douglas", 16 *U.C.-L.A. L. Rev.* 699 (1969).
327   "I'll be . . .", Bob Burleson and Jim Bowmer, "William O. Douglas—In Retrospect", 28 *Baylor L. Rev.* 211 (Spring 1976).
327   "Want to go . . .", Charles Reich, *The Sorcerer of Bolinas Reef,* (New York, 1976), p. 60.
327   "That is the . . .", WOD to FR, 8-2-(undated), FRP.
327   "Bill was a . . .", AI with Gene Marsh, McMinnville, OR, 8-26-76.
327   "You could see . . .", AI with Gilbert.
327   "I always felt . . .", Ibid.
328   "I would rather . . .", WOD, "People v. Trout: a majority opinion," *NYT Mag* 4-2-50.
328   "Set rock . . .", WOD profile, *The Oregonian,* 6-30-46.
328   "It is a . . .", *Time,* 2-1-54, p. 15.
329   WOD dedication, NYT, 5-18-77, p. B-1.
329   "in the name . . .", *Sierra Club* v. *Morton,* 405 U.S. 727 (1972).
330   "all of the noises . . .", WOD, *My Wilderness: The Pacific West,* (Garden City, NY, 1960), p. 9.
330   "If the sun . . .", Ibid., p. 83.
330   "Nursery . . .", Ibid., p. 135.
330   "Potbellied men . . .", Ibid., p. 94.
330   "We need . . .", Ibid., p. 101.
331   "The pull . . .", WOD, *My Wilderness: East to Katahdin* (Garden City, NY, 1961), p. 266.
331   "Civilization . . .", Ibid., p. 288.
331   "God made . . .", Ibid., p. 289.
331   "the modern Ahabs", WOD, *Farewell to Texas: A Vanishing Wilderness* (New York, 1967), foreword.
331   "When we think . . . , Ibid., p. 231.
332   "a shining jewel . . .", WOD, *A Wilderness Bill of Rights* (Boston, 1965), p. 10.
332   "once a proud . . .", Ibid., p. 13.
332   "at the heart . . .", Ibid., p. 23.
332   "The wilderness is . . .", Ibid., p. 31.
332   WOD's Wilderness Bill of Rights, Ibid., pp. 119–150.

Chapter Twenty-five: National Teacher

334   Meiklejohn's First Amendment philosophy, Alexander Meiklejohn, *Free Speech and Its Relation to Self-Government,* (New York, 1948).
335   "The unabridged . . .", A. Meiklejohn, op. cit., p. 91.

Page

335   "Full and free . . .", *Dennis* v. *U.S.*, 341 U.S. 494 (1951).
335   "The First Amendment . . .", *Beauharnais* v. *Ill.*, 343 U.S. 250 (1952).
336   "which have . . .", WOD, *An Almanac of Liberty*, (Garden City, NY, 1954) p. 125; Meiklejohn's criticism, A. Meiklejohn, "What Does the First Amendment Mean", 20 *U. of Chi. L. Rev.* 461 (1953).
336   "The command . . .", *Poulos* v. *New Hampshire*, 345 U.S. 395 (1953).
336   "In order . . .", *Superior Films Inc.* v. *Dept. of Education*, 346 U.S. 587 (1954).
336   "is so closely . . .", *Roth* v. *U.S.*, 354 U.S. 476 (1957).
337   "My views . . .", WOD to EC, 1-21-60, Edmond Cahn Papers (ECP), New York City.
337   WOD's fears about Yale, WOD to FR, 1-14-54, 2-9-55, FRP.
338   WOD on Frankfurter speech, WOD to FR, 1-14-54, FRP.
338   WOD on Shulman, WOD to FR, 2-9-55, Ibid.
338   "He said . . .", AI with Professor Steve Duke, New York City, 5-18-79.
338   "FF's boys", WOD to FR, 11-29-54, FRP.
338   "shows what . . .", WOD to FR, 3-29-(undated), Ibid.
338   "learning the . . .", WOD to FR, 11-11-(undated), Ibid.
338   Cahn letter, EC to WOD, 5-23-61, ECP.
339   "Dear Mr. Brown . . .", WOD to FB, 5-24-61, Ibid.
339   "This may . . .", WOD to EC, 5-24-61, Ibid.
339   "I don't know . . .", FB to WOD, 5-25-61, Ibid.
339   Cahn's elation, EC to WOD, 5-26-61, Ibid.
339   "more or less . . .", NYT, 1-19-58, VII, p. 3.
339   "no more than . . .", WOD, *The Right of the People*, (Garden City, NY, 1958), p. 45.
340   WOD's condemnation of balancing, Ibid., p. 51.
340   "legislative discretion", Ibid., p. 19.
340   "The philosophy . . .", Ibid., p. 35.
341   "And to us . . .", A. Meiklejohn, *Free Speech and Its Relation to Self-Government*, p. 32.
341   "the conscience . . .", WOD, *An Almanac of Liberty*, p. 42.
341   "more the small . . .", Ibid, foreword.
342   "Our philosophy . . .", Ibid., p. 125.
342   "Wiretapping . . .", Ibid., p. 354.
342   "The Fifth . . .", Ibid., p. 238.
342   "The Constitution . . .", Ibid., p. 42.
343   Florida A & M case, *Adderley* v. *Florida*, 385 U.S. 39 (1966).
344   Tinker decision, *Tinker* v. *Des Moines School District*, 393 U.S. 503 (1969).
345   WOD on "symbolic" speech, *Brandenburg* v. *Ohio*, 395 U.S. 444 (1969).
346   WOD on government eavesdropping, *On Lee* v. *U.S.*, 343 U.S. 747 (1952).
346   WOD 1952 dissent, *Public Utilities Commission* v. *Pollak*, 343 U.S. 451 (1952).
347   "natural rights", WOD, *The Right of the People*, p. 89. 1961 case, *Poe* v. *Ullman*, 367 U.S. 497 (1961).
348   1965 decision, *Griswold* v. *Conn.*, 381 U.S. 479 (1965).
349   Professor Kauper's criticism, Paul Kauper, "Penumbras, Peripheries, Emanations, Things Fundamental and Things Forgotten: The Griswold Case", 64 *Mich. L. Rev.* 235 (1965).

Chapter Twenty-six: Rich Man, Poor Man

350   "I'm embarrassed . . .", AI with a member of the Court.
350   WOD's colleagues' views, AI with members of the Court. (For this book, the author interviewed five members of the Court who served with Douglas.)

Page

350   WOD and his clerks, AI with WOD clerks.
351   "At work he treated . . .", AI with Duke.
351   "Well, that's . . .", Ibid.
351   "I felt . . .", AI with Duke.
351   "He [Douglas] didn't have . . .", Duke letter to author, 4-3-80.
352   "You would . . .", AI with a member of the Court.
352   "It was extraordinary . . .", Ibid.
352   "Felix had . . .", Ibid.
353   "The judicial conference . . .", Ibid.
353   "Douglas would . . .", AI with Fortas.
353   "At conferences . . .", Justice Tom Clark, "Bill Douglas—A Portrait", 28 *Baylor L. Rev.* 215, 219 (1976).
353   "I always . . .", AI with a member of the Court.
353   WOD's admirers and detractors, AI with members of the Court.
355   "Equal protection . . .", WOD, *We, the Judges,* (Garden City, NY, 1956), pp. 426, 427.
355   Background on school desegregation cases, Richard Kluger, *Simple Justice,* (New York, 1976).
355   "What's Douglas . . .", AI with Chester Maxey.
356   "Are you saying . . .", R. Kluger, op. cit., p. 567.
356   A state . . .", Ibid., p. 603.
356   Frankfurter's strategy, Ibid., pp. 599–603.
357   "impetuous and . . .", Ibid., p. 603.
357   Frankfurter and Bickel, Ibid., p. 615.
357   "This is . . .", Ibid., p. 656.
357   "separate educational . . .", *Brown* v. *Bd. of Education,* 347 U.S. 483 (1954).
357   "I will tell . . .", R. Kluger, op. cit., p. 603.
357   "all deliberate . . .", *Brown* v. *Bd. of Education,* 349 U.S. 294 (1955).
358   Background on Whittaker's replacement, A. M. Schlesinger, Jr., op. cit., pp. 376–378.
359   "I went up . . .", Ibid., p. 377.
359   "The scuttlebutt . . .", WOD to HB, 7-27-60, HBP.
359   "You wanted . . .", James E. Clayton, *The Making of Justice* (New York, 1964), p. 51.
360   Tennessee malapportionment case, *Baker* v. *Carr,* 369 U.S. 186 (1962).
360   "political thicket", *Colegrove* v. *Green,* 328 U.S. 549 (1946).
361   East Baton Rouge case, *Garner* v. *Louisiana,* 368 U.S. 157 (1961).
362   Hooper's restaurant case, *Bell* v. *Maryland,* 378 U.S. 226 (1964).
363   1951 poll tax case, *Butler* v. *Thompson,* 341 U.S. 937 (1951).
363   1966 poll tax case, *Harper* v. *Virginia Bd. of Elections,* 383 U.S. 663 (1966).
364   right to interstate travel, *Shapiro* v. *Thompson,* 394 U.S. 618 (1969).
364   right to counsel on first appeal, *Douglas* v. *California,* 372 U.S. 353 (1963).
365   "Of course, . . .", Kenneth Karst, "Invidious Discrimination: Justice Douglas and the Return of the 'Natural-Law-Due-Process Formula,' " 16 *U.C.L.A. L. Rev.* 716 (1969).

Chapter Twenty-seven: Three Wives

366   Father of the Year, *Publishers Weekly,* 5-27-50, p. 2297.
366   WOD craved adulation, AI with Mercedes Douglas Eichholz, Joan Douglas Nicholson.

Page

367　WOD's dancing, AI with Eichholz.
367　Meyer's criticism, Ibid.
367　WOD–Mercedes relationship, Ibid.
368　"What worries . . .", MD to HB, 8-14-56, HBP.
368　"Bill still . . .", MD to HB, 1-2-57, Ibid.
369　"Mercedes thought . . .", WOD to HB, 6-29-(undated), Ibid.
369　"I happened . . .", MD to HB, 6-29-(undated), Ibid.
369　McCormick's recollections, AI with McCormick.
369　"He started . . .", AI with Eichholz.
370　WOD and Joanie's meeting and courtship, AI with Joan Douglas Nicholson.
372　Mercedes's suspicions, Mercedes Douglas to Millie Douglas Read, 1-12-63, MDRL.
373　"twenty-year-old . . .", Ibid.
373　"My theory . . .", Ibid.
373　"miserable", Ibid.
373　"He'll probably . . .", MD to MDR, 2-4-63, Ibid.
374　"I called . . .", MD to MDR, 8-3-63, Ibid.
374　Mercedes and Robert Eichholz, AI with Mercedes Douglas Eichholz.
374　Mercedes's prediction, MD to MDR, 8-3-63, MDRL.
374　"Bill was . . .", AI with Kay Kershaw, Goose Prairie, WA, 8-22-76.
374　WOD note about Joanie, WOD to MDR, 7-31-63, MDRL.
375　WOD and Joanie's marriage, AI with Joan Douglas Nicholson.
380　WOD meets Cathy, AI with Trout.
381　"I loved . . .", Sandy North, "Justice Douglas' 23-year Bride Talks About Her Marriage," *Ladies Home Journal,* November, 1966.
381　WOD stunned Trout, AI with Trout.
381　"I was surprised . . .", Ibid.
381　WOD calls Cathy, AI with Cathleen Douglas, Washington, D.C., 12-20-76.
381　"actually . . .", Ibid.
381　Cathy's version of meeting WOD, Ibid.
381　"There was . . .", Ibid.
381　Cathy's background, Ibid.
382　"We understood . . .", Ibid.
382　WOD and Joanie, Joanie Douglas to Millie Douglas Read, 2-4-66, MDRL.
383　"Well, Mrs. . . .", Sandy North, op. cit.
383　"We hadn't . . .", Ibid.
383　"I don't . . .", Ibid.
384　Cathy's first press conference, WOD to MDR, 7-23-66, MDRL.
384　Sketch of Cathy, WOD to MDR, (undated), Ibid.
384　"sweetie", Sandy North, op. cit.
384　"Look at . . .", Ibid.
384　Cathy and WOD in Shangai, AI with Cathleen Douglas.
385　Cathy and WOD at hospital, Ibid.
385　"We planned . . .", Ibid.
385　"I'd rather . . .", Sandy North, op. cit.
385　"She's the . . .", AI with Millie Douglas Read.
386　"Here . . .", Ibid.
386　"These people . . .", Sandy North, op. cit.
386　"We intend . . .", Ibid.
386　"He even . . .", NB to MDR, 10-19-66, MDRL.
387　"I was . . .", WOD Jr. to MDR, 6-8-68, MDRL.

Page

387 "She's a star . . .", Cathy Douglas profile, *Washington Post,* 12-9-79.
388 "He made . . .", AI with Read.

Chapter Twenty-eight: Impeachment

391 "If they . . .", NYT, 7-19-66, p. 43.
391 "In all . . .", Ibid.
392 Ostrow's article, Los Angeles *Times,* 10-16-66.
392 "largely as . . .", Ibid.
393 Williams's charges, NYT, 10-18-66, p. 31.
393 "There is . . .", Ibid.
393 "a matter . . .", *Congressional Record,* 5-5-69, p. 11264.
393 WOD's letter, Ibid.
394 Donovan's letters, 11-16-66, HBP.
394 Harlan's response, JH to RD, 11-22-66, Ibid.
394 Black's response, HB to RD, 11-21-66, Ibid.
394 WOD's view of attack, Cathleen Douglas to Millie Douglas Read, 11-29-66, MDRL; Nan Burgess to Millie Douglas Read, 10-19-66, Ibid.
395 WOD told Warren, *Congressional Record,* op. cit.
395 Parvin on WOD, NYT, 12-17-70, p. 43.
395 WOD on Parvin, WOD remarks, 5-14-64, HBP.
395 "if compassion . . .", Ibid.
395 *Life* article, William Lambert, "Fortas of the Supreme Court," *Life,* 5-9-69.
395 Background on Fortas controversy, Robert Shogan, *A Question of Judgment* (New York, 1972).
396 "Of course, . . .", AI with Fortas.
396 WOD's advice, Ibid.
396 Fortas's fear, Ibid.
397 "I am sick . . .", NYT, 5-24-69, p. 1.
397 Barth's views, *Washington Post,* 5-18-69.
398 Background on Ford's role in Douglas impeachment attempt, Richard Sachs's analysis, *Congressional Record,* 11-26-73, p. 37965.
398 Ford investigation, *Washington Post,* 4-26-70.
398 NYT story, NYT, 5-20-69, p. 22.
398 WOD seminars, NYT, 5-22-69, p. 35.
398 WOD statement, NYT, 5-24-69, p. 1.
399 "I probably . . .", Ibid.
399 WOD letter, NYT, 5-26-69, p. 1.
399 "A manufactured case," Ibid.
399 "knew very little", *Newsweek,* 6-9-69, p. 36.
400 Warren on WOD and Fortas, Jack H. Pollack, *Earl Warren: The Judge Who Changed America* (New York, 1979), p. 299.
400 "It seems . . .", WOD to FR, 6-19-69, FRP.
400 Background on Haynsworth, James F. Simon, *In His Own Image: The Supreme Court in Richard Nixon's America* (New York, 1973), pp. 103–115.
400 "Haynsworth would . . .", Ibid., p. 104.
401 "There was . . .", Ibid., p. 112.
401 "none of his . . .", p. 111.
401 "If the Senate . . .", *Washington Post,* 11-8-69.
401 "The transparency . . .", NYT, 11-11-69, p. 46.

402 Impeach WOD effort, *Washington Star,* 12-21-69.
402 WOD publication, WOD, *Points of Rebellion* (New York, 1970).
402 "We must . . .", Ibid., p. 95.
403 "uninhibited, robust . . .", *New York Times* v. *Sullivan,* 376 U.S. 254 (1964).
403 "hackneyed," *The American Scholar* (Winter 1970–71), p. 188.
403 van den Haag review, 4 *Ga. L. Rev.* 830 (1970).
403 "political bankruptcy", WOD, *Points of Rebellion,* p. 53.
403 Background on Carswell, J.F. Simon, op. cit., pp. 115–124.
404 Agnew statement, Milton Viorst, "Bill Douglas Has Never Stopped Fighting the Bullies of Yakima", *NYT Mag.,* 6-14-70.
404 Ford reported, *Washington Post,* 4-26-70.
404 "Jerry was . . .", Ibid.
404 Ford's specific charges, *Congressional Record,* 4-15-70, pp. 11912–11927.
405 "An impeachable offense . . .", Ibid., p. 11913.
405 "The committee's . . .", Gerald R. Ford, *A Time to Heal* (New York, 1979), p. 93.
406 "It was . . .", M. Viorst, op. cit.
406 "sheer caricature . . .", NYT, 4-11-70, p. 33.
406 "I recommend . . .", Ibid.
406 WOD's friends' concern, M. Viorst, op. cit.
406 "We called . . .", AI with Simon Rifkind, New York City, 4-13-77.
407 "But we finally . . .", Ibid.
407 "under wraps", Ibid.
407 Rifkind's responses, *Congressional Quarterly Weekly Report,* 11-13-70, pp. 2788, 2789.
409 "seem so . . .", NYT, 12-16-70, p. 20.
409 Committee's findings, NYT, Ibid.; NYT, 12-17-70, p. 43; Judiciary Committee, Associate Justice William O. Douglas, Final reports of special subcommittee on impeachment resolution, 91st Congress, 2nd session, 1970.
410 Mason and Madison, Gerald Gunther, *Constitutional Law, Cases and Materials* (Mineola, NY, 1975), p. 451.

Chapter Twenty-nine: King Richard

412 Background on U.S. involvement in Cambodia, William Shawcross, *Sideshow* (New York, 1979); Arthur M. Schlesinger, Jr., *The Imperial Presidency* (Boston, 1973).
413 Background on history of presidential actions, "National Commitments", report of the Senate Committee on Foreign Relations, 1967; G. Gunther, op. cit., pp. 421–446.
414 Background on Holtzman suit in lower courts, *Holtzman* v. *Schlesinger,* 414 U.S. 1304 (1973).
414 "Lives are . . .", NYT, 8-2-73, p. 3.
415 Marshall opinion, *Holtzman* v. *Schlesinger,* 414 U.S. 1304 (1973).
416 WOD met attorneys, NYT, 8-4-73, p. 5.
416 WOD opinion, *Holtzman* v. *Schlesinger,* 414 U.S. 1316 (1973).
416 WOD opinions dissenting from denial of certs: *Sarnoff* v. *Schultz,* 409 U.S. 929 (1972); *DaCosta* v. *Laird,* 405 U.S. 979 (1972); *Mass.* v. *Laird,* 400 U.S. 886 (1970); *McArthur* v. *Clifford,* 393 U.S. 1002 (1968); *Hart* v. *U.S.,* 391 U.S. 956 (1968); *Holmes* v. *U.S.,* 391 U.S. 936 (1968); *Mora* v. *McNamara,* 389 U.S. 934 (1967); *Mitchell* v. *U.S.,* 386 U.S. 972 (1967).
417 Pentagon response, NYT, 8-5-73, p. 1.
417 Court reversed WOD, *Holtzman* v. *Schlesinger,* 414 U.S. 1321 (1973).

Page

417   WOD's response, Ibid., p. 1322.
417   Appeals court ruling, *Holtzman* v. *Schlesinger*, 484 F.2d 1307 (1973).
418   Criticism of WOD's action, Anthony Lewis column, NYT, 8-6-73, p. 31.
418   U.S. bombing mistakes, NYT, 8-7-73, p. 1; 8-8-73, p. 1; 8-10-73, p. 1.
419   WOD and LBJ friendship, Natalie Simon interview with Mrs. Lyndon B. Johnson, Austin, TX, 5-27-77.
419   WOD offer, AI with Joseph Rauh, Jr.
419   "Above all . . .", LBJ remarks, 5-14-64, HBP.
419   WOD remarks on LBJ, Ibid.
419   "Douglas gave . . .", AI with Sidney Davis, New York City, 5-15-79.
419   WOD dissents, see citations in notes for p. 416.
420   C.O. decision, *Gillette* v. *U.S.*, 401 U.S. 437 (1971).
420   "What was . . .", NYT, 5-26-69, p. 26; the reference was to the Court decision in *U.S.* v. *O'Brien*, 391 US 367 (1968).
420   WOD's suspicions about Nixon, AI with WOD.
421   Steel seizure case, *Youngstown Sheet and Tube Co.* v. *Sawyer*, 343 U.S. 579 (1952).
421   Nixon's imperial presidency, A. M. Schlesinger, Jr., op. cit., pp. 208–277.
422   Background on Pentagon Papers case, J. F. Simon, op. cit., pp. 180–214; Sanford J. Ungar, *The Papers & the Papers* (New York, 1972).
422   "You say . . .", NYT, 6-27-71, p. 24.
422   WOD-Bickel exchange, Ibid., p. 25.
422   Pentagon Papers decision, *New York Times Co.* v. *U.S.*, 403 U.S. 713 (1971).
424   Background on Powell and Rehnquist, J. F. Simon, op. cit., pp. 215–251.
424   Rehnquist's testimony, NYT, 10-11-73, p. 1.
425   Anti-war activists decision, *Laird* v. *Tatum*, 408 U.S. 1 (1972).
425   "proof that . . .", NYT, 10-11-72, p. 1.
425   WOD on standing, WOD, "The Bill of Rights Is Not Enough", 38 *N.Y.U. L. Rev.* 207 (1963); WOD opinions in *Flast* v. *Cohen*, 392 U.S. 83 (1968) and *U.S.* v. *Richardson*, 418 U.S. 166 (1974).
425   "This case . . .", *Laird* v. *Tatum*, 408 U.S. 1, 28 (1972).
426   WOD's loneliness, Cathy Douglas to Millie Douglas Read, 1-2-72, MDRL.
426   WOD attack, NYT, 10-16-73, p. 1.
426   Mink challenge, *Environmental Protection Agency* v. *Mink*, 410 U.S. 73 (1973).
428   Background on Watergate tapes argument, NYT, 7-9-74, pp. 1, 26.
428   "I thought . . .", Ibid., p. 26.
429   Watergate tapes decision, *U.S.* v. *Nixon*, 418 U.S. 683 (1974).
429   Other Justices drafted major portions, B. Woodward and S. Armstrong, *The Brethren* (New York, 1979), pp. 313–362; confirmed in AI with a member of the Court.

Chapter Thirty: Finishing Touches

430   WOD and colleagues, AI with members of the Court.
433   Background of El Paso Natural Gas case, B. Woodward and S. Armstrong, op. cit., pp. 79–85; confirmed in AI with a member of the Court.
434   "Art and literature . . .", *Paris Adult Theatre* v. *Slaton*, 413 U.S. 49, 70 (1973).
435   "we are a religious . . .", *Zorach* v. *Clauson*, 343 U.S. 306, 313 (1952).
435   Public school prayers, *Engel* v. *Vitale*, 370 U.S. 421 (1962).
435   Government loans of text books, *Bd. of Education* v. *Allen*, 392 U.S. 236 (1968).
435   Tax exemption, *Walz* v. *Tax Commission*, 397 U.S. 664 (1970).

Page

435 Swimming pool case, *Palmer* v. *Thompson*, 403 U.S. 217 (1971).
436 Moose Lodge case, *Moose Lodge No. 107* v. *Irvis*, 407 U.S. 163 (1972).
436 Vagrancy law, *Papachristou* v. *City of Jacksonville*, 405 U.S. 156 (1972).
437 *Gideon* v. *Wainwright*, 372 U.S. 335 (1963).
437 *Miranda* v. *Arizona*, 384 U.S. 436 (1966).
437 WOD 1958 opinion, *Crooker* v. *California*, 357 U.S. 433 (1958).
437 Counsel in cases of petty offenses, *Argersinger* v. *Hamlin*, 407 U.S. 25 (1972).
437 WOD dissenting, *Harris* v. *New York*, 401 U.S. 222 (1971), *Michigan* v. *Tucker*, 414 U.S. 433 (1974).
437 James case, *Wyman* v. *James*, 400 U.S. 309 (1971).
438 Background on abortion cases, B. Woodward and S. Armstrong, op. cit., pp. 165–189, 229–240; AI with confidential source (CS); confirmed in AI with a member of the Court.
441 Abortion decisions, *Roe* v. *Wade*, 410 U.S. 113 (1973); *Doe* v. *Bolton*, 410 U.S. 179 (1973).
442 Family and longtime friends shrugged, AI with Millie Douglas Read; Nan Burgess to Millie Douglas Read, 6-4-(undated), MDRL.
443 WOD and Hamilton, AI with Dagmar Hamilton, Austin, TX, 12-30-78.
446 WOD's stroke and hospitalization, AI with CS; *Time*, 4-7-75, p. 58.
447 Justices agree to delay, B. Woodward and S. Armstrong, op. cit., p. 358; confirmed in AI with a member of the Court.
448 WOD's press conference, *Time*, 4-7-75, p. 58; AI with David Beckwith, New York City, 2-17-77.
448 WOD's deteriorating condition, AI with Beckwith.
449 Justices' strategy, *Time*, 4-11-77, p. 80, confirmed in AI with a member of the Court.
449 "Bill's votes . . .", AI with a member of the Court.
449 "I would . . .", AI with Sandra Phillips Flax, New York City, 5-17-79.
449 "The Chief . . .", Ibid.
450 WOD in Yakima, *Washington Post*, 9-13-75.
450 WOD and Reich, Author's telephone interview with Reich, 4-20-80.
451 WOD returns, B. Woodward and S. Armstrong, op. cit., pp. 391–393; AI with CS; confirmed in AI with a member of the Court.
452 "Bill wants . . .", *Newsweek*, 11-24-75, p. 45.
452 WOD's memo to the Chief Justice, *Time*, 4-11-77, p. 81; confirmed in AI with a member of the Court.
452 "It was . . .", Author's telephone interview with Robert Deitz, 4-18-80.
452 Political financing challenge, *Buckley* v. *Valeo*, 424 U.S. 1 (1976).
453 WOD's view, AI with CS.
453 WOD's memo, B. Woodward and S. Armstrong, op. cit., pp. 398–399; confirmed in AI with a member of the Court.
453 "Bill is . . ." B. Woodward and S. Armstrong, op. cit., p. 399; confirmed in AI with CS.
453 WOD–clerk exchange, B. Woodward and S. Armstrong, op. cit.; confirmed in AI with CS.
453 "the tenth . . .", B. Woodward and S. Armstrong, op. cit.; confirmed in AI with CS.
454 WOD Jr's prediction, AI with WOD Jr., Washington, D.C., 2-21-77.
454 WOD request, WOD secretary, Rebecca Judge, letter to author, 5-15-78.
454 "Even at . . .", AI with Dennis Hutchinson, Washington, D.C., 4-19-77.
454 "We miss him", AI with a member of the Court.

INDEX

ABOUT THE AUTHOR

James F. Simon received a B.A. from Yale College and a
law degree from the Yale Law School. He has served as
correspondent and contributing editor of *Time* magazine,
specializing in legal affairs. He is the author of *The Judge* and
In His Own Image: The Supreme Court in Richard Nixon's America.
In His Own Image won the American Bar Association's Silver
Gavel Award in 1974. Simon has been a Visiting Lecturer in
American Studies at Yale University and a Harvard Fellow
in Law and the Humanities at Harvard University. He is a
professor of constitutional law at the New York Law School,
and lives with his wife and three children near New York
City.